THE WORLD'S LEADING CONQUERORS

ALEXANDER THE GREAT, CÆSAR, CHARLES THE GREAT,
THE OTTOMAN SULTANS, THE SPANISH CONQUISTADORS,
NAPOLEON

by

W. L. Bevan

Doctor of Political Science, Munich; Sometime Fellow of Columbia
University; Professor of History, University of the South

with portraits

NATAL PUBLISHING LLC
ARS LONGA, VITA BREVIS

CHARLEMAGNE
I.er du nom dit le grand, Roy de
France I.er Empereur d'Occident, né près
Mayence vers l'an 742, il mourut à Aix
la Chapelle l'an 814.
Desrochers ex.

Avoir par sa valeur et par son zele ardent
Sçeu vaincre les Saxons et les Mores d'Espagne
Esteint le nom Lombard, converti l'Allemagne
Et joint aux fleurs de lys l'Empire d'Occident
Sont les plus grands exploits de nostre Charlemagne.

Preface

The purpose of this volume is to present, in harmony with the popular character of the series of which it is a part, brief sketches of some of the most familiarly named men and well-known incidents in the history of Western Civilization. The plan upon which the work is constructed assumes that the broad highway of historical narrative must be followed, however attractive may be the deviations from it that offer themselves at almost every page. The story told here has been told often before and very frequently the telling of it has come from master hands of literature. It is no easy task to reproduce, in a condensed form, material so often handled under much more generous limitations of space than are possible in this work. An attempt has been made, however, to escape from the bald tabular method of recording historical happenings that is almost certain to make a continuous reading of text-book history an impossibility. This must be the apology for many omissions; not only had the temptation to generalize to be resisted in favor of what might be called a process of arbitrary selection but many things are passed over in order to give appropriate emphasis in treating the matters which do actually appear in a narrative. If the volume had aimed at comprehensiveness, many more conquests would necessarily have been described and the list of characters and leaders in large numbers of military campaigns could of course be almost indefinitely enlarged. One can say in any case that though such additions will naturally suggest themselves, there is less doubt as to the claim of the leaders and events selected to appear with the prominence here assigned to them. If there has been a guiding principle in the selection, it may be found in the deliberate choice made of widely different periods of history. What may be called the group conquest is best illustrated in the case of the Ottoman Sultans and the Spanish Conquistadors, whereas the personal factor of the conqueror comes intensively forward in the chapters describing Alexander, Cæsar, and Napoleon. Although the military aspect of the history of conquest has not been neglected, the other less visible elements that ushered in great changes in history have not been omitted. In the preparation of the volume some attempt has been made to incorporate methods, points of view, and material that might not be accessible to those not concerned with the range of literature to which the ordinary student of history must appeal. It is only fair, therefore, to express my obligations to the following works. In the chapters dealing with ancient history, Beloch's "Griechische Geschichte," Delbrück's "Kriegs Geschichte," Kaerst's "Geschichte des Hellenismus" and Heitland's "History of the Roman Republic" have been largely used. In the chapter on Charles the Great, apart from Hodgkin's well-known volumes "Italy and Her Invaders," I have drawn upon Hartmann's "Geschichte Italiens," Ranke's "Welt Geschichte," Hauck's "Kirchen Geschichte" and Lavisse's "Histoire de France." For the Ottoman conquest Professor Jorga's two recently published volumes, "Geschichte des Osmanischen Reiches," have been found especially useful because the author is thoroughly acquainted with the authorities both Slavonic and Turkish not previously accessible to Occidental scholars. In the chapter on the Spanish Conquest use has been made of Payne's "History of the New World," MacNutt's "Life of Las Casas," and in the narrative portion Garcia's "Character de la Conquista Española" has been found especially valuable. In the life of Napoleon, which offers the most serious difficulties in applying any accepted method of condensation, the well-known volumes of Fournier and portions of the "Histoire Générale" of Lavisse and Rambaud have been followed. Much help has been received from Professor W. P. Trent, the editor of the series; in the arduous task of revision, I wish to express my special obligations for time and work ungrudgingly given by my colleague, the Rev. S. L. Tyson of the University of the South, and I cannot pass over aid of the same kind received from Mr. Karl Schmidt of the New York *Churchman*.

W. L. B.
Sewanee, Tenn., *January, 1913*.

CONTENTS

ALEXANDER THE GREAT

I
INTRODUCTORY

Even in the critical time of the Persian invasion, the Greek peoples did not act together. The experiences of political individualism were too strong to be overcome, and the rooted tradition of local autonomy successfully resisted all attempts at larger plans of unity. It is not surprising that at a time when Greek thinkers regarded the development of the city-state as the highest field for human endeavor, Greek statesmen should have seen in the expansion of their native communities only a loose federation of subject cities to be exploited financially or for the purpose of adding increased military and naval strength, and not to be subjected to any formal centralized control.

As time went on the old solidarity of the Greek city-state was sapped in the fight of social classes and political parties. Not only were Athens, Sparta, and Thebes frequently at war with one another but in each one of these states there were at work factions dominated by revolutionary aims. Nothing was regarded as fixed except that the community must be self-sufficing, it mattered little in what way. It seemed as if the troubled relations of Greek political life might go on indefinitely after the Persian invasion had been repelled.

No Greek statesman for a hundred and fifty years, say roughly from 500 B.C. to 350 B.C., the most brilliant period of Greek history, regarded the kingdom of Macedon as anything but a negligible quantity. Macedon itself was a land that lay on the boundaries of the Hellenic world. Its people were held to be half Hellenic and half barbarian. Even to-day scholars are not at one on the question whether the Macedonian dialect can be reckoned as properly belonging to Greek speech. But it was this alien power that ended in bringing Greece to a kind of unity, a unity based on the force of arms. The most remarkable feature of this achievement lies in the fact that it was accomplished by one man, Philip of Macedon, who began his victorious career in 359 B.C. by repressing internal disturbances at home and by dealing effectively with his warlike neighbors, the Illyrians and the Thracians. The divisions in Greece gave him the opportunity of intervention there. He posed as the friend of the oligarchic party in various Greek communities, and made it his aim to oppose by diplomacy and by war the most important center of Greek democracy, Athens. The final struggle between the free states and the Macedonian monarchy took place at the battle of Chæronea, August, 338 B.C. Philip won a decisive victory, because he had spent years in training a professional army that proved irresistible when it faced the best citizen soldiers of Athens, Thebes, and other smaller towns which, persuaded by the eloquence of Demosthenes, stood side by side in the defense of liberty. Philip survived his victory only a short time, dying in 336 B.C. as the master of Greece and leaving to his son Alexander the heritage of his unique achievements.

ALEXANDER

II
THE CONQUEST OF GREECE

Alexander's succession to the throne of Macedon seemed secured by his father Philip's sincere personal affection for him. His confidence in Alexander's ability, even in his son's early youth, was manifested in the assignment to him of the most responsible positions under his father's directions. Philip saw to it that his son should be carefully educated by placing him under the charge of Aristotle. Good reports must have come of his precocity, because Philip, while he was occupied in the siege of Byzantium, handed over to Alexander, then only sixteen years old, the administration of Macedon. Two years later, at the battle of Chæronea, already mentioned as marking the downfall of Greek freedom, the youth was placed at the head of the division of the army which took the offensive at a critical part of the engagement, and it was through this important command that the questionable honor of striking the decisive blow in the defeat of the allied forces of free Greece was ungrudgingly conceded to him.

Philip, unattractive as his character was in so many ways, stained as he was by savage passions and duplicity, at least performed conscientiously and effectively a father's part in preparing his son for the high position he was to take in the future. But the domestic situation of the Macedonian royal family was very far from being modeled on that described in the Odyssey as befitting the heroes and the leaders of men. Philip was lawless, and his numerous amours brought him both difficulty and notoriety, for in his irregular relations he did not scruple to disregard the customary conventions of Greek social life. On his return from his campaign for the subjugation of Greece, he became enamored of Cleopatra, a girl belonging to a distinguished Macedonian family, whose uncle, Attalus, had a high place in the government. Cleopatra's position made it impossible for the King to offer her the place of a royal mistress; accordingly he made her a legitimate wife. Olympias and her son Alexander left Macedon, the queen returning to her home in Epirus, and the crown prince withdrawing to the traditional enemies of the Macedonians, the Illyrians.

Philip, alarmed at the possibility of political combinations dangerous to his throne, came to an agreement with Alexander by which the latter was to return to his father's court at Pella, and Olympias' brother, the prince of Epirus, was induced to give up his hostility against his brother-in-law by a promise that he should have in marriage Philip's daughter, another Cleopatra. This alliance took place with great ceremony in the summer of 336, in the ancient royal town of Ægæ. Immediately after Philip prepared to set out to war with Persia. During the marriage festivities, however, he was assassinated by one of the members of his bodyguard, Pausanias, who in the confusion that followed almost succeeded in making his escape. Personal motives were assigned as grounds for this murder. Pausanias, it appears, had been deeply insulted by Attalus, the uncle of Philip's young wife Cleopatra, and failing to get redress from the King, had so revenged on him his injured honor. It has been asked why, if this were the case, he did not strike at Attalus rather than Philip. The probability is that Philip's murder was inspired by a woman's indignation.

It was suspected immediately after the event that it was a case of "cherchez la femme," and all indications pointed to the outraged Olympias as the author of the murder. Alexander himself was thought to have been concerned in his father's death, for his own rights of succession were endangered by the influence of Cleopatra over Philip, an influence no longer merely sentimental, since she had recently given birth to a son. For this infant she would naturally strive to secure the Macedonian crown, and Alexander would be left to play the uncertain rôle of Pretender.

Whatever happened at Ægæ, the fruits of the crime fell into Alexander's hands. He had been officially proclaimed his father's heir. Of Philip's sons he was the only one who had been tested on the battlefield, and he was also the one who had already shown capacity for leading the state in such crises as were bound to result from his father's murder. Philip's old companions in arms did not hesitate for a moment as to the proper choice of a ruler. Alexander was immediately recognized as king, and in the selection special weight was attached to the fact that his cause was urged by Antipater, one of Philip's closest friends and supporters.

In this way the young prince's road to the succession was made easy; there were no disturbances, and care was also taken that there should be no competitors for the crown in the future, for the young son of Cleopatra was killed. But these grim measures to establish domestic peace did not stop here. There was another line of Macedonian princes, descended from the dethroned family of Lynkestes; there were two members of this house who might, by making awkward claims at unsuitable times, give much trouble. These two, Heromenes and Arrhabæos, were both executed, on the ground that they had acted as accomplices with Pausanias in the conspiracy against Philip. They had a brother Alexander, whose life was spared only because he was a son-in-law of Antipater and had hailed Alexander as the new king immediately after the murder.

By these deeds of violence, Alexander became the acknowledged master of Macedon, but the prospects outside his own country were anything but favorable. In Asia, Attalus was at the head of the Greek cities. As the uncle of Cleopatra he would naturally be a most bitter enemy of Alexander. The uncertain future in Macedon was not lost on those Greeks whose liberties Philip had so recently destroyed, and whose acquiescence in the rule of Macedon was due only to their fear of the conqueror. Now they were ready to throw off the yoke, needing no excuse, but only an opportunity of rising, which the advent to the throne of an untried youth made most hopeful. A revolt broke out in Ambrakia and the Macedonian governor was driven out. Thebes was preparing for a similar outbreak, and there were plain signs of restlessness in Ætolia and in the Peloponnesus.

Athens was the city to which all the opponents of Macedonian rule looked for sympathy and support. The peace party there, who had gained adherents among the Athenians because of the moderation shown by Philip after his decisive victory at Chæronea, now lost ground because patriotic hopes sprung anew to life at the unexpected death of the man who had shattered the traditional system of Greek city autonomy.

Every Greek regarded Macedon as an alien and semibarbarous power, and one can sympathize with their view. Demosthenes was the leader of the patriotic party in Athens, and all attempts to undermine his popularity only put the partisans of Macedonia in a worse light in the eyes of the Athenians. Whenever he was judicially attacked he came out of the trial in triumph.

Besides, the personal ascendancy of Demosthenes protected the minor politicians who joined him as opponents of the friends of the Macedonian monarch. Hyperides, who was responsible for a decree calling every Athenian freeman, slave, and ally under arms for the defense of the city against Philip after the defeat of the Greeks, was brought to trial for his action and, despite the eloquence of the pro-Macedonian orator, Aristogeiton, was acquitted.

The current of popular emotion was even more plainly revealed when the time came to deliver the oration, at the Attic feast of the dead, to commemorate the citizens fallen at the battle of Chæronea. The honor fell to Demosthenes, the one man whose implacable hatred to the Macedonian dynasty and all its works was known to everyone. Attempts were made in Athens to reform the terms of military service by arranging that all citizens should be called out to defend their country, and at the same time money was spent in putting the fortifications of the city in a state to resist an army composed of skilled troops and provided with the siege artillery of the time.

But care had been taken not to invite attack while Athens was yet unprepared. At the marriage feast of Ægæ appeared an Athenian deputation bringing a golden wreath to Philip and a copy of a decree, passed formally by the city, by which it undertook to surrender anyone in its jurisdiction who should dare to plot against the king. When the news of the assassination reached Athens, Demosthenes appeared in the council in festal garb, and solemnly thanked the gods for the deliverance done at Ægæ. He considered that Athens had nothing to fear from the silly youth who now was ruling over Macedon.

But Alexander showed that the great orator had not taken his enemy's measure. By the rapidity of his actions, he checked all attempts to revolt. Suddenly appearing at the head of his army in Thessaly, he received from the Thessalian allied cities the position of commander-in-chief, as his father had done before him, and moving rapidly south, he reached Thermopylæ, where he summoned the Amphiktyons, and meeting no opposition, was declared by them guardian of the temple at Delphi. Marching farther south to Thebes, he prevented, by his presence with an overwhelming force, any anti-Macedonian movement; and when the Athenians sent a delegation to greet him, he was tactful enough not to ask for further guaranties of good behavior on the part of the city they represented.

The Hellenic league, which included all the Greek states south of Thermopylæ and all the islands which had once owned the supremacy of Athens, met again at Corinth and renewed with Alexander the same agreement that had previously been made with his father, a treaty of offensive and defensive alliance, and the chief command by land and sea was assigned to the new king, as his father's successor. After this triumphal and peaceful progress, Alexander returned home, where his barbarian neighbors were giving trouble by revolts against his authority.

In order to bring himself in contact with the Greek opposition to Alexander, Attalus, one of the two commanders of the Macedonian army in Asia, had entered into relations with Demosthenes, only a short time after Alexander's succession. As Cleopatra's uncle he took a leading part in engineering a conspiracy intended to supplant Alexander by Amyntas, the young son of Perdikkas, the elder brother of Philip, who by the traditional usage of the Macedonian monarchy was entitled to succeed Philip. The success of Alexander in Greece convinced Attalus of the futility of his schemes, and he therefore tried to make advances to the young ruler. But Alexander was not to be placated, and, as a deviser of conspiracies in his own interest, he showed that he had nothing to learn from the practised hands of the Macedonian nobles.

It would have been extremely unwise for Alexander to have shown himself openly an enemy of Attalus, who enjoyed much popularity in the army. Accordingly he made a show of friendship by graciously accepting the advances of Attalus, and at the same time he despatched an associate, Hekatæus, on whom he could rely, with directions to assassinate him. The treacherous deed was made the easier, because Parmenio, joint-commander with Attalus in Asia Minor, facilitated the plans of the assassination, despite the fact that Attalus was married to his daughter. The tribal interests of a half-barbarous people had full sway among the Macedonians, so Parmenio, who had throughout his life been conscientiously loyal to the Macedonian monarchy, did not scruple to sacrifice his daughter's husband, when it appeared that his son-in-law was plotting to supplant the regularly accepted monarch of his people.

Alexander's difficulties were being quickly dissolved by crime and bloodshed. The Macedonians had none of the political experiences common to the free Greek communities, and assassination was regarded both as an ordinary expedient for removing opponents, and as the logical method of rounding off a policy that was complicated. With Attalus removed, Alexander could proceed, without further hesitation, to strengthen his position at home. Amyntas, the young pretender, was executed, and with him all of the relatives of Attalus and Cleopatra. In this Borgia-like program of eliminating possible claimants to the throne, only the stepbrother of Alexander, a half-witted lad, Amidæus, was spared. Later Alexander's mother, Olympias, forced her rival, the queen-widow Cleopatra, to commit suicide.

With this orgy of crime, the reign of Alexander was ushered in, and one reads with astonishment to-day the thin and specious apologies which would excuse the young ruler, the real instigator of these atrocities. As a matter of fact he early acquired the habit of assassination; unfortunately he never unlearned it. Whatever may be argued in behalf of his people, who were uncivilized, nothing can extenuate this early exercise in crime of the pupil of Aristotle. When we survey his record of one year we perceive that hatred of his deeds must have been the test of patriotism and good citizenship among the Greek communities, who might well see in him the typical tyrant of their political theories.

Alexander's violent preparations for a peaceful reign were successful. During his lifetime the tranquillity of Macedonia was not disturbed. Greece had been brought by the display of military supremacy to a position of servitude; all that needed to be done before he took up his father's program for the invasion of Asia, was to bring the western tribes on his northern frontier to reason, and to force home upon them the realization of the power of Macedon.

In the spring of 335, Alexander left Amphipolis, and by a rapid march of ten days reached Mount Hæmus in the thick of a population which had never recognized the supremacy of Macedon. They tried to defend themselves in their mountain passes, but Alexander soon forced his way through, and on the top of the highest mountain, celebrated his victory by setting up a thank offering to Dionysus. He then gave his attention to various mountain tribes with whom his father had had trouble, who had never before been subjugated, but who now met a decisive defeat at his hands. An island on the Danube, where the tribesmen had placed for security their wives and children and property, proved, however, impregnable. The young king showed himself from the first a master of strategy, for although he could not capture the island, he executed rapid movements along the river, beating the Getæ who were defending the passages, and when the Triballi had come to terms, he marched up the Danube, and then, crossing the eastern passes of the Hæmus range, returned to Pæonia.

Alexander's absence in the north in this untiring campaign against barbarian tribes, whose homes and habits were hardly known to the civilized states of Greece, was taken advantage of by his enemies. While he was fighting on the Danube, the King of Illyria, Kleitos, whose people had given trouble to Philip and whose father had fallen in battle with the Macedonians, rose in revolt. Several tribes farther north on the Adriatic coast joined with the Illyrians in this anti-Macedonian movement. Without a moment's hesitation, Alexander turned to deal with his new enemies, and in order to do effective work, penetrated far into the mountainous region of Illyria. The Macedonian army soon found itself in a hazardous position, surrounded on all sides by hostile tribes. By skilful strategy, Alexander withdrew his troops from the danger that threatened them, while they were besieging Pelion in the face of superior numbers, and when he found that the Illyrians were following him, he quickly turned on them, administered a decisive blow, and forced Kleitos to seek a refuge in the territory of the Taulantines, one of the tribes which had been co-operating with the Illyrians in their resistance to his army.

In the meantime, the presence of a Macedonian force in Asia Minor had awakened the Persians to the danger confronting them of an invasion from Greece. Its full meaning was hardly appreciated, and the new situation was interpreted as only another example of the type of attack so frequently made by the Greek communities ever since the time when the Persian invasion of Greece had been successfully blocked. It had always been found possible to avoid a serious attack from Greece on the Persian Empire by playing off one Greek state against another. This well-tried expedient was now used again. Letters were sent from the King of Persia to the states of Greece urging them to rise against Macedon, and offering large sums of money to subsidize the revolt. Sparta alone responded to the invitation; Athens and the other states, which had just renewed a formal alliance with Macedon, seemed to realize the hopelessness of an anti-Macedonian movement, and refused to accept the offer of Persian money. All that the representatives of the great king could accomplish in this direction was to leave in the hands of Demosthenes the sum of three hundred talents, with the understanding that he could use his own discretion in employing it to the best advantage in the interests of Persia.

The action of the great Athenian orator in accepting the Persian gold has been severely criticised and warmly defended. It must be remembered that to him Alexander appeared only as the destroyer of Greek liberty and not as the protagonist of Greek culture, a position which can be understood only as the result of his conquests in the East. There was no reason why an Athenian patriot should have been willing to destroy the Persian Empire at the cost of the enslavement of his own city.

The perils and difficulties of the Illyrian campaign were magnified by the rumors which reached the Greek cities. It was even reported that Alexander had been slain and his army destroyed. This report was soon followed by an uprising in Thebes against the Macedonians. The leaders of the Macedonian faction were murdered and the Macedonian garrison in the citadel closely besieged. The democratic constitution was then restored and Theban officials were elected according to the old constitutional forms. At this juncture, Demosthenes used some of the Persian treasure to purchase arms, which he sent to Thebes to aid its citizens in their contest for the restoration of their independence.

While the Thebans were most active, the rest of Greece was not slow in showing its antipathy to Macedonian control. Athens prepared itself to do battle for Greek autonomy; the isthmus of Corinth was occupied by an army raised from among the Arcadian cities, with Mantineia at their head. And the people of Elis and Ætolia showed that they would be ready to aid the Thebans.

But before any common plan of resistance could be prepared, Alexander and his army had passed the frontiers of Bœotia after a remarkably rapid forced march, undertaken as soon as the news of the defection of the Thebans had reached him in Illyria. It took him but fourteen days in all to cover the distance from the scene of operations in Illyria to the gates of Thebes. He was willing to come to terms with the Thebans, offering them easy conditions provided they would admit his troops into the city; but the mass of the inhabitants preferred to cast in their lot with those who were in favor of resistance.

The exiled citizens of Thebes knew they would receive short shrift at the hands of the son of the man who had driven them from their native city. The chances of successful resistance were overestimated, but Thebes had formerly led a forlorn hope in its contest with the Spartans; and, as the unexpected had happened before, the Thebans, who were preparing to withstand the Macedonians can hardly be blamed for recalling the glorious memories of the battle of Leuktra. But they were now dealing with a new, vigorous army, not with a Spartan force spoiled by routine. As no help could be looked for from the outside, the situation was altogether different. The result proved that the Thebans of Alexander's day had inherited indeed the valor, but not the intelligence, of the generation of Epaminondas and Pelopidas.

The Macedonian garrison still held out in the Kadmeia, the citadel which lay in the southern part of the city, near the gate of Elektra, through which passed the road to Athens. Its walls were an integral part of the fortifications of the city. The object of the Thebans was therefore to cut off all communication from the Kadmeia by building about it inclosing lines. This operation Alexander aimed to prevent, and with Perdikkas at the head of a contingent of Macedonian mountaineers, he succeeded in breaking through the Theban line of defense, and finally forced his adversaries back to the walls of the city. They were closely pursued in this retreat, and, as they entered the gate in disorder, the Macedonians were able to force their way into the city at the same time. Another division of the Macedonians found little difficulty in entering the Kadmeia, and from this point of vantage they quickly descended into the city. The Thebans made an attempt to rally in the market place, but the rout was soon general. After the city was overrun by the Macedonians and their allies, it was noted that the people of the smaller Bœotian towns signalized themselves by their acts of cruelty done on the now defenseless Thebans, from whose tyranny they had suffered in the past. Six thousand men, it is said, perished in the taking of Thebes, while the Macedonian loss did not exceed 500. (September, 335 B.C.)

Alexander called together his allies to settle the fate of the conquered. The decision was a horrible example of rancorous hatred, for he allowed the smaller cities of Bœotia, smarting, as we have seen, under the sense of long grievances, to work their will on their once powerful neighbor. The town was to be razed to the ground, only the house of Pindar being spared. The sole part of the fortifications of the town to be retained was the Kadmeia, which remained as a military post with its Macedonian garrison. The Theban territory was to be divided among the allies, and all the captive Thebans, men, women, and children, with but a few exceptions, were to be sold as slaves. Those Thebans who escaped from the city were to be outlawed, and no Greek city would be permitted to receive them. The only positive items in this ruthless decree were the provisions for restoring Orchemenos and Platæa, places which Thebes had once treated with the severity now meted out to her.

Such a catastrophe, as the result of a defeat or a siege, had never before been witnessed in Greece, and the impression produced was one of unmitigated terror. It was not simply the misfortunes of the existing Theban community, or the material loss from the annihilation of property. Thebes had the closest associations with the heroic age of Greece, its name was interwoven with the stories of gods and heroes. Kadmus had founded it; within its limits Dionysus and Herakles had been born. The city which had shattered the power of Sparta was left desolate, and the plow passed over the ground where it had once stood. It seemed according to a contemporary as if Zeus had torn the moon from the heavens.

The impression made throughout Greece by this barbarous deed was universal; no one dared to think of resistance to Alexander. There was a general desire among the various cities to place themselves in a favorable position with the conqueror. The Arcadians condemned to death those who had advised that aid should be given to the Thebans; in other places the partisans of Macedonia were received back from exile, and haste was made to acquaint Alexander of the general desire to meet his wishes.

The Athenians were celebrating their most solemn religious festival, the Eleusinian Mysteries, when the taking of Thebes was announced. There was widespread consternation, because it was assumed that the next move of Alexander would be made against Athens in order to punish its citizens for their anti-Macedonian sentiments. The celebration of the festival was abandoned; the inhabitants of the open country took refuge within the city walls, in anticipation of the ravaging of their lands, and the fortifications surrounding the city were fully prepared for defense. In spite of the plain dangers involved in showing sympathy for the defeated Thebans, fugitives from that city were received with an open-handed hospitality, and their needs cared for without stint. But at the same time an opening for maintaining amicable relations with the victor was preserved, by sending a formal embassy to Alexander to congratulate him on his return from Illyria and for his quick victory over the rebels in Thebes.

The true situation of affairs in Athens was an open secret. Alexander knew the part played by the Athenians in preparing for the Theban revolt; he knew, too, that they had been on the point of actively and openly co-operating with the Thebans, and that the plan had been frustrated only by the rapidity with which he had moved on the city. Yet the young ruler showed himself unexpectedly placable in his treatment of Athens. There is no reason to attribute his attitude to mere generosity of sentiment in favor of the city because of its glorious past. There were more practical reasons; the siege of Athens could hardly be successful except through command of the sea, and any attempt of this kind would most likely have been frustrated or at least rendered doubtful by the intervention of the Persian fleet.

Instead of advancing into Attica, Alexander stopped to parley, and agreed to abstain from hostilities on condition that the Athenians should promptly expel the Theban fugitives, and also should surrender to him the men who had been lately responsible for the anti-Macedonian direction of the government. It is to the credit of the Athenians that the first condition was without a negative rejected; and as to the second there were many of the anti-democratic faction who would have been glad to get rid of their opponents by agreeing to this indirect demand of the Macedonian king that the government of the city should be handed over to his partisans. Phokion, one of the distinguished and revered members of the oligarchic group, was willing to accept the condition unreservedly; but Demosthenes and Demades, another popular leader, successfully urged the assembly of the people to vote against it, and even Phokion agreed to head an embassy to acquaint Alexander with the decision of the Athenian citizens. The king showed himself ready to compromise, for the success of his schemes against Asia depended largely on the good will of Athens and its fleet. It was finally arranged that the Athenian anti-Macedonian military leader Charidemos should be banished, a proposal to which it was all the easier for the Athenians to accede, because he was not a native Athenian. This officer and several others withdrew to Asia and took service under Darius.

III

THE CONQUEST OF PERSIA

Now that the pacification of Greece was effected by the restoration of Athens as a member of the Macedonian confederacy, Alexander, without visiting that city, marched to the isthmus of Corinth to arrange for the various Greek contingents for his expedition to Asia, and after receiving from the oracle at Delphi a reply encouraging him to carry out his grandiose scheme of conquest, he retired to Macedonia to spend the winter before setting out on his march against the Persian Empire.

Of the details of his proposed invasion nothing is known beyond the fact that his original scheme must have been considerably modified as he penetrated farther into Asia. His geographical knowledge of the interior of the empire could hardly have been sufficient for an orderly mapping out beforehand of the course he actually took. That was entirely governed by the extraordinary series of events which marked the various stages of his expedition. His design was to dethrone the Persian king and secure possession of the country. To do this effectively the first step was to conquer Asia Minor, to get under his control the remoter provinces of Syria and Egypt, and then to advance on Babylon and Susa. That there was immediate necessity for setting his army on the march was plain to him, because of the dangerous position of the Macedonian forces already in Asia Minor. The Persian general, Memnon, had checkmated Parmenio, who was recalled, and the prospects of Macedonian success were blighted by the defeat of another Macedonian general Kallás in the Troad. Before Alexander left his own kingdom, the authority of the Persian government had been generally restored throughout the whole of Asia Minor.

In the spring of 334, Alexander marched to the Hellespont with an army numbering altogether 30,000 infantry and 4500 cavalry. Of these, 12,000 infantry and 1500 cavalry were from Macedon; contingents from the allies made up the rest. There were besides 160 warships, of which Athens furnished twenty. Alexander's chief military adviser was Parmenio, whom Philip, his father, had declared to be the only Macedonian general he had discovered in many years. Of the subordinate officers the most noteworthy were Philotas, who was in command of the Macedonian cavalry, and Nikanor, who led the álite of the Macedonian infantry (the so-called Hypaspistæ, or the Bodyguards). During the absence of the king, the administration of Macedon and of the subject states was left in the hands of Antipater.

The incompetence of the Persians in aggressive resistance was manifest from the first. They were far superior to the Greeks at sea, and if they had

11

made intelligent use of their fleet they could have prevented Alexander's army from crossing the Hellespont. Indeed, orders had been issued the year before to the coast cities that their ships should be kept in readiness in anticipation of an invasion. But so slipshod was the administration in the loosely governed provinces of Persia that their great fleet was unable to put to sea when Alexander reached the narrow arm of water which divides Europe from Asia. He had no difficulty in passing; indeed Parmenio was left to superintend this operation, while the young king visited the cities of the Troad rich in legendary lore, and made a pilgrimage to the tomb of his reputed ancestor, Achilles.

The Greeks soon began their march down the coast. The satraps of the neighboring provinces had in the meantime gathered together all the troops available in the Propontis and had joined the army of Memnon. From the statements made in contemporary sources, it is not possible to gather the numerical strength of the army which now opposed Alexander's advance; it is certain, however, that in infantry the Persians were weaker than the Greeks, while it is probable that they were also outnumbered in cavalry.

They were certainly aware of their weakness, because Memnon advised against a stand-up battle, suggesting instead that they should retire into the interior, wasting the country as they went, and so hinder the rapidity of the enemy's march until their own fleet appeared; then the war could be carried into Greece and Alexander forced to retreat. But this prudent strategy was not acceptable to the Persian satraps, who preferred active measures that seemed to offer a chance of preventing Alexander from getting a firm foothold in Persian territory.

They prepared to offer battle by taking up a position on the river Granicus, a stream flowing down from the northern slope of Mt. Ida to the Propontis. It seems as if the Persians, conscious of their weakness, selected a battlefield where their enemies, with a river in front of them, would find it a matter of some difficulty to attack. They may have supposed that Alexander would hesitate to advance under such unfavorable conditions. The Macedonian army was so disposed that the heavy-armed infantry held the center while the wings were formed by the cavalry and the bowmen. Alexander himself was with the picked Macedonian cavalry on the right wing; next him were arranged the hypaspists, extending towards the middle. This wing, comprising cavalry, bowmen, and heavy-armed troops, appears to have crossed the river first and to have put to flight the Persian cavalry. That the Persians used horsemen here and not bowmen seems strange. Cavalry were of little use in preventing an advance up the steep slope from the stream.

First the Persian horse were put to flight by the right Macedonian wing, commanded by Alexander, who took an active part in the hand-to-hand conflict; then the phalanx of Greek mercenaries on the Persian side, who had stood by hitherto without taking any part in the engagement, were attacked in front by the Macedonian phalanx and on the flanks by the cavalry and bowmen and, being thus prevented from making any real resistance, were hewn down or taken prisoners. The Macedonian loss was so small, eighty-five horsemen and thirty foot soldiers, that it would seem that probably the Greek mercenaries, instead of resisting their own kinsmen, allowed themselves to be taken prisoners. The brunt of the battle was borne by the Persian horsemen, who fought valorously, and in the obstinate scrimmage with them Alexander was in considerable personal danger. Two of the satraps lost their lives on the field. The Greek prisoners were sent in chains to Macedon, and of the booty taken, 300 suits of armor were sent to the Parthenon at Athens as a thank-offering, a visible reminder to the Greeks of the victor's progress. (May-June, 334 B.C.)

The fruits of the victory were immediate: several of the principal cities surrendered, among them Sardis, with its impregnable citadel, and Ephesus. In both places Alexander was greeted as a deliverer from Persian tyranny; democratic government was restored, and a beginning was made for organizing a massacre of the oligarchic faction. This Alexander prevented, making it clear by his intervention that he did not wish to alienate the sympathies of the propertied classes in Asia. Of the other Greek cities in Ionia and Æolis, only one gave serious trouble, Miletus, which looked to the Persian fleet for aid. It was occupied besides by a strong garrison of Greek mercenaries. Alexander's fleet, however, appeared at Miletus before the Persian fleet, which was on its way from Cyprus and Phœnicia, reached the scene of action. When this fleet came up, it tried in vain to entice the Macedonian ships into an action, and remained idly by while Alexander besieged Miletus and finally took it by storm.

The sole stronghold still left to Persia in the region was Halicarnassus to the south. Hither the Persian fleet repaired, and here, as the place was strongly fortified and well manned with troops, Memnon planned to establish a base for further operations by sea against Greece itself. But Alexander declined to take the risk of meeting the Persian fleet in a naval engagement. Winter was at hand, and most of the Macedonian ships had been sent home; there was only a small squadron left, and the king marched south with his army to besiege Halicarnassus by land.

The problem before him was anything but easy, for Halicarnassus, besides being strongly fortified, had through the presence of the Persian fleet free communication with the outside. It could be supplied with food, although the opportunity of obtaining mercenary troops from Greece was made difficult through the fear of Macedon. The city walls were surrounded with wide ditches and these Alexander filled up, in order to give access to his siege engines. Several breaches were made, but the first attempt to storm the place failed, and the defenders of the city erected new fortifications in place of those that had been cut down. They also made a sortie, trying to destroy the siege engines, but were repulsed with loss. Memnon saw that the town could no longer be held, and by night embarked his troops, carrying them to Cos; but before he left he set fire to the abandoned town. Alexander immediately entered, showed himself merciful to its citizens, and proceeded on his march, leaving a division of 3050 men to watch the citadel of Halicarnassus, which evidently he did not think of sufficient importance to besiege now that the

Persians had only a small number of troops in the neighborhood, in Salmakis and on the island Arconnesus.

The whole of the province of Caria now ceased to resist, with the exception of a few places on the coast. A part of the Greek army, under the orders of Parmenio, were sent into winter quarters in Lydia, while Alexander advanced through Lycia and Pamphylia, without meeting any real resistance, and marched by the way of the mountainous country of Pisidia, among a population never conquered by the Persians, and in the spring of 333 joined Parmenio at Gordion, the ancient capital of Phrygia. From here the route of the army was through Cappadocia by the narrow pass called the Cilician Gate, by which the road from the interior plateau crosses the Taurus on its way to Tarsus. The garrison which occupied the pass fled on the approach of the Greek army, Tarsus itself was abandoned, and the whole province of Cilicia was occupied without resistance.

In the meantime, however, Memnon had not been inactive, and he was putting to good use his superiority in naval strength. Several islands had either been occupied or were making preparations to join the Persian general, and even in continental Greece the anti-Macedonian influence was being felt. There was no question that Memnon's arrival on the shores of European Greece would be the signal for a general abandonment of the Macedonian cause. Athens even sent an embassy to Darius, although the city did not dare to join the Persians openly. In the midst of these successes, Memnon was taken ill and died. Those who succeeded him in the command showed none of his capacity. The fleet was kept in inactivity, and though on land some small successes could be put to the credit of the Persian arms in Asia Minor, the soldiers operating there were soon directed to join the main army of Darius in Syria, now being collected to meet the advancing Greeks. When the news of Alexander's victory at the Granicus reached the interior of the Persian Empire, Darius began to draw together a large army, and leaving Babylon in January, reached northern Syria in autumn. Alexander was still in Cilicia, detained in Tarsus by a severe illness, and on his recovery busied himself with the conquest of some of the coast cities. But when he heard of the advance of Darius, he marched trough the narrow pass near the coast which connects Cilicia and Syria, and commenced the siege of Myriandros, the first Phœnician city on the road. He evidently reckoned on Darius meeting him in the level places of northern Persia, where the latter's cavalry could be used to its best advantage, but Darius showed a keener strategical instinct than is usually associated with Persian generalship. While Alexander was taking the coast road south, Darius' army made a northerly movement, passing over a difficult mountain region, and so appeared in the rear of the Macedonian army on the level plain near Issus. The Persians had a strong position; on their right was the sea, and on their left a chain of mountains. On the front they were protected by the deeply worn bed of the river Pinarus. They had also constructed a line of earthworks.

The preliminary operations of the Persians were conducted with great intelligence. By them Alexander was cut off from his base and his position was desperate, unless he could restore his line of communications by a successful engagement. This was no easy matter, for the mountain defile, the Assyrian Gate, had to be passed through, a place where the mountains and the sea are so close that there is room only for a road. Darius had an excellent position but failed to make any use of it. Without attempting to interfere he allowed Alexander to march through the narrow strip of land between the mountains and the sea and to change from a column formation into regular battle array.

It took the Greek commander the whole night to make the journey from Myriandros, a place south of the defile, to the level country on the banks of the Pinarus. As Alexander's army debouched on the plain, the cavalry and the light-armed troops sent against them by Darius failed to arrest their progress. The Persians were outmanœuvered from the start, for on the plain, which had very narrow limits—a little more than two miles wide—Darius could make no use of his superior numbers, nor was there opportunity for bringing to bear to any purpose the Persian advantage in cavalry. It was possible for Alexander to extend his own line of battle just as far as the enemy could, and the nature of the ground protected him against any enveloping manœuver. Thus the disposable forces, on either side, were equalized, and on account of the superior training and skill of the Macedonians, there was little doubt from the first as to the issue of the fight.

On the Greek side the left wing was commanded by Alexander in person, and it was made up of the Macedonian cavalry, the hypaspists, and a part of the ordinary infantry. The vigor of their onslaught was irresistible, and the Asiatics opposed to them gave way after a short struggle and fled. The whole Persian center was disorganized, even Darius avoiding capture with difficulty. His chariots, his royal robes, and his arms fell into the hands of the victorious Greeks. In another part of the field Parmenio, who was in command of the left wing of the Greek army, had no easy time in withstanding the charges of the Asiatic cavalry, and also when the Macedonian phalanx undertook to storm the heights which were occupied by Greek mercenary troops on the other side, they were repulsed with considerable loss. Fortunately, Alexander, after defeating the division opposed to him, was able to use his infantry to attack the mercenaries on their rear, and they were forced to withdraw from the field. They retired in good order, but the Persian cavalry proved inefficient, and were repulsed with great loss. In their flight they demoralized the reserves which had been placed by the Persians immediately behind the line of battle. The Persian army ceased to exist as a military entity and the fugitives were saved from further pursuit only by the early nightfall of the autumn season. Darius was able to bring together on the other side of the Syrian mountains 4000 men, most of whom were Greek mercenaries, and with a small force he recrossed the Euphrates. The main body of the Greeks, attached to the army of Darius, made their way to Tripolis in Phœnicia and from there sailed to Cyprus. (October, 333 B.C.)

After the battle the Persian camp was occupied by the Greeks, and among the captives were the mother of Darius and his wife, Stateira, and her children. These members of the royal household were treated considerately. Their presence with the Greek army was a most valuable asset, and a few days after his defeat Darius began to open negotiations for the purpose of having the captives restored to him. Alexander showed no unfriendly spirit, and received an embassy with formal proposals of peace from Darius. The conditions were, that all of the country west of the Euphrates should be ceded and the large sum of 10,000 talents given for the return of the royal captives. In addition to this, as a pledge of good faith, it was proposed that Alexander should receive one of the king's daughters in marriage. The offer was a proof that Darius realized how deep was his humiliation and how small the chance of successful resistance to the conqueror.

Liberal as the terms were, it must have been plain to Alexander that to make peace now was to leave his work half finished, especially as the first half was the more difficult. In it he had defeated the best soldiers under the command of Darius, and there was nothing more to fear from the Persian fleet, its most important units being withdrawn to protect Syria, nor was a rising in Greece likely to be attempted. The news of the battle of Issus had made the anti-Macedonian faction in the Greek cities see the purposelessness of counting on the co-operation of Persia. At the Isthmian games the representatives of the Hellenic confederation voted Alexander a golden crown as a defender of the liberties of Greece.

Alexander answered the proposition of the Persian king in a stern mood, fully conscious of his strength. His letter to Darius, which has been preserved, is a document that speaks in no uncertain tone. "Your ancestors invaded Macedonia and the rest of Greece, and without provocation inflicted wrongs upon us. I was appointed leader of the Greeks and crossed over into Asia for the purpose of avenging those wrongs; for ye were the first aggressors. In the next place ye assisted the people of Perinthus, who were offenders against my father, and Ochus sent a force into Thrace, which was part of our empire. Further, the conspirators who slew my father were suborned by you, as ye yourselves boasted in your letters. Thou with the help of Bagoas didst murder Arses (son of Ochus) and seize the throne unjustly and contrary to the law of the Persians, and then thou didst write improper letters regarding me to the Greeks, to incite them to war against me, and didst send to the Lacedæmonians and other of the Greeks, for the same purpose, sums of money (whereof none of the other cities partook but only the Lacedæmonians); and these emissaries corrupted my friends and tried to dissolve the peace which I had brought about in Greece. Wherefore I marched forth against thee who wert the aggressor in general. I have overcome in battle first thy generals and satraps, and now thyself and thine host, and possess thy land through the grace of the gods. Those who fought on thy side and were not slain but took refuge with me, are under my protection and are glad to be with me and will fight with me henceforward. I am lord of all Asia, and therefore do thou come to me. If thou art afraid of being evilly entreated, send some of thy friends to receive sufficient guaranties. Thou hast only to come to me to ask and receive thy mother and children, and whatsoever else thou mayest desire. And for the future whenever thou sendest, send to me as to the Great King of Asia, and do not write as to an equal, but tell me whatever thy need be, as to one who is lord of all that is thine. Otherwise I shall deal with thee as an offender. But if thou disputest the kingdom, then wait and fight for it again and do not flee; for I will march against thee, wherever thou mayest be."

Darius now set about collecting another army and made no more peace proposals. He gathered the fragments of the force that had been beaten at Issus, and to this were added contingents drawn from all the furthermost parts of his empire still in his hands. The army so formed was almost exclusively Asiatic, for of Greek mercenaries there were only the soldiers, a few thousand all told, who had followed him in his flight. No others could now be secured. Darius' new plan was to await the approach of Alexander on the plains of Assyria, where the Persian cavalry could be used with most effect.

On Alexander's part there was no haste in turning to the interior. Instead of following Darius, he remained on the sea coast, while Parmenio was sent to Damascus with half the Greek army, to seize the treasure left there by Darius before the battle of Issus. Alexander with the rest of the army turned south to the conquest of the great island city of Phœnicia, which unlike its smaller neighbors had refused to surrender and had declared its neutrality to Alexander. Tyre was the center of Persian sea power, and so long as it remained independent its fleet could be used against the Greek king, either on the sea itself or as an instrument for creating disturbances in continental Greece.

The siege of Tyre involved special difficulties; not only were its walls high and strong, but it was situated on an island separated from the mainland by a shallow body of water. As Alexander had no fleet adequate to conduct aggressive operations from the open sea against the city, he planned to bring up his siege engines against the walls from the land side, by building a causeway over the shallow body of water. The defenders of the town tried repeatedly and with great bravery to prevent such an approach from being made. Tyre's own commercial competitors, Cyprus and the less important Phœnician cities, including Sidon, placed their navies at Alexander's disposition, and with their ships he began to operate from the sea. The situation of the town was desperate, but its people made a defense as desperate and as resourceful as their daughter city Carthage in later days against the Romans.

When the causeway was finally constructed, the walls on this side, being 150 feet high and enormously thick, were not damaged by the siege engines. Accordingly Alexander changed his plans quickly; the engines were mounted in vessels and a breach was effected in one of the battlements extending along the harbor. While the Macedonians were now able to penetrate the city, they met with heavy resistance from the besieged townsmen, and the occupation of Tyre was only effected by the protection of Alexander's naval allies, who forced an entrance into the two harbors, and so drew off a portion of the defenders from the side where the Greeks were making their attack. The stubborn defense cost the Tyrians 8000 men, and of the prisoners 3000 were sold as slaves. On the Macedonian side the loss was small, only amounting to 400 men, but no mention is made of the losses of the allied fleets. The siege of Tyre lasted seven months, the city falling in July, 332. The long delay was worth while, for the successful issue showed how invincible was the generalship of the Greek leader. By the possession of the city he held the key to the control of the eastern Mediterranean.

On the way south he met with no resistance except from the strong citadel at Gaza, which withstood him for two months and was finally taken by storm. The march to Egypt could now be safely undertaken, as the whole sea coast from the Hellespont south was in the hands of the Greeks. Egypt itself had no love for its Persian masters. It had not long before been autonomous for fifty years, and it had been brought back under the régime of the Great King under circumstances of repression that made its inhabitants greet Alexander as a liberator. The Persian governor, seeing the folly of resistance, gave up the strong places, and Alexander passed the winter in the country. During his stay he founded the only good harbor on the coast, the city which still bears his name. This undertaking was not the boastful action of a conqueror, solicitous of the praise of posterity; it was a keen-sighted scheme to divert from the Phœnician towns of Syria the control of the Mediterranean trade. Within half a century Alexandria had become a great commercial emporium, the center of Greek science and learning, and for three hundred years it continued to be the richest and largest city in the world.

As the members of the old Egyptian monarchy had proclaimed themselves sons of Ammon, Alexander, in order to regularize his position in the newly conquered province, made a visit to the temple of Zeus Ammon, traveling across the desert with a small company of troops. He was greeted by the priests of the temple as the divinely accredited ruler of Egypt, but the exact words of the response of the oracle were not communicated. They were kept as a mystery, but the divine honors claimed afterwards by Alexander were always connected with this mysterious attestation of his claim that his father was no earthly parent, but Zeus himself.

Darius, meanwhile, was in no position to interrupt this series of successes in Syria and in Egypt. He had no army there prepared to take the field, but he did try to interfere with the Greek lines of communication in regions more remote from the present scene of operations. Antigonus, left in Phrygia as its governor, was attacked by a force composed of some of the soldiers who had fought on the Persian side at Issus, as well as of contingents from Cappadocia and Paphlagonia. But the attempt was unsuccessful. Antigonus showed remarkable military ability, for with his small force he defeated the Persians and added to the region under him the country of Lycaonia, which had never submitted to Persian rule. In the spring of 331 Alexander left Egypt for his march to the interior of the Persian Empire, and by the middle of the summer he crossed the Euphrates near Thapsacus, and from there, taking a northerly direction through Mesopotamia, he passed the Tigris on the 20th of September.

The advance of the Greek army was continuous, little resistance being offered to its progress. It seemed to be the aim of Darius to do nothing to prevent Alexander from penetrating into the interior. If the Greeks were defeated there, they would be cut off from retreat, and in case the Persians again failed, there would be a chance for the vanquished to withdraw in security to the mountainous country to the north. Alexander has been criticised for delaying so long in his occupation of Syria and Egypt; indeed Parmenio had urged him to accept the terms offered by Darius after the battle of Issus, a suggestion which called forth from Alexander the reply "that he would do it if he were Parmenio." But the small number of soldiers under his command showed the strategy he followed to be as cautious as his conduct of the expedition was daring. If he had gone straight on after the battle of Issus, he would have been obliged to detach enough men from his main army to act as a corps of observation in Syria and Egypt, and this would have left him hardly more than 20,000 men.

In the meantime he had received accessions of numbers, so that when he came to confront Darius for the second time he had under his command about 47,000 men. The engagement took place at Gaugamela (October, 331 B.C.), not far from the ruins of Nineveh. Darius had made some attempt to give an improved armament to his foot soldiers, supplying them with longer spears and swords so that they might fight the Macedonian phalanx on more equal terms. Besides this, he had provided chariots armed with scythes and a small number of elephants, which could be effectively used only in a level country. But his chief hope lay in his cavalry, of which he probably had 12,000, while Alexander had but 7000.

The Greeks had had four days' rest in a fortified camp before they were drawn up in battle array, and besides this the ground between them and the Persians had been carefully reconnoitered, in order to discern if the enemy had constructed concealed pits to confuse the cavalry charge. There was no way of protecting the flanks of the army, so Alexander placed a reserve force behind with orders to move towards the right or the left, according as the expected turning movement from the Persians might develop. The Greeks moved forward on the 30th of September, with Alexander leading the Macedonian heavy cavalry and the bulk of the phalanx. He directed his attack against the enemy's left wing, but as he did so he was charged on the flank by the Scythian and Bactrian horse. He sent against them the reserves previously mentioned, and himself engaged the Persian infantry, who had lost heart when they were attacked by the Macedonian cavalry. The manœuvers with the scythe-bearing chariots did no damage, for the Greeks made way for them to pass through their ranks, and re-formed again as soon as they had rattled past. The onslaught of the phalanx proved irresistible; the Asiatic foot could not withstand its superior armament and discipline. The Persian center was broken and again Darius had the ignominious experience of a headlong flight. The Persian cavalry, left to battle alone, was soon demoralized and could not hold its ground.

Parmenio's experience with the left wing of the Greeks was different, for he had difficulty in keeping his position against the Persian horse. He could not follow Alexander's advance, and hence there came to be a great gap between the two positions of the army. In this open space the Persians precipitated themselves; the Greek lines in battle array were forced farther apart and their camp occupied. It was a most dangerous position, but the barbarians, instead of using their advantage, busied themselves in plundering the Greek camp. Alexander turned from pursuing the Persian center to help the hard-pressed left wing, and on his way met the enemy's cavalry, now on their way back with the booty of the Macedonian camp. He tried to cut them off from their main body, but they fought with desperation and succeeded in breaking through. In the hand-to-hand fights one of Alexander's closest friends, Hephæstion, was wounded.

The danger to the left wing was now over, for the Persian commander Mazæus, on hearing of his king's flight, had ceased the attack on Parmenio, who now occupied the Persian camp, while Alexander resumed the pursuit of the main body, anxious to get Darius into his hands. He marched with great rapidity, reaching on the day after the battle Arbela, at which place the supplies and treasures of the flying Persians were discovered. But the Great King had made good his escape to Media, where, owing to the mountainous character of the country, it was useless to pursue him farther. The results of the battle were impressive materially and emotionally. The Persians had no heart to continue the war. Their army was destroyed, 10,000 prisoners were in the hands of their enemy, and the road to their capitals, Babylon and Susa, lay open. All this had been won by Alexander at a small cost, only 100 Macedonians having fallen, and the whole loss of the Greek army did not exceed 500 men.

Alexander marched to Babylon, which was surrendered without resistance by its inhabitants, who welcomed him as a liberator. Religious differences had made the citizens regard the Persians as oppressors, and Alexander won over the Babylonians by acting as the protector of their national religion. He rebuilt the Babylonian temples and also showed a placable temper by keeping the Persian Mazæus as satrap of the province of Babylonia. Without delaying at Babylon longer than was necessary to conciliate the inhabitants, Alexander passed to Susa. Its citadel offered no resistance, and with its surrender the town and its treasury, amounting to 50,000 talents ($60,000,000), became the property of the conqueror. (December, 331 B.C.)

The next stage of the conquest of the interior of Asia was the occupation of the country called Persis, the homeland of the Persians. To reach it a difficult country held by Uxian hillmen had to be passed. These were proud of their independence, for they had never paid tribute to the Persians, and they now occupied their mountain defile, prepared to dispute the passage of the Greeks. They were easily circumvented by Alexander's strategy, and brought to reason. Farther on, the access to Persepolis was strongly defended by the Persians, but Alexander forced his way through devious mountain roads and took the capital without trouble. The national treasure, equivalent to 120,000 talents, fell into his hands.

Up to this point the march of Alexander had been through territories which the Persians had themselves acquired by conquest, and which had been long exploited by their satraps. The populations were, therefore, not inimical to the new conquerors. Indeed, as we have seen in many cases, the latter were greeted as deliverers from the heavy yoke of the Persians. On its side, the Macedonian army had been kept under strict discipline, and the lives and property of the people through whom it had passed were carefully respected. But Persepolis was really in the enemy's country, the cradle of Persian rule, and there was no chance of reconciling its inhabitants by kind treatment. They were now to feel the brunt of real warfare. The city was given up to plunder, and the royal citadel of the Achæmenian kings was burnt down in a drunken revel. This ruthless act has been condemned, and it does appear to have been the result of a moment of excess, not planned as part of a policy of repression, for Alexander ordered the flames quenched, though he himself had cast the first firebrand that had set the costly cedar work of the palace in flames.

These various military operations lasted far into the autumn. When winter came the sorely tried and traveled Greeks took four months' rest, and from this point begins another stage in the expedition, for Persis was regarded as sufficiently pacified to allow the bulk of the army to march into Media. Here Darius was preparing to make a last stand, but his efforts to collect a new army had the somewhat pitiful result of bringing to his standard a force of not more than 3000 horsemen and 6000 foot soldiers. As the Greeks approached, he fled before them, recognizing the hopelessness of resistance. He seemed minded to take refuge in the extreme limits of what had been his empire, the province of Bactria. Without striking a blow, Alexander occupied Ecbatana, the last of the great Persian capitals.

All that now remained was to round off the conquest by capturing the person of the defeated monarch, and to force the satraps of the eastern provinces to accept the new régime. This program offered no serious military problems, but it was bound to consume time and required patience. Many of the non-Macedonian Greeks were now sent home, after receiving generous rewards for their service, and Parmenio was left at Ecbatana, while Alexander with the best of his troops set off to pursue Darius. Hurrying on by Ragæ, a place a little to the south of the modern capital of Persia, Alexander found there that the royal fugitive had already passed through the Caspian Gates into the regions of Parthia. Bactria was still much farther to the east. The followers of Darius, with the exception of a few faithful Greek mercenaries, determined to hand over their unlucky monarch as a prisoner to the satrap of Bactria, Bessus, a kinsman of his, and to trust to his initiative to organize a national resistance more effectively than Darius.

When Alexander, after a stay of several days at Ragæ, heard that his old antagonist was a prisoner he hurried on, taking rest neither by night nor by day, and finally came up with the barbarians, who now preserved no semblance of discipline in their retreat. When Bessus and the other conspirators saw Alexander approaching, they ordered Darius, who was probably carried in a litter, to mount a horse and accompany them. When he refused, they stabbed him and rode off. He was found dying at a spring near the road, by a Macedonian soldier. By the time Alexander reached the place the end had come. All that he could do for his fallen foe was to throw his own cloak over the body and order it to be sent with befitting honor to the queen mother. The last member of the Persian monarchy, which had become a world power under Cyrus, was buried in the royal tombs at Persepolis.

IV

THE INVASION OF INDIA

The death of Darius did not delay the activity of Alexander; he was all the more stirred to pursue Bessus when it was announced that the satrap of Bactria was claiming to be the successor of Darius and had assumed the insignia of royalty. But the regions close at hand had to be pacified, so Parmenio was sent to occupy the country near the southwest coast of the Caspian Sea. Alexander himself had to retrace his steps to deal with a rebellious satrap who had previously sent in his submission.

On the march southward, the province of Drangiana was taken without resistance, but the conqueror's stay at the capital, Prophthasia, was marked by a mysterious tragedy. It was reported to Alexander that Philotas, the son of Parmenio, was plotting against him. An assembly of the Macedonian army was summoned, and the charges laid formally before them. Philotas admitted that he had known of a plot to assassinate Alexander, but had kept it secret. This reserve was treated as treason, and Philotas was put to death by the soldiers. This semi-judicial act was followed by the murder at Alexander's command of his faithful lieutenant, Parmenio, for which there was no excuse, as he had never been charged with complicity in the guilty knowledge of his son. But Alexander probably judged that the execution of Philotas would inaugurate a blood feud familiar to Macedonian life, and he resolved to take no chances.

The road to Bactria selected by Alexander led him through modern Afghanistan and across the Hindu Kush mountains. But first he turned to the south in order to secure Seistan and the northwestern portion of Baluchistan, known at that time as Gedrosia. The winter of 330-29 he spent in the south of Seistan among a friendly people, the Ariaspæ, to whom, on account of their hospitable reception, he granted autonomy. Among the Gedrosians, their neighbors, he set up a satrapy, with a capital at Pasa.

In the spring, the Greek army pushed on to Arachosia, almost directly south of Bactria, where the king founded another Alexandria, probably on the site of the modern Candahar. At the foot of the high range of the Hindu Kush, a complex mass of mountains which divides southern from central, eastern from western Asia, called Paropanisus, the army passed the winter, and yet another city, named after their leader, was founded somewhere to the north of Cabul, Alexandria of the Caucasus. In the early spring the difficult mountain ranges which protected Bactria were crossed, the troops suffering much from the cold and from the lack of food. They were obliged to subsist on raw meat and on herbs instead of bread. After resting the army, Alexander led them on through an arid plain to Bactria, the chief city of the satrapy. (329-28 B.C.)

Bessus, the pretender, had tried to hinder the progress of the Greeks by laying waste the country in front of them, but as soon as they drew near, his horsemen deserted him and he fled across the Oxus. Alexander lost no time in following him up. The pursuit carried him through Sogdiana, where he crossed the Oxus on the rafts, made of inflated skins, such as are still in use to-day. The river was passed at a point where it was not a mile wide, at Kilif, and from thence the road was taken to Maracanda, a town whose old name is now thinly disguised as Samarcand. Bessus was deserted by his supporters, who thought that they would be glad to secure peace by his surrender. They abandoned him, and he was found by a division of the Greek army in a walled village, and was finally sent in chains to Bactria, after Alexander had charged him with the murder of Darius, his kinsman and benefactor.

The ardor for annexing the Far Eastern division of the Persian Empire to his rule spurred Alexander on, now that the rebellion of Bessus had so unexpectedly failed. He purposed to make, not the Oxus, but the Tanais his frontier on the northeast. The resistance seemed easily overcome; the seven strongholds of the Sogdians were occupied, and on the banks of the Jaxartes, or Tanais, at a point which is the gate of communication between southwestern Asia and China, the pass over the Tian-shan mountains, Alexander set the boundary of his conquests in this direction, by founding a new city called Alexandria the Ultimate, in later days Khodjend. While he was planning his new town, the country rose in revolt, for the chieftains of Sogdiana had no mind to lose their freedom. The small Macedonian garrisons left in the strongholds a short time before were overpowered, and the city of Maracanda was being besieged. The news of the revolt had spread far and wide, and the various Scythian tribes were hurrying to join in driving out the invaders. Alexander quickly recovered the strongholds, burning five of them, but at Cyropolis there was stout resistance, and he received a wound. The inhabitants of all were removed and forcibly transplanted as citizens of the new Alexandria. (328 B.C.)

It was not possible to go to the rescue of Maracanda because of the threatening attitude of the Scythian tribes, who were preparing to descend upon Alexandria, which was only separated from them by the river Tanais. The danger of being rushed by these barbarous hordes was imminent. The new city, therefore, was made capable of resistance; in the short period of twenty days it was surrounded with walls of unburnt clay. But Alexander determined also to strike terror by aggressive action. He brought up to the banks of the river engines which threw stones and darts among the enemy and forced them to retreat from the stream. Then the Greek army crossed, and the Scythians were soon routed. The king, with his cavalry, pursued them some distance in their own territory. The heat was intense and Alexander was made dangerously ill by drinking the water along the line of march.

On his recovery he had to deal with a difficult revolt in Sogdiana, again led by Spitamenes, who had figured in the previous uprising and who this time had succeeded in cutting off a detachment of Macedonian troops sent in pursuit of him. It is recounted that the fear of a disaster made such a serious impression on the conqueror that he covered the distance to Samarcand, over 150 miles, in three days. Spitamenes did not wait to try conclusions with the Greeks, but abandoned the siege, drawing off hurriedly in a westward direction, closely pursued by Alexander.

The Persian leader and his Scythian supporters were driven into the wastes across the river Sogda, and Alexander, after ravaging the province of Sogdiana, crossed into western Bactria and passed the winter at Zariaspa, one of the chief cities of that region.

While residing here, the trial of the pretender Bessus was begun. He was condemned to mutilation and to die on the cross at Ecbatana. This type of punishment was alien to Greek feeling and tradition, but it is not necessary to say that Alexander's apologists have argued the necessity of conforming to the habits of Oriental races when they are to be ruled successfully by outsiders. Alexander himself, as he had never assimilated the best traditions of Greece, seemed ready enough to adopt Oriental customs either to heighten his own dignity in Persia or to impress the Persians that he was the legitimate successor of Darius.

The colloquial axiom, "the longest way round is the shortest way home," can be applied to the science of government and politics, and it is more than probable that the Hellenization of Asia would have had less of the pinchbeck quality if Alexander had been trained in Sparta rather than in Macedon. In any case, we know that his abandonment of the homely traits characteristic of the relations between a Greek commander and his soldiers made him unpopular, and that, especially, the favor shown by him to the Persians who sided with him was distasteful to the Macedonians. His execution of Parmenio savored of oriental despotism, and during this winter there were open signs of discontent in the camp. (328-27 B.C.)

The winter quarters were changed to Maracanda on account of the restlessness among the natives, and in the relaxation from the strict discipline the soldiers and their leaders spent much of their time in carousing. On one occasion when Alexander and his companions were excited with wine, the king was made indignant at some slighting reference to his military exploits made by his foster-brother Clitus, who appealed to some verses of Euripides which signify that the army does the work and the general reaps the glory. Alexander in his drunken passion hurled a spear at the offender, and Clitus fell dead. The fatal issue of this drunken quarrel was followed by three days' passionate remorse, and Alexander lay in his tent sleepless and refused food. The fact that he had murdered his intimate friend could not be glossed over even if the army were willing to exculpate their leader, by giving Clitus a post-mortem trial, or by their ascribing the act to the Dioscuri, whose festival was being celebrated at the time.

The excitable temperament of Alexander, unfortunately, cannot always be ascribed to intemperance in drink. He began to be intoxicated with the idea that he was a semi-divine being, and he undertook to act the rôle of an avenging deity, in executing a ruthless sentence of destruction on a small Greek colony in Sogdiana, where dwelt the descendants of the people of Branchidæ, who generations before had betrayed to the Persians the treasures of a temple of Apollo not far from Miletus. The act had never been forgotten, and now Alexander caused all the inhabitants of the place to be massacred, and every vestige of it to be destroyed. An action like this was alien to the spirit of free Greece, and it marks the king's progress in Oriental despotism. It is all the more a witness to his personal degradation that the Milesian men in his own army, to whom Alexander wished to leave the decision, could not themselves agree on the fate of the Branchidæ, and hence the initiative in the massacre was due to the savage sentiments of their leader.

The pacification of Sogdiana took some time, owing to the rugged nature of the regions in the southern part of the province, but the campaign is chiefly noteworthy because it resulted in the marriage of Alexander with Roxane, the daughter of a native chieftain who had gallantly defended against the Macedonians a mountain fastness called the Sogdian Rock. It had never been noted in the career of the youthful conqueror that he was susceptible to the influence of women. Hence this sudden attachment was as unexpected as it was unpopular in the army. They disliked to have their king ally himself with an alien, and their lack of sympathy was accentuated because Alexander chose to marry his bride after the fashion of her country.

The influence of the Oriental environment was seen also in the introduction of Persian court ceremonial. The king desired to make the custom of obeisance to royalty used by the Persians applicable also to the Greeks. Callisthenes, a nephew of Aristotle, who was attached to the army as official historiographer of the campaign, earned Alexander's resentment because he sturdily refused to adopt the Persian ceremonial in the king's presence. He was soon afterwards charged with being involved in a plot to murder Alexander, which originated because of the resentment held against the king by the royal pages, when one of their number, Hermolaus, was flogged and reduced from his position for a breach of etiquette in a boar hunt at which Alexander was present. Callisthenes, apparently because he was an intimate friend of Hermolaus and therefore assumed to be an accomplice in the plot, was hanged.

Three years had now passed since the death of Darius; Alexander had done in the interior of Asia a work which no western conqueror has accomplished since on so large a scale. Even to-day the effective occupation by Russia of the lands once included in the Persian Empire falls short of Alexander's achievement, because Afghanistan, included in his conquests, is still an autonomous state. It will have been already noticed that much attention had to be given while the Macedonian army was in these Far Eastern provinces, to their protection against the nomad tribes on their frontiers. These operations in Bactria and Sogdiana were a necessary part of the conquests of Persia, since these remote provinces acted as a barrier against the savage tribes of the central Asiatic steppes, who might at any time by joint action overrun the civilization of the regions south of them. The special care shown by Alexander in the construction of settlements in this region is an evidence of his desire to make them centers of civilizing influence by which the restless herdsmen might be trained to orderly methods of life. The experiment failed, but it was a brilliant vision—a vision which might have become a reality if the conqueror had lived the normal span of years.

The beating down of all opposition in the enormously extensive empire which the defeat of Darius had laid at his feet had now been accomplished. If Alexander had been a statesman and nothing else, he would have stayed his hand, because the consolidation of the territory he had overrun was a work demanding the time and the talents of the greatest genius. But Alexander had not the temper of a Roman proconsul, capable and zealous to solve large political problems. He was young enough to be influenced by the spirit of adventure, and unlike Cæsar and Napoleon, had sometimes no deeply laid scheme in his military exploits.

There was no political or military necessity summoning Alexander to the conquest of India, but there was the irresistible charm of novelty exerted by the unknown, the ambition to penetrate into regions untrodden before by any Greek, and with this feeling of the conqueror the modern world is able to sympathize. He was lured also by the legendary stories of the visits to India of the god Dionysus and the hero Herakles. The mystical, superstitious traits in Alexander's character could easily be stimulated, as we have already seen, to emulation with the divinities of his people, and he was also glad to afford proof that he could effect a conquest attempted without success by Cyrus and Semiramis.

The actual military difficulties of the undertaking were not great, for though the Indians were brave and warlike, and though they had a well-populated land to draw from, they were not a national unity. As the Indian states were constantly at war with one another, there would be an opportunity of securing allies in the peninsula. There was no difficulty in securing recruits for the expedition, although it is true a large detachment of the army had well-understood motives for desiring to be left in Bactria; but some of the best Asiatic warriors from these regions were enrolled, 30,000 in number, and the levies with which Alexander now prepared to descend on India were certainly twice as great as those with which he had left Macedon seven years before. His army was now a great cosmopolitan community, an organism resembling the mercenary armies of the Middle Ages, in the times of the Condottieri. It was self-supporting and self-sufficient in more senses than one, for it included artisans, engineers, physicians, diviners, literary men, athletes, secretaries, clerks, musicians, as well as a host of women and slaves.

Most of the states in northern India at this time were inhabited by what is often called an Aryan stock, the descendants of a succession of waves of emigration through the northwestern hills from central Asia. They had given up their nomadic life and reached the agricultural stage. The Brahman caste system, with its asceticism, and with its power of directive guidance in the state, according to the dictates of a religious sect, already dominated the life of India, and the country as a whole was made up of small principalities and village communities with no common bond of union.

Alexander effected his entrance into this new world by marching from Nicæa (probably to be identified with Cabul) along the Cabul river and then proceeded through the now well-known Khyber Pass. For the purpose of securing his communications much time had to be spent in warfare with the brave inhabitants of the Himalaya Mountains. Many fortresses were taken, the most remarkable of these exploits being the capture of the rock of Aormas, which probably lies on the right bank of the Indus, some sixty miles above the junction of that river with the Cabul. The two tribes whose resistance gave the most trouble were the Aspasians and the Assacenes, dwelling in localities which can now be identified as being parts of Chitral in the Pangkan and Swat valleys.

This hard preliminary campaign lasted all the winter; in the spring the Indus was crossed and a three days' march was made eastward to Taxila, a rich country, whose prince, along with lesser princes, gave a friendly welcome to the conqueror. But this friendly attitude was not taken by Porus, the ruler of the region farther south, who sent a formal defiance to Alexander, and prepared to resist the invaders by collecting an army of from thirty to forty thousand men. With this he encamped on the river Hydaspes and prepared to contest its passage. Alexander transported the boats, which he had constructed for crossing the Indus, to the Hydaspes, and took up a position on the right bank of the stream, near Jalalpur, in view of the army of Porus, who had collected a large number of elephants, a formidable obstacle to the effective use of the Greek cavalry. (326 B.C.)

In the face of an enemy so placed the transit of the river was impossible, for the edge of the stream was slimy, making an insecure footing for the soldiers, and the horses, terrified by the presence of the elephants, could not be kept in control and would certainly be lost. Besides, Porus kept a sharp eye on all the fords near his camping ground. Alexander kept the enemy busy by making various feints as if he were about to attempt to pass the stream. It was the rainy season, and the Indian soldiers and elephants were kept in battle array at the threatened points, exposed for hours to the force of the wind and rain. Porus began to think that the Greeks were afraid to force the passage, and these manœuvers were continued until he was off his guard.

Some sixteen miles below the Greek encampment, where the river made a bend, there was a wooded island which hid the right shore from observation. Taking advantage of this, and also of the fact that on his side of the river there was a thick forest, Alexander managed to bring his boats, which were made of skins, to a place opposite the island, and at the same time he marched some of his troops down the stream, leading them by a detour some distance from the bank, in order to prevent the enemy from detecting his operations. The rest of the Greeks were left at the original camping ground or were posted along the river at different points, with directions to cross and aid him at the proper moment.

The actual crossing of the division under his command was done under his own eyes. Regiments of heavy-armed men were left on the right bank in anticipation of a possible rear attack by Abisares, prince of Cashmir, who, it was known, had promised to assist Porus in resisting the invading army. The passage was facilitated by the stormy weather which prevailed during the night. The Indian outposts heard nothing, and Alexander led the way safely past the island to the opposite shore, where, though some difficulty was caused by mistaking an islet for the mainland, the cavalry were disembarked and put in battle array. The whole number of troops under Alexander's command were 6000 hypaspists, 4000 light-armed foot, 5000 cavalry, including 1000 Scythian archers. In the meantime the Indian outposts had ridden away to announce to Porus what had happened and to prepare him for the news of the Greek advance. Alexander went swiftly forward, taking with him all the cavalry, and he soon met and defeated a detachment of 1000 Indian horsemen and 160 chariots under the command of the son of Porus.

The Indian king himself was advancing with the bulk of his army, and he drew up his line of battle as soon as he found a piece of sandy ground suitable for displaying the cavalry and elephants. In front he placed 200 elephants at intervals of 100 feet, and behind them his infantry to the number of 20,000. In the wings his cavalry were drawn up, about 4000 in all. Alexander placed the pick of his army, the hypaspists, immediately in front of the elephants. The use of these animals in battle was still a strange sight to the Greeks, and the Indian fighting line seemed to them like a city wall with towers. Porus did not think that his foes would venture to advance through the spaces left between the elephants. He argued that the horses would be terror-stricken and the foot would be met by the Indian foot soldiers if they tried to attack the elephants from the side, and that they would hesitate to move directly against them for fear of being trodden down by their onslaught.

Exactly how the Indian infantry were armed is left uncertain. They probably had not the solidity of the Greek phalanx and were depended upon only to cover the work of the elephants. Alexander kept his infantry in reserve until he was able to confuse the line of the enemy by a cavalry attack. His cavalry he directed to spread out and attack not only in front but on the flanks as well. This manœuver was executed with practised precision, and neither the Indian chariots nor their horse could withstand the furious onslaught of the Greek squadrons, and soon retired behind the elephants with the Macedonians in close pursuit. As the elephants wheeled round, passing through the infantry in order to meet the Macedonians, the quick advance was blocked; the horses could not be induced to charge. They were obliged to retire; then Porus, on his side, vigorously attacked both the Macedonian cavalry and the phalanx.

The fight was now a general one. The Greek authorities paint this stage of the battle in superlative diction, describing how the elephants pressed through the thickly packed masses in front of them, rending and trampling the soldiers and horses as they went, while the engines on their backs scattered destruction far and wide. But the Macedonians finally won by striking down the elephants' drivers and destroying the turrets they were in, and so wounded the beasts themselves that they ceased to attack. With the elephants rendered useless, the chance of victory for the Indians was gone. Their infantry was not sufficiently disciplined to make any use of the confusion caused in the Greek ranks by the work of the elephants. Besides, the Macedonian cavalry had in the first stage of the engagement got so far into the Indian lines, that they remained not only on the field of battle, but actually were, as the engagement advanced, behind both the enemy's infantry and the elephants as well. When the Indian cavalry tried to take a hand in the fight and leave the part of the field where the elephants were in action, the Greek horse, having a superiority in numbers, forced them back.

The Greek infantry phalanx had been ordered by Alexander to keep its ground, but when the cavalry fight made it impossible for the Indians to move forward, the Greek foot soldiers drew away from their first position, where they were liable to a frontal attack by the elephants, and driving the elephants back, exposed the enemy to an attack by the Macedonian horse. Unprotected as the Indians were on both sides, they could not escape defeat, and at this point of the battle they suffered severely; most of the elephants and King Porus himself were taken prisoners.

The Greek historian, Arrian, says that the Macedonian loss was only 310 dead, mostly horsemen; but as other authorities add 700 foot soldiers, it seems likely that the battle was a stubborn one, for there were only 11,000 men engaged in Alexander's army. The fact, too, that the use of elephants became customary in the wars fought by Alexander's successors, some of whom were present at the battle of Hydaspes, proves that the fight with Porus must have made an impression on his opponents, and this places it in a different category from the easier victories over the Persians. Alexander treated his defeated antagonist with magnanimity and erected his kingdom into a vassal state; but as safeguards of his loyalty, directed that two garrison cities, Bucephala and Nicæa, should be established in his domains, one on either side of the Hydaspes near the site of the battle. A lieutenant, Crateros, was left to carry out these building plans, while Alexander turned to the conquest of the neighboring tribes. The only notable difficulty was the taking of the town of Sangala, the chief citadel of the free and warlike Cathæans, which had been strongly fortified and which had to be taken by storm.

The general result was that the Punjab was annexed to Alexander's empire and placed in the hands of vassal princes. From this region the Greek army advanced to the river Hyphasis, reaching it at a point higher up than its junction with the Sutlej. This was the extreme limit of Alexander's march. He would have gladly gone farther, for the whole of India might well have become a subject state; but the army had suffered from the discomforts of the rainy season, and they were weary of campaigning. The horses were worn out, the armor and accoutrements in bad condition. The temper of the troops, devoted though they were to their commander, left no doubt that they would mutiny if Alexander refused to turn back. He told the officers he would go on himself, and that they could return to Macedonia and let the Macedonians know that they had abandoned their king in a hostile land.

But appeals and threats alike failed to convince the army that their view of the situation was unreasonable. The sacrifices were found to be unfavorable, and persuaded by this intimation of the disfavor of the gods, the king consented to return. On the bank of the Hyphasis twelve altars were erected of large size, as lofty as the walls of a city, to mark the limits of Macedonian conquests, and as a thank-offering to the gods for their protection through the hazards of long-continued warfare in strange lands. The army then retired to the Hydaspes.

Alexander was an explorer as well as a conqueror, and his disappointment at this enforced withdrawal from the prosecution of his march must have been that of a man who was within reach of the goal and just failed to attain it. According to the geographical notions of his day, he was near the certain limit of the world; he knew nothing of the great Indian peninsula, and of course nothing of the vast extent of Siberia or the Chinese Empire. He supposed that the Ganges flowed into an eastern sea which was continuous with the Caspian and which washed the shores of Scythia and the base of the high mountains he had lately passed through. On the river Hydaspes, a fleet had already been under construction; as soon as it was ready he embarked on it a part of his best troops, while the mass of the army, in two divisions, moved down the stream. The route followed was along the Hydaspes to its confluence with the Akesines, then down this stream to the Indus and the Indus itself to the Delta.

From the military point of view, this concluding stage of the Indian expedition offers little of special interest. The inhabitants of the country either submitted to or fled from the Greek army, and various strongholds were taken by storm. In an assault on one of them, held by the Malians, who dwelt in the southern Punjab, the king, who had pressed forward in the midst of the enemy, found himself separated from the main body of his followers and was dangerously wounded. In the region the army traversed several colonies were founded; another Alexandria rose at the point where the Akesines flows into the Indus, and at Pattala a harbor and navy yard were built. The conquered portion of India was organized in three satrapies, one of which was under Porus, who had a free position as a vassal prince, for in his territory there were no Macedonian garrisons.

But the real subjugation of the country had not been effected by the spectacular march through it; as soon as the Greeks turned their backs, an uprising took place. Before the whole army reached Pattala, a part had been detached with directions to march west to Arachosia, and to wait in Caramania till it was joined there by the main division. The fleet was placed under the command of Nearchus, a Cretan, who was to take it along the coast of the Indian Ocean and finally into the Persian Gulf. Alexander, at the head of the rest of the army, took the road through Gedrosia.

The difficulties of the return were considerable. The men under Alexander suffered terribly in passing a desert country before they reached, after sixty days' slow progress, the capital of Gedrosia, Pura. In the farther stretch to Caramania there was also exhausting work, but these trials marked the end of the expedition, for Crateros, who had led the rest of the troops by Arachosia, soon arrived, and news came of the landing of the fleet after a skilfully managed cruise of seventy-five days through unknown waters on the coasts of Caramania. A year had now passed (325 B.C.) since the beginning of the return home from India. During the course of the winter the army returned to Susa, thus concluding this remarkable adventure of Far Eastern conquest.

V

ALEXANDER'S EMPIRE

It had now been five years, from the summer of 330, since Alexander had left Ecbatana in pursuit of Darius. His presence was urgently needed, for the government of the empire was in chaotic state so far as the central administration was concerned. Fortunately the attempts at an uprising had generally been feeble, and were easily and loyally suppressed by the satraps where they did occur. Only one gave trouble, a revolt in Bactria, initiated first of all by Greek mercenaries and taken up by the native inhabitants as far as the border of Scythia. This lasted some time, and peace was not restored until after Alexander's death.

But the maladministration of the conquered provinces was more serious than these uprisings. During Alexander's absence in the Far East there had been boundless liberty in the financial plundering of the people. Peculation was the rule everywhere, and it was common to the Persian official class, to whom the government of the satrapies had been intrusted. Trained as these officers had been in maladministration and corruption, they had no notion of following different standards, simply because there was a different ruler. While Alexander was in Bactria he had been forced to deprive several satraps of their governments. It was time for the strong arm of the king to be felt, and there was no doubt about his intentions and aims. Many Persian satraps were executed and their places taken by Macedonian officers. But while Alexander had been away the infection had spread to European office-holders, both military and civil. We hear, for example, of the death penalty being inflicted on Greek commanders of the troops in Media, who had plundered graves and temples and had signalized their rule over the subject population by systemic oppression.

Among the guiltiest of this class was the minister of finance, Harpalus, who treated the state's money as his private property, had brought over from Athens a company of gay comrades, and was living the easy, reckless life of an Oriental satrap. His previous record had been anything but clean; before the battle of Issus he had been obliged to return to Greece and had only come back to Asia because he had received the royal pardon. He knew that there was no chance of finding the king amenable to excuses or explanations; so with 5000 talents taken from the treasury, he raised a body of 6000 mercenaries and departed for the sea coast, hoping to stir up a revolt. The scheme was a pitiable failure; no satrap held out a hand to him; and finally Harpalus sailed to Athens, where he had influence and could count on a welcome, because of the strong anti-Macedonian feeling in the city.

Alexander showed his appreciation of the lesson of Harpalus' official career by ordering the governors of the provinces to dismiss all soldiers they had collected on their own authority. Now that the period of military expansion was closed, the king devoted himself to the organization of the empire, following the lines he had worked out originally, which tended to the amalgamation of the Greek and Persian elements. This ideal survived the experience of maladministration, and Alexander held fast to it, despite the opposition of the officers of his army. He seems to have believed firmly in the possibility of educating politically the Asiatic peoples so that they could be ruled without display of despotic power, and he was just as firm in trusting to the loyalty of the Persian ruling class to carry out this program of interracial conciliation. In doing so he failed to take account of the Persian's deep-rooted dislike of the Greeks, which with Oriental wiliness his new subjects could conceal, but which was ever present as an inducement to them to take advantage of the first opportunity that offered to throw off the yoke imposed upon them by the conquest.

Alexander planned to make his scheme a success by marrying the daughters of the Persian official class to the Macedonian officers. He led the way by claiming, as the successor of the Great King, the right to have more than one legitimate wife, and after his return from India he added to his royal household a daughter of Darius, Stateira, and a daughter of Ochus, Parysatis. Alexander's close friend, Hephæstion, received another daughter of Darius, and altogether eighty of the high officers in command of the Macedonian army were married to Persian women of high degree. The wedding festivities were made a national affair, and took place at Susa on the same day with great ceremonial, all the brides receiving from Alexander marriage portions. The Macedonian private soldiers, who followed the example of their chief on this occasion, were richly rewarded.

It is said that the officers were as dissatisfied with the matrimonial schemes of the king as they had been with his plans for further conquest in India; in any case, it is known that on the king's death there was a general movement among them to get rid of their Persian helpmates. The discontent among the rank and file of Alexander's followers with his program of social equality between Greek and Persian could not be appeased, even when he paid their debts at the time of the "Union of the Two Races" festival, an act of bounty which cost him about $5,000,000. The hostility to Persian influence was accentuated by the introduction of foreign troops into the army. This was naturally a step required by the necessity of raising a force greater than Greece could possibly supply. That thinly populated country must have been already drained to the point of exhaustion by the demands already made upon it to fill up the losses during the years of constant campaigning. And as a matter of fact, we know that a year and a half after the passage of the Hellespont with 35,000 men, Alexander led to battle at Arbela about 60,000, and in the years during which the expedition was moving in the Far East, the various additional troops must have equaled altogether 50,000 men. The substitution of Persian contingents for Greek soldiers was a matter of plain necessity. They received lower pay, they cost less to feed, without considering the saving made in the high cost of transportation of bodies of men from continental Greece to the interior of Asia.

Orders had therefore been given to draw 30,000 young men from the conquered provinces and to prepare them for military services according to Macedonian methods. A further and more radical stage in the amalgamation policy was reached when Persians were enrolled in the Macedonian phalanx and Asiatic horsemen in the élite regiment of the Hetæroi; even in the life guards distinguished Persians were received, and the command of that force was assigned to a warrior from Bactria, Hystaspes.

These leveling measures were more than the Macedonian veterans could endure, and they became openly mutinous when Alexander proposed to dismiss those who had been longest in the service. The whole army stood together and told the king that they would serve no longer, and that he would see how he could do without them, now that he had his Persians to serve under him. Alexander then set to work to organize purely Persian regiments on the Macedonian model, a Persian life guard, a Persian squadron of Hetæroi, and a Persian phalanx. This satisfied the Macedonians, and they were farther placated by being given precedence over the various Persian units of the army. Under these conditions, the veterans were willing to be dismissed, and they received one talent as a bonus and full pay until they were actually on Macedonian soil. Moreover, the king agreed to provide for the education of their children. Ten thousand men on these terms returned to Greece.

A more effective means for bringing together the two races on an equal footing was the establishment of military colonies throughout the empire. At an early stage of the expedition this had been adopted as the readiest way of keeping peace in the conquered territory. Tyre and Gaza, after the native population had been sold into slavery, received a new population of Greek origin. We have already noted the extension of this scheme in the Far Eastern provinces and in India. Altogether seventy cities are said to have been founded by Alexander. These colonies, though primarily intended for military purposes, became centers of industrial communication and of civilization. The case of the Egyptian Alexandria is so well known that it does not require to be stressed. Less familiar are the proofs of Alexander's sagacity as a founder of flourishing towns in other parts of his empire. Alexandria, on the Persian Gulf, continued through the whole period of antiquity to be the greatest emporium of the whole region of Mesopotamia. Alexandria in Arcia (Herat) and Alexandria in Arachosia (Candahar) are still to-day important towns in Persia.

Despite his absorption in military interests, Alexander found time for looking after the economic development of his empire. The Indian Ocean was opened to commerce by the remarkable voyage of Nearchus which concluded the Indian expedition. Attempts were made to circumnavigate the Arabian peninsula, and, though they failed, yet a considerable portion of the coast was explored. The Caspian Sea was also the scene of exploring adventures, because it was supposed to be a part of the vast ocean by which the earth was surrounded. The Tigris was freed from obstruction and made navigable; the ancient irrigation canals in Babylonia were restored; and a beginning was made in constructing a harbor near Babylon.

Equally farsighted was Alexander's foundation of a unified monetary system for the empire. Under Persian rule the custom had been for the satraps to coin silver money, while the coinage of gold was reserved to the Great King. The result was that each province followed its own customs and financial chaos prevailed. Alexander reserved the minting privilege to the general government; even where provincial coining was permitted, the coins were of the same general type and bore the name of the king. The only exception to this rule is found in the case of the autonomous Greek cities on the western coast of Asia. This new monetary system was based on that of the Athenians; the bimetallic basis, as it had existed in the Persian Empire, was abandoned and the silver standard, as used at Athens and Corinth, took its place. The reformed monetary system of Alexander continued down to Roman times.

The large hoards of precious metals, which fell into Alexander's hands during the course of his conquests, not only gave occupation to his mints, but also freed him from financial anxiety. He had begun the expedition in a state of insolvency, for he had a debt of 1300 talents with only seventy in his war chest to cover it. The maintenance of the army required a monthly expenditure of 200 talents, and to this 100 talents had to be added for the fleet. The provinces in western Asia, the first fruits of his victories, could not supply a sum so large, and it was lack of money which caused Alexander to give up his fleet in the autumn of 334. After the battle of Issus and the conquest of the rich province of Egypt, there was soon a surplus where there had been a deficit, and Alexander was able to send considerable sums of money to Antipater to help him out in his campaign in Greece.

Rich as were the Persian treasures, they were heavily and constantly drawn upon by the ever-developing military needs of the conqueror. The whole force under arms, including the very numerous garrisons, must have equaled 100,000 men. This meant at least an expense of 7000 talents; to this large sum must be added the drains caused by Alexander's generosity, by official peculation such as that of Harpalus, and by the gifts to old soldiers, who were richly rewarded. The royal household, which was organized on the Persian model, was most expensive; the royal table alone costing 600 talents. Of course, the receipts were large, probably from fifteen to twenty thousand talents annually, but Alexandria's budget was far from balancing; and at the time of his death, there were contained in all the treasuries of the empire only 50,000 talents, about $70,000,000, a small sum when the size of the empire is taken into account.

In administering his domains, Alexander showed great conservatism; he made few changes, he allowed each of the countries which acknowledged the Great King as its overlord to retain its particular institutions. One important modification he did introduce into the loosely organized and haphazard

Persian system of rule, the division of power. The Persian satrap was generally the sole governor, having in his hands the civil, military, and financial administration. Alexander limited him to matters of internal administration, appointing a financial officer and a military commander armed with considerable powers. After the return from India, there was a further innovation made by the appointment of a Chiliarch, as the supreme director and head of the provinces, with a place immediately after the monarch himself. This official was a part of the governmental machinery of the Persian Empire, holding in it the place of a Grand Vizier. It was given to Alexander's friend, Hephæstion, but after his death it was left vacant. The most trusted servant, the actual head of the administration, was the Chief Secretary Eumenes from Cardia, a man of first-rate military and civil capacity; he was unfailingly loyal to his master, and after Alexander's death, suffered many vicissitudes because of his devotion to the Macedonian royal house.

Alexander was not satisfied with the rôle of conqueror; he wished to give his rule in the East that trait of legitimacy which the popular Oriental mind required as a stimulus to its loyalty. It was impossible for him to be King of Persia by the grace of God, for it was the might of his own hand, not the right of succession, that constituted him the heir of Darius. This Gordian knot of politics he solved in his own direct fashion by directing that divine honors should be paid to him by the subject populations. The custom of apotheosis originated in Egypt, but it was not alien to Greek thought, according to which no deep distinction existed between man and divinity. The mythical heroes of the Greek people, whom all allowed to have once been men, were everywhere honored with altars and sacrifice. Asclepius and Herakles sat on Olympus with the greater divinities of a purely spiritual origin. It had become not unusual in the age preceding Alexander to accord divine honors to the living. Such had been the case with Clearchus of Heracleia who had been greeted as the son of Zeus, and with Dionysius the Younger who had caused himself to be honored at Syracuse as the son of Apollo. Alexander's achievements, far greater in comparison, gave him a right to this distinction during his lifetime; his divine origin had, besides, been attested by the Erythrian Sibyl and by the oracle at Branchidæ; with this theological and official stamp all that remained to be done was to give the accepted belief a concrete form. The cult of the conqueror became a part of the state religion in the Greek communities throughout the empire. Whether Alexander took the initiative in this form of adulation we do not know; he certainly did not discourage it, and on his return from India he did not reject the adulatory form of congratulation expressed by many Greek states, who instead of sending formal deputations, presented the so-called "theories" usual when the festivals of the gods were celebrated. Athens at first resisted this form of transcendent courtesy, but finally, in order to avoid offending Alexander, it was resolved in the year 324 to enrol the conqueror among the gods of the city under the designation of Dionysus. So this debasing custom took root in Greece; the monarch became, by a noxious fiction, differentiated from the rest of mortals, and the infection spread from

Greece to Rome, and later on became crystallized in Christian civilization, through the example of the Byzantine court, and under the form of monarchy by divine right has not yet disappeared.

After the dismissal of the veterans from the army at Opis, Alexander withdrew from the plains of the Tigris, and according to the custom of the Persian monarchs spent the summer in the highlands of Media. He passed the time in relaxation; nautical and athletic festivals were held, in which celebrities from Greece took part. When the cooler weather began, there were expeditions to repress the bandit hill-tribes who dwelt between Ecbatana and Susa, people whom the Persians had never succeeded in bringing under control. Afterwards, the king returned to Babylon, where he received deputations from the Greek states and even from Italy. It was thought that an expedition to the west was being planned. But the king preferred to give his immediate attention to Arabia and, by conquering it, to open at last a direct road of communication between the interior of Persia and Egypt.

By June both the fleet and army were ready to start. A great banquet was given in honor of Nearchus, the admiral who was to undertake the adventurous voyage from the Persian Gulf to the Red Sea. The king withdrew from the feast and spent the rest of the night in a carouse with a friend, Medius. He rose late in the morning and another night was spent in excessive drinking. The following day he was attacked with fever; he could not walk and had to be carried on a couch to the altar, to make the customary sacrifices. He spent the day discussing the plans of the expedition with Nearchus. In the evening he had himself conveyed across the river to a garden villa, hoping for relief from its quiet isolation. But for six days the fever continued, the king being able only to attend the sacrificial ceremonial. His condition grew worse, and he was taken back to the palace; he slept a little, but the fever did not abate, and when his officers visited him, they saw that he had lost the power of speech. There was confusion among the soldiers, for it was rumored that their leader was dead; they clamored to be let into the palace, and passing by the bodyguard they circled past the bed of the dying monarch; but he was not able to speak and only signified by movements of his hands and eyes that he recognized them. Some of those about him spent the night in the temple of Serapis, awaiting an indication of the god that he might be transported to the temple as he lay and be healed by divine help. But they were warned, it is said, by a voice that he was not to be moved, and on the evening of June 13th he died, before he had completed his thirty-third year.

During the years of Alexander's conquests, the history of the Greek states sinks into insignificance. After the battle of Issus all hope of defeating Macedon by a combination with Persia was abandoned. The confederacy sent congratulations, and only Sparta stood aloof. Its king, Agis, even ventured to declare war, but, after a few small successes, he was defeated in the battle of Megalopolis, losing his life in the field. Sparta then sent hostages to Alexander and was generously treated. Later on he interfered again in the affairs of Greece by directing the confederation to take back the Greek exiles, 20,000 in number, and so mark his overlordship by an era of good feeling.

Only two states objected, Athens and Ætolia.

The only exciting incident in continental Greece was connected with the flight of the faithless finance minister, Harpalus, who came to the coast of Attica with 5000 talents, a body of mercenaries, and a considerable fleet, hoping to stir up a revolt. But the Athenian politicians were too cautious to be drawn into an intrigue which would certainly have proved dangerous. They seized Harpalus and took his treasure, proposing only to surrender this money to officers expressly sent by Alexander. Half the money taken disappeared and there was no official record made of the sum received. Demosthenes was involved in the scandal, and he emerged from it with a besmirched reputation. Harpalus escaped and was soon afterwards murdered. Demosthenes was condemned, imprisoned, and escaped. But Greek feeling was not sensitive about a case where it was plain that a man had appropriated stolen money for the good of the state, and Demosthenes was praised as a patriot.

Alexander's conquests, both in method and in achievement, were but the elaboration of the groundwork laid down by Philip his father. The army that conquered Persia and invaded India was trained in the campaigns of continental Greece, and without this preliminary training in Europe, its spectacular successes in Asia would not have been possible. Up to the time of Philip of Macedon, warfare in Greece had achieved only negative results. It was not systematized, no extensive imperial rule had come to the victors through any of the decisive battlefields, for these military successes were never followed up by a consistent scheme of conquest. Philip changed all this, and he brought his developed army and his new political policy into close connection. Demosthenes himself remarked this contrast, for he said that King Philip fought his wars not only with a phalanx of heavy-armed men, but with light infantry, archers, and cavalry.

The old campaigning schedule, which consisted in ravaging the enemy's territory for a few months, a set battle in the open country, and a withdrawal to winter quarters, was no longer observed. If the Macedonian king did not find his enemy in the field, he besieged his towns, using siege engines to bring him to terms. Summer and winter were alike used for operations when the old array of citizen amateur soldiers had given place to the professional fighters. Alexander's victories were won not only on the battlefield, but through the quick following up of his victories; the enemies' power of resistance was annihilated by the rapidity with which a defeated army was pursued and never allowed a chance to gather itself together again after it was beaten. These cavalry marches in the rear of a retreating enemy, or the suddenly delivered attacks on a foe preparing to resist, attacks made irrespective of mountains and deserts, were as military achievements no less remarkable than the set battles and the sieges of strongly walled cities and citadels. Supremely characteristic of Alexander's strategy was the pursuit after the battle of Gaugamela, when numbers of horses fell on the road from exhaustion.

As a general, Alexander did great deeds and did them in an heroic style. He was a warrior distinguished by personal bravery, filled with the ardor of combat, eager to be in the thickest of the fight, and yet the physical passion of the fighter in no way dulled the acute intelligence of the general, or made him indifferent to the mastery of details in preparing for battle or in following a victory up after it had been won. He showed strategical knowledge in approaching the enemy and knew how to overcome the natural difficulties in his way. So we see him unhesitatingly marching through narrow defiles and organizing different classes of troops according to the changing conditions which confronted him. He showed high capacity in selecting his base, in looking after his communications, in providing for and provisioning his men. When all was ready, and not before, these cautious provisions gave place to the impetuous onslaught in battle and the untiring pursuit of the defeated enemy. But the duties of generalship, complicated as they were, were not allowed to interfere with the "joy of fighting." Alexander in every fight led his cavalry in person; whenever a breach was made in a fortification he was in the first rank; whenever a town was taken he was the first to scale the wall.

He seemed instinctively to have taken in the significance of the enlarged scale on which warfare under him was conducted. He had to solve untried problems, due to the vast extent of territory he traversed, so different in every way from the restricted limits of continental Greece. The students of strategy have especially admired his originality in the systematic following up of a victory, an element in successful warfare not dreamed of by the citizen generals of Greece. In the Peloponnesian war it never occurred to the Spartans when they had defeated the Athenians to besiege Athens. But after Issus, a most decisive victory, Alexander showed the utmost resourcefulness in the long seven months' siege of Tyre, and finally took it by storm. The same mobility of generalship is noted in India, where he did not hesitate in the face of a division of elephants, an unknown arm in warfare, to cross a river and deliver a frontal attack.

The army, which never failed to respond to the ever-developing visions and schemes of its commander, until he had carried it to the eastern limits of the known world in his career of conquest, was at the very beginning of Alexander's career trained for any military project he might propose. It was composed of seasoned officers and men, who had proved their mettle and gained their laurels under Philip while he was bringing his army to the highest pitch of excellence. In the list of great Greek military leaders, Philip is placed by the side of Epaminondas, the Theban, the man who revolutionized the Greek art of warfare by a fine stroke of genius. It had been noted that in the Greek battles, where the phalanx had become the controlling factor, its right wing was frequently victorious in both opposing armies. This phenomenon was simply due to the fact that the Greek heavy-armed soldier carried a shield on his left arm and naturally tended to move in an oblique direction towards the right hand. The chief innovations introduced by Epaminondas were the strengthening of the left wing by increasing its depth—it was made fifty men deep—and the holding back of the right wing as the whole phalanx advanced in battle array. With the increased depth of the phalanx, the front was necessarily shortened, and in order to prevent flanking operations, Epaminondas made great use of cavalry, in protecting the flanks of his men from an encircling movement on the part of the enemy, whose phalanx, since it was not so deep (being the old shape), would stretch out on both sides beyond the lines of the Theban line. As a general, Philip accepted these new tactical principles originated by Epaminondas, and applying them to Macedonian conditions, made of the Macedonian army a wonderfully effective military machine.

Macedonia was peopled by peasants and herdsmen, and up to Philip's time they were an untrained mass, insufficiently armed, not able to contend with the armies of the rest of Greece. There was a landed aristocracy in Macedon, forming a special warrior class, who fought as cavalry. Using these elements and adding to them Greek mercenaries, King Philip had created a military force far superior to any that Greece had ever seen before.

The Greek cavalry moved in loose formation, the horsemen wore armor, and as arms they had a shield, sword, and spear, the spear being used rather for throwing than for striking, as is the case with the modern lance, with the whole momentum of the moving mass, man and horse. The troops of the Macedonian cavalry, formed of the nobles of the land, were called the followers of the king, "Hetairoi." They bore a shield and a spear for casting or thrusting, and a sword, and were always given a crucial position in an engagement. As contrasted with Greek cavalry generally, the Macedonians showed superior training and discipline; they moved together and behaved in a fight, not as individual warriors, but as tactical units, and were controlled in their movements by a single will. Such development of cavalry was unfamiliar to the Greek republics, which confined themselves to the technical training of the phalanx.

The Macedonian foot were the special creation of Philip, and were named by him "the followers on foot." They fought in the ordinary phalanx formation, but closer together than was usual, and used long spears, so that several lines were enabled at once to engage in actual hand-to-hand fighting. The spear was so constructed as to weight, thickness, and length that it could reach the opposing line and yet be firmly grasped. The ordinary spear was somewhat over six feet in length, but the Macedonian phalanx depended for its success not so much on man-to-man fighting as on the irresistible impact of the whole. When it was acting on the defensive, it was virtually impenetrable. Its disadvantage was in its lack of individual initiative; the soldiers were machines rather than fighting men. It was heavy in its movements and could be thrown into disorder more easily than the older Greek phalanx with its looser formation. The élite corps, the hypaspists, were more lightly armed than the men in the phalanx, and so moved more freely. In Alexander's battles they were the connecting link between the cavalry and heavy mass of the phalanx, which advanced slowly forward. As managed by Alexander, these various arms seem to have worked admirably together, all sharing in the activity of a general offensive movement. It should be added that Alexander was also indebted to his father for much of the advance made in the art of besieging. He constantly used siege engines, and we have noticed how much he depended on their successful employment at Tyre and Halicarnassus.

Posterity has justly selected the epithet "great" as most fitting to be coupled with Alexander's name, and he has this honor for more than one reason. It is perhaps less contested than in the case of any other of the world's leading personalities, Charles the Great alone excepted, for Charles, like Alexander, introduced a new age of the world's history. Great as were the successes of Alexander, they constitute less of a claim on the personal admiration of posterity than his knightly qualities as a warrior, and the charm and impetuosity of youth. His great victories were won between the years of twenty-one and twenty-five. In the space of thirteen years there are crowded together events and achievements that would exalt the longest life of the greatest man.

His sudden and premature death did him a kind of poetic justice, because his temperament cannot be coupled consistently with the characteristics of old age or even with the middle period of man's life. His body and his brain had been under a tremendous pressure, which even a strong constitution could not resist. It was this restive youthfulness that spurred him on to adventures which were purposeless when looked at from the point of view of the mature statesman, such as the expedition to India, an uncalculated move not to be understood except as due to the stimulus of an explorer's curiosity and the desire to accomplish a feat unheard of before.

The impulsiveness and emotionalism of Alexander in combination with his military genius produced results unprecedented in history. His career is that of a Homeric hero on a larger stage. It is not surprising that his conquests almost defy criticism and make a personal estimate seem artificial. He did so much that it apparently makes little difference what he was, for his actions speak for themselves, and they tell their tale like a fairy story, without any need of analysis. It is obviously unfair to look for constructive statesmanship in a career so short, when almost every month was occupied with military campaigns either planned or in execution. When his life was ended, Alexander was still a young man with a fresh and vigorous intelligence, open to new impressions. It is hazardous to infer (as Grote does) that he would have spent his life in acts of military aggression or that he would have sunk to the position of an Oriental despot, little differing from the Persian kings to whose title he succeeded. It is safer to put aside these pessimistic historic prognostics of what might have been, and to recognize that Alexander, provided he kept his mental powers undulled by drink, would have remained a Greek and not become a Hun or a Vandal.

His enthusiasm for absolutism was, when one considers his age and how deeply he was involved in military plans and schemes, less of a reflection on himself than a curse to his followers and successors, who kept faithful to the personal tradition of their leader and made the Hellenization of Asia untrue to so much that was best in Greek political life and thought. It was, as Ranke says, a break in their whole national history, for the Greeks to have extended over them the kind of authority which was in no way different from that against which they had contended in warfare for a century. But it must be remembered that Alexander had only just begun to rule over Asiatics; he had receded before his death from pressing his theory of amalgamation to its logical conclusion, and quick as he was to feel instinctively the meaning of new conditions, it may be fairly supposed that he would have come to recognize the value of Aristotle's profoundly wise advice to him, that he should behave to the Greeks as a leader or president and to the barbarians or non-Greeks as a master.

We may put to one side all the ingenious speculations as to what might have happened if Alexander had reached the ordinary limit of human life, a line of thought which Livy seems to have originated, when he tried to foretell for his age what would have happened if Alexander had taken up the rôle followed later by his relative, Pyrrhus. It is only necessary to say that, so far as Greek affairs were concerned, Alexander was the son of his father. His public career began when, as Philip's son, he put the finishing touches to Philip's program for dominating the free states of Greece. So long as Alexander lived, the lines of Macedonian supremacy, the outcome of the battle of Chæronea, remained clear and fixed. The destruction of Thebes was but the epilogue of Philip's own career. The sentimental vein in the nature of Alexander made him patient with the somewhat childish and ineffective hostility shown him by both Athens and Sparta, venerable names as protagonists in the secular struggle with the Persians, whose mantle had now fallen on his broader shoulders.

In Asia his conquests, rather than his half-thought-out plans for racial amalgamation, were decisive of future political development. There was an expansion of Hellenic culture throughout the East, marked by the common use of the Greek language and by a general absorption of the special traits of Greek social usages and sympathies. The civilization, so wrought out and transplanted, lost the creativeness and the spontaneity of the small communities of continental Greece. The Hellenic spirit lost its potency, if we may so phrase it, and in the sphere of government especially exhibited disheartening symptoms of selfishness and greed. Economically, the opening up of Asia meant enlarged facilities for the commercial exploitation of a vast and rich territory. It ushered in a period of great industrial fortunes, it increased opportunities for communication both by land and sea, it established higher standards of comfort and taste among populations who had lived a crude, colorless, and isolated existence. On the basis of Alexander's conquests a grandiose cosmopolitanism was built up in Asia which cast down tribal and racial boundaries and made it possible for masses of plain people to gain a livelihood under tolerable conditions.

CÆSAR

I
CÆSAR'S BEGINNINGS

The progress of an imperial power is obscure even when the foundations of its greatness are associated with some great military leader or lawgiver, but when one has to give a reason why some one political community becomes the point of centripetal attraction, and gathers about it, either by fear or devotion, the support of large masses of mankind, the efforts of historical analysis are frustrated at almost every point.

The rise of the small town community on the Tiber, about whose name there centered for nearly two thousand years the dread and the reverence of the progressive nations of the world, is veiled in legend. Why did not Palestrina, or Cori, or one of the numerous Etruscan cities to the north, become the germ of a world-wide rule? Of course the answer of the economist is that just because Rome is situated on the Tiber, its position gave it possibilities of advancement denied to the ordinary hill towns of Italy. This explanation may be taken as sufficient only when one allows that the burghers of Rome set out to accomplish what they did, not only because they were traders, but because the imaginative and grandiose factors in commercial enterprise must have worked in a singularly sensitive and highly organized social medium.

If the rise of the republic of Rome is difficult to account for, even more difficult is it to explain why such a community endowed with great generals, great statesmen, and great patriots, found it impossible so to modify their republican institutions that the manifest advantages of a sane and well-balanced democracy might be retained unimpaired, and might be extended at the same time to conquered races and nations. The rigidity of Roman republican institutions led to grave and demoralizing social disorders. The victories of Roman arms abroad were accompanied by political degradation at home. It must have been felt as a shock when a local government, admirably devised to promote civic virtues and secure just administration, was found, just as soon as Rome got the better of her numerous enemies, to be such a convenient protection for misrule.

As early as the last twenty-five years of the second century before Christ, the machinery of Roman government seems to have been recognized as inadequate to perform its functions. Constitutional methods and precedents were inadequate to solve the agrarian question, nor was there in the state, as an organism, sufficient force either to check an oligarchy of wealth or to impose restrictions on the personal ambitions of successful military leaders such as Marius and Sulla. Some of the fundamental principles of the Roman republican system were now treated as legal fiction. There had been years of civil war, for not only had Rome been attacked by groups of Italian towns associated with her for several hundred years, but Roman citizens had been divided among themselves in a way that would have been unthinkable in the

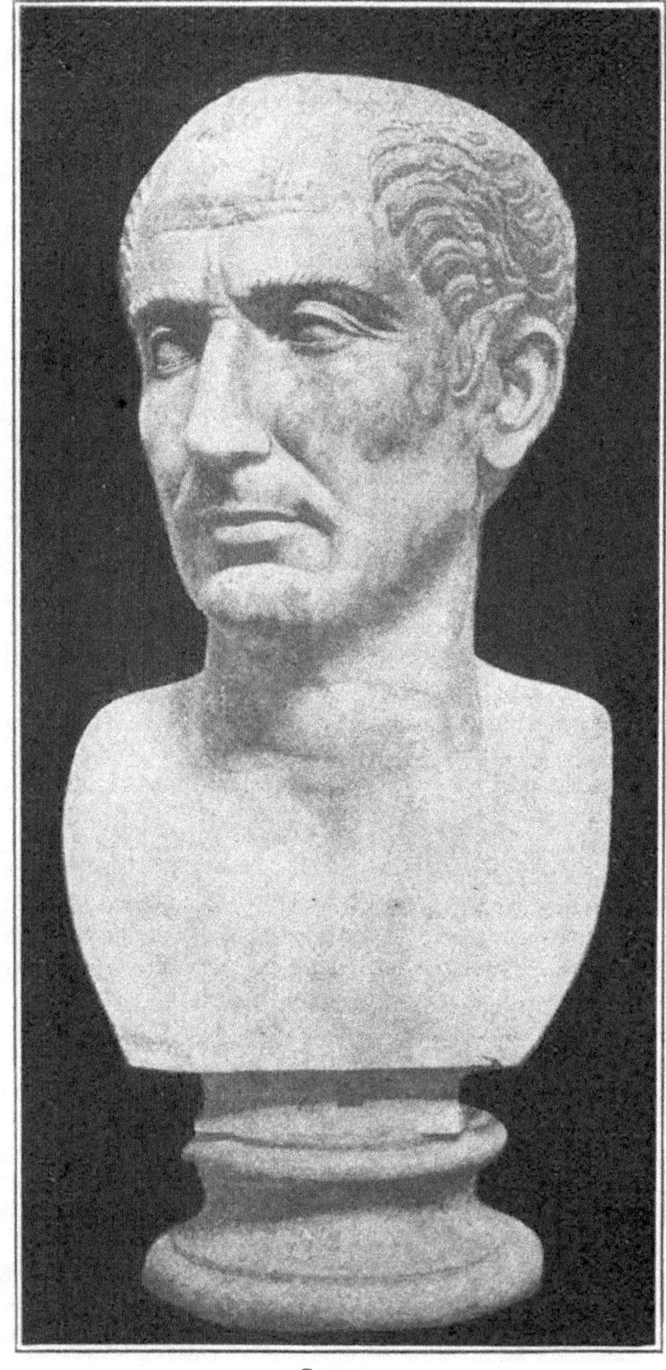

CÆSAR
(Naples, Museum.)

period of the Punic wars.

One would like to know the personal political convictions of the opposing leaders, Marius and Sulla. The probability is that neither of them looked much farther ahead than does a representative of "boss" rule in America, who would be very much surprised if asked whether he would like to see the principles of the political ring incorporated frankly and definitely in the Constitution of the United States. It is certain that after the death of Sulla, though personal rule had come to an end, there was no effort made to prevent its re-emergence. The question was rather—from what quarter it would emerge. The common opinion was that the popular general, Pompeius, distinguished by his victories in the East, would come to take the place left vacant by Sulla's death. He had none of the antipathetic personal qualities of the late dictator, therefore he was regarded as a man of principle, and accordingly, fitted to supply the personal element in Roman administration which most people seem to have felt was needed.

But all these calculations were soon upset. Pompeius, rapidly elevated to greatness along a smooth road of easy gradients, trusted to his friends in Rome to overcome all the political obstacles in his way there. While he was still acclaimed the great military champion of the Roman Republic, he soon found himself face to face with a rival—a man who set himself forward purposefully to revive the popular platform of the Marian party.

Caius Julius Cæsar, born July 12, 100 B.C., had no natural affiliations with the popular side of politics represented by Marius. So far as descent was concerned, he was an aristocrat of the aristocrats, belonging to an ancient patrician *gens* which traced back its legendary origin to a divine being—the goddess Venus. Of the early years of Cæsar only a little is known; and that little is handed down in the form of anecdotes the value of which lies in the incidental light they throw on his travels in the eastern part of the Roman world. It would be more interesting to know something of Cæsar's education than of his capture by pirates off the coast of Asia Minor—an accident used by his ancient biographers to prove what everybody knows—that he was a brave man even in the most hazardous circumstances. His early years could not have been spent carelessly, for he acquired a remarkably sound education. His literary tastes must have been the result of long discipline. His manysidedness and intellectual facility were fully recognized by his contemporaries. Even Cicero, who claimed to have spent his youth as a model "grind," tacitly allows that Cæsar's intellectual equipment was fully the equal of his own. The years of study were a necessity as well as a diversion. It was not safe even for a brilliant young man, while the truculent Sulla was dictator, to show practical interest in home politics, especially if his sympathies were with the Marian party.

And Cæsar was from the first a partisan of Marius. He was pledged to this political faction by family ties as well as by personal conviction. Marius's wife was Cæsar's aunt, and Cæsar himself had made the alliance with the Marians closer by taking as his wife the daughter of Cinna, one of the most active of Marius's supporters. During the Reign of Terror caused by the proscriptions of Sulla, Cæsar, because of his relations with the democratic party, had with difficulty escaped the dictator's vengeance, and while Sulla continued to control the Republic Cæsar found it prudent to withdraw into obscurity, from which he only emerged when the revival of the democratic tradition could be safely undertaken. Then he took the first opportunity that offered itself to make a declaration of loyalty to Marius, the old leader of the democracy. It was at the death of his aunt, Marius's widow, that he delivered a funeral address in which he praised Marius's principles and achievements. (68 B.C.) This challenge made to the dominant party by the young politician was a bold stroke. His speech was the sensation of the hour, and the glowing words which expressed his purpose of working for the restoration of the Marian democracy won for him the warm approval of the popular party. Not long after this Cæsar was chosen to his first elective office, that of Ædile, in 65 B.C., a somewhat irregular proceeding, for he was two years short of the legal age. He used his term of service in order to increase his favor with the democracy, and he showed a keen political scent in discovering ways and means by which he could keep himself constantly in the foreground as the champion of popular rights, earning a reputation for lavish expenditure of money by giving public games, fairs, and gladiatorial shows. It was not difficult at this time to win the favor of the Roman democracy. Pompeius, who controlled the army and through his position as commander-in-chief exerted a preponderating influence on the government, was on the point of completing the destruction of the upstart empire of Mithridates and bringing the Asiatic provinces with firm hand again under the sway of Rome. There stood in Cæsar's way as a competitor for political honors only the second-rate personality of Crassus, the richest man in Rome, who, somehow, despite his belief in the venality of the populace and his readiness to act upon his belief, seemed never to have struck the popular imagination powerfully enough to acquire the momentum of the genuine demagogue.

Cæsar had great advantages through his family connections; his position as the legitimate heir of Marius made him already a central figure in the political life of the city, and even Crassus found it advisable to work for him and with him, by advancing him large sums of money to cover the lavish expenditure of the three years' ædileship. Cæsar was already looking beyond Rome and its purely local interests. That he had no confidence in the kind of government under which he served is shown by pretty clear intimations that he was aware of the existence of a plot, intended to reduce the power of the senatorial oligarchy to zero. It is certain, too, that Cæsar worked hard to secure a military command in Egypt, which was not yet a Roman province and, therefore, could furnish him an admirable vantage ground by its wealth and by its strategical position for blocking the plans of Pompeius, who was working through control of the senatorial oligarchy for a revival in his own hands of personal rule after the Sullan model. This design of Cæsar was a bold one and conceived with a large vision. Its aim was to provide a stronghold for the democracy should the central government, as seemed likely to happen, be manipulated by an irregular dictatorship. The plan may have been suggested by the career of Sertorius in Spain, where this successful opponent of the Sullan régime had so long offered a refuge to all those who were enemies of the oligarchy that ruled the capital. It was characteristic of Cæsar's confident temperament that he was willing, without previous military training, to undertake a hazardous adventure that meant certainly a conflict with the seasoned generals of the oligarchy.

A further indication, if any were needed, of the purpose of the new leader of the democratic party to treat Pompeius as the danger point on the horizon, was a proposed scheme of an agrarian legislation by which a board was to be created with extensive military and judicial power for the purpose of selling all the properties and territories acquired by the state since the year 88, along with all of the war booty and confiscated revenues now in the hands of Pompeius. To this measure was added a clause intended to transform the bill into a popular manifesto for the colonization of Italy with small landholders, and therefore constructed on the lines of those earlier agrarian laws which mark the commencement of the struggle of the Roman democracy with the capitalistic oligarchy two generations before Cæsar's time. This agrarian legislation was defeated by Cicero, who in this case, as often elsewhere, championed the interests of the moneyed classes. He who was now Consul and was posing as the Grand Conciliator, praised Pompeius as the strict constitutional champion, and characterized Cæsar's agrarian legislation as revolutionary. In the face of the Consul's opposition Cæsar hesitated to press the matter and withdrew his bill. (64 B.C.) As this is the first legislative act brought forward under Cæsar's influence, it is interesting to note that his later political methods and policies are anticipated in it. His Agrarian Law, when analyzed, contains two elements. There is the purely personal feature, more or less cleverly concealed in various clauses of the measure so constructed as to forward the political interests of its author, and, secondly, one can detect in Cæsar's plan for agrarian reform a keen-sighted appreciation of existing social and economic needs. This last showed itself in the provision that the surplus population of Rome should be employed as cultivators of the soil. Cicero's methods of defeating the bill by appealing to party prejudice were as essentially demagogic as were Cæsar's plans for winning popular support for his measure. The only difference between them was that Cicero was working in the interest of a capitalistic oligarchy, while Cæsar directly aimed at the establishment of personal rule under the protection of an irresponsible commission with unlimited powers. The campaign against the dominant party was not, however, allowed to drop because of the withdrawal of the Agrarian Bill. Cæsar, through one of his lieutenants, brought impeachment proceedings against the murderer of a democratic leader who had distinguished himself in the last days of Marius. It was part of his pin-pricking policy, meant to intimidate the senatorial faction, and the aim was clear, for the Senate had by a decree relieved the murderer of responsibility years before. Nothing came of the impeachment, but it went on record as showing Cæsar's loyalty to the democracy. His next proposal was especially gratifying to the admirers of Marius, because it involved the removal from the children of the victims of the Sullan proscription the disqualification by which they were prevented from holding public office.

Soon after this, in the spring of 63, when there was a vacancy in the office of Pontifex Maximus, the supreme head of the religion of the city of Rome, Cæsar became a candidate. There were no religious qualifications necessary; the office had no more relation to personal belief than that of a prince bishop of the later history of the German States, when territorial princes added the episcopal to their other titles. Cæsar was one of the most advanced free-thinkers in Rome. But he felt no incongruity, and apparently no one else did, in his desire to figure as the director of the traditional religious usages of the capital. The position meant so much to Cæsar that, heavily indebted as he was, he refused to withdraw his name, when a large sum was offered by an opposing candidate on condition that he would retire from the contest. The office of Pontifex Maximus carried with it a number of powers with great political possibilities, because in addition to controlling the property attached to the college of priests over which he presided, the Pontifex had important jurisdiction in religious questions, the determination of religious scruples, and the charge of the Calendar. All of these matters were intimately connected with the Roman legislative procedure and also with the judicial system as worked by the Roman magistrates. Moreover, it was a life position, and one's only surprise is that Cæsar's administration of the office was not attacked by his enemies. As a matter of fact, his career as an official religious leader is marked by beneficent reforms in the Calendar and by a solid contribution to the science of chronology.

There was some difficulty in the election, for it had been placed by Sulla in the hands of the members of the college. But this measure was repealed, and when the people became the electors, Cæsar had easily the majority of the votes over his two conservative opponents. The year 63 had not been, as we have seen, a happy or tranquil one for the men in power; there had been a constant series of attacks made upon them, and they had been forced to stand steadily on the defensive.

Before the time for the consular elections the extreme wing of the popular party appeared to have got out of hand. They selected for their candidate Catiline, a leading spirit among the criminal and corrupt order of Roman society, who had contested the election before and had been defeated. Cæsar had already energetically supported Catiline, but in the latter's second attempt to be elected Consul, it seems clear that Cæsar's support was at best half-hearted. Cæsar had come to know the reckless nature of Catiline's program, with its appeal for a general canceling of debts and its general attack on all capitalistic interests. The scheme, however, did win the approval of the discontented classes, and the occasion for carrying it through was favorable, because Pompeius, the only man with a military force adequate to act forcibly on behalf of the senatorial oligarchy, was absent still in the East. It was understood that Catiline, if he obtained office, would use it to inaugurate a social revolution; if he were defeated, it was planned that violent methods should be used to force a change of government on the oligarchy. An army was to be collected in Italy, the city was to be set on fire, and in the confusion the reins of government would be taken by Catiline and his followers.

The plot was shrewdly defeated by Cicero, who was given by the Senate unlimited powers, after a state of siege had been proclaimed. Catiline escaped from the city, taking refuge with his army, which had been collected near Florence; but several of the other conspirators were taken prisoners in Rome, and the question of their fate was brought up before the Senate. Cæsar had by report been implicated in the conspiracy, but Cicero refused to follow up these suspicions. Accordingly, in the senatorial debate, Cæsar appeared rather in the light of a cross bench statesman than as a firm supporter of the revolutionary leader.

It must be remembered that the Senate had no right to condemn a man to death or to banishment. A general in the field could inflict the death sentence without appeal, but no magistrate within the precincts of the city could do so; there was an appeal from his decision to the people legally assembled. Cicero wished to get from the Senate an authoritative opinion, as to whether under their previous decree of martial law he could exercise in the city the summary rights allowed to a general in the field. Cæsar spoke after the consular members of the Senate, all of whom had declared for the administration of the extreme penalty. He opposed it in a careful and statesmanlike speech, using his opportunity for putting himself on record as the upholder of the democratic view of the constitution.

As no verbal report of any other of Cæsar's speeches has come down to us, it is interesting to give an extract from Sallust's version, which may be taken as an accurate outline, for, owing to Cicero's personal interest in the matter, the whole proceedings of the Senate during this crucial debate were taken down in shorthand. After deprecating the use of rhetoric as likely to prejudice the judgment, and remarking that eloquent pictures of the horrors of war and rebellion were alien to the matter in hand, Cæsar's words were: "And indeed, for the crimes we have to deal with, no penalty is in itself too cruel; death at least cannot be so, for it puts an end to the misery of this life and brings no torment in another. But the penalty will be looked on as cruel, simply because it is unconstitutional. It has been over and over again forbidden by express legislation to scourge or kill a citizen without trial. You do not propose to scourge these men, presumably because the law forbids it. Why, then, do you propose to put them to death? Both penalties are equally illegal. I must remind you also of the precedent your action will create. Once place such a power as you claim in the hands of a government and you cannot put a limit on its use; it may be and will be used against good and bad alike, as it was by the Thirty at Athens and in our own recollection by Sulla. I do not fear this now or with Cicero as Consul; but I will not answer for the power of the sword in the hands of future Consuls. Let us abide by the law and not seek in a panic to overrule it. My advice is, not indeed that we let these men go, and thus increase the resources of Catiline, but that we commit them for life to close custody in the largest Italian towns, securing them by holding over each town the heaviest possible penalty in case they should escape. And I further propose that we pass a decree embodying our opinion that no proposal touching them shall be made henceforth either in Senate or assembly; and that disregard of the decree shall be treated by the Senate as high treason against the state."

The hint of a reaction was not an oratorical commonplace; it was suggested by the recent history of Rome itself, and proved most effective, for even Cicero's own brother, Quintus, who followed Cæsar, expressed his agreement with him. Cicero himself, in his reply, took a rather wavering position, paying special attention to the practical proposals of Cæsar, which so many modern historians have decided to be weak and specious. But these have forgotten that, even if Cæsar's plans for keeping the prisoners as perpetual ticket-of-leave men in various Italian communities offered no effective guarantee that they would not escape, there was no especial reason for fearing their presence again in Rome after Catiline and his army had been destroyed. None of the conspirators was a man of first-rate ability, and besides, the experience of unsuccessful conspiracy has almost as strong an educational effect as imprisonment. Many Paris communards settled down as peaceful citizens.

Cicero made an unfortunate experiment at this juncture. The Senate listened readily to the summary appeals for justice to traitors made by Cato, but Cicero's execution of the Catilinarians was stored up against him in the popular mind, and much of the good he might have done in his political career was frustrated by his weakness in identifying himself with the blind passion of the reactionary party. For the moment, however, Cicero carried the people with him; they lost their heads, alarmed by the wild tales of conflagration and massacre. Cæsar's life was in danger, because he had pleaded for a policy of moderation, and it must be allowed that the words of his speech did not represent a pose. The principles he stood for in 63 he adhered to after the civil wars were over, when a word from him might have initiated a proscription after the Sullan model.

II
ALLIANCE WITH POMPEIUS AND CRASSUS

The year following the suppression of the Catiline conspiracy was one of uncertainty. Pompeius was returning home after his six years' stay in the East. The question was whether he would play the rôle of a new Sulla. It seems generally to have been expected that he would. There was no army in Italy strong enough to resist his will; certainly the force which had overcome Catiline near Fiesole was quite unequal to such a work. The question was, who were to be his friends and what policy would he pursue. One of the general's emissaries appeared in Rome, and made it clear that Pompeius could not be used as a mere tool of the senatorial party. Cicero made tactless overtures to secure his favor, and met with a cold reception.

Cæsar showed more diplomacy, paying the general the compliment of requesting him to finish the Capitoline temple, one of the chief shrines of the civic religion of Rome. This duty came within Cæsar's province as Pontifex

Maximus, and besides as Prætor for this year he held a position which made his influence useful to the returning general. Both the scheme for the restoration of the temple and a measure for recalling Pompeius to the city, which was supported by Cæsar, were opposed by the Senate, and the discussion led to such violence that the Senate suspended Cæsar from his functions as magistrate, and only restored him when he had personally intervened to quiet the passions of the mob.

Though Cæsar's year of office was over (61 B.C.), and the time had come for him to administer Spain as Proprætor, that being the province assigned him, he delayed his departure. There were many grounds for this course. Pompeius had been keeping his own counsel as to his future plans, and required watching. Cæsar had difficulties with his creditors; he had long been heavily in debt, and his year of office, with its sensational political activities, must have severely drained his resources.

But the chief cause which delayed his journey west was the violation, in the House of the Pontifex Maximus, of the sacred mysteries of the Bona Dea by a young Quæstor-elect, Clodius, who was suspected of being the lover of Cæsar's wife, Pompeia. A scandal involving the head of the state religion was a serious matter, and Cæsar lived up to the rôle assigned him by sententiously remarking that Cæsar's wife ought not even to be suspected and by seizing this opportunity of divorcing her. The step satisfied public opinion at the time, but the dignity of the act is somewhat lessened in the eyes of later critics from the fact that the Pontifex Maximus himself was, even according to the flexible standards of Rome, notorious for his moral laxity.

When Clodius' trial was held, Cæsar diplomatically denied that he had any certain knowledge of the case. Politics were so much involved in this trial that proscriptions might have been initiated. Clodius was a figure in the popular party, and, in the end, by the common method of bribing the judges, an acquittal was secured. Pompeius, in the midst of this exciting time, had arrived in Rome, thus giving Cæsar an opportunity of taking the measure of the over-praised Eastern conqueror. Before Cæsar left for Spain, mutual advances had taken place, and he felt sure that Pompeius would not ally himself with the senatorial party. Cæsar also continued to be on good terms with the millionaire Crassus, and before leaving Italy he borrowed from him eighteen hundred talents to satisfy the demands of creditors.

Of the period of Cæsar's rule in Spain little is known; but his service there was valuable to him because, while contending with the hardy hill tribes, who were constantly in arms against the Romans, he received a training in war that afterwards stood him in good stead. He showed himself, too, an able and conscientious administrator, regardful of the condition of the provincials, who had suffered from the loss of property and from heavy taxation during the unintermitted war that took place while the government at Rome was destroying the home-rule system set up by Sertorius. The beneficent character of Cæsar's administration showed itself in his friendly relation with the free city of Gades, where he was called in to reform the local laws and to settle factional disputes. The prosperity of the town in after years may reasonably be supposed to have dated from this period. Even Cicero speaks in glowing language of Cæsar's supervision. The generous character of his treatment of the town is seen in its admission twelve years afterwards to the full Roman franchise. One of the most distinguished of the citizens of Gades, Balbus, became Cæsar's confidential agent and secretary, serving in this capacity for many years without a break. After his master's death, Balbus rose to be Prætor and Consul; he was the first enfranchised foreigner who held these highest offices in Rome.

All the affairs relating to his provincial government were set in order in the spring of 59 B.C., when Cæsar set out for Rome to be there in time for the consular elections, which were usually held in summer. He had two objects in view: one to secure the dignity of a triumph, the official stamp of a successful military commander; the other to present himself as a candidate for the consulship. It was impossible for him while holding a military command to appear within the walls and formally solicit the votes of his fellow-citizens. He therefore asked for permission to become a candidate without fulfilling the formal conditions, and this request the Senate refused to grant. Cæsar solved the difficulty by sacrificing the triumph; he resigned his command and entered the city as a private individual.

But now the opposition to him took another form. A determined aristocrat, M. Calpurnius Bibulus, who, apart from his political tenets, had a long-standing personal grudge against Cæsar, was put up by the senatorial party as his colleague for the consulship, and was elected by the lavish use of money. Cæsar's next move in this game of political strategy was a master stroke of astuteness; he formed a close combination with Pompeius, whom the senatorial party had just irritated by vetoing all his pet schemes, among them an opportunity of a second consulship and a plan to reward his soldiers by a distribution of public lands. As a third member of the alliance Crassus was introduced, a valuable asset because of the great financial backing he could give. He saw a chance for promoting his political advancement with two such colleagues to help him. It was a frank system of give and take; there were no strong personal ties between any of the three members of the junta, but they had at least a common opponent, the senatorial party.

An effort was made, though it was unsuccessful, to detach Cicero from his friendly relations with the aristocratic majority in the Senate; as he declined the invitation, the new political machine became a triumvirate, the union of three influential persons to overcome opposition and to prevent the wheels of public business from being blocked by the endless methods of obstruction ever ready to be employed in the complicated system of Roman government, where the checks were more numerous than the balances. It simply meant that these three men, and not the reactionary senators, should decide on the distribution of provinces, on the candidates for offices, and on the command of armies. From the record of all three, it was clear that the technique of the constitutional system would not be treated with great reverence, for all were practical politicians and had definite personal ambitions to gratify.

As Consul, Cæsar began his year of magistracy with a policy of studied moderation. He tried to get on with Bibulus by showing him marked consideration in the way of official precedence, and his first reform of senatorial practice concerned a subject which might well have been taken as a non-controversial matter, the publication of the Senate's proceedings. Cæsar proposed that a summary of each debate should be exposed to view in the Forum. It was an intimation to the senators that they must hold themselves responsible to public opinion.

The next proposal was to make some arrangement by which the veterans of Pompeius' army should be supplied with public lands. These lands had to be acquired by the state from private owners, so the proceeds of the extensive conquests of Pompeius' conquests in the East were to be applied to this purpose. The Senate refused to listen to any agrarian measure; the very name frightened them. Cato obstructed, trying to talk the scheme out in the Senate. Cæsar, who had as little respect for parliamentary procedure as Cromwell, put a stop to this copious oratory by placing the speaker under arrest. He was soon released, however, in deference to the pressure of his colleagues.

In the face of the hopeless opposition of the Senate to the Consul's legislation, the only course left to pursue was for Cæsar to present his legislation directly to the popular assembly, without the authorization of the Senate. This method was extraordinary, but not absolutely illegal, and it had been employed by reformers since the time of Tiberius Gracchus. There were, of course, grave objections to it, for measures could be rushed through without proper discussion, and it is well known that hasty legislation is often dangerous, even for those who promote it. A specially drastic feature of the agrarian bill was the clause which compelled senators and all officers, to be elected in future, to swear to be faithful to its provisions.

In this way Cæsar hoped to secure his measure from being abrogated when the year of his magistracy was over. This clause was not, however, a new expedient, but it was now being used in a new way to prevent the claim that prerogatives of the Senate had been violated by passing legislation without consulting its wishes. Pompeius promised to support the bill by arms if violence were resorted to on the other side. A Tribune exercised his right to veto on the measure, when it was introduced in the popular assembly, but this old constitutional check was contemptuously disregarded. Also, when Bibulus, the conservative colleague of Cæsar, interfered by formally delaying action in the measure, he was forcibly removed from the Forum by some of Pompeius' veterans. Bibulus was equally powerless when he invoked religious scruples of a technical kind, for Cæsar was Pontifex Maximus as well as Consul. Bibulus' interpretations of signs and omens were ruled out as irregular. Even when the bill was passed by the people, he kept up opposition in the Senate and tried to induce the senators to declare the agrarian law null and void. They, however, were not prepared to join him in such a hazardous undertaking, so in disgust he withdrew for the rest of his term into private life. His retirement led the people to remark jokingly that the two Consuls for the year were Julius and Cæsar, not Cæsar and Bibulus.

The passage of the agrarian democratic measure, as it stood, was undertaken to fulfil engagements made with Pompeius, whose troops were especially concerned in this distribution of lands. Equally personal were the measures passed by the people to regularize the situation of the territories in the East, where Pompeius, after his conquests, had acted on his own initiative in making treaties, imposing taxation, and settling the terms of local administration. The personal relations between the two triumvirs were now drawn closer by the marriage of Cæsar's daughter Julia to Pompeius; she was at this time twenty-two years old, and as long as she lived she prevented any open rupture between her husband and her father.

In another legislative enactment Cæsar attested his loyal interpretation of the triumvirate compact rather than his desire to forward the public interests of the state. Crassus desired that the farmers of the taxes in the province of Asia should be relieved from the contract which they had made with the government. It was a shady piece of business; even Cicero, who was not apt to be critical where capitalistic interests were involved, called the scheme of Crassus shameful. It was defeated in the Senate by the determined efforts of Cato. The measure was afterwards jammed through the popular assembly in a form which relieved the taxgatherers of one-third of their financial burden.

This was really a shrewd move to separate from the senatorial party the whole mercantile class, who normally acted solidly with them. They now looked upon the triumvirate combination as favorable to their interests, and so deprived the Senate of a solid support at a time when that body needed every element of the population in its unequal struggle with the triumvirs.

Much more worthy than this act of special legislation was a measure for dealing with extortion on the part of provincial administrators. The Roman governors and their subordinates treated the provinces as legitimate spoil, by which they could balance the large amounts spent at home in political corruption. This system offered the most unwholesome example of ring rule. Every man in public life had a good chance of ruling a province at some time in his career, and there was no inducement to touch a well-tried system which had proved profitable to all concerned.

Cæsar's law was a blanket measure, evidently drawn with great intelligence and showing the familiarity of an ex-provincial official with the concrete needs of the situation. It extended the jurisdiction of existing courts for cases of provincial extortion, in regard to the definition of the crime, the persons liable, and the penalties to be imposed. All the methods of extortion were brought within the scope of this act. The governor and his official staff were held liable, and the punishment, hitherto chiefly imposed by damages, was increased to deprivation of the right to bequeath property, and in some cases expulsion from the Senate and exile were inflicted on offending officials.

Good as this legislation was, it contained a political element which prevented it from meeting the whole situation of provincial misrule. The triumvirate, we have seen, made a distinct bid for the favor of the mercantile classes when the previous bill was passed relieving the taxgatherers of Asia from the full extent of their contract. This new law only concerned the administration of senatorial officials; it did not put an end to extortion, nor did it stop the avenues of public corruption, because the financiers, the men who gathered about the official ruling class, were left to ply their nefarious trade unmolested.

But Cæsar's consulship broke the power of the senatorial aristocracy, which had been on the decline ever since the death of Sulla. By his alliance with Pompeius and Crassus a continuity of policy was secured, under which the old republican principle that cessation of office meant also cessation of power came to an end. The main business at the close of his year of service as Consul was to arrange that the system he had started should continue to work smoothly. The two candidates for the consulship were pledged supporters of the triumvirate. An even more important tool was the active and unscrupulous Clodius, who had made himself notorious because of the Bona Dea scandal. He was made a Tribune, and as such became the local agent in Rome of the triumvirs' interests. He signalized his entrance into office by abolishing the small payment still exacted on the state distribution of grain to the people, and he organized the masses into guilds, each under a district leader, so that the populace could be controlled and could be worked together either as a political machine or as a mob, whether to vote or to do deeds of violence according to the password of their leader.

The Senate, in arranging the assignment of provinces in B.C. 59, had tried to diminish Cæsar's influence by giving him for his work as Proconsul the duty of attending to the internal condition of Italy. This meant that he would have no military force at his command, and that he would be expected to devote himself to the supervision of roads and public works. The senatorial arrangement for rendering their chief opponent innocuous was simply an invitation to him to treat it as non-existing. It was proposed to set the Senate's action aside and to give Cisalpine Gaul and the adjoining province of Illyria to Cæsar for a period of five years.

When the new measure was before the popular assembly, the Senate, under pressure from Pompeius, voted that in addition to Cisalpine Gaul in the Celtic region on the Italian side of the Alps, the Gallic province, with an ample army and suitable staff, should be assigned to Cæsar. It was known that there was restlessness among the Gauls and the Germans, who were on the borders of the prosperous Roman province in southern Gaul along the lower Rhone. This was, of course, an opportunity for real proconsular duty, but probably no one who voted for the assignment realized the possibilities of the command which now fell into Cæsar's hand.

But before setting out for his province (58 B.C.), Cæsar remained near at hand to supervise Clodius' arrangements for muzzling the Senate; it was not safe for the new Proconsul to absent himself from Rome until affairs there had been brought so under control that there would be no chance of a senatorial reactionary movement. Clodius first abolished the use of indefinitely prolonged obstruction, a practice involved in the religious privilege of "watching the heavens" for evil omens, and a method of delay normally used to prevent the assemblies of the people from being held. The next step was to hinder the Censors from making a combination to remove from the Senate partisans of Cæsar. This purpose was secured by another law of Clodius that made it impossible for the Censor to strike from the roll of the Senate anyone, except on a formal accusation, and no member could be removed even then unless both Censors acted together.

Cæsar attempted also to conciliate Cicero by offering him a staff appointment; on this being refused, as it was desirable to deprive the senatorial party of the oratorical talents which gave Cicero a hold on the people, Clodius was allowed to bring charges against him in connection with the execution of the Catilinarian conspirators. The terms of the new law were perfectly general; it simply outlawed any person who had or should hereafter put to death a Roman citizen uncondemned, that is, without due trial and sentence. Cicero took the hint and fled from Rome. At the same time the uncompromising senatorial obstructionist Cato was "kicked upstairs" by being given an appointment as commissioner to supervise the annexation of the island of Cyprus. Ample time was allowed him, and it was arranged that when he had finished with Cyprus, he should go to Byzantium and settle some unimportant disputes in that free city. With Cato kept busy at a long distance from Rome, and with Cicero out of the way, there was little to fear with Clodius acting in the rôle of "boss" of Rome.

III

THE CONQUEST OF GAUL

Very soon after the flight of the great orator, Cæsar, who had been watching with his army the proceedings within the city, started for his province of Gaul. The country which was to be the scene of his labors as governor, and in which through successive campaigns his reputation in generalship was to be made, was larger than modern France, for it extended to the Rhine, the Alps, and the Pyrenees. Only a part of it was familiar to the Romans, and for this reason one of the most striking proofs of Cæsar's skill as a commander is the ability and certainty with which he penetrated into regions unvisited before and therefore unfamiliar to him except by the hearsay stories of the casual traveler. The province had originally been occupied by the Romans in the struggle with Hannibal, because it secured their land communication with Spain. In its southern part it was well developed and civilized, but the limit of Roman rule northward was marked by the valley of the Rhone, and the famous city of Lyons had not yet been founded, which was later on the headquarters of Roman power in Gaul.

Much trouble was being experienced from Germanic invaders farther north, who were crossing the Rhine and were in great numbers occupying the fertile lands to the east of them. The Gauls themselves had no cohesive power of resistance; they were constantly quarreling among themselves, and it seemed only a question of time when the Germans, uniting with the Gauls, who were certain to become subject to their rule, would overwhelm the peaceful and civilized inhabitants of the Roman province. The situation required immediate attention, for the Ædui who lived between the Loire and the Saône were calling on the Romans as allies for help and protection against their neighbors, other Gaulish tribes, who with the aid of the German king, Ariovistus, were threatening to take their land. Besides, it was reported that the Helvetic and the German peoples were contemplating a migration on a large scale, induced to leave south Germany by the prospect of finding better lands farther west.

The country as a whole was in a state of unrest; the unconquered mass of the free tribes, extending from the fringe of Roman occupation in the south to the North Sea, might easily become dangerous to the countries under Roman occupation on the other side of the Pyrenees and the Alps. Up to the time of Cæsar's advent, the government at Rome had shown singular apathy; a few resolutions had been passed, directing that the allied tribes should be aided, but no additions were made to the army in the province. The emotional temperament of the Gauls made them subject to quick changes in their point of view; unless something were done quickly, even the allies of Rome would have to be counted on the other side. It was easy for them to drop their present allegiance, for they were as a mass a servile population, guided by an aristocracy of nobles or knights, and by a widely extended and mysterious guild, the Druids, who each year held a solemn assembly in a sacred place in the center of the land.

The general difficulties of coping with the situation were great when Cæsar took command, but the special details of the position as it confronted him increased the obstacles in the way of prompt action. There was but one legion beyond the Alps; the other three were far away in Aquileia at the top of the Adriatic. It was fortunate for him that he could draw on the reserves of Cisalpine Gaul, the richest part of Italy, the province which extended over the plains of Lombardy to Tuscany. This province was filled with a hardy race of yeomen cultivators, a mixed population, having its origin in the conquered Celtic tribes and in genuine Roman colonists.

Nowhere else could there be found a better recruiting ground for the legions, and nowhere also, on account of the general intelligence of the inhabitants, would the personal qualities of a general find a more immediate response. The tactfulness of Cæsar had already been put to the test in the arena of political life; he had learned how to make friends and to hold them. Apart from the technical gifts of military art, the personal charm of Cæsar's character was a great factor in securing for him an army made up of devoted troops and officers. They trusted him, and they were held to him as a leader, because he seems from the first to have been able to establish close relations of a spontaneous and genuine type with those who were under him. His army was not a mere fighting machine, but an organism reflecting the individual driving power and coolness of the man who led it.

The series of campaigns in Gaul begins with Cæsar's successful blocking of the migration of the Helvetii. All that is known of the details of the strategy employed by the Romans is derived from Cæsar's own report, which has been frequently criticised as intentionally obscure and misleading. It must be remembered that the famous commentaries on the Gallic wars were hurriedly dictated, and were meant to tell the public what the commander-in-chief wished them to know and nothing more. For example, many modern authorities are agreed that the numbers of the migrating Helvetii are very much overestimated by Cæsar and that the real purpose of their migration was artfully concealed. Napoleon, who was a past master in falsifying military records, declared that the campaign against the Helvetii as narrated by Cæsar was incomprehensible.

The real situation in Gaul prior to the migration seems to have been as follows. As we have said, Ariovistus, the German king, was in control of the central part of the country. This overlordship was burdensome to the Gauls, who paid him a yearly tribute. A prince of the Ædui, Divitiacus, had turned to the Romans for help, but his request was rejected, for Ariovistus, during Cæsar's own consulship, had been acknowledged as king and formally declared an ally and friend of the Roman people. There was another party among the Ædui, led by Dumnorix, the brother of Divitiacus, who favored throwing off the German yoke, and urged a general uprising of the Gauls, unassisted by the Romans.

Not far away from Æduan territory were the Helvetii, who were independent of the rule of Ariovistus, and with them the autonomous party among the Ædui entered into friendly relations in order to secure them as allies against the Germans. The Helvetii were to be persuaded by their leaders to migrate to western Gaul, and it was arranged that, when the whole tribe was slowly passing through the land of the Ædui, there should be a rising against Ariovistus. The Ædui could count on the assistance of the Helvetii, because as future occupants of Gallic territory the immigrants would have no desire to be dependents of the German king.

This situation and this program were known to Cæsar before he left Rome, for he was in communication with the pro-Roman party among the Ædui. It was of course his object to frustrate this plan of driving out the Germans without the help of Rome, because it was to his interest that Roman overlordship should take the place of German control. The request of the Helvetii to be allowed to pass peacefully through Roman territory came just in time. It gave Cæsar the opportunity of defending the frontier and strengthening his army.

As soon as the Helvetii were refused a passage through the Roman province, they started directly for the land of the Ædui, crossing over the Roman territory, and so they abandoned the fiction of a migration to the west. In the meantime, by the liberal use of money, the pro-Roman party among the Ædui had got the upper hand. Accordingly when the Helvetii, whose rear division had been attacked by Cæsar as they were crossing the Saône, reached the land of their would-be allies, they were treated as enemies by the Ædui, who were now calling on Cæsar for help to resist the invaders. The Helvetii, willing to return, desired to come to terms with the Roman general, but they refused to accept the Roman conditions as to hostages. They started to retrace their steps by following a more northerly course on their return in order to take advantage of the mountainous country, as a protection against an attack on the part of the Romans.

Cæsar followed warily; his own troops were indeed strengthened by Æduan cavalry, but these, on the first engagement, had fled before the enemy. It was obvious their loyalty could not be depended upon, and significant, too, that Dumnorix was in command. When an attempt to surround the Helvetii with two Roman legions failed, Cæsar withdrew to Bibracte, the Æduan capital, to replenish his army and probably to prevent the defection of his allies. The Helvetii might now have returned to their old home unmolested, but they were embittered against the Romans, who had shown constant hostility to their movements, whether they advanced or retreated, and they were quite willing to treat with the patriotic party among the Ædui, who asked them now for help against the Romans. They turned back therefore, with the purpose of attacking the Romans as they were marching towards Bibracte.

The actual number of the Helvetii engaged in this operation cannot have been very great, for their wagon train was in a very short time collected, formed, and turned into an improvised citadel. Their movements before, during, and after battle show that the number 368,000 given by Cæsar is enormously exaggerated. Altogether, including allied forces, Cæsar's army may be reckoned at 40,000 men. There were six legions (36,000 men) and allied cavalry to the number of 4000.

When the Helvetii approached, the brunt of the fighting was assigned to four legions of veterans; the rest, the fresh recruits and the allies, were placed behind the line of battle and directed to protect the camp. As the Helvetii attacked the four legions, who were advantageously stationed on the slope of a hill, they were thrown back; but, as the legions advanced, these in turn were vigorously attacked on their flanks. The battle was hotly contested, the Romans taking the offensive both in the front and on the sides. Slowly the enemy withdrew, and it was dark before the Roman army took the massed wagons by assault. After the victory, Cæsar remained on the field of battle for three days. The Helvetii fled towards the east and a few days later surrendered, most of them being sent back to their old homes. The Helvetian overthrow was a useful stroke; it made a decided impression on the Gauls, who were now able to take the measure of the new commander of the Romans.

The next move was to break the power of Ariovistus. Cæsar represents the suggestion as coming from various Gallic deputations, who besought him to help them cast off the German yoke. But it is obvious that the presence of Ariovistus in Gaul was incompatible with the purpose of Cæsar to subjugate the entire country. All negotiations with the German chieftain proved futile; he insisted on keeping the Gallic tribes as his tributaries, and simply asked to be let alone.

Cæsar took his army to the east and came into contact with the Germans in the neighborhood of Belfort or in southern Alsace; it is impossible to determine the locality with precision. Ariovistus collected his wagons into a fortified camp on an elevation a short distance from the position of the

Romans, using his advantage to break up by cavalry sorties the Roman line of communication. His plan appears to have been to force the Romans to withdraw and to attack them on their march. The German leader took full advantage of the mobility of his troops, and his cavalry proved too strong for the Gallic horse on the side of the Romans. All attempts to draw Ariovistus from his camp failed, until Cæsar divided his army, placing two legions in a fortified position, where they could more efficiently protect the line of communications. This smaller camp Ariovistus tried to take by storm, and failed.

When the main Roman army advanced, and began to threaten the wagon citadel of the Germans, Ariovistus determined to give battle. The battle itself was won through the superior discipline of the Romans; once during its progress the left wing was in danger, but it was saved by the prompt action of the younger Crassus, who was in command of the cavalry. Cæsar with the right wing carried all before him. As to the numbers engaged, it was Napoleon's opinion that the Germans were not stronger than Cæsar; the probability is that they were weaker. Ariovistus' whole army, though with it he controlled a large part of Gaul, need not have been more than 20,000 men. They were, of course, a better trained fighting force than anything the Gallic tribes could create, and it was not difficult, using the divisions among the Gauls, to establish an effective overlordship with a small, well-disciplined army.

Apparently the bulk of the German army was destroyed; Ariovistus, however, succeeded in making his escape beyond the Rhine. The defeat of the Germans had important consequences; before the opening of the campaign against Ariovistus, news had come from the north that the Suevi, an important German tribe, were about to move across the Rhine. The knowledge of the fate of Ariovistus forced them back again into the depths of Germany.

During the winter Cæsar crossed the Alps to attend to the administration of the Cisalpine province, leaving his troops quartered in Gaul under the command of his trusted lieutenant, Labienus. He raised two new legions, and when he returned northward it was already plain that the pacification of the country was far from complete. The Gauls feared the expansion of Roman power, and there were rumors of an uprising to be led by the tribes of the Belgæ. Cæsar marched directly to the danger spot, and taking advantage of tribal jealousies, induced the Remi, whose territory lay between the Maas, the Oise, and the Maine, to accept the alliance and protectorate of Rome. (57 B.C.)

This was a wise move, for it was clear from reports on the spot that the whole Belgic confederacy, representing the most warlike of the Gallic tribes, were up in arms. The fate of Ariovistus, the year before, had shown that the only way to resist the extension of Roman rule in Gaul was by tribal combination. The Belgæ thoroughly realized their danger, and when Cæsar passed their frontiers, they opposed him with a large allied army composed of contingents of all the neighboring peoples.

The great difficulty was to keep such large masses of men together and to provide them with food. In the time of Marius, the Germanic invaders, the Cimbri and the Teutones, in order to secure provisions as they went, had divided into several smaller groups, each one of which was beaten in detail by the Roman general. Cæsar's strategy was to be governed by the same principles; he meant to wear the Belgæ out and to refuse to give battle until they had lost their unity, until each dissevered fraction might be drawn into action without support from the rest. Cæsar having recruited two new legions, in all there were eight. Besides, there served under him a variegated band of allies, Numidians, Cretans, men of the Balearic Islands, and Gallic cavalry.

Altogether the Roman fighting host may be reckoned at fifty to sixty thousand men, with camp followers, perhaps nearly one hundred thousand in all. To keep such a body in the field for a considerable time meant a carefully organized system of transportation and economic equipment. A strongly fortified camp was constructed on the north bank of the River Aisne, where the soldiers were kept in good discipline. The remains of extensive fortifications, in the form of ditches eighteen feet wide and nine or ten feet deep, and a wall with palisades twelve feet high, were found on the site of Cæsar's camp by the archæologists who worked under the direction of Napoleon III.

The camp was in the country of the Remi, who had, as we have mentioned, become allies of the Romans; it was their town Bibrax which the Belgæ first attacked, hoping to induce Cæsar to leave his fortified position to repel them. He remained, however, where he was, sending sufficient help in the way of defensive artillery to enable the townsmen to defend themselves and to force the Belgæ to give up the siege. They then turned to attack the Roman camp. Cæsar drew up his army, but neither side had any desire to come to close quarters, as in front of the camp there was a considerable stretch of swampy ground. The Belgæ then tried to cut off the Roman line of communications, but this involved crossing the Aisne, and its banks were closely watched by Cæsar's men. A few horsemen and war engines were sufficient to deter them from making the attempt.

If the Belgæ had crossed with their whole army, they could have carried out their purpose; the Roman communications would have been broken, but the Romans could have gone ahead, and the Belgæ, outside of their own land, had no way of maintaining their supplies. The only thing to do was to surround the Roman camp from all sides and starve it out. Even with their superior numbers, which Cæsar gives as 306,000, this was a difficult operation, for the enveloping lines, owing to the country being traversed by two rivers, would have been large. In any case the Belgæ recognized that they could not keep the field long, and when they heard that Cæsar's allies, the Ædui, were invading their country, they decided to withdraw, the confederated tribes engaging to help one another if Cæsar's army invaded their territory. The retreat of the Belgæ was so unexpected that at first the Romans took it for a feint meant to provoke them to leave their camp.

As soon as the news was well authenticated, the cavalry pursued the retreating barbarians, keeping up a series of irritating attacks. The Belgic strongholds surrendered soon after; only three tribes, the Nervii, the Viromandui, and the Atrebates, tried to strike a blow for Gallic freedom. They fell upon the Romans, while they were arranging to encamp in a woody country on the Sambre, and caused almost a panic. The allied troops fled in confusion, but the legionaries held their ground, getting themselves in line, and as they were far superior in numbers to the Nervii, they soon got the upper hand of them, although there was some sharp fighting and for a time two of the legions were hard pressed. It was part of the Roman general's strategy not to face a superior force. This point is apparent in the previous campaigns, but, as a military writer, Cæsar had no scruples in manipulating his figures for popular consumption. When the Nervii made peace unconditionally, they represented themselves, according to Cæsar, as having only 500 men left out of an original 60,000 capable of bearing arms; a few years later they appear again in the Commentaries as having a considerable army. They also sent a contingent of 5000 to Alesia at the close of the Gallic war. Probably a just estimate of the fighting force of the Nervii would give them 30,000 men, because the whole population of the district could hardly have been more than 150,000 souls. They occupied a territory of four hundred square kilometers, and with the slight density of population in Gaul, they could not have numbered more than the figures given above. Even in the Italian peninsula, which was more thickly settled, there was altogether a population of not more than three and a half millions and a density of only twenty-five per square kilometer. The Roman legions who opposed the Nervii in this last fight numbered at least 40,000 men.

Dwelling east of the Nervii were the Aduatuci, said to be descendants of the survivors of the former Cimbri and Teutones, whom Marius had destroyed. They had promised to help the Nervii, but had come too late for the battle. Now they withdrew to their chief fortress, but when they saw themselves being enveloped in the complicated and scientific siege works of the Romans, their hearts failed and they surrendered before the final assault was made. What they had not been able to do openly they hoped to accomplish by treachery, for they reserved a part of their arms, at the time they made their submission, and when the Romans were off their guard at night, made a sudden attack upon them. They were defeated with heavy loss, and the next day, in order to make an example of them, Cæsar sold the whole tribe, men, women, and children, into slavery, 53,000 souls in all.

After the Belgic campaign was over, Cæsar laid plans for the further expansion of Roman control in Gaul by sending one of his lieutenants to Armorica, modern Normandy and Brittany, to secure the submission of the inhabitants. Moreover, seven legions were placed in winter quarters along the Loire, ready to use the stream to transport themselves to the territory of the Veneti, the chief tribe in the west of Gaul. (56 B.C.)

The announcement of Cæsar's great success made a profound impression in Rome; new and unknown domains were being annexed, and the people were granted an unprecedented space of fifteen days for a public thanksgiving. During the winter the general himself took up the detailed work of governor of the Cisalpine province, and also made a tour of Illyria, which had been previously unvisited by him. It was filled with a hardy and brave population and might well be used for drawing auxiliary troops for his army.

In Gaul the situation of affairs showed that the people of Armorica could not be depended upon, though they professed loyalty to the Romans. Young Crassus, who commanded a garrison encamped at the mouth of the Loire, when he found his soldiers suffering from lack of supplies, sent some of his officers to collect provisions from the neighboring districts supposedly friendly. The Veneti seized these men, and refused to give them up except in exchange for their own hostages in the hands of the Romans, and they proceeded to bind themselves together for common action, showing their desire to repudiate the sovereignty of Rome. Cæsar's reply to the challenge was to order the preparation of a fleet of ships to be put into service the following summer against the Veneti, whose chief seats were along the sea coast.

It was not possible for Cæsar to direct these operations in person, for affairs in Rome demanded his presence on the southern side of the Alps. Clodius had mismanaged the affairs of the democratic party in Rome, had proved headstrong, had alienated Pompeius, and had been unable to prevent the return of Cicero from exile. The cause of the senatorial oligarchy was progressing, and a danger point was reached when Crassus drew away from Pompeius, of whose popularity he was jealous, and when Pompeius himself felt that his talents and his position as conqueror of the East were not being sufficiently recognized. Cato, too, was returning from Cyprus, and could be relied upon to give the triumvirs trouble in his rôle of professional obstructionist.

As there was talk already in Rome of the recalling of Cæsar, a consultation between the triumvirs was imperatively needed. Lucca in Tuscany was selected for the place of meeting, which took place in April, 56. A great crowd of officials, magistrates, and senators were present to receive orders from the triumvirs or to hear particulars of the conference. Cæsar by his diplomacy managed to remove the causes of estrangement between Crassus and Pompeius, and the details of a common policy were arranged. By the conference at Lucca, through the adroit manipulation of Cæsar, the old combination that had begun to work haltingly, owing to the estrangement between Crassus and Pompeius, and also to their common lack of political acumen, was re-established and its details settled.

The main thing was to muzzle the Senate; with this done, it would be safe for Pompeius and Crassus to carry out their plans for securing an important province each, together with a military command for a long term of years. The arrangement was that the other two triumvirs (Cæsar of course returning to finish the subjugation of Gaul) should be Consuls in 55; and after their year of magistracy was finished, Pompeius was to have the two provinces in Spain, and Crassus was to go to the East, where there would be a chance of achieving military distinction in a war with the Parthians. In the local affairs of Rome care was taken that Clodius should be kept from continuing his line of irresponsible action, and Cicero was drawn into the sphere of Cæsar's influence by his brother being given a subordinate military command in Gaul.

Cæsar, when the conference was over, soon returned to the front, to deal with the Veneti in such an effective way that by their example the Gallic tribes might be taught the risks of braving the power of Rome. Divisions of the army were sent to various points of Gaul, where it seemed likely there might be sympathetic uprisings of the populations in favor of the national movement, led by the tribes about the Loire. The Veneti had against them Cæsar himself, and the problem of their subjugation offered some novel difficulties. Their fortified places were usually on headlands; sometimes inaccessible from the mainland except by ship. The country was cut up by many estuaries, and the Veneti, who were practised sailors, showed great mobility in their movements. They withdrew from one post to another, easily cutting themselves off from attack as the Romans, who were not familiar with the country, advanced to meet them with the hope of forcing a decisive engagement. Their power could be destroyed only in a naval battle, and it required both patience and ingenuity on Cæsar's part before his men could be trained to meet the enemy in their own waters, or even before a fleet could be built suitable to overcome the special difficulties of navigation on the shores of the Bay of Biscay, so unlike the conditions in the Mediterranean. The fleet of the Veneti was finally destroyed; their ships were rendered helpless when the men on the Roman fleet cut their rigging with long poles having at the end sharp hooked knives, and boarding parties disposed of the warriors on the decks. Many of the brave tribe were put to death when they submitted, and the rest were sold as slaves.

In the meantime the operations of the subordinate commanders had been successful, and conspicuous results had been reached in Aquitaine, where the younger Crassus had brought all the tribes to accept Roman sovereignty. Indeed the only failure to be registered this year was Cæsar's own expedition in the far northern part of Gaul between the Somme and the Rhine, the dwelling place of the Morini and the Menapii. These tribes took refuge in their forests and could not be dislodged, and even some incidental defeats failed to break their obstinacy.

The new year, as it opened, with news of a German invasion on a large scale, brought fresh anxieties to the commander. It was told him that warlike tribes living in and about the Thuringian forest were on the move towards the west, and that others had even crossed the Rhine, dispersing the Gallic tribes in their progress. In Gaul there was a disposition in some quarters to welcome them as deliverers; already some of the Gallic tribes were in communication with them on a friendly basis. (55 B.C.)

Cæsar marched to meet the Germans, and in a conference with their leaders told them they must leave Gallic territory, at the same time offering to make an arrangement by which they could receive land on the right bank of the Rhine. They seemed disposed to accept these terms, but soon hostilities were precipitated because, while the terms were being discussed, the Germans attacked some of the Gallic cavalry attached to Cæsar's army. The Romans moved suddenly, and according to Cæsar's own account, butchered in cold blood men, women, and children to the number of 430,000, a hearsay number of course, but there is no reason for doubting that there was a massacre. No Roman was killed and few were wounded. Even in Rome, notoriously insensible to deeds of blood, this wholesale butchery caused disgust. Cato proposed that Cæsar should be given up to the barbarians as an act of justice. But the Senate contented itself with decreeing honors for the victory, although it was proposed, but not carried, that the operations in Gaul should be investigated by a commission.

To finish up the moral effect made on the Germans by the massacre of their kinsmen, Cæsar built a trestle across the Rhine, transported his army into German territory, and for a short time his soldiers were employed in laying waste the country contiguous to the river. He had no intention of penetrating to the interior of the country, and soon returned to Gaul, after destroying the bridge he had built.

This year's campaign had been marked by daring adventures; it was to have a spectacular close in the expedition to Britain, an island known in a general way to traders from Gaul, but never yet visited by a Roman official or by a Roman army. Cæsar affected to believe that resistance to Roman rule in Gaul was being supported from Britain. In any case a protectorate of the island seemed to offer great material advantages, for exaggerated reports were in circulation as to its wealth and fertility. The expedition was only a partial success. A few tribes made their submission, but the troops had to be hastily withdrawn, because Cæsar desired to be back on the mainland before the equinoctials set in, as the fleet had already severely suffered in a storm.

In the winter preparations were made on a large scale for a second crossing, a large body of transports being prepared and collected at Portus Itius (perhaps Wissant, near Cape Grinez). The troops in the meantime were carefully trained in handling newly constructed vessels specially planned for the waters of the narrow seas. During the winter the periodic signs of disaffection among the Gauls were again plainly visible, this time the Treviri were intriguing with the Germans. An advance in force from Cæsar was needed to put a check to the rising hopes of the anti-Roman party, whose chief, Indutiomar, was forced to give hostages for his good behavior. Much discontent was caused by the necessity of sending contingents to the army; besides, the legions were a burden on the food supplies of the land. The feeling against foreign control grew so strong that Cæsar determined to take some of the Gallic chiefs with him to Britain, to keep them under personal observation. Dumnorix, the Æduan, tried to secure common action among all and to induce the other chiefs not to embark. Only Dumnorix, however, withdrew when the fleet was about to sail. A party was sent back to pursue him. When he resisted, he was slain.

The second expedition to Britain was on an unprecedented scale. There were five legions, two cavalry troops, and an armada of 800 vessels to carry them. The British tribes withdrew from the coast, and there was some fighting, as the Romans made their way inland to attack various British strongholds. Some of the tribes submitted, but the Roman victories were more apparent than real; the camp around the fleet was attacked, and as the army returned, it was continually harassed by an active enemy, who dogged each stage of the march, but refused to come out and fight in the open. The chief result of the invasion was the collection of reliable information about the people and their customs. The island was not occupied or formally conquered for nearly a century. The captives that were taken were brought over to the continent and sold as slaves. (54 B.C.)

When the expedition returned, the troops were distributed through Gaul in winter quarters as camps of observation, not more than a hundred miles from one another; Cæsar's own headquarters being at Amiens. The scene of the first disturbance was in the northeast; a Roman garrison on the march from one camp to another was cut off, and only a few stragglers were left to tell the tale. Cicero's brother Quintus, the commander of another garrison, was attacked, and no message could be got through the hostile tribes of the Nervii to tell Cæsar of his desperate straits. Finally news was carried by means of a Gallic slave whose master, a Nervian refugee, promised him his liberty if he were successful.

Cæsar, with one legion and with a division of horsemen, arrived just in time to save the beleaguered garrison. The Gauls were severely handled when the Romans pushed through their lines to reach Cicero's camp. The news of the relief caused dejection among the other Gallic tribes, who were about to attack isolated Roman garrisons. Labienus alone had trouble with the Treviri, but managed to ward off the blow, inflicting upon them in turn a crushing defeat, and slaying their leader, Indutiomar. The rest of the winter and summer campaign was spent in various expeditions directed against the Gallic tribes whose loyalty was suspected. It was designed to make a special example of the Eburones, who had cut off the Roman legion the preceding year. They were doomed to destruction, and the neighboring tribes were invited to come and enjoy the plunder. Some of those who came preferred to attack the Romans first, and Cicero's camp again fared badly by a sudden raid, made by the Sigambri, a German tribe, who had crossed the Rhine, invited by the prospect of plundering the Gauls. This mistake confused the whole original scheme, and it resulted in the escape of the leader of the Eburones, Ambiorix, an implacable foe of Rome.

When the winter of 53-52 came on, Cæsar's sojourn in the Cisalpine province was passed during a season of much anxiety. Rome had been disturbed by factional fights between Clodius and his opponent, Milo, in which the popular demagogue met his death. There had been a drawing together of the senatorial party, and Pompeius, who was now looked upon as the chief bulwark against anarchy, had been intrusted by the Senate with extraordinary powers, enabling him to call for a general levy of men of military age throughout Italy. Julia, the wife of Pompeius, was dead, and with her vanished the one strong personal link between the two triumvirs, for Crassus had perished in the East fighting against the Parthians. The news of the troubles in Italy spread rapidly in Gaul, causing the restless tribes there to believe that Cæsar would be kept on the southern side of the Alps, and that, with the commander-in-chief away, there would be no trouble in bringing about a successful revolt, provided there were common action throughout the whole country. The essential condition was to unite all the Gauls against Roman control, and this had already in a large measure been accomplished by the king of the great tribe of the Arverni, Vercingetorix, now at the head of a confederation extending over the whole of the central part of the country. It was difficult to overcome the particularistic tendencies of the Gauls, but this new chieftain at least understood the difficulties and made a brave effort to counteract them. He showed also a sense of the strategical needs of the situation by advising the Gauls to make use of their superiority in cavalry and to cut off the Roman communications; another feature of his scheme was to lay waste the country and force the Roman garrisons to withdraw as they were gradually starved out.

A necessary part of the program was the fighting of a decisive battle on a large scale. Vercingetorix had the men at his command, for he had won over the Ædui, who from the first had aided the Romans in their conquests. Cæsar's plan was to take the various tribal strongholds one by one; he succeeded in the case of Avaricum, the capital of the Bituriges. He then sent Labienus against Lutetia with four legions, while he advanced with six to lay siege to the chief city of the Arverni, Gergovia. Cæsar's army was not strong enough for the task; the plan of attack failed, and the Roman legions were saved only by a quick junction with Labienus.

The whole army was soon withdrawn from central Gaul in order to protect the Roman province from attack and also to secure for Cæsar a position where he could establish a fortified camp, from which it would be difficult to be dislodged, and where he could depend upon a regular source of supplies. He selected a place on the Saône, where he could threaten the Æduan territory and be so protected that it would be dangerous for Vercingetorix to follow him. On the march the Romans were vigorously attacked by the Gallic cavalry, but, as they had with them a detachment of German horse, they were beaten off, and the Romans quickly turned the tables, pursuing the Gallic army and finally enclosing it in a hill town, Alesia (Alise Ste. Reine).

Preparations were now made for a long siege. It was a complicated affair, because Cæsar had to provide against attacks both from the beleaguered army and from the Gauls, who were hastening to aid their natural champion. The lines of contravallation were sixteen kilometers long, those of circumvallation twenty; the space between the Roman army and the town was filled with artificial obstacles, meant to prevent the successful use of infantry. The force under Cæsar numbered about 70,000 men and included eleven legions. Cæsar reports that there were 80,000 men imprisoned in Alesia, while to the Gallic relief army is assigned 250,000 infantry and 8000 cavalry. Probably there were not more than 20,000 men altogether in Alesia, for provisions were scarce. This is the number that Napoleon I would give to the inclosed army, and he further remarks that the relief army in its manœuvering and in its camping operations behaved as if it were equal, not superior in strength, to its adversaries.

Cæsar had five or six weeks of leisure before the relieving army appeared. The first part of the decisive engagement was marked by a cavalry battle, in which Cæsar's German horse proved superior to the Gauls. Then a night attack on the inclosing lines was tried and failed. A daylight struggle afterwards took place along the weakest part of the Roman fortifications, Vercingetorix and the relief force making coincident attacks. The Gauls from the outside were driven off by a skilfully delivered movement on their flank, executed by Labienus, which forced them to withdraw, and at the same time Vercingetorix moved back into the city, and soon recognizing his hopeless position, surrendered. The fall of Alesia marks the completion of the Gallic wars. The spirit of the Gauls was broken; there were afterwards various punitive expeditions, but with the collapse of the great rebellion the country became pacified and accepted its position as a Roman dependency.

IV

THE BREAK WITH POMPEIUS AND THE SENATE

Cæsar's government of Gaul was now drawing to its close. He had added to the Roman dominions a territory larger than the two original provinces assigned to him. The question now was, what next? The precedents on this point were clear enough; they were written large in the lives of other recent conquerors, Marius and Sulla. But the senatorial party had no intention of allowing Cæsar to return to Rome with a free hand; it was to be a struggle between the self-interests of a narrow oligarchy and a clear-headed effort to attain personal control of the machinery of the government. On neither side was regard for legality given much weight. Both Cæsar and the senatorial party used without scruple illegal means; both at the same time claimed hypocritically to represent the side of law and order.

As a matter of fact, the old governmental methods of the Republic were adapted only to the conditions of a city community with a homogeneous population. There had been a breakdown years before Cæsar's time, and the question now was who should benefit from this chaotic situation. The senators meant to get Cæsar out of Gaul, reduce him to the ranks of a private individual, and then ruin him by some legal prosecution in connection with his eight years of provincial rule. The chief asset of the Senate was Pompeius' jealousy of Cæsar as a rival of his military glory; he was soured because he could not get the position and the influence for which his early record had marked him out. Pompeius was proconsul of Spain, according to the arrangement made at the last meeting of the triumvirs. It was only carried out nominally; he had no intention of losing his control of Rome, a control which depended on his presence at the center of affairs. Contrary to all precedent, he governed his province by means of deputies. He was also in special charge of the corn supply, a position valuable as a means of propitiating the people with votes. He arranged to have a five-year extension of his proconsular power in Spain, and his influence on the Senate is shown by their willingness to allot him 100 talents a year for the maintenance of his troops. He used his patronage exclusively to advance his own personal interests, oblivious of the compact with Cæsar, showing altogether that, while he meant to stand outside the law, the chicanery of legislation could well be used to block the path of his rival.

Cæsar, who had not forgotten to retain the favor of the Roman populace by entertainments and benefactions, and who had all the skill of a party boss in retaining the allegiance of friends and followers, had three very strong allies back of him, leaving aside his natural superiority in capacity and in shrewdness to Pompeius. His conquest of Gaul, followed as it was by a very judicious treatment of the conquered tribes, gave him the support of a warlike population ready to act on his behalf. Moreover, the reduction of the country had unlocked a store of wealth, which was naturally in his hands; the slaves alone, collected from the captives, represented as capital a very large sum of money. Then there were the seasoned legions on whose loyalty he could depend.

The rival claims of the two leaders reached an acute stage when Pompeius, now Consul, passed legislation by which an interval of five years was required between service as a provincial governor and as a magistrate in Rome. Cæsar's term of office expired in B.C. 49; he had received leave to stand for the consulship and had requested to be left in possession of his provinces till the end of 49. Now in Pompeius' legislation there was required, unless special permission were given, personal candidature, and also the Senate was given authority to relieve provincial governors at any time during the last year of their service. Cæsar might find himself relieved of his proconsulship before he had been elected Consul. It would be a dangerous position for him to confront a rival armed with extraordinary powers, while he was only an individual citizen. There were further grounds of irritation because the senatorial party refused to recognize certain administrative acts of Cæsar, by which he had extended the franchise to various provincial towns. In arranging the question of provincial succession there was much delay. Pompeius hesitated to accept the Senate's drastic measure, by which Cæsar would be relieved long before he could be elected Consul. He made a show of conciliation by shortening the interval and also by promising to resign his own command before the expiration of his term if the Senate so desired. Cæsar's agent in Rome, the Tribune Curio, displayed much ingenuity in obstructing all measures aimed at his chief, and it was plain from the way the political game was being played that Cæsar's minimum, service as Proconsul till the end of 49, and entrance into the consulship on January 1, 48, would be the watchword of his partisans. In all other respects he showed himself ready for conciliation and compromise. When two legions were asked for the Parthian war, they were promptly sent, and no protest was made at their being kept at Capua, when they were no longer wanted in the East. Curio, too, was ordered to cease blocking the vote of money to pay Pompeius' troops.

But the senatorial party were not ready to make terms; it seemed to them that with the co-operation of Pompeius they could place Cæsar in an *impasse*. They miscalculated his personal popularity and his military strength, and now were all the more confident, because they were successfully intriguing with Labienus to detach him from his chief.

The weakness of the senatorial clique was its obvious insincerity in claiming to be the representative of the party of law and order. It was absurd to object to Cæsar stepping directly from the proconsulship to the consulship as an irregularity, when Pompeius had held both offices together; indeed he had been twice Consul within four years, entirely in contravention of the required legal interval of ten years between the holding by one individual of the highest magistracy.

Marcellus, one of the Consuls in B.C. 51, a determined opponent of Cæsar, brought matters to a climax by denouncing Cæsar in the Senate as a brigand and asking that he should be called a public enemy unless he gave up his province by a fixed date. These motions were made as a result of the debate whether a successor to Cæsar should be appointed; they were carried by an imposing majority. An equal majority rejected the motion that Pompeius should be required to resign.

Curio, who had as Tribune interposed his veto on the first motion, then offered a resolution by which both commanders should be required to resign. This was carried by 322 to 320, but no effect was given to it; probably it was vetoed by a Pompeian Tribune. Through private channels, efforts were being made to prevent a break between the two rivals; on account of Pompeius' well-known indecision of temper, the senatorial clique resolved by a bold stroke to prevent further negotiations. Marcellus, on the 9th of December, using as a pretext the rumor that Cæsar was on his way to Rome with his army, tried in vain to get the Senate to declare Cæsar a public enemy and to authorize Pompeius to take command of the troops in Italy and protect the state. Indignant at the timidity of the senators, he took matters in his own hands, virtually declaring war on his own responsibility, for he handed over the two Italian legions to Pompeius, with the command to march against Cæsar. Pompeius, though this action of the Consul was unconstitutional, accepted the commission; at the end of the month he was still confident that Cæsar would drop his claim to the consulship and that so peace would be restored.

Cæsar acted cautiously; he sent for additional troops from Gaul and also despatched a message to the Senate offering to resign all his provinces and his army, provided Pompeius would do the same. In case of refusal, he said he would be compelled to take measures for asserting his own rights and the freedom of the Roman people. Curio was sent with this ultimatum to Rome; it was only with difficulty that the letter was read. A motion was passed that at a fixed date Cæsar should give up his army and that his non-compliance would be treated as an act of war. There was, of course, the usual obstruction from Marcus Antonius, a Cæsarian Tribune; the final decree by which martial law was introduced and the magistrates called upon to see "that the commonwealth took no harm," was not passed till the seventh of January.

(49 B.C.) Lentulus, the Consul, in the meantime had advised the obstructing tribunes to leave the city if they valued their personal safety. It was this verbal threat which put in Cæsar's hands the very useful plea that he was acting as the defender of the freedom of the Roman people.

The military strength of the two parties was, from the senatorial point of view, altogether on their side; they had, they reasoned, the whole empire to draw upon for recruits, while Cæsar had only his own province. The difficulty of the senatorial position was, that their forces were not together when the war broke out. Of Cæsar's original thirteen legions, two were now under Pompeius' command; besides this, the latter had in Spain seven legions of well-seasoned troops; in Italy he had the two legions already mentioned, which originally belonged to the army of Gaul; and another in a state of creation.

Cæsar's chance lay in prompt action, in administering a decisive defeat before Pompeius could get his scattered men together. While the negotiations were in progress, he had only one legion in northern Italy; but two had been sent for, and when they were at hand Cæsar had, with his allies, about 20,000 men, a force considerably superior to that of Pompeius, who was especially careful not to lead Cæsar's old legions against their former commander. With one legion of newly recruited men he could do nothing; the consequence was that in Italy there was practically no resistance to Cæsar's advance. When some of the newly created cohorts joined him, the senators with their commander fled to Greece.

The moral effect of the abandonment of Italy and the capital was a great asset for the Cæsarian party. The critics have condemned Pompeius because he failed to relieve the senatorial troops inclosed by Cæsar in the town of Corfinium in the Abruzzi. It was a discouraging blow at the very commencement of the struggle for the senatorial party to see their soldiers and one of their chief partisans, Domitius Ahenobarbus, left to their fate. But Pompeius was in no position to give help; if he had attempted to give aid, he would have been defeated and captured.

Instead of pursuing Pompeius across the Adriatic to Greece, Cæsar turned away to the conquest of Spain. Even if transports were lacking, he might have doubled round the Adriatic coast through Illyria, his own province. He might soon have got the control of the entire East before a sufficient force was collected to oppose him. But if he had done so, in the meantime Italy would have been exposed to an invasion from Pompeius' Spanish veterans, for the senatorial commander would undoubtedly have betaken himself there and acted on the offensive. By the time Cæsar could reach Antioch, in Syria, Pompeius could have occupied Rome. Cæsar therefore consistently followed the principle of striking at the enemy's force where it was concentrated and prepared for effective work.

Several of the legions newly formed from Italian recruits were sent to Sardinia, Sicily, and Africa as crucial points, from which a descent might be made on Italy; others were left in Italy itself. Of the veteran legions from Gaul, three were despatched to Marseilles, which had taken the senatorial side, and six were taken to Spain. There were seven Pompeian legions in the peninsula under three different commanders, Afranius and Petreius in the north, Varro in the south. Varro, the celebrated antiquarian and scholar, was not an enthusiastic partisan of Pompeius; there seems to be no reason, except his desire to be neutral, why he should have weakened the Pompeian forces in the north by keeping his legions in the south. In any case, the five legions near the Pyrenees, as if conscious of their weakness, remained on the defensive, although for a time they were opposed only by two legions of Cæsar's.

Cæsar's force was undoubtedly numerically superior, for there was a considerable contingent of allies, German and Gallic, both horse and foot. The plan of strategy adopted by the Pompeians was to keep Cæsar in check until Pompeius' preparations in the East were completed, that is, to wait until he could come to Spain to direct the operations there in person, or could make a diversion by attacking Italy with the troops raised in the East. No attempt was made by Pompeius' lieutenants to stop Cæsar's passage through the mountain passes of the Pyrenees. This, in any case, would have been a questionable operation and apt to cause a division of strength in the opposing army.

The first point of conflict between the two armies was at Ilerda, 150 kilometers south of the Pyrenees and about forty north of the Ebro. There was a stream in front of the town, crossed by a stone bridge, and near this stream, on a height south of the town, the Pompeians placed their camp. They were well supplied with provisions; and they commanded the access to the bridge. As the stream had a strong current and was liable to the sudden changes of a mountain torrent it would be unsafe for Cæsar to make a temporary bridge to keep in contact two separated portions of an enveloping army. Cæsar could not afford to leave this strongly encamped force in his rear, for the way would be open to them to invade both Gaul and Italy. In case of defeat the Pompeians might make a further stand, with an advantageous position on the banks of the Ebro.

For some time the Cæsarian army under Fabius remained inactive before Ilerda. Two bridges had been built across the stream, but one of these the current had carried away, and at one time two of the legions were in considerable danger while they were foraging on the southern bank. When Cæsar took over the command both bridges had gone, and the Pompeians, by using the stone bridge, could prevent any further bridge building. Food supplies from the north were cut off, and the Cæsarians were hard-pressed for provisions, having exhausted all the food in the neighborhood of their camp. Cæsar managed finally to relieve this trying situation by building a bridge outside the range of the operations of the Pompeians, who never dared to get too far away from their camp. His next move was to try to cut them off from the city, their base of supplies, but this failed. They were secure where they were, but they grew alarmed when some of the native population joined Cæsar's forces; there was also a prospect of a period of low water in the river, when Cæsar could use a ford and so completely envelop them.

Under such conditions they resolved to abandon their camp and retire to the Ebro to make there another stand. The retreat was accomplished without much difficulty, except from cavalry attacks, which delayed their progress toward the river, which they would have reached five miles south of Ilerda. They had covered most of this distance when Cæsar's legions suddenly appeared ready for attack. In spite of the difficulty of crossing the stream at Ilerda, Cæsar's men with great valor had braved the dangers of the swift current and had marched with such rapidity that they caught up with the Pompeians before sunset. Afranius and Petreius soon found themselves outmanœuvered by their opponents, the way to the river being closed to them. The only alternative now was to fight or surrender. After some hesitation, perhaps due to divided counsels in their own camp, they abandoned the attempt to reach the Ebro and returned to their original camping ground at Ilerda. (August, 44 B.C.)

Cæsar, in the meantime, held his hand, though his soldiers earnestly wished for a pitched battle under such favorable circumstances. It was a civil war, and Cæsar had no taste for the kind of butchery practised on the barbarians in Gaul on so many occasions. The Pompeian commanders soon capitulated; the best force of his opponents had now by Cæsar's superior strategy been put out of action, as effectively as if it had been beaten on the battlefield. Such a victory is practically unique in military annals. The Roman army at Trasimene and at Cannæ, the Prussians at Jena, and the French in 1870-71 were annihilated as military units, but only after hard-fought battles.

Cæsar in this brilliant campaign of forty days deprived his antagonists of an entire and efficient army without striking a blow. He was all the time ready to fight, and the absence of a battle was due to the fact that the commanders on the other side were completely out-generaled. The operations followed one another with the system of moves on a chess board. The losing party saw the uselessness of a fight and the victor had no desire to shed blood needlessly.

Easy terms were imposed upon the vanquished; the only conditions made being that Afranius and Petreius should dismiss their troops on the way back to Italy. Varro, in southern Spain, who had none of the temperament for command, and who was waiting to see which was the winning side, soon found himself deserted by the provincials; even Gades, where he had contemplated making a resolute stand, declared for Cæsar. The most serious feature of the campaign in the West was due to the obstinate resistance of the people of Marseilles; they held out for several months and surrendered only when they were exhausted by pestilence and famine. With this siege ended, Cæsar was free to return to Italy.

In general, the first stage of the war was in favor of the Cæsarians; Sicily had been abandoned by Cato, and the only dark spot on the record was the decisive defeat in Africa of Curio, who had unwisely attacked the Pompeians near Utica while they were being aided by a Numidian king. On the way to Rome Cæsar had to handle a case of mutiny in one of the legions, the ninth. The soldiers complained of the strict discipline under which they were kept, as no plundering was allowed. A signal example was made of them, for the whole legion was disbanded and the men only taken back on condition that they gave up their ringleaders. Of these one in ten were taken by lot and executed.

During his residence in Rome, in the interval between the first and second stages of the war, Cæsar was returned as Consul for the coming year (48), after serving a few days in the extraordinary capacity of Dictator. Some new legislation was passed, extending the franchise to provincial populations, and an effort was made to relieve the financial situation produced by the civil war. Money was scarce, interest was high, there being, owing to the general uncertainty, a good deal of hoarding of specie; but nothing was done to encourage the wild rumors of a revolution after the Catiline model, under which there would be a general cancellation of debts. Practically the whole administration of civil affairs was in the conqueror's hands. Only a few senators were left, most of them having fled to Pompeius' camp in Greece, where their presence was a considerable annoyance to their leader, who found in them inveterate critics and grumblers, anxious to give advice on military matters of which they were supremely ignorant.

Cæsar's undivided authority was useful to him; before he left Italy he had his consular powers enlarged and the city could be left without fear, as his own partisans were in control. Cæsar's Spanish victory had given him, on land, decided superiority over his opponents. He had now, in addition to the eleven old legions, seventeen new ones, mostly composed of Pompeian troops, who had transferred their allegiance as the fortune of war had changed. Two had been lost in the disaster in Africa under Curio. About half of his whole strength, twelve legions and 1000 horse, he collected together at Brundisium, intending to sail from that port and meet Pompeius' army in Epirus. The rest of his forces were scattered about in Italy, Sicily, Gaul, and Spain.

To oppose to the Cæsarian main army, the senatorial party had only eleven legions; two of them had originally served under Cæsar, the rest were recruited in the East or were old units filled out by fresh additional soldiers. Pompeius' chief hope, after the defeat of his army in Spain, lay in the possession of a superior sea power. In this respect he had decidedly the advantage, for besides the Roman fleet there were the ships of the dependent Eastern states, while Cæsar's ships in the Adriatic had been either captured or destroyed. Cæsar had, it is true, ordered new ones, but he had no seagoing population to draw from, to secure sailors. Marseilles, it will be remembered, had taken sides with Pompeius and had only been captured with difficulty.

When Cæsar reached Brundisium, he found there were not enough ships there to transport his army to the Greek coast. He adopted, however, the bold plan of using what transports there were, and so, taking advantage of a favorable wind, carried half his available force, seven legions and a corps of cavalry, to the other side. The whole operation took only from twelve to fifteen hours. Pompeius had not brought his land force to the coast of Epirus, and his fleet, as it was the winter season, had not counted on Cæsar's making the passage at that time. Yet when Cæsar landed, the situation was anything but favorable for him; Pompeius' army had reached the principal harbor of Epirus, Dyrrhachium, and his fleet had destroyed part of the transports and was keeping vigilant watch to intercept the rest, if they attempted to leave Brundisium with the legions which remained there. Cæsar was cut off from his base, but Pompeius dared not attack him, though his army was numerically superior. The two armies faced one another in inaction, Pompeius waiting for reinforcements, and Cæsar hoping that there would be a chance for the rest of his army to join him, although the way through Illyria was impracticable, the country being mountainous and the population of uncertain loyalty.

On the other hand, the attempt of the Pompeian fleet to blockade Brundisium failed. After waiting two months, Marcus Antonius succeeded in making the passage, at a time when weather conditions made it impossible for the enemy's ships to interfere with the landing. With this accession of strength, four legions and additional cavalry, Cæsar's force was now superior to that of his opponent; but Pompeius was strongly intrenched on the shore, close to a city well supplied with provisions, and by means of his fleet, in communication with the rest of the world.

The problem of supplies on Cæsar's side was a difficult one, since the neighboring country was nearly exhausted. It was probably this reason which induced him to divide his force by sending some three and a half legions into the interior of the country, partly to intercept a Pompeian relieving army under Scipio, and partly to operate in Greece itself with a view of winning adherents for his cause. With the remainder he proceeded to inclose Pompeius' camp, not so much to force a capitulation, which seemed hopeless because at any time they wished the Pompeian fleet could carry the army away, as to produce a moral effect on the Pompeians, who would be dispirited everywhere, when they learned that their leader was not acting on the offensive.

The siege operations proved calamitous; Cæsar's veterans suffered a severe defeat, and in some places the lines of the inclosing fortifications were destroyed. The other side, elated by victory, were now prepared for a decisive battle. This hazard Cæsar declined to take; instead of this he gave his troops time enough to recover from the effects of their defeat and then moved off from the coast, taking the road to Thessaly in order there to join the other detachments of his army, who were occupied in trying to force Scipio to an engagement.

He was soon followed by Pompeius, and the great pitched battle of the year took place on the plains of Thessaly. The two sides were far from being evenly matched; probably Pompeius had 40,000 legionaries and 3000 cavalry, while under Cæsar there were 30,000 legionaries and 2000 horse. When the armies came in sight of one another, there was some preliminary manœuvering to get the advantage of a favorable position, but finally Pompeius advanced some distance from his camp on level ground, and Cæsar, who was about to march away rather than attack under unfavorable conditions, decided to give battle. Pompeius' right wing rested near a brook with precipitous sides. Relying on this to protect his flanks, he placed the light-armed infantry and the cavalry, under the command of Labienus, on the left wing with directions to make a vigorous onslaught on the troops opposed to them. If the enemy gave way, they were then to attack the legionaries on the sides and rear; in the meantime, Pompeius' own legions were ordered not to advance but to await, where they were, the attack from the other side. It was hoped that Cæsar's men would be in confusion before the hand-to-hand conflict began, as the distance they would have to traverse was greater than was usual in the battles of this period.

Probably all of Cæsar's cavalry were disposed in such a way that they faced the opposing cavalry. In order to compensate for his inferiority of numbers in this arm, he had trained some of his best legionaries to fight interspersed with the cavalry, after the practice among the Germans. The cavalry were separated, too, by a division of 3000 men, and behind his whole order of battle there was a considerable reserve force. It was to be supposed that, even without the assistance of this last support, his seasoned veterans would withstand the enemy for a long time. This expectation was all the more likely to be realized, just because of Pompeius' orders that his own infantry were to be held back from engagement and should maintain their own ground, while his cavalry were at work.

The battle opened with the cavalry charge on the Pompeian side. Cæsar's German and Gallic horse, as they were instructed, withdrew, and as soon as the Pompeian horse followed them, the 3000 men placed previously to support them, attacked the Pompeian cavalry in the flank. This manœuver was immediately followed by a quick action on the part of Cæsar's cavalry. They swerved about, attacked in their turn those who had just been pressing them, and forced them back in confusion. There was not time enough for Pompeius now to get together a mass of infantry to protect his cavalry. The hand-to-hand conflict immediately began, Cæsar's whole force of infantry throwing themselves on the opposing legionaries, who now no longer had the support of their cavalry. The pressure on the front and sides was too much for the Pompeians; first the left wing gave way and then the entire army. (August 8, 48 B.C.)

The crucial feature of the whole battle was Cæsar's skilful disposition of the 3000 men, placed, as some authorities describe it, in a kind of ambuscade. It was this that upset the whole plan of Pompeius' massive cavalry charge. The intelligent manœuvering of the Gallic and German horse, first giving way, then returning to charge superior numbers, is an illuminating illustration of the discipline prevailing in all arms of Cæsar's force. The close of the battle was followed by the occupation of the Pompeian camp. The commander himself fled in deep dejection from Greece, and met his death by an assassin's hands, when landing from a boat on the coast of Egypt. As a military leader he had proved himself in this war unimaginative and sluggish. He was a master of the technique of warfare, but failed to make use of his opportunities; he seemed to have worked out his own campaign in advance, and to have followed the scheme with deliberation, but in other respects he was resourceless, both when the advantage was his own and when the enemy made mistakes.

With two very much reduced legions and a few horse, Cæsar pursued his rival to Egypt, where he was too late to take him alive. But the factional contests in Egypt as to the royal succession and perhaps, too, the desire to get his hands on the Egyptian treasury, induced the conqueror to use this opportunity of asserting Roman sovereignty over the dependent kingdom. It proved to be a rash step, for the Egyptians were fanatically attached to their autonomous position, and Cæsar's small force was in great danger, not only from the Egyptian army, but also from the turbulent Alexandrian populace, who tried and almost succeeded in shutting him up in part of the city, and in preventing supplies and reinforcements coming to him by sea. At times the Romans were in great danger; there were furious combats in the city and in the harbor, and it was not till many months had passed that Cæsar was master of the situation. It took all the resources of his versatile genius to hold out until large enough reinforcements came from the East to bring the Alexandrians into subjection.

The whole winter after the battle of Pharsalus was spent in this way, and when the war was over in March, there was three months more delay in Alexandria, owing, it was said, to the fascination exerted over the conqueror by the famous Egyptian queen, Cleopatra. During the summer preparations were made for an extensive expedition throughout the Farther East with a small body of men, the design being to pacify the Oriental provinces. This proved not very difficult; most of the problems were solved by diplomacy and only one battle was fought, that of Zela, in Pontus, with Pharnaces, king of Pontus, who had taken advantage of the civil war to try to set up an independent rule over a large part of Asia Minor.

While Cæsar was absent in the East, his cause in the West had been far from successfully handled by his lieutenants. The Pompeian fleet had given great trouble on the Italian coast and in the Adriatic Sea. Affairs in Spain had been hopelessly muddled by a corrupt and tyrannous governor, who angered the provincials and got into trouble with the native tribes. In Rome the victory at Pharsalus had been followed by great activity on the part of the Senate and popular assembly in heaping additional honors on Cæsar. He was made Dictator with virtually unlimited powers. The administration, so far as any semblance of legality was concerned, seemed to have gone to pieces, while Cæsar was having his troubled experiences in Alexandria. No provision had been made for filling up the magistracies, and the conduct of affairs fell into the hands of an irresponsible agitator, Dolabella, Cicero's son-in-law, who prepared a social program containing, as its chief items, canceling of debts and remission of rents. There were serious riots in the city, the mob becoming so powerful that even the Cæsarian Senate had to call on Marcus Antonius, Cæsar's chief local lieutenant, to suppress the violence by the use of military power.

When Cæsar arrived in Italy from the Orient, there was much to be done and not much time in which to do it, because all the irreconcilable partisans of Pompeius, trusting in the help of the Numidian king, Juba, had gathered in Africa, where, since the defeat of Curio, they met with no opposition in their control of the country. During Cæsar's stay in Rome, there were various measures passed, some to relieve the financial crisis, others to provide against disturbances of public order, while political rewards had to be distributed to his followers in the way of nominations to the Senate, or by the creation of additional places among the magistracies. On account of the government's embarrassments, there was a resort to the policy of forced loans, both from individuals and from communities. The private property of Pompeius and some of his adherents was sold at public auction, a questionable proceeding which gave rise to a good deal of unpleasant jobbery among Cæsar's friends, who bought the property in, and then, depending on their influence with their all-powerful master, tried to evade payment. (47 B.C.)

More serious than these matters of local politics was the sullenness of Cæsar's troops, which developed into open mutiny when they were ordered to make ready for the coming campaign in Africa. They refused to budge until the promises of money and land made them before the battle of Pharsalus were strictly carried out. Cæsar dealt successfully with the situation; he had no cash to give them, but he discharged them, calling them citizens and not soldiers, and assured them at the same time that all of their demands, with back interest, would be paid as soon as he returned from Africa to celebrate his triumph. The veterans were placed in a dilemma; they could not turn against Cæsar, for their hope of reward lay in his success. Most of them were taken back as volunteers for the African campaign. Before leaving Italy, Cæsar again arranged to become Consul for the year 46, at the same time making arrangements for the distribution of provincial charges. One assignment was especially noteworthy: a pardoned Pompeian senator, Junius Brutus, nephew of Cato, at the time in arms against Cæsar, was appointed to Cisalpine Gaul.

A year and a half had passed since Pompeius' defeat at Pharsalus, but his cause was being energetically upheld in Africa, where his partisans were making a final stand. It was here that Scipio, Labienus, Cato, Afranius, and Petreius gathered together with the forces that remained, ten legions in all, no inconsiderable force in itself; but there were besides a large contingent of well-trained cavalry and heavy- and light-armed troops, supplied by Juba, king of Numidia, who was implacably hostile to Cæsar's cause, and who meant to use the divisions of the Romans for the purpose of carving out for himself an independent kingdom. The only danger point, apart from an attack from Italy, lay further west, where the two Mauretanian kings, Bocchus and Bogud, acted together as a check to the power of the Numidians. They were able to carry out their policy intelligently, because they had the help of a Roman adventurer, Publius Sittius, suspected of being an accomplice of Catiline, and for this reason an enemy of the remnant of the senatorial party in Africa.

Cæsar landed in Africa in December with only a small force, and for a time he had to maintain himself in an intrenched camp on the coast. His six legions were made up of raw material, and it was impossible for him to take the offensive, until his veterans, who had been sent for, arrived. The situation was saved by Sittius, who made a diversion in the West, and so drew off Juba to the defense of his own kingdom. Among the provincials, the Cæsarian cause began to be popular, for they saw in it a protection against the nationalist schemes of Juba. Moreover, the Roman aristocratic commanders had treated the population of the province with scant consideration, so there were many desertions to Cæsar's side. Owing to the incompetent strategy of his opponents, who do not seem to have known how to handle their fleet, communications with Italy were kept open. It was Cæsar's purpose, after the veteran legions arrived, to compel Scipio to give battle. This he refused to do, until his hands were forced. When Cæsar began the siege of the important seaport town of Thapsus, Scipio was obliged to come to the rescue, and a pitched battle was fought early in April, in which the Pompeian force was completely routed. Cæsar's troops occupied the enemy's camp, and despite the entreaties of their commander, a wholesale butchery by the legionaries followed the fight.

The campaign was soon completed. Utica, where Cato commanded the garrison, surrendered, after their leader, seeing the ruin of his cause, had committed suicide. Scipio perished at sea, Varus and Labienus succeeded in making their escape to Spain. Even Juba was ruined by the misfortunes of his allies, for his own subjects rejected him on his return, and he and Petreius met deaths by suicide. After setting the affairs of Africa in order, and annexing the kingdom of Numidia as a province, Cæsar returned to Rome after an absence from the capital of 180 days. (46 B.C.)

V

CÆSAR SUPREME

With his return begins the period of Cæsar's full autocratic power in the largest sense of that term; honors extraordinary were heaped upon him and the whole machinery of government was in his hands. He was perpetual Tribune, and so might check all legislation which did not meet his approval. Moreover, he was made sole Censor, which position included not only the guardianship of manners and morals, but also gave him authority over the composition of the Senate, and the even more valuable supervision of contracts and financial affairs. Besides this there was the dictatorship and the consulship. No opposition could come from the religious side, for he was Pontifex Maximus and a member of all the religious colleges.

His position was not so novel as the way he used it. Sulla also had established personal autocratic rule, and Pompeius, who was looked to by the conservatives to preserve republican government, had been completely oblivious of constitutional traditions when they clashed with his interests. Cæsar did not abdicate as did Sulla, nor did he hypocritically veil his purposes as Pompeius had done. There was much ostentatious display in the way of triumphs, festivals, games, and largesses, to celebrate the conqueror's victories, nor were deeds of cruelty absent in the Gallic triumph. Vercingetorix, who had spent six years in a Roman dungeon, was put to death in accordance with old-fashioned republican brutality.

Some citizens felt disgust at the extravagant expenditure of the autocrat, but this kind of discontent was not so deep as the resentment caused among the upper classes by the introduction of a virtual monarchy. Their point of view is vividly presented in Cicero's correspondence during the closing years of Cæsar's rule. He suffered all the more intensely because he had to belie his own principles and live on friendly terms with the man who had destroyed his ideals and robbed him of his chances of political distinction. Cæsar advanced oblivious of criticism, safe in the possession of uncontested powers. There were many things to do, and there was nothing to which he hesitated to set his hands. It was not a time to follow the maxim, "quieta non movere."

Among the most difficult problems was the allotment of land to the discharged veterans. The plan followed was not to establish them in new colonies, but to incorporate them in existing communities. Apparently private rights were respected, for no serious complaints are recorded. A much-needed reform was taken in hand when Cæsar, using his power as Censor, reduced the number of those who received the dole of corn from 320,000 to 150,000 persons. Equally creditable was the extension of the Roman citizenship to non-Italians, special classes being chosen for this privilege, such as medical practitioners and teachers. Other measures were economic, such as the restoration of customs duties, or had a social aim like the attempt to extend free labor where slaves were commonly used. Municipal administration received special attention, rules being made for the maintenance of streets and lanes, for the control of wheeled traffic, and to prevent public ground from being occupied by the erectors of stands and platforms.

In general, the exceptional position of the city of Rome was not preserved; rather, provincial towns were organized after the model of the imperial metropolis. Probably it was this bold step in reducing Rome to the level of other towns, a proceeding strictly in harmony with Cæsar's consistent and established policy of equal and fair treatment to the provinces, that led to the idle bit of gossip that he thought of transferring the capital to the East, to Alexandria or Troy. Criminal legislation was stiffened by adding to the recognized sentence of exile forfeiture of property as a penalty. Care was taken that Roman citizens should not travel abroad for a lengthy period, a provision probably intended to protect the provincials from the presence of needy individuals who would make use of official favor for questionable financial schemes. But perhaps the most striking of all these measures from the personal point of view was a law restricting the tenure of provincial governorship. There were to be no more chances open for a series of campaigns under one leader such as Cæsar had waged in Gaul.

Under this personal government there was little place for a Senate except as a registering body, and Cæsar did not always allow it to perform even this humble function. It came to have a make-believe existence. Decrees were drawn up in its name that had actually never come before it, and the conqueror's unpopularity with the Senators was increased by the introduction of new members, who had no aristocratic traditions to maintain.

As an example of the versatility of his mind, no better one can be given than the fact that Cæsar's work in bringing order out of chaos was extended to reorganization of the old Roman calendar, under which the year lasted only 355 days, and attempts were made to make the solar and civil years coincide by the occasional introduction of an intercalary month, a process often guided by political or superstitious motives. Since experienced scientists from Alexandria were called on as experts, Cæsar's reformed calendar of 365 1/4 days with an intercalating day every fourth year was sufficiently accurate to stand for centuries, and with a slight correction is still in use in the civilized world.

The machinery of legislation, important and sound as it was, was not entirely depended upon to reveal the whole policy of the ruler. Cæsar is said to have explained in his public speeches that his ideal was not a despotism, but the paternal rule of a father over his children. He tried to live up to this standard, making a noteworthy display of doing so by his generous treatment of his adversaries during the period of the civil war. Some of his most truculent enemies were pardoned by an act of grace, a treatment which induced Cicero to try his hand again at the kind of decorative oratory he had displayed in his early panegyric on Pompeius. Popular as this clemency was, it did not shelter Cæsar from severe criticism when he renewed his amour with Cleopatra, now summoned to Rome, it was said on his invitation, and it was supposed that he was about to marry her, a foreign queen, as the first step to the attainment, by regular process, of regal power for himself.

Invincible as Cæsar was in war, and conciliatory as he was to those who had served against him, there was still a body of Pompeian partisans in Spain, Labienus and Cnæus Pompeius among them, who felt that there was reason for resistance and a chance of success. Cæsar's governors in the peninsula had proved incompetent either to hold the loyalty of the provincials, or to prevent the mutiny of the troops when the Pompeian leaders appeared on Spanish ground. All they could do was to clamor for their leader's presence. He left Rome hurriedly in December, 46. This, his last campaign, was conducted with an army inferior in numbers to that of his opponents. It was an arduous struggle, characterized by conspicuous barbarity on both sides, for neither depended on Roman legionaries alone. The Pompeians had native allies and liberated slaves, and both sides were helped by auxiliary troops from the wild tribesmen of Mauretania. After winning and taking the town of Cordova, Cæsar forced the eldest son of Pompeius to fight a pitched battle at Munda. (March 17, 45 B.C.)

The two armies met here in a life and death struggle, Cnæus Pompeius appealing to his men to avenge his father, while Cæsar's veterans, responding to the battle cry of Venus the Victorious, the patron goddess of the Cæsarian house and its mythical foundress, made it plain that the cause for which they fought was also a personal one. Neither side could look for quarter; Pompeius had already shown his temper by cruel dealings with the provincials who had opposed him, and Cæsar's men were not likely to deal mercifully with those who had rekindled the flame of civil war and so deprived them of a well-earned peace. Both in attack and defense each side showed equal bravery and obstinacy. For some time the issue seemed dubious; Cæsar to rally his own men had to take sword in hand and engage in the thick of the struggle. Finally, when the Pompeians made a change of their order to help the wing of their army which was being hard pressed by the tenth legion, the movement gave the Cæsarians a chance to put their opponents in confusion and finally to flight. On the Pompeian side 30,000 are reported to have been slain; among the dead were Labienus, Cæsar's right-hand man in the Gallic campaign, and Cnæus Pompeius himself, who escaped from the field but was taken and put to death afterward.

Before the return to Italy the affairs of the Spanish provinces had to be set in order; special favors were distributed to the loyal communities in the way of franchise or immunities, and this reconstructive work seems to have been accompanied by financial exactions. The return to Italy was not made until September, and for a whole month Cæsar remained outside the walls of Rome. To mark the victory at Munda there was nothing tangible to do in the way of increasing the autocratic power of the supreme and all-embracing magistrate and executive; there were, however, no visible limitations to the servility of the Senate and Assembly. Fifty days' thanksgiving, yearly games commemorative of the victory, special distinctions of dress, extraordinary honorific titles, a state residence on the Palatine, built after the model of a temple of the gods; special statues in holy places connected with communal worship, all these were voted, and most of them accepted by the conqueror.

After the Spanish war, gold and silver coins were minted, having on one side the laurel-crowned head of Cæsar, with the inscription Cæsar Imperator, and on the reverse the figure of conquering Venus, lance in one hand and on the other a Victory. The conqueror was now treated as being beyond the ordinary human standard. This recognition of superhuman qualities is made plainer in an inscription, placed under a relief of Cæsar (introduced on a metallic map of the world), which reads, "he is a demigod." The Oriental idea of deification, opposed as it was to the whole genius of government in Rome, was now adopted there. With Julius Cæsar began the custom of deifying the supreme ruler of Rome, and it is significant that, although he refused a ten-year consulship, he did not protest against this use of religion for the purpose of adulation.

Now that the supreme authority was unassailably placed in the hands of a single individual, who was protected in its exercise from any legal opposition in Rome, Cæsar showed no hesitation in taking the full responsibility of his position. The Western provinces had for some time been practically under his personal control. He was virtually the founder and the creator of the Roman Empire in the West. The foundation laid by him lasted for hundreds of years. But as military lord of the Roman world he had also to deal with the situation of the East. There especially the extension of the Parthian rule was dreaded, and also anticipated, for the moral effect of the defeat of Crassus a few years before had been immense. Cæsar saw that a war in the East could alone restore the prestige of Rome, and also that it was not safe to leave the conduct of such a war in other hands. His plan was first to conquer the Parthians, and through their territory to reach the Caspian Sea. Afterwards by the way of the Black Sea he meant to march along the Danube, where there were wild tribes which had to be taught to respect the power of Rome, and finally to return to Italy by the way of Germany. Such was the mighty program now developed in the vision of the conqueror. In its details it bore the marks of the bold imagination and the political sagacity which characterized his genius, but the immediate necessity was to bring the Parthian war to an end, and so restore confidence on the Eastern frontier. After the return from Spain the transfer of the bulk of the Roman army to the East was being prepared for.

It was in connection with this purpose that there first arose, apparently, the idea of conferring on Cæsar the title of king. It was said that an oracle of the Sibylline Books had declared that only a king could get the better of the Parthians in war. Such a designation was especially antagonistic to Roman political principles; personal rule was tolerated, but not divine right by family descent. Some preparations had been made for the introduction of this alien conception by the act of the Senate, according to which the title "Imperator," associated directly with the name of Cæsar, should pass to his legal heir. The road to a succession being now marked out, the whole question of the title could not long be left undecided. Imperator was locally understood, but made no claim on subject races. To test popular feeling, Marcus Antonius offered the Imperator a diadem, the insignia of royalty. This was refused, but it was noted that the offer did not call forth the enthusiastic response that was anticipated, nor was Cæsar's rejection of the symbol openly deplored. Still, the desire for some accommodation with the terms of the oracle was not abandoned. It seemed possible that in Rome Cæsar might bow to public opinion by employing only the title of Imperator, while in the provinces he could exercise royal powers and use the royal title. It was supposed that some arrangement of this sort would be made by a regular decree before he set out for the Parthian campaign.

Opposition was bound to develop at this point from the convinced republicans in the Senate; they were strongly represented there, and Cæsar was responsible for their presence. He had gathered about him men of both parties, making a special effort by his generosity to win over some of the most convinced of the senatorial partisans who had followed Pompeius and had fought the victor to the end of the African campaign. But even Cæsar's own appointees and adherents were by no means reconciled to the program which would openly do away with the republic; they wished it still to exist as an institution, and they had no wish to provide for the continuance of personal rule beyond the terms of Cæsar's own life.

The party of Pompeius was by no means inactive; they wrote freely as apologists for their own side, and they did not hesitate in their intrigues to hold up Cæsar as an ambitious autocrat guilty of cruelty on the battlefield, and now that peace was restored, using his claims to mask his aim to establish a tyranny. These views were found among the Senators. Cæsar either thought he was unassailable or reckoned on their gratitude as an obstacle which would separate their theory and their practice. This attitude was only one example of a general want of alertness that seemed to characterize the conqueror after the close of the Spanish campaign.

All the old republican antipathies against royalty were called into life. Cæsar's statue was now seen on the capitol between the figures of Rome's ancient kings. Another statue, that of Lucius Junius Brutus, the founder of the republic, recalled to men's minds the quick and ready method of dealing with kings and tyrants. This old-fashioned republican doctrine was not lost on a disciple and nephew of Cato, Marcus Brutus, who had made peace with Cæsar after the battle of Pharsalus. He claimed to be a descendant of the famous liberator, and by this very fact had influence in heading any movement against the new autocratic system. His personal abilities were of a mediocre order; but he was obstinate and self-consciously vain of his integrity, and could be paraded as a concrete argument to strengthen the republican cause, when others might hesitate to take extreme steps.

But the real motive power in the organization of the conspiracy against Cæsar was found in Caius Cassius, also holding prætorian office like Brutus. The two had not before been friendly, although both were partisans of Pompeius. Cassius, with his dark and gloomy temperament and sarcastic tongue, was not likely to accept the sententious pomposity of his brother Prætor at that high standard of value exacted by Brutus from his friends. What drew them together was their common republican sympathies. Brutus was asked by Cassius what would be his attitude at the next meeting of the Senate when the question of the royal title would be discussed. Brutus replied that he would not be present. Cassius said that Brutus's position as Prætor imposed upon him the obligation of attending the meeting. At this Brutus answered that if he went he would defend the cause of liberty.

Such was the basis of the understanding between the two, and the agreement for common action was accepted, not only by the remnant of the old Pompeian party, but by those as well who called themselves the partisans of Cæsar. Even Caius Trebonius, who had served the cause of Cæsar in the city and on the battlefield for many years, agreed that the freedom of the Roman people was to be preferred to the friendship of an individual. He had once before spoken plainly to Marcus Antonius of Cæsar's ingratitude and of the misfortunes of the republic, but had found no sympathy. Another of Cæsar's companions in arms, Tullius Cimber, felt personally injured because the commander had exiled his brother.

Both sides had grievances. The Pompeians were not to be won by tactful treatment to accept Cæsar's schemes, while his own followers often felt that their allegiance had secured no more favors from him than the open enmity of his former opponents. All experienced the common pressure of an exalted and unlimited authority, and were prepared to act together. The exact details of the conspiracy are obscure; they must have been arranged between the 15th of February and the 5th of March, on which date the Senate was to be called together in a building erected by Pompeius, to decide whether Cæsar was to be allowed to bear outside of Rome the title of king. The conspirators were at one against accepting such a proposal.

Cæsar seemed not to realize his danger, since he paid no attention to the warnings that came to him. His mind was filled with the prospect of the Eastern war. Everyone realized that another victory would render all opposition unavailing. The conspirators would have to act before Cæsar could set out for the new campaign. In the plan to be followed the leading Senators were all accomplices. The way would be easy, provided Cæsar's fellow Consul, Marcus Antonius, who could be relied upon to defend him, were prevented from coming to the Senate. Trebonius was to see that Antonius was detained and kept occupied elsewhere, while another of Cæsar's friends of long standing, Decimus Brutus, undertook the necessary persuasion of the dictator should the latter hesitate to come to the Curia.

Cæsar, as had been arranged, took his seat in the consular chair; the place next his was vacant, his colleague not being present. There was no time to be lost, for Marcus Antonius might appear at any moment. Tullius Cimber, showing much vehemence, drew near to the Consul, making a plea for the return of his brother from exile. As Cæsar hesitated, the prearranged signal for the murder was immediately acted upon. Cimber with both hands tore apart Cæsar's toga; at the same time Casca aimed at his neck a blow which glanced and struck the breast. Cæsar appears to have thought that it was only an act of personal vengeance from which he could protect himself. He sprang to his feet, snatched his toga from the hands of Cimber, and threw himself on the arm of Cassius, at the same time defending himself with the stylus of his tablet. He was strong and active, and might have got the better of his two antagonists, but as he turned on Casca he received a wound in the side, then several others from the conspirators as they closed in upon him. No one of the Senators, whom he had created, came to his help. All was over in a moment, for he made no further resistance when he saw the arm of Marcus Brutus, specially bound to him by personal favors, raised to strike. He fell at the feet of the statue of Pompeius, his body pierced by twenty-three wounds. The corpse was brought back to his dwelling by three slaves in the litter in which he had been carried to the Senate. All the rest of his retinue of clients and friends had fled.

The assassination, its method of accomplishment, and the men who planned and carried it out, bound as all of them were by some kind of obligation to the conqueror, can hardly win sympathy even from those who hate autocratic rule, and think the man who destroys a democracy beyond the law. The conspirators had not the personal character of the traditional tyrannicides of Greece. There is something of a pose in the whole action. Brutus and his fellows were representing a clique and cannot be called in any sense the executors of the will of the people. It would have been more fitting if the old precedent followed in the legendary expulsion of the former kings of Rome, banishment, had been adopted here. After all, Cæsar was giving the

Roman empire a better kind of government than the Senatorial oligarchy. The cause of the conspirators was weak, and the men who carried it out, as events soon showed, were even weaker than their cause. Only verbally were the interests of republicanism represented by the murderers of Cæsar. The Senate and People of Rome existed as they had done of old; but the elements in each were different. In the people of Cæsar's days there was nothing that resembled the ancient community of the plebeians. Military expansion had long since destroyed the old civil constitution; the assemblies in the Forum were legal only in name, for they disguised the irregularities of mob rule, giving opportunities for violence and corruption on the largest scale. Even the Senate was virtually a new creation filled with Cæsar's enemies and certainly incapable from its membership of preparing a genuine restoration of republican institutions. It had stood, even before the civil war, at a time when the oligarchy of wealth and descent had recovered its lost ground through the patronage of Sulla, for governmental inefficiency.

The one man with genius and creativeness adequate to restore a practical republican government was Cæsar himself, and to him republican ideals meant nothing. He was a realistic statesman, who saw the road to monarchy as the short cut to good government, and took it unhesitatingly. At no point in Cæsar's career is there any evidence that he believed in anything but personal rule. Alike skeptical of higher appeals and with a contempt for shams, he never wavered at any stage in his well-planned pursuit of autocratic power. His fight with the Senatorial oligarchy, who alone blocked his way, was conducted with the directness of a military campaign. There was little personal feeling, for he treated men as pawns, whether they were friends or enemies. When their power to help or to oppose him was gone, they were of no significance; so, at the close of the civil war, it was easy to exercise a clemency or a patronage which meant little. There was a superficial amiability in these acts which indicated a contempt of individuals rather than spontaneous humanity. His cold, clear-cut character seemed to work out problems in a bloodless atmosphere alike free from prejudices and from prepossessions.

Cæsar's benefactions and his enmities were alike self-centered. The whole force of a nature extraordinarily versatile and incessantly active was turned to one end, and the various stages of his political career are explained by the closing years of his life. It was his purpose to overthrow the Senatorial aristocrats. The purpose was a most worthy one, and it is difficult to see how it could have been done except by extra-legal means, for the Senatorial faction made the laws, and so held all the cards in their hands. Their motto of government was "Heads I win, tails you lose"; and the claim of legality with such a leader as Pompeius, who had no respect for the constitution, was altogether disingenuous. Cæsar was a shrewder politician than any member of the Senatorial faction, far more brilliant in conception and far quicker in action than his rival Pompeius. After clearing the field of his opponents, he showed less creative capacity than in his preparatory work.

Of course, the time was short between his murder and the close of the last campaign in the civil war, but the government he established was a kind of sham republicanism after the Sullan model, only with a different center of gravity. He seems to have planned a better system of administration, and meant that it should be worked in a way regardful of the public interests of a great empire; but the machinery was to remain the same, except that the various magistracies were either to be held by himself or filled by men of his own selection. The shadow of republicanism was to cover a monarchical rule, and in this respect the conservatism of Cæsar was epoch-making, for it continued to influence the whole genius of the Roman imperial system for centuries.

As a general Cæsar was fortunate in having at his command an army which represented the result of years of technical training acquired in the almost continuous campaigns of the Romans. He did not have to create his army; the material for his conquests was ready to hand. He added nothing new to the art of war as it was already known, but the legion under him had a commander of great versatility, who understood how to use it to the best advantage under any given conditions. This genius in providing for the maintenance of his army repeatedly gave him the advantage over the enemy in the Gallic wars, for it enabled him to defer the decisive engagement until all conditions were favorable for his own side.

Another characteristic of his strategy was his skill in using fortified camps. He was a born engineer, and the engineering feats of his campaigns are evidently recounted with great satisfaction in his "Commentaries." It is evident that they played a decisive part in securing success both during the Gallic campaigns and in the civil war. Indeed, one of the most important contributions of the Romans to the art of warfare was superior technique in fortifications, and in protection of camps, aided by which the defensive of a numerically smaller force could be made to balance the offensive of superior numbers. The sole method of overcoming such resistance was by starving out the army placed in a fortified camp. In his campaigns Cæsar showed remarkable versatility in using the argument of hunger as well as the argument of the sword, and he was quick to turn from one to the other as occasion required.

He seems never to have burdened himself with a pedantic following of rules. Plutarch tells us he had read the accounts of Alexander's great victories. So far as his own "Commentaries" are concerned, there is a studied vagueness, which, as has been mentioned, often leaves important points in obscurity. He is very sparing of giving personal reflections on the progress of the war he is describing. It is noteworthy, therefore, that he once blames Pompeius for repressing the enthusiasm of his troops, saying that it is the general's business to encourage the emotional element in battle.

He is also fond of calling attention to the rôle played by fortune or chance, and so he has been often blamed for the risks he was willing to take because he trusted too much to luck, and it is said that he conducted warfare in the spirit of a gambler. Like Napoleon, he appears to have believed in his star, but the references to fortune in the "Commentaries" are probably a literary device intended to impress a popular audience who, though they had lost belief in the gods of polytheism, were ready to recognize an incalculable and mysterious element in human life.

But there was in his strategy more than a spontaneous brilliancy adequate to rescue him from the difficulties of a position he had not anticipated. In his campaigns we see evidence enough of caution and calculation. Especially in the matter of numerical superiority he was careful not to allow himself any hazards in a decisive engagement. The battle of Pharsalus is the only one in which it is certain that he won a victory with an army inferior in numbers to his opponent. In this case nothing else could have been done, for Pompeius, who was in control of the sea, would have removed his army from Greece if he had been outnumbered. There was but one way of forcing a pitched battle under these circumstances, and it was part of superior strategy to induce an enemy relying on superior numbers to confront troops superior in quality. But such chances Cæsar only took when obliged. There was little of the bravado element in his wars. The situation was outlined beforehand. The almost mathematical result bears witness to the presence of that same type of cool reflection which in the political side of his career makes the founder of the Roman Empire something of an enigma. It is hard to believe that a man can be just as unfeeling and unethical in statesmanship as when he is directing the movements of masses of troops. Cæsar's genius stands for an abnormal development of intellectual power disciplined to serve the ambitious purposes of a man bent on enjoying personal rule, who, to a unique degree, had measured the capacity of other men and himself.

CHARLES THE GREAT

I
INTRODUCTORY

Out of the chaos in Western Europe due to the collapse of Roman provincial rule in the fifth century, there came into being various Teutonic states. They all bore the mark of the early tribal organization of the German peoples and took up the work, more or less successfully, of assimilating the orderly elements and traditions of Roman polity. In the Italian peninsula the permanence of these political creations was short-lived, except in the case of the Lombards, who maintained an enduring rule, largely because they adhered to a crude policy of isolation and set well-considered limits to their desire for expansion. In Spain, the Goths, despite the predominance of the Roman provincial element, succeeded, with the help of the Church, in attaining a fairly centralized organization for several centuries until it was swept aside by the irresistible pressure of the Moslem conquest. To the North, in France, which was first of all the seat of various Teutonic peoples, the Franks, under the astute leadership of their tribal monarchs, gradually absorbed all the territory of the old Roman province of Gallia, adding to it the land to the east which had been the home of their ancestors before they had crossed into the Roman province.

Chlodvig, the founder of the Merovingian line of kings, was not a ruler of the type of Theodoric the Ostrogoth. In contrast with the Teutonic kingdoms of Italy and Spain, the Merovingian showed a stubborn conservatism. After Chlodvig's death there was no man of first-rate ability during the period of Merovingian rule with the dubious exception of Dagobert. These were long years of division, lawlessness, and bloodshed. The Franks kept possession of their conquests, but the royal line produced a succession of weak and helpless rulers who showed themselves incapable of casting aside the traditions of tribal rule. The demand for centralization was recognized and met by the representatives of the noble family of Heristal who, because they were landlords over wide estates, became, as mayors of the palace, *de facto* possessors of sovereign authority. To them the Frankish chieftains throughout the land looked for leadership, and did not look in vain, for their efficient statesmanship soon arrested the disintegrating tendencies of Merovingian rule, and gave their people such an amount of cohesive strength that they became the foremost representatives of Teutonic power in Western Europe. It was the House of Heristal which saved the Franks from the fate of the Visigoths, for it was Charles the Hammer who met the Moslem host on the field of Poictiers and swept them back across the Pyrenees.

Charles' son, Pippin, carried on the work of his father; he was strong, courageous, and cautious, a thorough type of the opportunist statesman, willing so far as he was concerned to control his people under the title of Mayor of the Palace, while the titular dignity of king was kept intact in the Merovingian family. The bloodless revolution which made Pippin a monarch *de jure* from a ruler *de facto*, was due to outside pressure, and this pressure came from the See of Rome, which appealed to him for help as the representative and most powerful Catholic leader in Western Europe after the Emperors at Constantinople had alienated the population in Italy by the part they played in the Iconoclastic controversy.

The Popes of the eighth century, seeing the inability of the Eastern Empire to protect its Italian possessions, and unwilling to give them support against the aggressions of the Lombards, were face to face with a difficult problem. They did not wish to be absorbed in the Lombard kingdom, and were just as much afraid of seeing any restoration of power to the hands of the Emperor's representative, the Exarch of Ravenna.

Pope Stephen played a bold stroke of genius when he crossed the Alps to ask the ruler of the Franks to save the religious capital of Western Christianity from capture at the hands of the Lombard kings. Nor was his political sagacity yet exhausted, for he persuaded the Mayor of the Palace to regularize his own position by taking the title of king under the sanction of the Holy See. This was an ambitious design, unprecedented in the earlier pages of Papal history. Even Gregory the Great had no thought of bestowing the royal crown on any Teutonic tribal chieftain. The action was evidently suggested by the plan prepared some years before, when, with the coöperation of the Pope, it was proposed to revive in Italy a native Italian emperor to lead the people of the Peninsula against the church policy of Constantinople. This scheme was from the beginning a forlorn hope, and it had turned out to be a failure. There was not sufficient military strength in Italy, apart from the Lombards, to back up a revived Emperor of the West, and it is clear that the Lombards would have made short work of any such ruler, even if there had not been among the Italians a party who looked up to the Exarch of Ravenna as the natural head of their civil government.

The negotiations with Pippin ended successfully. The Pope's prestige was enormously increased. Instead of looking forward to becoming the captive of a Lombard king, he became himself the bestower of royal dignity on a man who had at his disposal such vast military power that the passage of his army across the Alps into Lombard territory brought about the reduction of the Lombard kingdom to a status of dependency on a Frankish ruler.

Pippin, as a loyal churchman, followed the Pope's counsel, but he seems to have done so with distinct reservations. The traditional Frankish policy had been the complete subordination of the Church to the State. It is no wonder then that many of the Frankish nobles disapproved of Pippin's act, which reduced their monarchy to a gift from the hands of the Pope. Pippin did all he could during the rest of his lifetime to keep clear of further Italian complications. He never crossed the Alps again, and he was very careful not to depress the Lombard power in Northern Italy and so give Stephen an excuse for demanding additional territory. As a temporal ruler the Pope's authority had been substantially increased by the cession of lands which he had claimed from him on the basis of the so-called Donation of Constantine— a fictitious instrument which Stephen appealed to when there arose the question of the disposition of the territory once belonging to the Exarchate of Ravenna. According to the legend, Pope Sylvester, the contemporary of Constantine, when the capital of the Empire had been removed to Constantinople, had received from the Emperor extensive donations of Italian territory, both on the Peninsula and on the adjacent islands, over which he was to rule with the power of a temporal sovereign. To Pippin, this legendary Donation, because of its presumed sanction at the hands of a revered Emperor and Pope, was sacred. He was willing to be an instrument in carrying out the terms of the sacrosanct compact, but he refused to go farther than this, and for the rest of his life he maintained an attitude of reserve in according additional favors to the Holy See.

Pippin's reign came to an end as calmly as though the line of descent had been unbroken. Even the evil traditions of the Frankish monarchy with respect to the inheritance of the crown were not cast aside. Just as Cromwell and Napoleon felt the weight of custom in their relations with the members of their families, when they were arranging to perpetuate the power of their own creation, so Pippin, the diplomat, the cautious statesman, could do, or at least did nothing to alter the bad and impracticable tribal custom of division of patrimony. This practice caused the downfall of the Merovingian line, and had started the revolution by which the fortunes of the House of Heristal had been assured. This is only one of many anomalies which followed the breaking up of the administration of the Roman Empire, and which testified to the absence of initiative on the part of the Germanic peoples when they were called upon to solve problems of government, for which they had had no preparation. Rulers who did not hesitate to show their individuality in other ways proved fearful of violating tribal customs on questions of divisions of property and family precedence.

The new line of Frankish rulers had apparently learned nothing from the vicissitudes of the elder house. At the death of Charles Martel, the division of the kingdom between his two sons would have certainly endangered the sovereignty of his family had not the difficulty been averted by the abdication of Carloman the elder. Yet Pippin, on his deathbed, had not scrupled to make the same blunder of dividing the realm between his two sons, Charles and Carloman. Almost immediately after their father's death the heirs, apparently mutually suspicious, separated from each other, and had themselves separately proclaimed kings by the Frankish nobles, and received anointment at the hands of the bishops, Charles at Noyon, Carloman at Soissons.

The diplomacy of the dead ruler was revealed in the kind of disposal he made of his realm. It was an equal division only on paper; for the arrangement of the shares was such that the elder son was left with such manifest superior advantages as to territory that the younger brother could not venture to compete with him. As his share Charles had the part of his father's kingdom from which the Frankish hosts derived their chief military strength, viz.: the lands from the Main to the English Channel. Besides this, he received the western portion of Aquitaine, the province whose conquest had cost Pippin a hard struggle of seven years, and which, therefore, might become a dangerous center of warlike enterprise if it were placed entirely in the hands of the younger brother. Carloman had as his share the Suabian lands on both sides of the upper Rhine, and the entire Mediterranean coast from the Maritime Alps to the frontier of Spain. In addition to this there came to him the eastern half of the territory adjacent to such towns as Clermont, Rodez, Albi, and Toulouse.

In geographical extent there was but little advantage on the part of the elder brother, but the territory of the younger from a military point of view was far inferior. Carloman in case of war would have against him, under the command of Charles, the whole military power of the Franks. There was no pretense of friendship between the two new rulers; it seems they had never been friendly. The reason of the alienation may have been because the birth of Charles preceded the formal transfer of the Frankish crown to his father. He was, therefore, the son of a Mayor of the Palace, while Carloman, though younger, was son of the King of the Franks.

The question of the duration of external harmony between the brothers was of especial importance in its effect on the situation in the Italian peninsula. Some of the Frankish nobles had by no means approved of Pippin's policy of opposition to the Lombard kings, and had criticised his willingness to protect the integrity of the dominions of the Pope, whenever he was appealed to from Rome for aid. The efforts of the Queen Mother Bertrada were evidently intended to promote a better feeling between the Franks and the Lombards, for she personally arranged a marriage between Charles and the daughter of Desiderius, the Lombard king. The protests of the Pope were unavailing when he urged, from a decidedly interested point of view, that Charles should marry a wife from his own people; although he recalled the oaths taken, when the two Frankish rulers were children, that they would have the same friends and the same enemies as the Church.

The whole situation, political as well as personal, was suddenly changed by the death of Carloman in 771, and by domestic difficulties in Charles' own household which led to an alienation from his mother and caused the repudiation of his Lombard wife. Immediately after his brother's death Charles was acknowledged as sole king throughout the Frankish territories, and the alliance with the Lombard party in Italy was brought to an end. Gerberga, Carloman's widow, and her sons betook themselves to the court of Desiderius, which now became a natural refuge for all who were discontented with the new ruler of the Franks.

II

CONSOLIDATION OF RULE

In the meantime, Pope Stephen, the man who had made the Frankish alliance the cornerstone of papal diplomacy, had died. (772.) He was succeeded by Hadrian, who proclaimed his purpose to follow the rule of peacemaker in the complexities of Italian politics, and so to induce Romans, Franks, and Lombards to live in mutual harmony. Despite his pacific intentions, he was unable to tolerate the military aggression of the Lombards on the cities in the Patrimony which had been turned over to the Pope by Pippin, including Ravenna itself.

Papal protests against this invasion proved useless. Desiderius threatened to appear with his army before the walls of Rome itself, and he actually approached as close to the city as Viterbo, having in his army the young heirs of Carloman, whose claims to their father's inheritance he wished to have legitimatized by having them anointed by the Pope. He was deterred from carrying out his plan, and the Pope met the daring of the Lombard leader with a formal warning, that the king and all his host would be placed under the ban of anathema if they entered the territory of Rome. Desiderius therefore withdrew.

To the Frankish delegates who appeared in Rome to investigate the condition of affairs between the Pope and Desiderius, Hadrian probably explained that his difficulties had been occasioned by his refusal to anoint the pretenders, Carloman's sons, at Desiderius' request. There would not be wanting, also, appeals to Charles to fulfil his solemn engagements to stand by the Roman See. Desiderius, in his interview with the envoys, treated them curtly; he was evidently looking forward to settling the issue with Charles by arms. There was not only the difference with the Pope, due to Lombard aggression on the papal cities, but he must have felt aggrieved because Charles had refused to live with his daughter. There was also the fact that at the court of the Lombard king, Carloman's children had been received and were being used in the rôle of pretenders, as tools in an intrigue against the ruler of the Franks.

Desiderius had prepared for invasion from the North by fortifying the pass at Susa, the "débouchement" in northwestern Italy of the road regularly taken by the Frankish army when they invaded Italy. But while methods of military defense were being looked to, Desiderius saw the need of preparing for the coming struggle by consolidating his rule over his adherents and dependents. The important Duchy of Benevento was allied with him by the bonds of family relationship. The Duchy of Spoleto was less important, as it had lost in territory and in independence during the reign of Desiderius, but means were taken to conciliate the Church by gifts to important abbeys. Indeed, so numerous were these alienations of the royal lands to ecclesiastical foundations, that the king's policy in annexing cities and territories in the Patrimony of the Pope had become as much an economic as a political necessity, for the owners of the alienated land could only in this way be compensated for their losses. The abbeys were of strategic importance; many of them, and these the largest, were situated on the inner lines of communication. The cities and castles were still surrounded with their Roman walls, and under the Lombard monarchy the many roads and bridges had been kept in order.

On the other side of the Alps, there was less unanimity as to the necessity of the Frankish army passing the frontier. Charles' plan of intervention was agreed to by the Frankish nobles, though the opposition against an Italian expedition had always before in Pippin's day had a strong backing. But, in order to show a temper amenable to compromise, Charles offered to continue peaceful relations with Desiderius, on condition that the sum of 14,000 solidi be given as an indemnity to the Franks. This offer was refused. A general assembly of the Frankish host was held at Geneva by Charles, and after dividing it into two parts, the army passed over into Italy by Mont Cenis and by the Great St. Bernard. Again Charles stopped to treat with Desiderius, but to no purpose.

The Lombards withdrew from their strongly fortified position where the Alpine passes widen out into valleys, and it was rumored that the Frankish army, aided by Lombard treachery, had found by-paths to avoid the strongly held Lombard camps and had marched down into the plain after Charles had stayed some time at Novalese, an abbey richly endowed by his family, where he took provisions for his march.

In the meantime, Desiderius had fled to Pavia, his capital, preparing for a long siege. Most of his army was now scattered; a portion of it retreated, accompanying his son Adalghis, with the widow of Carloman and her children, to Verona, the strongest of the Lombard citadels. But the Lombard resistance was most ineffective; the Beneventines apparently took no part in the wars, while the people of the Spoletan duchy, deserting their duke, took the oath of allegiance to Hadrian, and many places in central Italy surrendered to the Pope.

Charles began the siege of Pavia at the end of September, purposing by the capture of their chief city to end completely the dominion of the Lombards, and so to finish the work left half done by his father. Leaving the bulk of his army in front of the walls of Pavia, he took a division of Frankish troops and entered Verona without opposition. Adalghis fled to Constantinople. Carloman's wife and heirs were now in the hands of the conquerors.

There was no longer fear of opposition from other Lombard towns. The siege had already lasted six months, but the town was well provided with food, and was too strong to be taken by assault. Charles now left the siege with a large escort in order to celebrate the Easter festival at Rome. He was the first Frankish sovereign who had visited the city. Pippin, his father, notwithstanding his close alliance with the Church, had always scrupulously avoided making the pilgrimage to Rome, probably because he did not desire to pass through Lombard territories.

Charles was received with the honors ordinarily given to the Exarch of Ravenna. As he entered St. Peter's, the choir sang the anthem, "Blessed is He that Cometh in the Name of the Lord," and there were many public demonstrations of friendship between the Pope and the King. But it is worth noting that Charles asked the Pope's permission to enter the city, and great care had to be taken to prevent acts of violence between the residents of the city and the visitors from the North. The most important step taken before Charles left the city to return to Pavia, was the formal transfer to the Pope of a document signed by Charles and his nobles, authorizing the retention by the Pope of the existing patrimony of the Holy See, and also engaging that all private property belonging to it should be restored.

Pavia held out stoutly, though sorely tried by famine and pestilence; but there was no hope of relief. Finally, Desiderius surrendered his capital and his person at the beginning of June, 774, and with this surrender the independent Lombard monarchy ends. Charles, from this time forth, took the title of King of the Lombards. The Lombard chieftains crowded into the city to do him homage, and when he crossed the Alps, he took with him Desiderius and his family, not forgetting the royal treasury of the Lombards.

Charles had been mindful of his obligations to the Pope, and regarded himself as bound to carry out the policy of his father. But he plainly had no thought of turning over any large share of the territory of the Italian peninsula into the hands of the Roman See. In Rome it seemed to be expected that the friendly and generous ruler from across the Alps would make Hadrian master of the whole of middle Italy. But now that Charles was ruler of the Lombards he showed that in dealing with the Italian situation he did not intend to be guided by idealistic politics. Charles also put an interpretation on his title of Patrician that made it clear he meant to be the predominant factor in the states under the Pope's control. He behaved as master in cases affecting the Pope's territory when Hadrian's rights over Ravenna were resisted by the Archbishop of that city; and he also exercised his sovereign authority over Spoleto when the Duke rose in revolt against the Franks.

III

THE CONQUEST OF THE SAXONS

While Charles' intervention in Italy may be considered as the logical outcome of the policy inaugurated by his father, his long struggle with the pagan Teutonic tribes, spoken of loosely by contemporary historians as the Saxons, was part of a program of expansion for which he alone was responsible. Dwelling in a territory extending from the Elbe, on the East, nearly to the Rhine, on the West, the Saxons in three tribes formed a primitive confederation occupying the various divisions of Germany known in modern times as Hanover, Brunswick, Oldenburg, and Westphalia. Beyond the Elbe there was a fourth section of the Saxon stock extending over a territory nearly coextensive with the modern Duchy of Holstein. Though the name suggests a plausible identity, the Saxon territory of the eighth century had no connection with the present kingdom of Saxony, which only to a small extent comprises land that once belonged to these ancient Saxons. Though unlike their kinsfolk to the West, the Saxons held to their old tribal creed, they were in no sense savages, for they had long since abandoned a nomadic life and had become settled tillers of the soil. But probably the primitive institutions of the Germans described by Tacitus still existed among them, and, from the point of view of the Franks, they must have seemed undesirable neighbors, largely because of their obstinate attitude toward all attempts to convert them to Christianity. As the missionaries who undertook the task were either Franks themselves or acted under the patronage and support of Frankish rulers, the feeling toward the Saxons was anything but friendly, especially as since the time of the Merovingians on several occasions the Saxons had recognized the Franks as their overlords, by paying tribute. It is probable, too, that the Saxons were not very scrupulous in respecting the frontier of their Western neighbors. There must have been frequent raids to annoy the Franks, though there is absolutely no proof that the Saxons ever contemplated invading Frankish territory by expeditions organized on a large scale. The situation had, however, been serious enough to call forth active intervention from Charles's father Pippin, who, in 753, had advanced as far as the Weser, where, by an overwhelming display of military strength, he had forced the Saxons to pay tribute and not to oppose the preaching of Christian missionaries in their territory.

Five years later, in another expedition, Pippin advanced beyond the Weser, occupying the Saxon strongholds between that river and the Lippe, and again securing from the Saxon chiefs promises that the terms on which peace had been made should be carried out.

The religious conditions of the peace were especially obnoxious to the Saxons, who were firmly attached to the faith of their fathers. They had a simple form of nature worship, that displayed itself in a passionate reverence for trees and mountains, regarded as the concrete expression of the powers governing the world. The new expedition of the Franks practically took the form of a crusade; for Charles saw in the gods of the Saxons only demons inimical to the Christian faith. Starting from Worms and accompanied by a large number of ecclesiastics, who were to war against Saxon paganism, the Frankish army, seemingly, met not resistance, and Charles took and destroyed without difficulty the Saxon shrines Irminsul and Eresburg. He withdrew, satisfied now that there was no hindrance in the way of winning the land to Christianity. The character of the expedition is accurately indicated in a brief sentence from the life of Sturm: "He [Charles] gave the servants of the Lord power for teaching and baptizing."

The Saxons, before the Franks retired beyond the Rhine, renewed the terms of peace previously concluded with Pippin, gave hostages for their good behavior, and seemingly made no protest against the introduction of the Church hierarchical system in their land. But the war with the Lombards gave the Saxons the opportunity of casting aside their pledges; they did not desire Frankish ascendancy, and, still less, Christian missionaries. The real situation on his Eastern frontier was so patent that as soon as the Italian expedition had ended with the annihilation of the Lombard kingdom, Charles (775) set out to war on the Saxons, resolved either to force them to accept Christianity or to destroy them as a people. His attack was skilfully and rapidly managed; one of their strong places, Sigiburg, was taken, and Eresburg, previously captured, was turned into a Frankish citadel. The Saxons hesitated to strike back until the Franks were withdrawing across the Weser. Near Brunisberg, where they contested the passage of the Frankish army, the Saxons were outnumbered and decisively beaten. Marching with picked troops Charles advanced into the territory of the Eastphalians, where their leader, Hessi, hastened to take the oath of fidelity to the Frankish monarch and gave hostages. The same method of forcing a capitulation was tried successfully with the Saxon tribe, the Angarians.

But meanwhile, the Westphalians had assaulted the Frankish camp in their land, and had been able to occupy it partially. They were forced, however, to withdraw, and while they were retreating they were met by the division of the Frankish army under Charles, and were defeated; so they were obliged to accept the same terms as the Eastphalians and the Angarians. Within a short period the overlordship of the Franks had come to be recognized by the three leading tribes of the Saxon people.

It only needed the outbreak of fresh disturbances in Italy to show how imperfect had been the so-called pacification of the Saxons. When Charles was drawn away beyond the Alps by an attempt to revive the Lombard kingdom, his absence was immediately taken advantage of by the Saxons, who rose in revolt against the Franks. Even the fortress at Sigiburg was hard pressed. An imposing army was gathered by Charles at Worms in 776, with which he crossed into Saxon territory and again occupied Eresburg. His authority was soon restored. Bands of Saxons comprising whole families came to the Frankish camp as humble petitioners and willingly allowed themselves to be baptized. There were evidently two parties among the Saxons, one willing to carry out the conditions of peace, the other ready by any subterfuge to reject them. The irreconcilable faction finally lost heart and withdrew.

In 777, Charles held in Paderborn his first general assembly; here appeared Saxons from all parts of the land and solemnly pledged themselves willingly to give up their freedom and their property if they denied the Christian faith and broke their oath of allegiance. But such verbal assurances were not more binding than they had been before.

More expeditions (779 and 780) were necessary, and in 780 specific steps were taken to intensify the ecclesiastical organization already felt as a burden by the unwilling converts. The land was divided into parishes, and provision was made for systematic preaching and for the administration of baptism.

Along with the expansion of the Church, the secular organization of the Franks went hand in hand. The country was placed under the supervision of counts, the leading Saxon chiefs being appointed to the positions. In one of the capitularies assigned to this time, the slightest deviation from Christianity is treated as a most serious crime. The murder of a deacon is punished by death, while an assault on a count only entails confiscation of property. Similar severity is exercised against those who are guilty of sacrilege, who break into churches, or who violate the rule of fasting.

There seemed to be a fear at this time lest the popular Saxon leader, Witikind, who had failed to appear at the assembly, might organize a pagan revival, and so head a successful revolt against the Franks. This fear was realized, for the drastic character of the new religious legislation only provoked the opposition it was designed to meet. Witikind soon returned to his people and quickly organized a revolt. The character of the struggle showed itself in attacks on the Christian missionaries, and in the destruction of the newly erected churches, the places selected for bishoprics and abbeys suffering most. This insurrection was for a time successful, and a Frankish army, through the divided counsels of those who were leading it, was defeated and forced to retreat. But the personal appearance of Charles on the field was enough to turn the tide and was followed by the defeat of the Saxons and by pacification according to the familiar terms.

The question was what to do with those who had taken up arms. It was decided to put to death all who had united with the heathen against the Christians. This merciless penalty was applied in its fullest rigor. Those who were taken captive in the revolt numbered in all four thousand; and of these, five hundred were beheaded at Verden, a savage act of retaliation which disgraces the memory of Charles, and which even the crudeness of the times cannot excuse. Besides, it did not accomplish its purpose, for it only embittered those who were related by kin or by friendship to the massacred Saxons. The revolt against the Franks hitherto had never been universal, but now the whole people rose en masse with sudden determination. Yet even with this temper they were not hardy enough to take the offensive; so, while they were preparing to resist, Charles, by a quick movement, surprised them, and divided their army by his unexpected onslaught. But the first battle, though unfavorable to the Saxons, was not decisive. The second ended in a complete victory for the Franks, who took many prisoners and much booty. The backbone of Saxon resistance was now broken, and Charles with his army marched through the whole territory as far as the Elbe.

In all these Saxon campaigns, three victories stand out above the rest, dividing the monotonous levels of revolt, conquest, and pacification. The first, at Brunisberg, opened a way into Saxon territory for the Frankish army; the second, at Bocholt, brought about the suppression of a partial insurrectionary movement; the third, on the Hase, settled the fate of paganism in Germany. But the state of the Saxon country required constant watching, and we find Charles taking up his station at Eresburg in 784-85, ready to repress any incipient movement of revolt.

At Paderborn the Frankish assembly was attended by the Saxons, and this meeting was signalized by further extreme measures to protect the Church. The defenders of their independence met with all the more harshness because they were sturdily loyal to a primitive ancestral faith. Charles saw in them only worshipers of evil spirits,—men who are charged in the capitularies with the practice of offering human sacrifices and with eating human flesh. In his ruthless dealings with the Saxons, Charles was the champion of a higher civilization fighting against a lower, but one must at least question the legitimacy of his policy, specifically because it claimed Christian aims and professed Christian sanction. But we know it seemed righteous in Charles' own eyes, and his satisfaction was increased when he received, after the long military campaigns were over, the Saxon Witikind, and his companion in arms, Abbio, as voluntary converts to the Christian faith. With his baptism (785) Witikind drops into obscurity, and we only hear that his descendants became known for their loyalty to the new religion.

From 785 to 792 the Saxons did not stir; they sent regularly their assigned contingents to the army of the Franks, and they took no part in the Bavarian troubles. However, at the beginning of the expedition against the Avars in 793, there was a fresh revolt, marked, as the previous ones had been, by the destruction of churches, the massacre of priests, and the return of the people to idolatry. From 794 to 799 the Franks under Charles were busy each year in enforcing Frankish rule in Saxon lands by a specially thorough military occupation of the country.

Further drastic measures of pacification were required, for whenever Charles returned West to his own domains, he took with him a large contingent of the conquered people, men, women, and children. Lands were given them, and so the natural racial traits of Saxon unity were destroyed and their fidelity to paganism broken. It is estimated that a third of the population was removed, and the extent of this enforced emigration may be judged from the fact that in 804 ten thousand men were deported from two districts of Saxony and their land given over to some of Charles' Slavic allies who had rendered efficient services to him during these wars against their hereditary enemies. The Saxons gave up the fight only when their strength was broken, and when the last adherents of paganism yielded to superior force. Only then was the country from the Elbe to the Atlantic under the sway of a single sovereign, and united by the profession of the same faith. The conquered land was effectively occupied, and the loyalty of the inhabitants to Charles' empire was secured by the establishment of three richly endowed bishoprics, Bremen, Münster, and Paderborn, under whose supervision the work begun by the Frankish armies was completed.

IV

OTHER MILITARY ACHIEVEMENTS

The struggle with the Saxons lasted thirty years in all, and its completion brings us almost to the end of Charles' reign. In order to close our survey of the military operations by which the integrity of the Carolingian Empire was preserved, or its frontiers enlarged, it is necessary to take up the narrative of various warlike expeditions and operations which demanded the ruler's attention while the Saxons were making their heroic struggle to cast off the Frankish yoke.

Hardly two years after the destruction of the Lombard monarchy, there was such unrest in the small Duchy of Friuli, which was ruled over by Hrodgaud, that a punitive expedition was needed to restore order. Apparently Hrodgaud was intriguing with other Lombard leaders to procure the restoration of the exiled son of Desiderius and so to reëstablish Lombard independence. The project failed. Hrodgaud's allies among his own people withdrew support. Adalghis, the "pretender," did not leave Constantinople to head the revolt, consequently the Duke of Friuli was obliged single-handed to meet the avenging Frankish army. The revolted cities were soon captured; Hrodgaud himself appears to have lost his life on the battlefield, and after this short campaign, which took place in the early months of 776, Charles crossed the Alps in June to take up again the conquest of the Saxon lands.

This Lombard revolt, although it was an incident, and involved only a small territory, was followed by stringent measures of repression. Paul the Deacon, the Lombard historian, tells of the treatment of his brother, who, it seems, took part in this insurrection. "My brother languishes a captive in your land, broken-hearted, in nakedness and want. His unhappy wife, with grieving lips, begs for bread from street to street. Four children must she support in this humiliating manner, whom she is scarce able to cover even with rags."

Much more serious than this outbreak among the Lombards was the disaffection of Tassilo III, Duke of Bavaria, who resented Charles' aim to turn a nominal suzerainty into an effective control. United closely to the Frankish ruler by a common descent from Charles Martel, Tassilo, whose family, the Agilolfings, had governed Bavaria for two hundred years, had no mind to sacrifice the autonomy of his people. Even under Pippin he had showed that he placed a very loose interpretation on the ties of vassalage which bound him to the Franks. After Charles' accession he continued his policy of isolation, showing by his failure to render assistance in the campaign against the Lombards that he did not recognize any obligation to further the ambitious schemes of his overlord. During the revolt of Friuli he observed an attitude of neutrality, an act which, coming from a vassal, could signify only that the Duke of the Bavarians claimed an independent position. Such a claim Charles was in no mood to allow. In 780, during one of the intervals in the progress of the Saxon conquest, Charles, accompanied by his wife and his sons, Carloman and Louis, spent Christmas at Pavia, the Lombard capital, and in Easter, 781, visited Rome, where the royal children received baptism at Pope Hadrian's hands, and were raised by the ecclesiastical ceremony of anointment to the royal dignity, Carloman taking the title of King of Italy, and his brother Louis, that of King of Aquitaine. During this stay at Rome, the relations of Tassilo to the King of the Franks were discussed by Charles and the Pope. The result was that a joint deputation was sent from both Charles and Hadrian to Bavaria to remind its ruler of his obligations as a vassal of the Frankish kingdom. Tassilo soon after appeared personally at Worms to renew the oath previously sworn to Pippin. Hostages were exchanged on both sides, but the tension continued. We find Tassilo, a few years later, in 787, sending representatives to Rome in order to secure the Pope as an intermediary to establish an agreement with Charles and put an end to the mutual irritation of both parties. The terms offered by the Bavarians were not regarded as acceptable by the representatives of Charles, and the Pope himself solemnly appealed to the Duke to fulfil his promises as a dependent ally and so avoid the evils of war.

After his return from Italy Charles held his court at Worms and summoned Tassilo before him as the first step in acknowledging the overlordship of the Frankish monarch. In the eyes of Charles, swift dealing with a disobedient vassal was all the more necessary, because Tassilo, by his marriage with the daughter of Desiderius, might easily make himself the center of a revival of pro-Lombard feeling in Italy. Three Frankish armies from different quarters invaded Bavaria, and Tassilo soon found himself forced by this display of superior strength to give up his dreams of independent power. He formally resigned his duchy and received it back again from Charles' hands, at the same time taking an oath as vassal and giving hostages, among whom was his own son. But not long after this Tassilo, who complained openly that his position of dependence was insupportable, was charged by members of his people with intriguing with the Avars. He was accused of treachery, and was condemned to death by legal process. But the sentence was reduced by Charles' intervention to imprisonment in a monastery. His wife and children met a like fate, and from this time on Bavaria was treated as Frankish territory. Like Saxony, it was divided into jurisdictions under counts and placed under the supreme military control of one superior official.

The overthrow of Bavaria as a separate power laid the foundation of a consolidated Germany, North and South, and, as in Middle Germany, there was the same system of counties and bishoprics. Unity was still far from being thoroughly realized, but that the germ of national consciousness was already present is proved by the readiness of the Bavarians, after the loss of their ruling duke and their autonomy, to coöperate with the Franks in resisting the attacks of the Avars.

Just at the time that the tension in Bavaria was reaching its acute stage, the situation in the Lombard Duchy of Benevento, whose Duke Arichis seemed to be taking his cue from Tassilo, demanded attention. There were no actual hostilities, for the presence of Charles in the duchy was enough to bring the turbulent Duke to reason. His position of vassalage was marked by a payment of an annual tribute of 7000 solidi. The duchy was mildly treated by Charles because it was useful as a buffer against the provinces of the Eastern Empire, with which his relations were far from being always friendly. The result was that the Beneventines played a double rôle, sometimes befriending the Greeks and rejecting the Frank overlordship, and on other occasions engaging in hostilities with their Southern neighbors, as allies of the Franks. There were a number of Frankish expeditions necessary to keep the Lombards of Benevento and their dukes in mind of their duty as a vassal state, and once there was a noteworthy failure of Frankish arms in 792, when the campaign they had begun in the territory of the duchy was abandoned.

Apart from the campaigns in Saxony, in Italy, and in Bavaria, necessary to the integrity of the Frankish empire, there were various frontier wars undertaken, not for the purpose of incorporating fresh territory, but rather to impress upon contiguous peoples the power and prestige of Frankish arms. The occupation of Bavaria brought Charles in contact with the Avars, and his control of Aquitaine gave him as near neighbors the Moslems of Spain, those enemies with whom his grandfather, Charles Martel, had tried conclusions on the historic field of Poictiers.

This defeat had been inflicted on the conquerors of Spain at a time when the Ommayad Caliphate ruled over a united Moslem world. But the great internal revolution had broken this unity in 750, eighteen years before the accession of Charles. The last Ommayad Caliph, Merwan, after the great battle of Mosul, had been obliged to flee from Damascus to Egypt and had there met his death. Shortly afterward eighty members of his house were massacred by treachery at a banquet. Only one of the family escaped, Abderahman, the son of Merwan, who, after many adventures, reached Morocco, and was there invited to assume the rule of Moslem Spain, where the jealousies of the Emirs, the lieutenants of the far-distant Caliph in the East, had produced an era of misgovernment and faction.

So began in 755 the Caliphate of Cordova, and with it the most brilliant period of Mohammedan rule in Spain. But Abderahman was not accepted as supreme head of the Spanish Moslems without active protest; the Eastern Caliphate of the Abbasides had many supporters in the peninsula, and it was to Charles that they appealed for aid in resisting the Ommayad house. Naturally, the internal disputes of the Spanish Moslems constituted by themselves no ground for Frankish intervention. But the appeal was reinforced by promises that various Spanish cities would open their gates if Charles would undertake to cross the Pyrenees with an adequate army. This offer was made to Charles by Moslem envoys, who appeared before him at Paderborn, where he was holding a formal assembly (placitum) of the Frankish host during the early course of the Saxon war. The prospects of valuable territorial acquisition prompted the ruler of the Franks to embark on this hazardous expedition. There is no proof whatsoever it was undertaken to aid, as a kind of crusade, the feeble kingdom of the Asturias, where the heirs of the Visigoths were still maintaining the Christian cause against the Moslems.

In the spring of 778 the Christian army in force, containing contingents of Lombards and Bavarians, as well as Franks, crossed the Pyrenees, part of it passing into what afterwards became the Kingdom of Navarre, while the second division moved along the Mediterranean coast. Both were to meet at Saragossa, but before the junction was made Charles laid siege to Pampeluna, which had previously belonged to the small Christian kingdom of the Asturias. The city was taken, and at Saragossa hostages were received to guarantee to the Franks the possession of certain towns between the Ebro and the Pyrenees. With this inconclusive result the aggressive part of the campaign ended. Probably Charles hesitated to penetrate further into the country after hearing that Abderahman had lately defeated an army of Berbers who had come over to Spain to help the cause of the Abbaside Caliph. It was now evident that the prospects of the opponents of the Ommayad house were anything but brilliant, and it must have seemed advisable for the Frankish army to withdraw from Spanish territory. Summer had already begun before Charles turned his face homeward, after leveling the walls of the city of Pampeluna to the ground to prevent its inhabitants from revolting against him.

It was during this retreat that the famous disaster befell the arms of Charles, to which literary history has given an importance beyond its real deserts. On the 15th of August, at Roncesvalles, while the main army was slowly winding its way among the defiles of the mountains, the Basques applied to the Franks the guerrilla tactics they had successfully used against all the invaders of Spain, Roman, Gothic, and Moslem in turn. They made a sudden attack on the rear guard, and this division of the Frankish army was utterly cut to pieces. Many of the closest followers of Charles here met their death, among them Roland, prefect of the march of Brittany, of whom we know nothing apart from this brief notice in the contemporary histories, but whose exploits were celebrated in popular legend, where, under the glamour of poetical description, he has come to occupy a place as a warrior and hero almost the equal of Hector.

The defeat remained unavenged, for it was realized that the pursuit of the Basques in their mountain fastnesses was impossible. This expedition into Spain not only accomplished little in the way of permanent conquest, but served to provoke the Moslems to successful reprisals extending over a series of years in the Southern part of Gaul. The country was harried by the invaders, and towns as important as Carcassonne and Narbonne were attacked and the country about them ravaged. Dissensions among the Moslems themselves brought a respite, and, aided by insurgents against the authority of the Cordovan Caliphate, the Frankish officers in Aquitaine later on extended the sphere of Frankish influence far into the Iberian peninsula. Before the end of Charles' reign Navarre and Pampeluna were again occupied, and he could number Barcelona among the cities of his empire.

After the conquest of Bavaria, the campaign against the Avars, a people closely allied to the Huns, was brought about by their threatening attitude on the Eastern frontier, where they showed such constant hostility to the peoples of German stock that in his military handling of the problem Charles had the ready coöperation of the Saxons themselves. After a preliminary campaign in 791, in which the Franks advanced as far as the confluence of the Danube and the Raab, the decisive struggle took place in 795, when the Frankish army, under Pippin, the son of Charles, taking advantage of dissensions among the Avars, succeeded in forcing the famous armed camp of the Khan called the Ring, and returned with an immense amount of booty stored there, the fruits of many successful raids on Christian towns and monasteries. In 809 the Avars, hard-pressed by the Slavs, were glad to place themselves under the Emperor, but their number had been so reduced by warfare that a contemporary historian speaks of their lands as being deserted, their treasures confiscated, and their nobility wiped out.

Operations against the Slavic tribes were taken up in earnest after the reduction of the Saxons, though we hear of one marauding expedition against them as early as 789. In 805 and 806 Slavic territory was overrun by Frankish armies under the command of the Emperor's lieutenants, and two strong outposts were established for purposes of military observation of their movements. These posts, on the Saale and on the Elbe, became the nucleus for the development of the German cities of Halle and Magdeburg.

After describing the wars of Charles, Einhard, his contemporary, gives a summary of the conqueror's achievements that deserves to be repeated: "Such are the wars," he says, "which this most powerful king waged during forty-seven years. For as many years as these he reigned in the different parts of the earth with the greatest wisdom and the greatest success. So the kingdom of the Franks, which he had received from Pippin, his father, already vast and powerful, nobly developed as it was by him, was increased nearly twofold in extent. Before his day this kingdom included only that part of Gaul which lies between the Loire and the Rhine, the ocean and the sea of the Balearic Isles, and that portion of Germany occupied by the Franks (who are called Eastern) whose country lies between Saxony and the Danube, the Rhine and the Saale, the river which divides the Thuringians from the Swabians. Besides this, the Alemanni and the Bavarians acknowledged the overlordship of the Franks. To these possessions Charles added by his conquests first Aquitaine and Gascony, all the chain of the Pyrenees, and all the territories as far as the Elbe. Then all that part of Italy which extends from the valley of Aosta to lower Calabria, where is the frontier between the Beneventines and the Greeks, in length more than a million paces; then Saxony, which is a considerable part of Germany, as long and twice as broad, it seems, as the portion of this country inhabited by the Franks; then the two Pannonias; Dacia, situated on the other bank of the Danube; then Istria, Liburnia, and Dalmatia, with the exception of the coast cities which it pleased him to leave to the Emperor, because of the friendship and the alliance by which they were united. Finally, all the barbarous and savage nations situated between the Rhine and the Vistula, the ocean and the Danube, much alike in language, different in manners, and in their method of existence, all of whom he overcame and rendered tributary."

V

THE RE-ESTABLISHMENT OF THE WESTERN EMPIRE

In order to present a general outline of the wars of Charles, we have been compelled more than once to pass beyond the crucial and culminating event of his career, his coronation as Emperor at Rome in the year 800, thirty-two years after he had become King of the Franks. All of his conquests are closely related with this elevation to a dignity revered for its venerable traditions, and yet the conquests alone were not in themselves sufficient to secure such an elevation. The acquisition of the imperial title was the result of a revolution, a change of policy, due as much to the intangible forces that move society as to the concrete details of the career of the Conqueror. Master of Italy as he was after the downfall of Lombard powers, this territorial control simply gave Charles the position once held by another great German prince, Theodoric the Ostrogoth. But Theodoric was not an orthodox churchman as Charles was. It was, therefore, the combination of the orthodox religion, which Charles inherited as the successor of the first Frankish kings, and his sway over the Italian peninsula which prepared the way for the great event of Christmas Day, 800, when he took his place in the line of rulers marked by the names of Augustus, Constantine, and Justinian.

Although close relations subsisted between the Papal territories in Italy and the Frankish overlord across the Alps, there was, nevertheless, in Rome a considerable degree of autonomy. Charles had no thought of exercising the rights of a sovereign on the basis of the title of Patrician, which he had inherited from his father, and on which he had acted when it came to a question of putting an end finally to Lombard autonomy. But it was only at such crises that the need of intervention was felt, and, as we have seen in the case of Pope Stephen, it was the policy of the Holy See to make use of the Frankish King when questions involving the dignity of the Pope could be settled in no other way. This policy was maintained by Stephen's successors, but it was not easy to induce Charles to undertake to handle thorny problems which involved the position of the Pope in his own city. There was no Frankish occupation of Rome, foreshadowing the condition of affairs there when another Emperor of the Franks protected the Pope from being overthrown by his unwilling subjects through the use of French bayonets. Rome, like other Italian cities, was often in a state of turbulence owing to factional divisions among its citizens. There was already a beginning of that rivalry among Roman families to secure the Papal throne to one of its members that so often brought degradation to the Papacy during the course of the Middle Ages. Upon the death of Pope Hadrian in 795, after a long pontificate of twenty-three years, Leo III became his successor, but it seems that the succession was not altogether satisfactory to the kinsmen of the dead Pope, for they soon proceeded to extreme measures against his successor, seizing his person and trying to blind him. Leo, completely terrorized, seems to have lacked supporters in Rome to defend him, and he sought refuge with the great King at his camp near Paderborn, in Saxony, which was being used as a center for the operations against the recalcitrant Saxon tribes. The matter in dispute between the Pope and his enemies at home turned out to be a complicated one. Charles, in his capacity as Patrician, listened to the charges and countercharges brought by one side against the other. It was evident that justice could not be done at such long range, and, therefore, the King, after sending Leo home under the protection of Frankish ambassadors, moved slowly down into Italy in the year 800.

Charles showed no haste to take up the obligation of settling the differences between the Pope and his discontented subjects. An expedition into Italy was always costly and troublesome. The situation, too, on the Eastern frontier needed his attention, because of the death of Count Gerold and of Erich of Friuli, on whom he depended for warding off the attacks of the Avars and the Slavs. There were matters also in the Western part of his dominions which required his personal supervision. His lieutenants had just won victories over the Bretons and in the Spanish peninsula. New schemes of expansion had to be worked out, and provision made for protecting the sea coast. Besides, he was interested in securing for Eastern Christians dwelling in the dominions of the Saracens, advantages which they were unable to attain through the intervention of the rulers at Constantinople. A way had been opened by the arrival at his court of a monk from Jerusalem, with presents from the Patriarch and relics from the Holy Places. There are hints also of his receiving representatives from the Byzantine province of Sicily, and of direct suggestions from influential quarters in the East, where the rule of a woman, the Empress Irene, was resented, that the great Frankish King should assume the imperial title. He turned his steps towards Rome only when he had made himself familiar with the special needs of the situation brought about by Leo's policy. Many of his intimate advisers, Alcuin, Engelbert, Am of Salzburg, and Paulinus of Aquileia, had evidently discarded for some time all thought of the possibility of the Frankish ruler assuming the honors and rights which the imperial position, to the minds of that age, could alone bestow. Now everything was changed; the Empire was the one political idea which was common to the German and to the Italian, and it was kept alive by the influence of churchmen, to whom the existence of the Empire was the necessary complement to a Catholic Church. Charles was already acting with a recognized power fully equivalent to that of an emperor. His rule was not local like that of other barbarian kings; the title was needed to complete the political evolution, just as really as it was necessary for his father, Pippin, to give up the rôle of Mayor of the Palace and become "de jure" King of the Franks. This point was made perfectly clear when the general assembly of Charles' dominions was held at Mainz in August, 800, and the Italian expedition was announced.

In Ravenna a stay of eight days was made by the invading army, and a detachment was sent off to pacify the Lombard Duchy of Benevento. Not far from Rome the King was greeted by the Pope, who then returned to Rome to prepare for the official reception of the ruler, which took place, on November 24th, with the customary ceremonies appropriate to the patrician rank of the visitor. Eight days afterwards, Charles having previously visited the Basilica of St. Peter's, explained publicly and officially the purpose of his coming to the city, viz.: to investigate the charges against the Pope.

This was an informal and personal process, for, according to the ecclesiastical canons, no one could officially judge a cause in which the Pope was concerned. But Charles' conception of his duties as Patrician meant no mere perfunctory examination. For three weeks there was a public hearing, like an extra-judicial examination before a referee, of the rumors and charges against Leo's conduct, a chance being given to each side to ventilate its grievances. It is significant that the Frankish King was won over to the view of his leading ecclesiastics, including Alcuin, that the charges against Leo were without foundation, and were only the product of personal enmity.

The difficulty was to give the decision such a form that, by avoiding a judicial character, it would not infringe upon the Papal prerogative, according to which the Bishop of Rome was not responsible to any earthly tribunal. The bishops themselves explicitly adopted this position by refusing to pass sentence on the head of the Church. After this principle had been accepted, the Pope could declare himself free from guilt. In so doing he was following a precedent set by his predecessors in like circumstances, Marcellinus,

Symmachus, and Pelagius I.

So he proceeded on December 23d to exculpate himself by formally declaring his innocence before a great assembly of secular and ecclesiastical dignitaries, expressly mentioning that the proceeding was voluntary and not required by the canons of the Church. In this way the immediate cause of the expedition of the Franks was disposed of, but Charles remained in Rome in order to provide for things needful in the administration of his Italian dominions.

On Christmas Day a multitude had gathered together to celebrate the festival. As the King rose from prayer at the Confession of St. Peter the Pope placed the imperial diadem upon his head. The congregation, acting under one inspiration, joined spontaneously in the acclamation, used in former days in Rome, and still customary at the time at Constantinople,—"Life and Victory to Charles the Pius Augustus, crowned by God, the great and peace-bringing Emperor."

Three times the formula was repeated. After this proclamation the Pope reverenced the new Emperor, genuflecting, as was the Roman custom, and probably this act of homage was repeated by all who were present. On the same day the Emperor's son, Karl, was anointed King by the Pope, just as his brothers, Pippin and Louis, had been elevated to the royal dignity twenty years before. A few days later the Emperor, sitting as supreme judge, condemned to death the Pope's accusers, sentences which, at Leo's request, were mitigated to deportation.

The biographer of Charles represents the ceremony of the coronation as a surprise, prepared by the Pope without consulting Charles, and so done not only without his will, but contrary to his desire. The Emperor, indeed, is reported to have said that, if he had known of the Pope's intention, he would not have visited the Basilica. These words may be interpreted as an expression of the usual formula of humility, frequent in ecclesiastical elections on the part of the successful candidate, or else they may mean that the Emperor objected to the way in which the dignity was bestowed. It will be noted that the act of placing the crown on his head preceded the acclamation of the people's choice. The details of the ceremonial were copied from the one used at Constantinople, where it had long been the custom for the Emperor to be crowned by the Patriarch. But, according to the political theory of the time, the imperial dignity was not conferred by the receiving of the diadem, but by the election of the Roman people and army, and by the formal act of homage done at the time. The Pope, by his presence, added more solemnity to the occasion, but his intervention added nothing in the way of legal validity to it.

Charles' own point of view is shown plainly enough in the fact that in 813 he proclaimed his son Louis Emperor and crowned him with his own hands. As he acted here without requesting the coöperation of the Pope, a purely lay method of conferring the imperial dignity may have appealed better to his convictions than that followed in his own case. But there could have been no improvised procedure in the ceremony at St. Peter's. Charles could not have been made Emperor against his will, nor is it possible to harmonize the details of the ceremony with such an explanation. How could the coronation have been an impulsive act on the Pope's part, taken without the Emperor's knowledge, when the diadem was in readiness, and the great congregation were prepared to repeat without confusion the words of acclamation? Such preparations must have had the consent of the Frankish ruler, for it is most unlikely that he should not have known of them. His own objections, therefore, were probably due to certain features of the ceremony actually carried out, those, namely, by which the Pope took the initiative. A stricter following of ancient precedent, at a time when no ceremonial change should have been introduced by which the legitimacy of the succession could be questioned, would have approved itself to Charles. An emperor had to be provided for the West, and scrupulosity in following precedents was desirable, especially in view of the doubt as to whether the Empress Irene could, as a woman, legally hold supreme power at Constantinople.

It must be remembered that there had been several attempts made in the seventh and eighth centuries to revive the connection between Rome and the imperial dignity. But they had failed because there was no considerable and acknowledged political force behind them. Now, under the extensive rule of the Frankish King, the elements required to give an actual validity to the imperial claim were present in an overwhelming degree. Charles was in control of most of the territory once belonging to the empire in Western Europe, and along the Eastern and Southeastern frontiers he had succeeded in extending its limits—a task unparalleled by the achievements in these same regions of the greatest of the Roman Emperors. The Teutonic peoples, who centuries before had made their first appearance as "fœderati," in the service of the Empire, were now component parts of it, and had definitely entered the sphere of Roman civilization. What Athaulf had deemed to be impossible, what neither Odoacer, Theodoric, nor the Lombard Kings had tried or dared to do, Charles had done, now that, advancing from the title of Patrician, which had been held often by the barbarian rulers, he claimed for the Germans the full right to the imperial name.

In its ecclesiastical relations the revived Empire differed from the old. The Pope had become a factor in the political evolution of the West in a way unknown to the age of Athaulf, Theodoric, or Odoacer. Gregory the Great had turned to the East as a subject of the Roman Empire, to ask aid of his legitimate Emperor; the bishops of Rome, in the eighth century, as equals, turned to the Franks, and of this alliance the ceremony of Christmas Day, 800, was the logical sequence.

For the Germanic peoples the coronation of Charles did not mean absorption into a unified system of absolutism, such as prevailed in the East; but it did mean that the predominant factor in their future was to be their relation in the logical sense to the Italian peninsula, and it is just this relationship in its various phases which was worked out in the Middle Ages, and so it may justly be called the distinguishing mark of the medieval period.

Charles' assumption of the imperial title did not imply that he ceased to regard himself as the head of a Germanic people, nor was there manifest on his part any intention to shift the existing Teutonic basis of his rule towards a Latin center. For several months after the coronation ceremony he remained in Italy, but the Alps were recrossed in the summer of 801, and during the rest of his life he never again set foot on Italian soil.

With the Eastern Empire, which might have been stirred to active hostility by the introduction of a rival claimant to the imperial throne, relations continued to be good. Embassies passed from one court to another, and it is reported by a Greek chronicler that Charles transmitted officially to the Empress Irene a proposal that the two empires should be united by their marriage. In 803 the Empress Irene died, after her deposition had been brought about by a palace revolution by which Nicephorus, the Grand Treasurer, was placed on the throne. In 806, for a short time, these peaceful relations were broken by a contention over the possession of Venice, whose commercial importance was beginning to be recognized. A Byzantine fleet appeared off the lagunes, but was unable to prevent the coveted islands from being taken by Pippin, Charles' representative in Italy, who brought the contest to a close in 810 by a combined attack on sea and land. In 812, as a compensation for acknowledging Charles as Roman Emperor, the Adriatic territories, Venetia, Istria, Liburnia, and Dalmatia, were restored to Byzantine rule.

VI

CLOSING YEARS

The period of conquests and warlike expeditions was almost over. One hears of the ravages of Scandinavian pirates, and of marauding incursions by Moorish corsairs along the extended coast line of the Empire. They seem to have remained unpunished, for Charles gave little attention to the development of a navy. In the years from 808 to 810 there were operations on a large scale against a threatened Danish invasion of the Northeastern frontier of the Empire. Some actions of an indecisive character were fought, and the preparation of a fleet sufficient to meet the Danish flotilla of two hundred ships was taken in hand. The prospect, however, of more serious complications was dissolved by a domestic revolution in Denmark, and for the rest of the Emperor's life peace prevailed between himself and the Danes. As time went on, the actual direction of military operations was left to the Emperor's two elder sons, Charles and Pippin, who seem, on the whole, to have harmoniously worked together in carrying out their father's plans.

The enforced inactivity of the Emperor brought forward the need of providing for the future administration of his domains. His eldest son, another Pippin, of illegitimate birth, was not on the list of those from whom the future rulers were to be selected. Years before, in 792, he had been discovered in a plot to dethrone his father, and had been sent to a monastery.

There were now but three heirs to the empire, Louis, in Aquitaine; a younger Pippin, in Italy, and Charles, in Germany, all intrusted with important charges by their father. In 806 a formal document was drawn up regulating the succession. Charles received the countries from whence the Franks had originated, Austrasia along with Neustria, and the East Frankish provinces; the younger brothers were to exercise independent power over the countries they already were administering. Besides this, Pippin was to take Bavaria, and Louis the Provençal districts and the largest parts of Burgundy. Charles directed that his sons should help one another against their enemies, internal and external; he also arranged the roads by which Italy should be approached in case of need, and provisions were made at the same time for securing independence in the fractions of the Empire. Among these dispositions, perhaps the most significant were that no "beneficium," or assignment of lands, should be made in any of the two divisions, save to individuals who were residents there, and that no man expatriated for his crimes should be received by the ruler of another territory. The inner unity of the three realms and their independence from one another was the master idea of this whole testamentary arrangement. These provisions were made by the Emperor after he had advised with his nobles. They seem to have harmonized with his own sense of justice, and, strangely enough, the ideals of family life predominated in cases where, beyond all other considerations, political acumen should have prevailed. The Emperor relied, so far as the unity of the Empire was concerned, on the loyalty of his sons to his own counsels and to one another.

The plan was soon frustrated by death, for within five years of the date of his division, Pippin and Charles had both died. The Emperor was old, and the question of succession was a more pressing one than ever. It was being discussed with equal interest by friends and foes alike. It must have been also a matter of the profoundest moment to the creator of the Empire, to make such dispositions as would, at least from his own point of view, secure its permanence.

At the end of the summer of 813, Charles, following the precedent of his father and grandfather, drew about him the most important of his officials, and prepared, with their approval, to provide finally for the succession. The disposition was comparatively simple, as only one of the three sons, Louis, who had enjoyed the privilege of Papal recognition, was still alive. He had succeeded, besides, in giving a practical demonstration of his capacity by his successful administration of Aquitaine. Therefore, he seemed entitled to the largest share of his father's dominions, the only difficulty being to determine the claims of Bernard, the legitimate heir of Pippin. It was, therefore, settled that he should receive Italy, and he was forthwith recognized as its King.

Only one question was now in doubt as to what extent the prerogatives of the imperial dignity should be passed over to the principal heir. This, as it was the creation of the Emperor, seemed to be under his personal control, so he accordingly prepared to make Louis co-Emperor.

The determination of the Emperor to advance his son to the imperial dignity, making him co-ruler with himself, appeared to have been unanticipated by the assembly. They applauded the design and greeted it as an illustration of divine direction. There was no longer any doubt that the central power would continue to exist. Louis was crowned with the diadem by the Emperor himself, and the act was dissociated from the precedent which had been followed in Charles' own case, so eliminating all question of Papal consent. Rome was not consulted, and Louis was allowed to return home to his own kingdom of Aquitaine. There could no longer, however, be any question as to his ultimately becoming the sole supreme ruler in his father's stead.

Charles may himself, as a political idealist, have believed that in this transmission he was guaranteeing the permanence of the system he had built up. But even apart from the unfortunate weakness and incapacity of his successor, it is doubtful whether personal rule of this type could have been perpetuated even in the Eastern Empire, with its crystallized traditions, and where an imperial dynasty, with recognized prerogatives and absolutism, endured from age to age. Even in the East there were frequent breaks in the succession.

The long reign was clearly drawing to a close. The Emperor's physical powers began to fail, and the malady, which proved a fatal one, appeared in alarming symptoms. The Emperor knew of his condition, and had disciplined himself with the common forms of devotion for the approach of death. After a hunting expedition in the autumn of 813 he returned to Aix and soon after had an attack of fever. His ordinary remedies, dieting and the mineral waters of the city, failed to bring relief, and pleurisy set in. Charles died on the morning of the 28th of January, 814, after having received the communion from the hands of his arch-chaplain, Hildebold. His body, after embalmment, was enclosed in an ancient Roman sarcophagus, still existing in Aix, with ornaments in relief which depict the Rape of Proserpine. Above the entrance of the vault containing it was placed this inscription: "Here rests the body of Charles the Great, mighty and orthodox Emperor, who enlarged nobly the realm of the Franks, and for forty-six years governed it with success. He died a septuagenarian, in the year of Our Lord 814, in the 7th indiction on the fifth day before the Kalends of February."

People told how marvels had foreshadowed the Emperor's dissolution, how for three days sun and moon were darkened, how the sky was filled by bright, unnatural flashes of light, how the roof of the Basilica at Aix was struck by a thunderbolt, and how the name of the Emperor, "Karolus Princeps," engraved on a golden crown, suspended in the nave of the building, faded from sight.

Later on, it was reported that the body of Charles had not been placed in a coffin, but that his tomb contained the body of the great ruler sitting upright on his throne, appearing just as he did in life, vested in the imperial robes, a diadem on his head, by his side a sword, his scepter in his hand, reposing with the book of the Gospels on his knees. Otto III was said to have entered the tomb and found the body so placed; but this supposed verification of the legend rests on a mistranslation of the text of an early chronicle.

Folklore soon amplified the career of the great ruler. In the medieval "Gesta," Charles appears as the brother of the Pope, the represser of disloyal vassals, a crusader and pilgrim to the Holy Land, a warrior of enormous stature, able with one stroke of his sword to cut in two an armed knight on his charger. In other legends he is presented as a famous wise man, the founder of the University of Paris.

The Emperor in person did not resemble the glorified image of him handed down by legend. There was no beard extending to his waist, nor did he wear the magnificent imperial vestments, heavy with precious stones; nor are the other attributes of the imperial dignity seen in his conventional portraits authentic, such, for example, as the scepter, the globe surmounted by a cross, the baton terminating in a knob of incised silver.

According to the most credible accounts, the Emperor was tall; as Einhard puts it, "not more than seven times the length of his foot." His neck was short, and he was, to use the expressive but inelegant epithet of our ancestors, "pot-bellied." His head was round, with large, active eyes, a lengthy nose, a large crop of hair, with a mustache, but no beard. His voice, we are told, seemed rather weak for such a large frame. Ordinarily, he was dressed after the Frankish fashion, in a linen shirt and short tunic, to which in winter fur was added; his legs were encased in leather bands; a blue cloak and a sword of expensive workmanship completed his out-of-door wardrobe. On ceremonial occasions he wore a diadem, adorned with precious stones, and when he was in Rome he conformed to local custom by wearing the chlamys, a long Roman tunic.

Charles was four times married. After his repudiation of the daughter of Desiderius, his wives were Hildegarde, Fastrada, and Liutgarda. The offspring of these various marriages were three sons, Charles, Pippin, and Louis, the children of Hildegarde; and five daughters, Rothruda, Bertha, Giselda, Theodrada, and Hiltruda. The girls were carefully trained in the various arts of domestic economy, and we are told, too, that in addition to skill in preparing stuffs for wearing apparel, they showed great interest in collecting for purposes of self-adornment "gold ornaments and many precious stones." These unusual maidens proved such valuable adjuncts to the household that their father refused to permit them to marry, with the result that three became abbesses, while two contracted irregular alliances. Rothruda secretly married Count Rovigo, and Bertha, the poet, Angilbert.

Life at court was anything but austere; even the Emperor himself could not be accused of being overscrupulous in his morals, for after the death of Liutgarda, in 800, he contracted several irregular alliances. Charles was fond of traveling; undoubtedly economic and political reasons may account for the number of royal residences. But his favorite seat was at Aix, which attracted him on account of its mineral springs. Here, in a cluster of buildings, secular and ecclesiastical, of his own creation, he was able to gratify his own tastes in amusements, which were swimming and hunting. He was fond of festivities, and liked to live surrounded by his large family, who helped him to enjoy the good cheer of his table and entered sympathetically into the natural atmosphere of a court which was without stiff convention, and which preserved in its naïve unconstrainedness the tastes of a great Teutonic tribal chieftain. But, while the wines, the abundant amount of solid food and numerous dishes of pastry, were well appreciated, there was serious conversation, and an opportunity was given to the "littérateurs" of the court to show their skill in verse or repartee. The Emperor himself reverenced learning, but his own education was anything but advanced, even for his own day. His intellectual interests were varied, theological speculation being especially attractive to him. He was fond of singing, and he spoke easily, clearly, and with an abundant diction. He knew Latin, and understood, too, a little Greek. When he was of adult age he studied rhetoric, logic, and astronomy. He liked to have the ancient historians read to him when he was at table, but his favorite book was St. Augustine's "City of God." Affable and easily approached, his guests found him personally interested in their affairs; he had a happy way of saying the right thing at the right time, but he was fully conscious that his position as Roman Emperor made him a successor of the Cæsars, and he never forgot that the religious consecration of the Church placed him, in a mystic sense, in the sacred line of David and of Solomon.

VII

THE CONSTITUTION OF THE EMPIRE

Though we speak of an empire founded by Charles the Great, the use of the word should not be allowed to lead us astray into comparisons or analogies based on merely verbal resemblances. Charles was not an emperor of the type known to the Roman Empire of the classic Christian period, nor as a ruler can he be compared with Russian Czars or Napoleon the First. Neither as king nor as emperor was Charles an absolute monarch. Both before and after the assumption of the more exalted title, the association of personal rule with the leadership of the armed host of the Frankish nation was so close and intimate that the ruler was not to be separated from the source of his authority. The house of the Karlings could not claim the kind of sanction given to the Merovingian princes, who were the hereditary rulers of the Franks.

When the power of the tribal kingship was broken, the Carolingian house took first the leadership of the armed Frankish host, and then the title of King; but they did so through, and with the consent of, the nation of the Franks. The Karlings were not true successors of the Merovingians. Their royal dignity had quite a different character; it did not rest on birth and custom, or the traditional reverence which comes from ancient and long recognized rights of succession. The army of the Franks gave the directorship over their nation to the father and grandfather of Charles, but the source of this authority remained with and through the army. The leader of the Franks, whether called king or emperor, ruled his own people, and the territory he gained, by the consent of the army of the Franks. Charles Martel divided his territories at his death, but he asked the army's consent, and when Pippin was crowned by the Pope, the act was again ratified by the army.

In the early years of Charles' own reign, it was the wish of the Franks that they should be guided by one ruler, not by two, and in all but one of the conquests of Charles, the principle that some portion at least of the annexed nation should ask him to be their overlord was accepted. Even in the case of the Saxons, where the resistance to the Franks was universal and unanimous, the purpose of Charles was not a personal conquest of a people to be governed afterwards as dependents under an absolute ruler. Rather, as Einhard expresses it, "that united with the Franks they might along with them be made one people." This declaration in itself explains the character of the empire founded by Charles. The closest analogy to it is to be found in the Ostrogothic kingdom of Theodoric; the difference being that Theodoric sought for allies among the independent tribal Germanic kingdoms, while the aim of Charles meant absorption of these kingdoms under the one ruling race of the Franks.

This principle is perfectly illustrated in the treatment of the Saxons after their conquest; the moment they accepted the rule of the Franks they were admitted on an equality with the Franks into the regular meetings of the armed host of the Frankish nation, and along with their conquerors took part in its legislative work. These primitive popular assemblies had originated as the Merovingian dynasty was drawing to its close, when it was realized that the people must provide for their own concerns because of the failure of the ruling house to govern efficiently or successfully. They were held generally in May at a royal villa or palace in the Rhine Valley, Aix, Worms, or Mainz. In theory every Frank was supposed to be present. Actually, only the great lords and the high ecclesiastics were at hand, and their followers stood for the people.

Only the most important personages were admitted to the deliberations. The laymen present were separated from the clergy, but sometimes the two orders sat together and went over in detail the measures prepared for them beforehand. Sometimes this process lasted several days. These informal sessions were visited by the Emperor, who passed among those present, talking familiarly to them, and asking questions as to the happenings and needs of the neighborhoods from whence they came. Outside the building were gathered a crowd of followers and retainers.

The Emperor, after taking the advice of his chief subjects, made his decisions, and the result was communicated to the people for their consent. This last act had become apparently a simple matter of form. The question submitted to the assembly had been prepared long in advance either by the immediate council at the palace, or by the autumn assembly, a body organized by Charles himself, which, when the matter was urgent, decided on questions of peace and war.

While nothing is known of the character of the deliberations of this smaller body, it is clear that measures, already settled by them, were brought before the May assembly, and so presented that the decisions taken earlier could be guessed. There were various names given to this larger body or general assembly, according to the character of the business that came before it,—conventus, placitum, synodus,—whether judicial, legislative, or ecclesiastic. It was a council of war and an executive cabinet; it was also a court of highest instance, a ministry of foreign affairs and of public worship.

At the assembly the members, great and small, made their fiscal contributions to the prince. The same vagueness, indicative of a crude and undeveloped stage of government, is seen in the legislative acts of the assembly, which appeared in the shape of what are technically called "capitularies." Analyzing them from the modern point of view, Guizot reckoned that there were of criminal or civil legislation, 273 items; of moral and religious, 172, and that of these, one hundred dealt with matters of canon law. The only distinction made by Charles himself in the capitularies was that some were new measures and were to be added to legislation already accepted, while others were to be used for the guidance of the higher imperial officials. The first class was valid only for the duration of the reign of the sovereign under whom they were passed. The last, for a year, but the additions to laws already existing had no time limitation.

These capitularies were not intended to supersede national or tribal custom and law. Each man was judged according to the laws of his own people, and in 802 the Emperor directed that the unwritten laws of the peoples under his rule should be collected. The capitularies were, therefore, supplemental and corrective to the national codes. For example, one of them, which, by the way, met such strong opposition that the Emperor was obliged to yield the point, was intended to remove the abuse of private vengeance.

Local administration was in the hands of the counts, and, as in the Merovingian period, the administrative unit was the county. Altogether throughout the whole Empire, there were three hundred counts; the districts which they administered varied in size, the authority exercised by them being judicial, military, and financial. Along with the count and closely associated with him is the bishop. As there was in the capitularies so much which concerned the sphere of the Church, the coöperation, in their official publication, of the bishop with the count was not unnatural. Moreover, in the Empire, in addition to purely religious duties, the bishop had the function of investigating certain categories of crime, homicides, incest, etc., and in a general way, he acted as adviser of the count.

Among the count's duties was that of defending the Church and, in trials for ecclesiastical offenses, he had to be present informally as assessor. The coöperation of the civil and ecclesiastical authorities strongly appealed to the Emperor, with his ideals of a Christian commonwealth; but in experience, the association of the bishop and the count, as local administrators, worked far from smoothly. So a capitulary of 801 mentions the Emperor's purpose to find out the reasons why bishops and abbots, on the one hand, and counts, on the other, are not able to assist one another.

The problem of defining the limits of the secular and religious spheres gave rise to constant difficulties, and the situation was further aggravated by the fact that in many cases the counts seemed inefficient and venal. They had to be warned not to hang offenders without trial, to be sober when they were sitting in judgment, not to receive presents, not to oppress freemen, not to usurp the right which belonged to the state, not to take the goods of the poor. Once a year the counts were summoned to the royal palace, and they were required to remain there long enough to lay before the Emperor a detailed record of their administration.

A special power of review over the counts was given to the "missi,"—a class of officials existing under the Merovingian Kings, but with power extended and regularized by Charles, especially after 802. The whole Empire was divided into "missatica"—the divisions under a "missus," which included several counties. For example, Western France made three of these divisions with centers at Paris, Rouen, and Orléans. The "missi," who were generally a count and a cleric, an abbot or bishop, made a general visitation of their district for a period lasting over a year, according to a fixed itinerary. They were expected to see that the royal authority was respected, by exacting a detailed oath of fidelity from all the inhabitants, and to take care that no one occupied the royal domain of forest or appropriated the royal revenue. They looked after the application of the directions contained in the capitularies, noted the general condition of law and order, saw that justice was done, and the rules of military service strictly carried out.

Much stress was laid on their judicial functions; when they arrived in a town they set up their court in the public place; the local bishop and count had to be in attendance, while the "missi" heard complaints and altered whatever judgments of the local officers seemed contrary to right and equity.

The "missi," as we have seen, were selected from the higher clergy and from the great landlords. Their persons were held to be inviolate and sacred; all the lower officials of the Empire were ordered to receive them with respect and give them ready help, and to attack them was a capital offense.

Theodulf, bishop of Orleans, one of the clergy performing the functions of a "missus," has left us an account of an official journey made by him to the South of France. He took boat on the Rhône with his companion, Leidrade, the archbishop of Lyons, and their work of inspection began at Avignon. They held their assizes at Nîmes, Maguelonne, Cette, Agde, Béziers, Narbonne, Carcassonne, le Razès, Arles, Marseilles, Aix, Cavaillon. The clergy and people hastened to take advantage of their presence, but Theodulf tells us they did so with no worthy motive, for they were prepared to buy their favor, each according to his means. The rich offered good coin, precious stones, valuable stuffs, and oriental carpets, arms, horses, ancient vases "of pure metal unbelievably heavy, on which a skilful graver had represented the fight of Hercules with the giant Cacus." The poorer citizens were ready to give red and white skins of Cordova, excellent fabrics of linen or wool, chests, and wax.

"Such was the engine of war with which they hoped to make a breach in the wall of my soul," the bishop says, intimating that they had learned the way by past experience. The custom of giving presents to officials was so firmly established that even the reforming bishop hesitated to interfere with it. Accordingly, in order not to offend the suitors, he felt constrained to accept articles of small value, such as eggs, bread, wine, tender chickens, and birds, "whose body is small but good to eat."

Little change was made in the ordinary forms of the Frankish judicial system by Charles; the count still continued to hold his tribunal as in Merovingian times, the freedmen of the county were expected to be present as assessors, but owing to the difficulty of securing an intelligent tribunal in this haphazard way, Charles instituted a chosen class of assessors called "scabini," who were to be taken from the class of "well-born, prudent, and God-fearing men." This body was both the judge and jury, as the count only acted as their presiding officer and pronounced the sentence formulated by them. From the verdict of this tribunal there was an appeal either to the King or to the judgment of God, the favorite form of which at this time was the test by the cross. In this test, the defendant, holding his arms in the form of a cross, had to stand upright without changing his position, while the clergy recited certain prayers. If any movement was made, it was taken as a sign of guilt.

In the palace the King himself often acted in the capacity of judge in the first instance, and he also heard appeals either in person or by proxy through the count of the palace. Considerable care was taken that the right of appeal should not be used indiscriminately. The palace officials had important governmental as well as personal functions; their general collective title was the "palatins." There was no Mayor of the Palace, the first place being held by the count, who, as has just been noted, had judicial duties. The administration of the palace was also in his hands. The religious services of the household were directed by the arch-chaplain; then came the chamberlains, treasurers, seneschals, butlers, constables, and the master of domestic functions. Counts of the palace are found in the command of armies; one of them being killed by the side of Roland at Roncesvalles, another in Saxony. Seneschals had charge of the kitchens, but they are also mentioned as valiant warriors. Butlers were also diplomatists, and we find a constable fighting the Slavs on the Elbe.

A real effort at division of labor is to be found solely in what might be called, with some elasticity of phrase, the Record Office, where notaries prepared the King's letters, charters, and acts of immunity. At their head was an ecclesiastic, the protonotary, or chancellor. He was a dependent of the arch-chaplain, and did not have charge of the seal, yet his position was especially confidential, as he kept the archives.

The King consulted the court officials, who, according to his pleasure, were gathered about him in an informal way whenever he saw fit to call them. But, besides this, we are told that Charles had always with him three of his counselors, chosen among the wisest and most eminent about him; without their advice he did nothing. To the royal household there were regularly attached a number of young men, the "discipuli," sent there to be educated, and the "comites," or personal retainers of the King, a continuation of a custom mentioned by Tacitus.

VIII
CAROLINGIAN CULTURE

The Emperor's solicitude in promoting learning has caused his reign to be spoken of as the Carolingian Renaissance. But Charles' intellectual interests were not those of a fifteenth century humanist. He desired the revival of letters because he saw in learning a means by which the Church, which, to his mind, was the organization of the state Christianized, might overcome pagan survivals, and take the lead in civilizing the various nationalities in his realm. The clergy and the monks were ignorant—they could neither preach nor teach. The Emperor planned a kind of Christian Athens, a new community of scholars, in which learning was to be the handmaid of religion. After he had assumed the title of Emperor, he recalled how closely the glory of letters was associated with the renown of the Roman world, and he desired his own reign to be signalized by the same elements of culture.

The point of view of this intellectual revival is indicated in the following letter addressed by Charles to Baugulf, Abbot of Fulda. "Know," he says, "that in recent years, since many monasteries were in the habit of writing us to let us know that their members were offering prayers for us, we noticed that in most of these writings the sentiments were good, and the composition bad. For what a pious devotion within was faithfully inspiring, an untrained tongue was incapable of explaining outwardly because of the inadequacy of scholarship. So we commenced to fear that, as the knowledge of style was weak, the understanding of the Holy Scriptures was less than it should be; we all know that if verbal errors are dangerous, mistakes in sense are much worse. For this reason we exhort you not only not to neglect the study of letters, but to cultivate them with a humility agreeable to God, in order that you may the more easily or the more justly fathom the mysteries of the divine writings. As there are in the sacred books figures, tropes, and other like things, there is no doubt that in reading them each one attains to the spiritual sense of them the more quickly, in proportion as he has received before a complete literary training.... Do not forget to send copies of this letter to all of those with you who are bishops, and to all the monasteries, if you wish to enjoy our favors."

It was not enough to rely on those already set in authority—they had to be placed under supervision themselves. Charles saw, as he expressed it, that he had to find men who had the will and the ability to learn, and the desire to teach others. Such leaders were selected from all nationalities, Anglo-Saxons, Irishmen, Scots, Lombards, Goths, Bavarians. The first to be attracted by the King's inducements of good pay and an honorable position were the grammarians, Peter of Pisa, and Paulinus, and Paul the Deacon, the poet and historian. But in influence all these were second to Alcuin, a native of England. Born in 735, he entered the School of York when Egbert, one of the disciples of Bede, was archbishop. Alcuin under his master Albert acquired the kind of encyclopedic knowledge that is handed down to us in the volumes of Isidore and Bede, the chief stress being laid on the Holy Scriptures, helped out by jejune rhetorical exercises, and scraps of physical science. He had read Latin literature, knew Greek, and was familiar with the great writers of Christian antiquity. The King was glad to secure such a prize, and the two became close friends. Alcuin acted as confidential adviser to the King, and was one of those who arranged for the coronation in 800.

There is a considerable body of literary work from Alcuin's pen, but nothing he wrote shows any originality. He was little more than a faithful transmitter of the learning he received. He set the seal on the traditional division of knowledge in its seven stages, or, as it was technically known, the seven arts: grammar, rhetoric, dialectic, arithmetic, geometry, music, and astronomy. His literary interests may be judged from the following dialogue: "What is writing?" said Pippin, one of the Emperor's sons. "The guardian of history," replied Alcuin. "What is speech?" "The treason of thought." "What engenders speech?" "The tongue." "What is the tongue?" "The flail of the air." "What is the air?" "The guardian of life." "What is life?" "The joy of the happy, the pain of the wretched, the expectation of death." "What is man?" "The slave of death, the guest of a place, a passing traveler."

These preciosities give one a depressing idea of Alcuin's ability. Yet it must be remembered that they were marvels to the obtuse and crudely trained minds of men whose chief occupation was war and the chase, and as an intellectual stimulus they were just as effective as are to-day the eagerly scanned columns of modern journalism.

Alcuin was made royal director of studies; he was schoolmaster of the palace, and from this circle of the King's friends originated the Palatine Academy, the members of which, in order to mark their efforts at imitating classic culture, adopted fancifully the names of ancient worthies. So Charles was called David, Alcuin was called Horatius Flaccus, and Angilbert, Homer. In order to extend their influence Charles promoted several of the members of the Academy to important positions in the Church, making them bishops or abbots.

The royal plans for promoting learning are indicated in a capitulary of March 23, 789. "Let," he says, "the ministers of God draw about them not only young people of servile condition, but the sons of freemen. Let there be reading schools for the children. Let the psalms, musical notation, singing, arithmetic, and grammar be taught in all the monasteries and all the bishoprics." These directions led to the creation of numerous monastic and episcopal schools, all ordered "according to the customs of the palace." Alcuin, in 796, withdrew to Tours, becoming the abbot of St. Martin's there, and planned to found a replica of the Saxon school at York, where he had himself been trained.

The success of the new educational policy owed much to Theodulph, a Spaniard of Gothic birth, who, in becoming bishop of Orleans about 798, proceeded to see that his clergy were industrious in reading and preaching. Schools were opened in town and country where children were educated without payment, though the parents were expected, if they were able, to make some return proportionate to their means. From a document written by another Carolingian bishop, it appears that parents were urged to send their children and allow them to remain at school until they were really instructed. In such provisions, it is possible to find a sketch for primary instruction, though it is not known how successfully or how widely it was developed.

Supplementing these lower schools were others of a higher grade founded in the more populous centers. In the episcopal and monastic schools there were accessible collections of books. Charles himself had a library attached to the palace. The size of some of these collections may be estimated from the fact that one monastery, St. Riquier owned two hundred and fifty-six manuscripts. We know, too, that abbots were accustomed in their election to give presents of books to their monasteries. In the lists of these donations, which have been preserved, are to be found chiefly Christian writers, St. Augustine being an especial favorite; some of the poets of antiquity also find a place, generally Virgil. The atmosphere of this revival of letters was predominantly Christian. There are extant, for example, numerous commentaries on the Gospels of this age, but they are of slight value, being mere transcriptions of previous authorities.

More successful was the new régime in the mechanical work of preparing better texts. One of the capitularies directs special care to be given in selecting copyists equal to their task. Both Alcuin and Theodulph were engaged in preparing a revised version of the Latin Bible, the latter scholar, with more discretion, using as his model the text prepared by the famous prime minister of Theodoric, Cassiodorus, after he had returned to his monastery in Calabria.

The historical literature of the period also shows the influence of this religious "Renaissance." Hagiographical works were popular, but in general critical ability was wanting in them. But some advance was made, for although the traditional lines of narrative are preserved, more biographical details are given and the style is improved. This type of Carolingian literature can best be studied in Eigil's life of Sturm, in the biographies of Gregory of Utrecht, by Liudger, and in Alcuin's "Life of Willibrord." Some of the annals compiled at this time follow preëxisting models, while others show a distinct improvement, especially the "Royal Annals," which were compiled under the influence of the royal "littérateurs." The most noteworthy of this type are the annals of Lorsch, which follow the course of contemporary history down to the year 829; they have been assigned without sufficient reason to Einhard, since it is known that works of a similar character, the "Gesta," of the bishops of Metz, were composed by Paul the Deacon.

The greatest monument of the literary revival is Einhard's "Life of Charles." Its author, who had studied at Fulda, and become a member of the court circle sometime between 791 and 796, was a favorite of the Emperor, and received as a gift several abbeys. Suetonius was taken as a model by Einhard, but was not slavishly followed. He oftentimes changes the phrases of his original, and, copyist as he is, he leaves on the reader the impression of freshness and vigor. Allowing himself to be guided by his original, he sets down much information which the ordinary medieval biographer leaves unmentioned.

Many letters of this time have been preserved, among the most interesting being the correspondence of Alcuin. Poetry was widely read, and all sorts of subjects were treated in verse. Especial attention was given to metrical inscriptions intended to be placed over the doors of churches or private houses, on walls, altars, tombs, and in books. The acrostic form was extremely popular and applied with great ingenuity. For the more serious poetic efforts, the most popular models were the Christian poets, Prudentius and Fortunatus. But pagan authors were by no means neglected, for Ovid, Virgil, Martial, Horace, Lucan, and Propertius all found imitators. Attempts were made to revive epic poetry, some of the writers, as in the case of Hugelbert, by no means doing discredit to their classical models.

While Latin was the official language, Charles did all he could to encourage his native Teutonic speech; he made collections of the folklore poetry of his own people, directed the preparation of a "Frank" grammar, and tried to introduce the custom of using the Teutonic names for the months of the year and winds. But throughout the greater part of Gaul the "Romance" tongue predominated, though educated people did not care to employ it. Charles' biographer tells us that the Emperor spoke it along with Frankish and Latin. At the Council of Tours, in 813, the bishops decided that the homilies should be translated into Romance in order to be understood by the congregation.

Warlike songs in the vernacular, celebrating the exploits of the Franks, are mentioned. The great deeds of the Emperor himself had this popular recognition, especially the expedition into Spain and the wars of the Saxons, which excited the popular fancy. That the actual combatants were accustomed to recount, in verse, both Frankish and Romance, the events they themselves had witnessed, is known from the case of Adalbert, a veteran of the wars with the Avars and the Slavs, whose narrative was taken down by a monk of St. Gall, and transcribed into Latin.

Carolingian art, like Carolingian literature, was pre-eminently religious. The revival of art was to a great extent a restoration, i.e., an attempt to keep already existing church buildings from falling into ruin. This process of destruction was due to the avarice and carelessness of the generations immediately preceding the founding of the Empire. New churches were also constructed, the work of building being laid on the various communities and superintended by the bishops and the counts. The Emperor's minister of public works was Einhard, to whom have been attributed, without sufficient ground, however, some of the greatest monuments of the period, the bridges at Mainz, the palace and church at Aix, and the palace at Ingelheim. Though the monuments of Carolingian architecture were scattered over a wide extent of territory, Germany, Gaul, and Lombardy, few have survived. Wood was used for both basilicas and country churches, especially in the Northern parts of the Empire, and such buildings were naturally not durable. Where stone was employed, restoration has so altered the original construction that few examples of the architecture of this period can be identified with certainty. The basilica type of church, usual in Merovingian France, was retained, but more attention was given to the technique of ancient art. Einhard, we know, read Vitruvius. An original feature of the Carolingian age was the lantern tower, square or cylindrical, erected at the transept crossing, and surmounted by a cupola containing the church bells.

Byzantine architecture was much admired in court circles, and the desire to imitate the earlier periods of Græco-Roman art led to a systematic plundering of the ancient buildings in the Italian peninsula, from which all sorts of architectural fragments, great and small, were carried across the Alps, to be incorporated, generally without much sense of proportion or fitness, in the newly constructed edifices. The most interesting example of this revived Byzantine architecture is the Emperor's own chapel at Aix, which still serves as a nave in the existing church. Workmen from all quarters of the civilized world were sent for to engage in its construction; marbles, sculpture, and mosaics were brought from Italy, chiefly from Ravenna. Eighteen years elapsed before the church was completed, and it was consecrated with imposing ceremonial by Leo III, on January 1, 805. It is a copy of the well-known church of St. Vitalis in Ravenna. Around an octagonal center, which measures fourteen and a half meters, there are galleries in two stories, to which access is given by turrets containing winding staircases. The Emperor's contemporaries were not conscious of the mistakes in the execution of this copy of a famous Byzantine model, and the chapel of Aix was spoken of by Einhard as admirable and of supreme beauty. It was followed by others in the same style, one of which, at Germain-des-Près, still preserves, despite restoration, distinct traces of the original design.

The age was remarkable, also, for the extension and building of monastic foundations. These buildings, as compared with the later monastic structures, followed a simple plan, with the church edifice forming the center of the complex. Around the square cloister were placed the common room, the school, the library, the refectory, and the dormitory. Near by were the abbot's home, the guest chamber, and the infirmary. An idea of the extent of these buildings may be had from the dimensions of a well-known French abbey, St. Wandrile, where the refectory and the dormitory measure 208 feet long by 27 feet wide. As to secular architecture, it is represented solely by the imperial palaces at Nymwegen, Ingelheim, and Aix.

The palace at Aix, like the church, has for its model a building at Ravenna, the so-called palace of Theodoric. As all of the dependents of the court had to be accommodated, the ground floor covered a considerable space. In the center were the apartments of the imperial family, the audience chamber, the baths. In a large wing of the building, connecting it with the chapel, there was room for the school, the library, the archives. In interior decoration stucco, mosaic work, and mural painting were used rather than sculpture, in which art Carolingian workers showed little skill. The Emperor, though he prohibited the worship of images, expressly directed the use in church of mural paintings, with subjects taken from the Scriptures. In the palaces the same art was used to illustrate the secular history of the Empire.

The Emperor's deeds were depicted on the walls and explained in poetical inscriptions. Mosaic was used for floors and wall spaces, and red and green porphyry were especially sought after for the decorative designs that often covered the interior of the cupola, as at Aix, where the Christ is represented on a gold background covered with red stars, blessing twelve aged men at his feet, and accompanied by two angels.

Work in the precious metals and in ivory was frequent in the churches, since each had a treasury, and a third of the income, saved from tithes, was assigned for religious ornaments. In these collections gold reliquaries with chased work and precious stones were specially valued; also portable altars and ciboria. The "ivories," of which interesting specimens are still preserved, are remarkable for the care displayed in continuing the traditions of this branch of Christian art, as practised both in the Eastern Empire and in Italy during earlier centuries.

Books are recorded also in the inventories of the church treasuries, and the specimens that have survived attest the artistic value of Carolingian calligraphy. The style of writing, under the influence of English and Irish models, is clear and free from abbreviations. Besides the miniatures, these manuscripts exhibit artistically drawn letters, effectively combined, and characters done in gold and silver on a purple background. There were a number of schools where the art of copying was taught, the most celebrated being at Tours, under the supervision of Alcuin. The national library at Paris has a beautiful example of this work in a book of the Gospels prepared for Charles in 781, by the monk Godescalk. In Vienna, in the imperial treasury, there is another Gospel book in similar style, which, legend says, was found on the knees of the Emperor when his tomb was opened.

In church music, the Emperor continued his father's policy of encouraging the Roman use of singing the psalter, as opposed to the Gallic custom. Masters were brought from Rome for this purpose and schools established at St. Gall and at Metz. There is still in the first-named place a Gregorian antiphonary, brought at this time from Italy, for the purpose of giving musical instruction after the Roman method.

IX

ECONOMIC CONDITIONS

Turning now to questions of economic development, one is impressed by the small part played by city life in the Empire, and by the industrial importance of the manor. The landed proprietor depended on his country seat for his support in the most real sense of the word. We find Einhard, while residing at the court at Aix, bidding his tenants send him flour, malt, wine, cheese, and other products, and he orders 360 bricks to be made in the country. Even the workmen, who are engaged in building work in the town, are to be sent from the "villa." Small estates had completely disappeared and agricultural communities were the exception. The villas were often placed near together, a tendency which led to the multiplication of country churches, whose existence up to this time is only infrequently mentioned in legal documents. It was this evolution from a union of "villas," or the country seats on great estates, which led to the creation of the villages. The growth of large estates may have been due to the impoverishment of the small landed proprietor, but other important factors in the change were the wide extent of frontier land and the growing importance of the monasteries. The monastic estates were of imposing size, as it was the custom for the small land owners to cede their property to the monastic communities, sometimes to escape taxation, but also from motives of ecclesiastical loyalty to those whom they looked up to as models of Christian virtue, and whose prayers they coveted as efficacious in healing all spiritual distress.

The importance of these institutions is revealed in the figures given for St. Wandrile, which had on its rolls 1727 manses, inhabited by a population numbering 10,000 souls. Luxeuil had 15,000 manses, and Alcuin, the abbot of St. Martin at Tours, is reported to have had on his domain no less than 20,000 serfs.

The celebrated Polypticon of Irminion, the abbot of St. Germain-des-Près, drawn up between 800 and 826, records the administration of one of these great monastic estates. The acreage belonging to the abbey was 26,613 hectares, and was spread over seven existing French departments. The parcels of ground numbered 1646; over 10,000 persons were employed, among them only eight freedmen, the rest being either serfs or "coloni."

Of the land, about two-thirds was arable and one-third wooded. The dues from the tenants were collected in money, cattle, poultry, wine, wheat, pitch, linen, mustard, woolen stuff, and thread, honey, wax, oil, and soap, instruments of wood and iron, firewood, torches. The annual revenue of the abbey was nearly $600,000, a sum which amounted to more than $20 per household.

But the largest landed proprietor was the King; and food, drink, and articles of clothing were supplied to the court by the villa system. The royal capitularies give the exact details as to the industrial administration of an estate. There were many outbuildings included in the royal villa, such as kitchens, bakeries, stables, dairies, etc. Fisheries, too, were encouraged. There were vegetable gardens and flower gardens, in which seventy-four kinds of plants were cultivated, among them many of the vegetables in common use at the present time, and sixteen species of trees, including fig, pear, apple, peach, and cherry trees. In the villa were found various kinds of artisans, smiths, workers in precious metals, cobblers, saddlers, carpenters, turners, rope makers. The women's apartments were provided with rooms artificially heated, and in them women wove wool and linen goods, and also prepared them for use by dyeing, although it must be noted that the range of coloring matters was limited. The staff was organized into a kind of industrial hierarchy under special officers, who supervised the work or kept the accounts. Over all stood the "mayor," who had the supervision of as much land in his district as he could visit in a day.

Care was exercised by the Emperor that these dependents should receive enough to live on; no one was to be reduced to poverty, and provision was made to protect all from unjust treatment at the hands of their superiors. The maximum price of staple articles, such as wheat and wine, was fixed; cornering the market was forbidden, likewise exportation from a given locality when crops were poor. The bishops and counts were charged to see that the owners of estates looked after the indigent, whether slave or free, lest any should die of hunger.

Economically the monasteries were really productive centers. Their artisans at first supplied only the needs of the monastic community itself; then, as there was a surplus, the abbots established industrial centers for wider distribution outside the monastic precincts. The oldest of such Carolingian factories, so far as we know, was St. Riquier, which contained special quarters for each trade. Indeed, many continental cities owe their origin to this industrial movement. The workingmen were organized in unions, guilds, or confraternities, whose purpose was primarily charity, resembling mutual aid societies, with features providing for insurance in case of loss by fire or shipwreck.

As villa manufacture was confined to articles of common need, more elaborate tastes had to be gratified by importation from places beyond the limits of the northern countries of Europe. The Emperor gave great attention to guarding the frontiers, so that foreign commerce could be carried on in security. The great trade routes followed the rivers. There was a regularly developed system of markets and fairs held near the cities and the monasteries, as in the case of St. Denis, near Paris, where for a space of four weeks goods were exposed for sale by traders from Spain, Southern France, and Lombardy.

In Germany and in the more remote portions of the Empire, near the Slavic frontiers, the government established shelters and exchange offices for the convenience of merchants, and strict care was taken that arms were not sold to the enemy. Chief among the entrepots of commerce was the city of Mainz, famous for its cloth manufacture. Charles planned to make of it the great imperial economic center, and in pursuance of this program provided for the construction of a wooden bridge over the Rhine. He proposed also to build a canal to connect the Danube with the Rhine. But the bridge was destroyed by fire, and the canal offered too serious difficulties for the engineers of his age to surmount.

Trade between the Empire and Great Britain and Ireland was encouraged. There was a lighthouse at Boulogne, and at Quentovia, now Étaples, a customs-house was established and placed under the supervision of Gerrold, a shrewd man of affairs, abbot of St. Wandrile. The constant stream of pilgrims passing from the islands was protected by the Emperor, and they proved useful in drawing closer the commercial ties with these remoter portions of the civilized world. Naturally the Mediterranean commerce was the more important, and the Emperor was careful to keep up good relations with Eastern princes, both Christian and Moslem.

Imports consisted of purple stuffs, silk cloaks of various colors, worked leather, perfumes, unguents, and medicinal plants, spices, Indian pearls, Egyptian papyrus, and even exotic animals, such as monkeys and elephants.

The cities in Southern France were especially frequented for trade, many of them having a cosmopolitan population. The Jews were valued for their business capacity, and also for their knowledge of languages and medical science. They were not allowed to own landed property, but no restrictions were placed on their loan operations, or on their commercial ventures.

A marked improvement is noted in the coinage. After 800 the bust of the Emperor appears with an indication of the Roman military cloak and the words "Carolus Imperator"; on the reverse is a temple with a cross and the inscription "Religio Christiana."

The financial administration of the government offered few complications, because the obligations on the state in the way of expenses were most limited. The chief item in the imperial budget, which preserved the personal and household character of the Merovingian period, was for the maintenance of the royal palaces, for the presents made by the king to churches, to foreign princes, or to the great officers of the Empire. Direct taxes were of the capitation type, graded according to the position of the individual taxed. The ordinary fiscal resources were made up from the income of the King from his own estates, from tributes paid by vassal nations, from war booty, obligatory annual gifts, and indirect taxes. The revenue from the royal estates, which were excellently managed, was considerable, and there must have been a large sum credited to the account of booty from the various successful wars.

The "benevolences," to use a term familiar in the constitutional and financial history of England, were not fixed, and the records speak in an indefinite way of the contribution offered by faithful subjects of the Empire in the annual assemblies. But it is plain that these so-called gifts included precious stones and valuable fabrics, as well as gold and silver.

The principal indirect taxes were in the form of personal service, rather than in money payments. Local taxation meant special work on roads, bridges, and making dikes. For the great bridge at Mainz, labor was called for from many localities, because it was an imperial work, intended for the common benefit of the whole Empire. Transportation dues are frequently mentioned in the Carolingian laws, as well as the right of "lodging," by which the inhabitants of a community were obliged to lodge and entertain the King and his officials on their travels, and to receive the representatives of foreign powers and others, to whom the royal privilege was given. A bishop, for example, had the right to receive forty loaves a day, three lambs, three measures of ale, a gallon of milk, three chickens, fifteen eggs, and four measures of feed for his horses.

The greatest difficulties of the government were not financial, but military, for the state of warfare was almost continuous, especially along the Alps, the Pyrenees, and from the Eider to the lower Danube. The summons for calling together the units of the military forces was either carried by means of direct envoys or by letters sent to the counts, bishops, and abbots, and sometimes by the "missi." These officials had to see that all those who were liable to service should be prepared to take their places when the call to arms was given. One of the "missi" writes: "let all be so prepared that, if the order to leave comes in the evening, they will leave without delay for Italy on the morning of the next day, but if it comes in the morning, in the evening of the same day."

The following letter, addressed to Fulrad, abbot of Saint Quentin, gives the full text of one of these summonses: "Know, that we have fixed this year our meeting place in the country of the Saxons, in the Eastern part on the River Bota, at a place called Storosfurt. For this reason we direct you to be at the said place on the 15th of June accompanied by all your men, well armed and well equipped, so that you may go under arms, wherever it seems good to us to direct you to march. We expressly recommend you, in order that you may see that the rest follow our directions, to proceed to the designated place, without disturbance, by the shortest road, without taking anything from the inhabitants but the grass, wood, and water you require. Let the men of your company march constantly with the chariots and the horsemen, and let them never leave them until they reach the meeting place, in order that in the absence of their master they may not be tempted to do evil." Late comers were punished by being deprived of rations for the time they were absent, if the period was short. They who failed to appear altogether were exposed to pay a heavy fine proportionate to their fortune. While on the march the troops, as we see by the terms of Fulrad's letter, were to receive from the inhabitants of the country through which they passed fire, water, wood, and lodging, but nothing else. They brought with them enough provisions to last three months, and arms and clothing for six months. Each warrior was expected to have a buckler, a lance or a sword, a bow with ten cords, and twelve arrows. Those who were better off brought with them a better type of shield, while the counts and those who served as substitutes for bishops and abbots, wore a breastplate and a helmet. Some of the soldiers carried slings, and, apparently, there were mounted divisions in the army. For certain necessary parts of war-material the counts were personally responsible, such as three kinds of battle-axe, skins, battering rams, also for the transportation of these, and for all things required to keep the various weapons in good condition, and for engineering tools.

It is interesting to note how these warlike preparations were arranged for. Ownership in land was the basis selected for apportioning the expense. But as the man who had only a small estate could not bear such an outlay, inequality of fortune had to be considered, and also the distance to be traversed to the place of meeting. These points were all kept in view by the legislation of the Emperor, but there was no systematic attempt made to meet these difficulties. There were special provisions intended to govern special cases. In the first place, the call to arms was rarely made general. This was only done on exceptional occasions, as in 773, for the Lombard war; in 775, in the war against the Saxons, and in 792, in that against the Avars. In 807 account was taken of the distance. The Saxons, for example, only sent one man out of six against the Spaniards and the Avars; one out of three was demanded against the Slavs; but in case of conflict with their neighbors, the Suabi, all Saxon warriors had to take up arms. There was also an apportionment according to race: the Franks were called upon to confront the Saxons, the Lombards and Bavarians marched against the Avars; while, in case of war with the Spanish Arabs, the Aquitanians, the Southern Goths, the Provençals, and the Burgundians had to make up the imperial army. In the war against the Slavs, the Emperor called upon the Eastern Franks, the Saxons, the Alemanni, and the Thuringians.

In 807 the Emperor made the following arrangement as to military service: Every man who owned three manses had to appear under arms; of two landowners, each one of whom had two manses, one was to provide the equipment for the other, and he who could go earliest had to appear for military duty. Of three landowners, who had but one manse apiece, one must go, while the other two were to provide the equipment, and so on, the same arrangement being applied to owners of smaller parcels of ground. Another year, the duty of serving in the army began with the owners of four manses. The working of this graduated system of service was left in the hands of the "missus," who made his arrangements in view of the prospective campaign.

It was evidently the Emperor's purpose to make the burden as light as possible for the small landholder, and at the same time the obligation to serve was extended to those who had no landed property. So we find it declared in 806 that "if there are six landless men who own each as much as the value of six silver pennies, i.e., a pound and a half of the metal, one has to serve and be equipped by the other five." But the freemen alone were not sufficient to fill up the ranks; for, under the strict application of this system, no one was obliged to serve who held land in dependence, or as a "beneficium" from a wealthy landowner, nor did the obligation rest on those who had surrendered their lands to the Church, or to a powerful layman, in order to receive it back again under the conditions of a "beneficium." This class were not wholly free, nor were they actually landowners.

The problem of keeping up the war strength without oppressing the small landowner was solved in the following way: Charles called together, under the following conditions, those who were his own tenants. "Let every freeman," he directed, "who owns absolutely four manses, or who holds them from another in the relation of a 'beneficium,' undertake to furnish his own equipment and join the army, either with his lord, if his lord is going there, or with the count." These distributions enabled the Emperor to get recruits who otherwise would have escaped service; the other more remote result was that the "beneficium" system received legal recognition, and in this way the Emperor himself coöperated in the disintegrating tendencies by which the feudalized state finally destroyed the imperial system.

The lot of the small landowner was made hard and unendurable under the terms of the imperial military regulations, despite the compromises intended by Charles to protect him. There was every inducement to the owner of a small holding to give it up. We find, for example, an imperial order forbidding freemen without permission from the Emperor to enter the clerical profession, "for we have heard," he says, "that certain of them are not so much actuated by devotion as by a desire to escape service in the army, and other public duties to the sovereign." The fact, too, that rules regulating this subject were extremely complicated, led to all kinds of abuses on the part of those who were intrusted with their execution. In a report made to the Emperor, we read that "the poor people claim that, if one of them is not willing to abandon his property to the bishop or abbot, or count, or 'master of a hundred,' these officials find occasion to have him condemned and compel him to go to the place where the army is mobilized, so that being reduced to misery he is forced, whether he wants to or not, to give up his property or sell it." It was added that those who had made this sacrifice were not disturbed.

The recriminations of the poor were directed against clerical and lay officers without distinction; and we hear of their grievances against bishops, abbots, and their legal representatives, as well as against the counts and other laymen. The Emperor's efforts proved futile, and he not only could not resist the movement of his age, but he found himself promoting the evolution he criticised. He actually gave exemptions under his own seal to a certain number of religious houses. The counts, on their side, made a practice of giving exemptions and dispensations from military service. The landlord was allowed a kind of authority over the tenant in questions in which the holding of land was not involved. The rule that each landowner must be conducted to the place of mobilization by the count was broken, and the landed proprietors were allowed to appear ready for service, at the head of their tenants and dependents, a distinct anticipation of the later feudal custom.

The mass of the people did not fail to let their sentiments be known when the Emperor proceeded to extend the privilege of quartering his functionaries on private individuals. The imperial officers were assaulted and their baggage stolen. There was much complaint, too, of the incessant calls to military service. Many sacrificed, therefore, their free status, which simply meant to them the constant obligation to be under arms, and they entered the ecclesiastical profession or became dependents of those who were more powerful. Carolingian legislation permitted the freeman to "commend" himself to whomsoever he would "after the death of his lord," and so that process began by which the central authority was robbed of its own subjects, the small, free landowners. Thus it was that the medieval régime took definite shape as a governmental hierarchy based on the possession of landed estates, great and small, worked either by serfs or by tenants, related to their overlord by various kinds of dependent tenures.

X

THE CHURCH

In his relations with the Church, Charles gave a liberal interpretation to his acknowledged powers of guidance and direction; the kind of rôle he was willing to undertake shows that he drew no hard and fast line between the secular and spiritual prerogatives of a monarch. For example, in the Adoptionist Controversy, he took the initiative himself in settling a troublesome problem of theological speculation. According to the Adoptionists, in Christ there are a divine personality and a human personality, which latter becomes by adoption the Son of God. This tenet was eagerly embraced in Spain, its two best-known adherents being Elipandus, Archbishop of Toledo, and Felix, Bishop of Urgel, the latter a city in the North of Spain under the authority of the Frankish King, who, therefore, immediately took steps to bring the subject in dispute before a council, assembled at Regensburg, "under the orders of the most glorious and orthodox King Charles." Felix was convicted of false teaching and sent to Rome to appear before Pope Hadrian. Though Felix was deprived of his bishopric he continued to be supported by the Spanish episcopate, who collectively wrote to Charles for his restoration. At Frankfort, in 794, a council of prelates from various Frankish sees met and listened to the King, who read the letter from the Spanish bishops. The council then heard a long technical speech from their ruler on the questions at issue. The Bishop of Urgel was again condemned, but the matter was not decided until a few years later, in 799, when a long discussion, lasting over six days, took place at Aix between Felix and Alcuin, the conclusion of which was that Felix allowed that he was overcome in argument, and published a retraction.

Charles was equally interested in two other religious controversies of his time, and he made his personal point of view predominant in spite of the weight of church authority on the other side. At the Council of Frankfort the bishops had received from Pope Hadrian the acts passed at the Second General Council of Nicæa dealing with the subject of image worship, a matter that had been debated with much violence in the East and in Italy for several generations. At Frankfort it was supposed, owing to an inability to understand the precise meaning of certain Greek words, that the Nicene Council had formally ordered the adoration of images, and its decrees were therefore rejected. The Emperor undertook the defense of the Western point of view, and in doing so did not hesitate to differ with Rome itself. He also took up an independent position on a more vital point. It seems that during Leo III's pontificate certain French monks residing in the East were charged with heresy because they inserted in the so-called Nicene Creed, in the article dealing with the procession of the Holy Spirit, i.e., where it is stated that the Holy Spirit proceeds from the Father, the crucial word "filioque" (and from the Son). The matter was taken up by Charles, and after this recondite theological point had been studied, the action of the monks was officially sanctioned by the Council of Aix-la-Chapelle, in 809, although the Pope refused to approve of any addition to the historic formula of Christian belief.

In considering the Frankish ruler's attitude towards the Papacy, it is well to remember that the later administrative system of the Curia, which made so clear-cut the antagonism between the secular prince and the ecclesiastical hierarchy in the medieval times after the age of Hildebrand, had not yet been developed. Charles reverenced the Papacy; indeed, the Pope's counsel and the Pope's words often played a decisive part in influencing his motives. He was a convinced believer in the Pope's right to teach the faithful, and he saw in him the guardian of apostolic tradition. It was to this tradition that he appealed when he condemned the Adoptionists at the Council of Frankfort. The specific rights of the Papacy, from this point of view, lay in its teaching function and in its liturgical usages, which were to be taken by the Christians of Charles' dominions as the correct norm of their practice. There was also a full recognition of the prerogatives of the Papacy in phases of administration and discipline, wherever ancient precedents could be cited. So we find Charles appealing, in the renewed disputes between the sees of Arles and Vienne, to the ancient directions of the Roman bishops governing this question.

But this recognition of the rights of Rome did not prevent Charles from regarding himself as the director of the Frankish Church. He speaks openly of himself as "the pilot of the Church in his domains," and when writing Leo III he explains his conception of the relation of the kingdom and the Papacy. "Our task it is, by the help of God, to protect by our arms outwardly the Holy Church of Christ from assaults of the heathen and from being wasted by the unbelievers and to establish it within by recognizing the Catholic faith. Your duty it is to support as Moses did, with uplifted arms our service in the battlefield, that the Christian people, being led through your petitions and prepared by God, may have constantly and everywhere victory over the enemies of His name." While Charles assigned to the Pope a religious activity and nothing more, he regarded his own guardianship over the churches as extending beyond questions of their material welfare. In 789 in a message to the bishops he stated that he wished to coöperate with them, using his power as a ruler, and working through his subordinates to improve things where improvement was possible. These were the principles he used in his Church policy. Just as in secular matters he was not absolute, but followed the laws and customs of the people over whom he ruled, so in regard to the Church he observed its canonical system with a reverence for its minute details. But his capitularies, as we have seen, are filled with ecclesiastical legislation, and in Church matters the King acted as the supreme authority. Even synods laid their decrees before him for correction, and to secure his authoritative sanction. There was little place for a fully developed Papacy in an ecclesiastical system worked along these lines, and there are no examples during Charles' reign of Papal interference in the administration of the Church in his own domains. The Pope, where and when he did act, did so in concert with Charles; even in cases of excommunication there was an understanding with the King; and often the extreme penalty was inflicted under his initiative. Even the exercise of discipline in connection with the episcopate was left in Charles' hands without any protest on the part of the Pope.

These religious activities of Charles seemed natural to his contemporaries. Alcuin says of him that he was armed with two swords, the one to smite false teaching in the bosom of the Church, the other to protect it from the devastations of the heathen. He speaks of Charles as a parent and teacher, under whose rule the Church is placed; yet at the same time Alcuin had the highest reverence for the Papacy and never thought of the possibility of conflict between the Pope and the Emperor. In Rome itself there was no formal acceptance of this Frankish conception of an ecclesiastical polity in which the Pope's place was that of a fifth wheel to the coach. Roman enthusiasm for the Emperor, as expressed by the Roman clergy, was limited to encomiums on him as protector of the Church. He was spoken of as the faithful ruler, who, by his energy and his benefactions, was doing valiant work for Rome and for the Papacy.

In matters of internal Church administration, the influence of the King was often paramount in questions affecting diocesan order. There was nothing revolutionary here, for the independence of the Church from the State implied a situation that was never dreamed of at this period, nor had it really existed since the time of Constantine. Theoretically, the choice of a bishop belonged rightfully to the clergy and to the laity of a diocese, but, as a matter of fact, the monarch controlled episcopal elections. These could not take place until the royal sanction had been secured, and the official in whose presence the electoral machinery was set in motion was an appointee of the King. The official papers recording the election had to be sent to the palace, and the successful candidate could not be consecrated except with the King's approval. Often Charles himself selected the candidate; besides, if a man were known to be favored by him, he would, on the strength of this fact, be elected. Where bishops were to be appointed for sees created in territory newly conquered from the heathen, they were named by Charles without the form of an election. What is true of bishops holds also with regard to abbots, who, on account of the great expansion of monastic life, were of more importance than a diocesan bishop. Church councils were summoned by Charles; he could preside over them, and only through his consent were the decrees they passed valid. Much attention was given to a systematic organization of the hierarchy. There were twenty-two metropolitical sees in the Empire, and the bishop was given real and effective charge of the clergy under him. Counties and parishes, throughout the imperial domains especially, were growing in number, and were placed in the newly acquired territories under an assistant bishop.

XI

THE EMPIRE WITHOUT AND WITHIN

The diplomacy, as well as the strategy, of the Emperor was worthy of a far-seeing and cautious ruler. He kept the frontiers of the Empire assured by fortifications, wherever there was prospect of direct attack from the Danes or the Slavs, and by such means saw to it that the tribes bordering on the lines of defense were kept in awe and reduced to a state of dependence. In other places where the more distant Avars and the Bulgars might ultimately give trouble, the Emperor had taken care to come to a friendly arrangement with the Eastern Empire for mutual protection. This understanding did not, it is true, prevent friction between the two powers on the Adriatic Sea, where on several occasions the armies had met to decide their differences by arms. But on neither side was there any intention of developing consistent schemes for conquering the territory of the rival emperor. Disturbances were local and the border population was itself uncertain in allegiance, and ready to accept the guidance of its interests in determining the direction of its loyalty. This kind of hesitancy was not found in Italy, which remained inviolably faithful to Charles' rule.

The rulers of Constantinople had no time nor inclination to repeat the experiment of Justinian and Constans during the reign of Charles; they were weakened by serious difficulties of their own, due to disputed succession and religious conflict, and to the need of constant watchfulness against Moslem aggression. It was fortunate for both empires that the Saracens were not united. This was the most decisive factor, indeed, of the history of this period. The East was freed from the type of attack which had kept Leo the Isaurian constantly on the defensive, and which only his high military talents were able to cope with, while in the West the inability of the Moslems to act together made it possible for Charles to expand his territory and to give the time needed for internal development in the consolidation of his rule.

It was one of the most permanent results of the activity of Charles as a conqueror that in the Spanish peninsula he strengthened not only the natural position of the petty and struggling Christian kingdoms, but by his personality made the ideal of a Christian ruler respected there, and so assured for the Christians in Spain a future which could be realized only when they had lived down their particularism and recognized the value of solidarity. But the wider field of armed conflict for the peoples included in his realm would have meant little, if it had not been accompanied by opportunities for real social progress.

The empire of Charles, though it was the concrete creation of an ideal government crudely understood and most inadequately worked out, illustrated the liberty-loving principles of the Germanic peoples who were gathered in its fold. In this respect, with all its imperfections, the rule of the great Frankish monarch is more closely allied to the political principles of modern times than were the more ambitious and more logical creations of the conquerors who preceded and who followed him. Unconsciously, it may be, his system of government gave scope for local diversities and recognized rights of deep-planted traditions with a generosity which is characteristic not of empires such as those of Cæsar and Napoleon, but of federal republics of the type of the United States, and the Federation of the Swiss Cantons. When he aimed at uniformity he did not lose sight of the fact that he was the ruler of heterogeneous nationalities, on whose good-will and coöperation the permanence of the Empire was dependent. The pressure of centralization was lightly exercised, simply because in the Emperor's mind the ideas of Roman rule had to pass through the medium of German tribal tradition.

There was no steam roller set to work to equalize, if not to pulverize, the component parts of his realm. The divisions were not destroyed, but were rather combined in a higher political unity. The kingdom of the West Goths was at least preserved, though it had less of a definite character than the

Lombard kingdom, which the Emperor took special pains to preserve in its integrity. Even the traditions of the Ostrogoths were allowed a value in so far as they stood for a strenuous opposition to the imperial policy of uniformity of administration and to the economic sacrifice of the local centers to the purposes of world politics. Lombard influence had overcome both Ostrogothic and Roman rule; it was irreconcilable, and stood for the stubborn and conservative standpoint that made the first Germanic invaders difficult to assimilate in the provinces of the Roman Empire, where by force of arms they became the ruling class. A similar obstinacy, with its preservation of the original political type, marked the Lombard kingdom and duchies which Charles had conquered. A picturesque example of local initiative was not crowded out by the Frankish overlordship in Venice; the seafaring community came into being in a favored spot, on the confines of the two empires, too remote to be crushed from Constantinople, and protected from the Western ruler by a few leagues of shallow sea.

The same centrifugal tendencies are seen in Southern Italy; and what is more important, in Northern and Central Italy, there was no attempt to stifle the germs of municipal activity which produced, later on, such marvelous fruitage in the Italian town life of the Middle Ages. The contrast between the Germanic and Roman elements in the Empire faded away gradually under the Emperor's administration, but Roman civilization could not be eclipsed, while the laws of Justinian continued to be quoted as a model, and while the Church with its general use of the Latin language was regarded as the chief adjunct and support of continuity in imperial rule.

The union of the Empire and the Papacy kept up that tradition of civilization by which the isolation of Germanic tribal life was swept aside, and the Germans learned that there were other governmental principles than custom, and began to see that might was not the only right. The institutions of the Church did more than preserve the ideal element for the individual and for society. They stood for continuity in securing the best achievements of classic culture in government and in learning, and prevented just that kind of social cataclysm which marked the progress of Islam, when it attempted to handle mankind in the mass. Reverence for the Holy Scriptures, however imperfect may have been the acquaintance with them, had a powerful influence in maintaining the connection of Church and State, and acted constantly against the divisive tendencies of racial rule.

The Celts of Western France, the remnant of the people who had once dominated the whole of Occidental Europe, were brought into the sphere of general European life, and the same opportunities were given to the Germanic peoples. Allied with the population of Latin origin, they extended their sway over a territory which before had never felt the influence of centralization. The union of the two elements was of momentous importance, and this achievement stands out as the abiding result of the Emperor's conquest. France and Germany made up a whole, in which the Teutonic element had a superior position, but without tyrannizing over the peoples of the Romance stock. In Burgundy and Neustria the elements of Latin blood were strongest, and the contrast gave a peculiar character to Austrasia.

The most significant factor of the Emperor's rule was that it offered a center of unity to the Teutonic tribes, consolidating them, where the Merovingian kingdoms, which also stood for the old Germanic tribal traditions, had shown complete incapacity. But under the Carolingian rule, neither the Alemanni, nor the Bavarians, nor the Saxons, could claim predominance, for the sovereign's authority was exercised apart from all these tribal influences, and yet at the same time the characteristics of the tribe, local sentiment, and customary law, were not broken up by the central government. The Teutonic local division, the "Gau," was no more interfered with than the Gallic "Civitas." The power at the top of all, formed by the armed hosts of the component parts of the Empire and by the clergy, was expressed in institutions that kept the body politic together. In the assemblies, all the different nationalities took part, and acted under the guidance of the single will of a single ruler, who was kept from the capricious action of a tyrant by his firm hold on the ideal of a Christian commonwealth. The principles of the whole imperial system harmonized with popular governmental traditions, and both in their social and in their religious aspects answered to the popular conceptions of membership in a world-wide church.

Charles, in his plans for the succession, looked forward to a ruling family controlling by descent a singularly heterogeneous collection of races. It is unthinkable, as an historical principle, that the traditions and customs of race and tribe could be long suppressed. Since the time of Germanic invasions they had been the most potent factor in the evolution of Western Europe; and, though they were kept in the background by the energy and character of the Emperor, it only needed a few crises to call them forth into activity. Out of the interplay of these tribal interests and racial divergencies has grown modern Europe.

A further weakness in the Carolingian structure was due to the relation of the secular and the ecclesiastical authority. The grounds of conflict, even in Charles' own time, were never far distant. The Emperor's diplomacy and personality smoothed the acerbities away, and his attitude of compromise found ready imitators in such Popes as Hadrian I and Leo III. There would have been a different outcome if, on his visits to Rome, he had been faced by a Pope of the temperament of Nicholas I. The possible independence of the spiritual power the Emperor did little to prevent by legislation. There was no way of avoiding such disputes, and the struggles for supremacy between Empire and Papacy attained their full development in the thirteenth century.

Charles, too, showed no willingness to deal radically with the customary laws of succession of the Frankish people, and in this sphere he was far more conservative than the Lombards or the Ostrogoths. The principle of division among the heirs rather than unity of territory, meant in itself a great danger. It would have caused trouble to Charles himself had not his brother been removed by death early in the reign. Yet the Emperor set a strong precedent for its recognition in his own disposition of the Empire among his three sons. The position of Louis was due to an accident, and the old question was bound to emerge again when the rights of his various children, as his heirs, came to be considered. Nothing was done to prescribe how the exercise of sole rule as Emperor was to be carried out when the subordinate rulers of his own house proved reluctant to obey their head.

The Empire plainly was only secure if its various rulers could consent to work harmoniously together; a division among them, a break between the Church and the State, the exaltation of the idea of nationality and race, were all possibilities which would surely destroy the integrity of Charles' imperial construction. The history of the century after his death shows the weak sides of the Emperor's benevolent optimism. He contemplated a great Christian republic directed by a family united in its members and guided by patriarchal instinct. In working out this program, Charles was an opportunist as well as an optimist; he took the component political factors as he found them, and introduced them as the stones of a mosaic, thinking more of the whole than of the parts, seemingly oblivious of the disparity of the elements he was introducing into the fabric. The distinctions of race were certain to become accentuated the moment the central power showed weakness and proved itself unable to be an effectual protection against anarchy within or attacks from the outside.

In its political creativeness the Emperor's work was framed on a smaller scale than he contemplated. He proposed an Empire, but he really founded kingdoms—the historic kingdoms of Western Europe. The inheritors of his system were the territorial monarchs, who took from him the conception of a supreme secular power closely united with the Church. The actual central authority established by Charles soon passed away, but the peoples included within it, endowed with the energy proceeding from him, as a source, survived and developed. The ground prepared by him was the foundation for the national kingdoms with whose vicissitudes and progress the course of civilization has been unalterably connected. He has been well named, therefore, the Patriarch of Europe, the Abraham in whose seed the political world has been blessed.

The ablest monarchs of Europe, both in the Middle Ages and in modern times, from Otto III to Napoleon, including Frederic Barbarossa and Louis XIV, all have felt the power of his personality. Napoleon speaks of him as his illustrious predecessor. Yet, as a politician, Charles was inferior to his father, Pippin, whose shrewdness in arranging momentous political combinations he did not inherit, and on the field of battle he was not the equal of his grandfather, Charles Martel. He never won a battle such as Poictiers, and with one or two exceptions the narrative of his campaigns shows nothing of the skilful and spectacular generalship of Belisarius.

In his wars no unusual gifts of strategy were required; no great mastery of tactics was necessary. But he was what one of his contemporaries declared, "the powerful fighter who smote the Saxons and humbled the hearts of the Franks and Barbarians, who had been able to resist the might of the Romans." His campaigns attest energy and obstinacy, a clear-sighted ability to see when and where a decisive blow must be delivered. He never lost his head in a dangerous position, and so he was able to take in a military problem in its various aspects, and while resting at one stage of a conflict, he could quietly prepare to overcome his adversaries in a second move.

His mind was well balanced, it worked logically and with a large vision, and he aimed at acting in such a way that the innumerable details of his work as ruler would be explicable and could harmonize as parts of a well-considered whole. He was general-in-chief, and he also realized as we have seen, Constantine's description of himself in relation to the Church, as "chief bishop for its external affairs." As a judge, Charles was the supreme court of appeal, and was in this capacity remarkable for his severity and unsparing attitude to the guilty. Though he was not a genius as an administrator, he showed industry and judgment in using and in improving such organs of government as were known in his day in Western Europe. As we have pointed out, his capitularies show him to us as a great landlord, familiar with agricultural methods, able to measure the economic needs of a large estate, and to act accordingly, possessing an extraordinary amount of practical energy and versatility.

There was no limit to his interests, and he brought in a high conception of duty. Up to the close of his life nothing was too small to escape his personal supervision; he kept count of the chickens on his personal estates, dictated his capitularies, and learned the art of writing, a rare accomplishment, and deemed among the Teutonic races the special work of a cleric. He presided over assemblies and councils, ordered the system of chanting in his private chapel, and hardly a year passed by that he did not visit one of the frontiers of the Empire. His mental capacity was characterized by something of the mobility which belonged to the Renaissance period, a trait not seen among medieval rulers, and perhaps paralleled only in the case of Frederick II. His talents were not employed towards futile ends; he economized them, and while he was open to impressions, he kept with scrupulousness his store of energy under control. He was free from Napoleon's defect of fitting all things as parts of a rigid system, and he knew when to keep his hands from disarranging a firmly established social order.

It may be that a larger measure of interference from him would have prevented the growth of feudal privileges which the land system of Western Europe was already producing. This evolution he did not oppose; in some cases his own acts furthered it. The court and "missi" under his direction became, as it were, observers and directors of a naturally developing type of local administration which the general ordinances of the Empire did nothing to repress. Feudal customs, still, of course, in their germ, were pressed into the service of the state, as for example when the lord was required to appear accompanied by his dependents at the general military assembly of the King. The Emperor was quick in reconciling local divergencies, and in discerning some easily practicable method of making seemingly irreconcilable factors contribute mutually to his ends. When a governmental order failed, he was fertile in discerning an immediate remedy, careless whether the innovation of a reform could be theoretically accommodated to the administration as it before existed. Wherever the structure he planned turned out faulty, he went to work with the spirit of an artist who thinks more of the safety of the whole building than of the harmony of its parts. His ideal of rule was always before him, yet there was none of the stage effect of which Napoleon was so fond. He did not try to impress upon others principles that did not attract his own sympathies. He believed in what he did and believed the way he was doing it was consistent with his own ideals of right, personal and social. The empire was to be a community guided by Christian standards, a visible embodiment of the City of God, as understood in his day.

The dream was a mighty one, and proved inspiring largely because it was impersonal. The Emperor stood as the champion, unselfish and devoted, of progress, so far as his age appreciated that much abused term. It was, at least, a reality in respect to the conscious effort on his part to moralize government, and by doing so to contribute to an ideal solidarity of men and races. Yet the task he had assigned himself was too great; and his work remained but an unfinished sketch, soon to be demolished in the troublous and hopeless reigns of his descendants.

The Ottomans

I
OSMAN

The empire of the Seldjoukian Turks by which the crusading conquests were destroyed, showed no greater powers of endurance than the other creations of Moslem rule; it did not escape the tendency to dismemberment due to the transfer of personal and autocratic control into the hands of rulers of mediocre ability. By the beginning of the fourteenth century the effect of disintegration showed itself plainly and definitely in Western Asia throughout the territory which had been won from the Emperors of Eastern Rome. One of the results of the expansion of the Mongol conquests towards the West was to hasten not only the division among the Seldjouks, but their speedy downfall. Their Sultans found no safety against the pressure of the Mongols on their territories, even though they combined with their Christian neighbors, with whom they had kept up for so long incessant warfare, against a danger which threatened annihilation to all races and peoples in the path of the Mongol hordes from the East. The Turks made peace with the Greeks at Nicæa, and even engaged the help of Frankish mercenary troops, but these counsels of despair did not save them from becoming tributaries to the Mongol rulers of Asia.

As early as 1243 the fatal course of the decadence was marked by constant defeat, and from this time on they were not able to defend their position. The Sultanate came practically to an end with the death of Masud II of Iconium, who was murdered by one of his emirs, though the Mongols continued the office, ruling under the name of Alaed-Din II, 1297-1307. Of the ten fragments which represented the former empire of the Seldjouks, one was controlled by Osman, from whose name the latest and most enduring effort to establish a Moslem world power takes its origin. Within the restricted bounds of a small emirate, whose most important point was the ancient city of Dorlæum, now called Sultan-Oeni, was trained and developed the people who were destined to make great European conquests lasting down to our own day, to threaten for many centuries Christian powers at their most vulnerable centers, and, finally, when their own ability to conquer and devastate had come to an end, to stir up such constant jealousies among the states which claimed the succession to their dominions in Europe, that some of the most disastrous and hardly contested wars in the nineteenth century have been due to their presence on European soil.

No more than in the case of Mohammed could such far-reaching consequences have been detected in the obscure beginnings of the people over whom Osman began to rule as an independent prince. Nearly a century before, his ancestor Souliman had led a migration from Khorassan; with tribal adherents numbering 150,000, he took possession of lands near Erzendjan and Akhlath; then came the invasion of the Mongols, which brought ruin to these plans of settlement. Souliman, in his flight from the invaders, was drowned as he was crossing the Euphrates at a place called to-day Turk-Mesari, the tomb of the Turk. On his death the nomads who followed his leadership were dispersed; even his four sons failed to keep together. Two returned to the place from which they had come, while the other two, Dundar and Ertoghroul, keeping four hundred families with them, occupied territories near Erzeroum. But as the proximity of the Mongols held out no prospect of peaceful possession, the two brothers continued their march westward, and finally put themselves under the protection of Ala-ed-Din I, Sultan of the Seldjouks. (1219-1234.)

According to the legendary account, while Ertoghroul was making his way West, he found himself on the top of a mountain ridge, where, looking down on the plain, he saw two armies about to engage each other. He decided to help those who were weaker, and adding his warriors to those who were giving way, he put the enemy to flight. At the close of the battle he found that he had brought victory over a horde of Mongols to the armies of Ala-ed-Din I, who, as a reward for this unexpected aid, gave the newcomers the mountain regions of Toumanidj and Ermeni as a dwelling place in summer, and the plain of Soegud for their winter quarters. Ertoghroul showed his loyalty to his new sovereign by undertaking successful raids against the outposts of the Greek Empire of Nicæa in parts adjacent to his own lands. Although under a Moslem overlord, Ertoghroul and his people still continued faithful to their ancestral polytheism, but he showed such great respect for the sacred volume of Mohammed, that it was not surprising when his son and successor, Osman or Othman (1288-1326), became converted to the religion of Islam.

This important event was connected with his marriage with the daughter of a cheikh belonging to the Seldjouks, Edebali, who, according to the legends of the Ottoman race, mysteriously foretold the future greatness of his son-in-law, and worked actively for the conversion of all his people. Up to this time the followers of Osman were nothing more than a band of nomads of mixed race composed of Turcomans, probably containing two Mongol elements. This change of religion not only gave them unity, but enabled them in the critical period of the Mongol conquests to act as a center around which were gathered all those of the Turkish race who held to Mohammedan orthodoxy. The first step was the absorption of the Seldjouks, a process natural enough because of racial affinity, but as time went on religious professions, not racial relationship, became so predominant a characteristic in Ottoman rule, that converts of all nationalities, Greeks, Slavs, Albanians, Roumanians, and Magyars, were absorbed without prejudice as to racial origin, and from the mere fact of profession of Mohammedanism were recognized just as fully as Ottoman Turks as if they had descended from the parent stock.

The social phenomenon of Western Europe, where the cohesive force of Christianity brought together people of Germanic, Celtic, and Roman origin, found its counterpart in this new national development of Mohammedan orthodoxy. It took place, too, just at a time when the old supporters of Islam, the Arabs, the Persians, and the Berbers had entered upon a stage of decadence. As a political power Islam was going to pieces, when new vigor was infused into it by a fresh and warlike race of barbarians, who, as convinced converts with all the fanaticism of a recently acquired faith, restored the simpler traditions of the Koran that had been lost or weakened, wherever the disciples of Mohammed were brought in contact with civilizing influences or wherever, in their mutual divisions, they had made terms of alliance with Christian rulers.

Predatory warfare was the training which gave the Ottoman Turks their irresistible power as conquerors; they were organized as an army disciplined and ever ready to strike. No better field for such training could have been found than the territory of Anatolia when the empire of the Seldjouks disappeared, and a condition of affairs arose, of which Northern Spain, at a somewhat earlier period, is a parallel instance of prevailing anarchy and local turmoil.

Some of the semi-independent fortresses under Greek commanders, who presided over narrow territories in the same way as the feudal seigneurs of Western Europe, were reduced by Osman. With these additions to his domains he had no hesitation in proclaiming himself an independent prince on the death of Ala-ed-Din. Soon afterward he conquered all the region near the river Songora, which gave approach to the sea coast and so offered an opportunity for equipping piratical expeditions that terrorized the islands and shores of the Greek Empire and the Latin states of the East. At this time the emirate under Osman covered the greater part of the ancient provinces of Galatia and Bithynia.

To this position of mastery must be ascribed the rapid acquisition of leadership by Osman. The territory he now governed was close to the important centers of Greek rule. Broussa, Nicæa, and Nicomedia were the specially selected points of attack in this effort to extend Moslem power over Northwestern Asia, which still remained in Christian hands. The prizes were great and the religious merit considerable; there was enough, then, to attract the most valiant warriors who joined the army of Osman from other emirates. Even mercenary troops of Greek, Slavic, and Latin origin served under the Turkish banner.

The plan of conquest showed skilful and cautious strategy. Osman adopted the policy of overshadowing the great fortresses of the Greek Empire by placing near them strongholds of his own garrisoned with men ready to surprise their opponents at the first favorable opportunity. Broussa soon found itself within the grasp of the Turk. There were two forts dominating its very gates, one on the east, the other on the west. An important town near it, Edrenos, was taken when Osman's son, Ourkhan, forced the city to capitulate, the inhabitants being given, in return for 30,000 pieces of gold, the right to retire with their property. The governor became a convert to Islam—a detail which is typical of the Turkish conquests. These new supporters found it to their advantage to change their allegiance. Such cases are often mentioned in these early years of the expansion of the Ottoman emirate, and they are indicative of a well-devised policy to sap the foundations of resistance.

Another even more striking example of the results of a change of allegiance from Christianity to Mohammedanism is found in the case of Mikhal-Koeze (Michael with the pointed beard), the Greek governor of the castle, who, after becoming a prisoner of war, was most kindly treated by Osman. The bonds of friendship between the two grew so strong that Mikhal embraced Islamism and signalized himself by his fidelity as an ally and subordinate officer. He is the ancestor of the family of Mikhal Oghli (sons of Michael), who in a long line of descent held the command of the irregular troops in the Turkish army.

The close of Osman's career had nothing to record in the way of an exploit equal to the capture of Broussa. In 1326 the conqueror died and was buried in the city, the possession of which marked the chief success of his remarkable reign. Here in after generations were shown the chaplet of rough-ground wood, the enormous drum given him by Ali-ed-Din, and the great carved double-edged sword wielded by the founder and champion of the Ottoman Empire. But the rapidity and importance of Osman's conquests had not changed the tastes of the tribal chieftain; all that he left to his heirs were horses, oxen, some sheep, a spoon, a salt cellar, an embroidered kaftan, and a turban.

Ourkhan, who followed Osman, proved that he had inherited his father's capacity for war and statesmanship. His brother was made vizier, with special charge of the organization of the army, which, in its various arms, preserved for centuries the marks of a military intelligence far superior to that shown in the organization of the armies of medieval Europe. The regular troops were divided into janitschars (foot soldiers), and spahis (horsemen), while the irregular forces had the same two divisions under the names of akindji and azabs.

The advance of conquest still went on upon a large scale. Soon Nicomedia, the ancient capital of Diocletian, surrendered to the Turks. In a battle at Maldepe the Greek Emperor Andronicus III suffered a defeat that led to the loss of all the Asiatic possessions of the Greeks. Nicæa, the second city of the empire, was obliged to yield to the conqueror, who gave the inhabitants the same terms as those accorded to the people of Broussa. The moral effect of this blow was immense, because Nicæa had been the starting point for the revival of Greek civilization and political rule after the taking of Constantinople by the Latins. It was also sacred as the seat of two great ecumenical councils. Now, the church where the Nicene Creed was proclaimed, became a mosque, and the city, with its name transformed into the Turkish disguise of Isnik, lost its historical identity. (1330.)

After the seizure of some small seaports on the Black Sea and the Propontis, the whole of Bithynia fell into Turkish hands. There were only the narrow straits between the Osmanlis and Europe; on the Asiatic side the only places which still belonged to the Greek Empire were Scutari and Philadelphia. As Ourkhan's dominions expanded, he followed his father's precedent in dividing the land into sandjaks (banners). Nicæa was intrusted, on account of its importance, to the eldest son, Souliman, who then, on his own account, resolved to attempt the passage into Europe. In his adventure he was accompanied only by a handful of companions; two rafts were constructed of the trunks of trees joined by thongs of leather, and with these a landing was made at Tzympe, which was seized without trouble, as the fortifications of the place had fallen into ruins (1356).

Not long after this event an earthquake shook the walls of Gallipoli and other neighboring towns, a misfortune which made them all an easy prey for Souliman's officers. When the Greek Emperor protested, Ourkhan answered that his latest conquests were due, not to his arms, but to the will of God that had been revealed in the earthquake. Gallipoli was the key to Europe, and it was not given up. Using it as a base, the Osmanlis commenced to make marauding expeditions into the adjacent country.

II
MURAD I

There followed in succession to Ourkhan, not Souliman, who died in one of the raids into Thrace, but Murad I, whose mother was a Greek. In some respects he was a greater leader than his father, Ourkhan; he is spoken of in the chronicles as eloquent, devoted to justice, and a strict disciplinarian. At the same time he was beloved by his troops because of his generosity. Although he had no education, not even the ability to read and write, he was known as a great builder of mosques, schools, and hospitals. When he had a document to sign he dipped four fingers in the ink, and, keeping them as far apart as possible, impressed them on the paper; the impression so made was worked up artistically into the imperial Osmanli seal. His success in warfare was due not only to his own valor, but also to the number of able commanders who conducted his campaigns under his directions.

The European successes of his elder brother could not be followed up immediately, because the notable victories of the Osmanlis had excited the jealousy of the remaining Seldjouk emirs in Asia. Ourkhan had himself warred with the Prince of Karasi and so been able to add Mysia with Pergamum to his territories. Now Murad's reign was opened by a contest with the emir of Karamania, another Ala-ed-Din, who stirred up many of the Osmanli dependencies to revolt. The city of Angora was the center of this insurrection. Murad overcame the rebels, placed a garrison in Angora, and adopted a policy of gradual absorption in order to keep the Seldjouk emirates from forming a coalition against him. One was ceded outright and a large part of another became the marriage portion of the wife of Bajesid, son of Murad. The situation in Asia, owing to the restlessness of the remaining emirs, who represented another branch of the Turkish stock, continued to be a source of difficulty for many years, and the final and complete conquest of the whole of Anatolia only took place when the European Empire of the Osmanlis was an accomplished fact.

The armies of Murad had now occupied Thrace; hence they were brought into immediate contact with the two strong Slavic nations on the Balkan peninsula, the Bulgarians and the Servians. These South Slavic peoples, after centuries of struggle for supremacy with the Eastern Empire, had been overpowered by the superior wealth, strategy, and civilization of the rulers of Constantinople in the beginning of the eleventh century. But the Latin conquest of Constantinople made it easy for them to regain the ground they had lost. In the course of the struggle between the Byzantines and the Crusaders, the movements towards independence among the Servians and Bulgarians were facilitated. After the year 1261 accessions of territory were made by both branches of the Slavic race. Besides contesting possession of Balkan territory with the Magyars they warred among themselves for the acquisition of lands in the Maritza basin and along the rivers Strouma and Vardar.

In this rivalry the Servians secured the greatest prizes in the way of territorial expansion. By the end of the thirteenth century they had reached the sea coast, and had occupied the region around the two lakes Ochrida and Prespa. About the same time the movement to expand their frontiers at the expense of the Greek Empire again became marked. Northern Albania was conquered and additional lands were seized in Macedonia. These successes led to a coalition between the Bulgars and the Greeks; but this scheme to block the Servians failed. There was a great battle at Velbouje, at which the Bulgarian army was completely crushed. The plan of the Servians was to secure the alliance of their rivals by a marriage between their leader, Stephen Douchan, and the sister of Tsar Michael, the head of the Bulgars.

Douchan is often called the Charlemagne of Servia, but the title is only true if measured by an unrealized dream. His reign marks the limit of Servian ambition; he looked forward to an imperial position under which the Slavs would become the heirs of the dignities and domains of the Byzantine Empire, a position they deserved because of the inability of the Greeks to defend their lands from the advancing power of the Turk. For a time the dream seemed on the point of realization, as Douchan's various campaigns against the Greeks were successful. The alliance with the Bulgars was maintained unbroken, and only a very small part of the European possessions of the Emperors at Constantinople remained intact. Thrace and a strip of Asia Minor was all that was left; there was every reason to urge Douchan to proclaim his overlordship in the regular way. Accordingly, on April 16, 1346, Douchan was solemnly anointed Emperor (Tsar) of Servia and Roumania by the Servian Patriarch Joannikos, at Uskup.

The next step was the conquest of the imperial city on the Bosphorus. This could not be effected without a fleet; neither Thessalonika nor Constantinople could be taken as long as their ports were open. Douchan turned to the Venetians for help, but they refused to encourage the formation of a new great power on the Mediterranean. Besides, the Turks now barred the way, for Gallipoli had been garrisoned. The Osmanlis, therefore, held the key to the Dardanelles. Undeterred, however, by these changes, Douchan girded himself for a final attack on Constantinople, when death overtook him suddenly on the 20th of December, 1355.

His successor, Ourach, was only nineteen years old, a young man of mild character, with none of the stern qualities needed to carry out the warlike plans of his father. His vassal lords had not lived long enough under a centralized system to understand its advantages even under a weak ruler. Without the strong personality of Douchan, the empire and the titular dignity of Tsar were only shadows. Less fortunate than the tribe of Osman, where the line from father to son maintained in unbroken succession under strong personal rule the clear-sighted aims of the founder, the Servians could not resist the forces of disintegration. Their country was mountainous, and hence the people were kept apart in small, isolated communities. There was no longer a vigorous leader to resist the centrifugal tendencies imposed by petty ambitions and jealousies; and only for ten years after Douchan's death did the external form of his empire last. As a barrier against the Turkish conquerors in Europe the Servians proved utterly ineffective.

With the Slavs eliminated the brunt of resistance naturally fell upon the Greeks; but they were now only an emaciated remnant of a great and long enduring empire that had worn out the Arab and Saracen and had held the Slav at bay. After the fall of the Latin rule at Constantinople (1261), the city became the capital of the reconstructed Eastern Empire; but the scale of this restoration was much reduced from its original grandeur. There were four groups of imperial territories: the Asiatic possessions that had been controlled from Nicæa, economically important as trade centers, but not great in extent; in Europe, the capital and Thrace; some towns to the North, such as Adrianople, a part of Macedonia, the peninsula of Gallipoli, Chalcidice, and a part of Thessaly; certain islands in the Ægean, Rhodes, Lesbos, Samothrace, Imbros, and the Peloponnesus in Greece.

These possessions, the feeble remnants of the realm once ruled by Basil the Macedonian, were surrounded by lands inhabited by numerous races. There were the Frankish lands in Greece, the Venetians in the Ægean, an independent Greek sovereignty in Epirus, Catalans in Thessaly, Genoese in the Black and Ægean Seas, and the parts immediately adjacent to Constantinople itself; the Seldjouk sultans at Iconium, and the autonomous empire of Trebizond. There were also the Slavic peoples in the Balkan peninsula, not to mention the more distant Christian kingdoms of Armenia and Georgia.

As a military power the revived Greek Empire was pathetically feeble. Its last great leader in war was Michael VIII, who had retaken Constantinople from the Latins, a conquest on a slight scale, since the Latins were even weaker than their opponents. The measure of Greek offensive is attested by the inability of any Greek Emperor to retake the Asiatic provinces from the Turk, to annex the Empire of Trebizond, to resist the Slavs in the Balkans, or to reoccupy the islands of the Ægean and drive the Franks from Greece. Even in the interior there was no effective administration. In every Greek city there were colonies of Italian merchants, either Genoese or Venetian, who formed independent communities under their own podestà. The army was filled with foreign contingents, who were not even mercenary troops, because the Empire could not afford to hire soldiers. They were auxiliary forces, organized as complete military units under their own natural chief, and were a constant menace. When they saw fit, they pillaged the country and sometimes fought among themselves. They were under no kind of control from the central or local authorities; within their own camps on the frontiers, in the provinces, even under the walls of the capital itself, they obeyed their own commanders and not the Emperor.

One of the most radical changes for the worse in the revived Greek Empire, a change that marked the contrast with the heroic period of Byzantine military enterprise, was the lack of a fleet. For his naval operations the Emperor depended on the Venetians or Genoese, a most unsatisfactory arrangement, for, owing to the jealousy of these two commercial states, if one were the ally of Constantinople, the other was certain to be on the opposite side. In 1296 the Venetians, after defeating their rivals at sea, laid siege to the Pera and Galata sections of Constantinople, the seat of the Genoese colony, and in setting fire to the quarter destroyed many Greek houses. Later on, the Genoese revenged themselves by massacring the Venetian residents of Constantinople.

The anarchy was increased when, owing to rival claimants to the throne, open civil war broke out, as it did frequently in the course of the fourteenth century. Cantacuzene, an official in the imperial palace, who became rival Emperor, while Anna of Saxony was regent during the minority of her son, John V, after the death of his father, Andronicus III, allied himself with the Servians and with the Seldjouk emir of Konia. Anna tried to strengthen her side by calling upon Ourkhan, the Osmanli Sultan. In the war that followed the Turks were authorized to seize the citizens of the empire, and the rival governments placed at the disposition of their Mohammedan allies seaports and vessels. The captives taken were sent to Asia and sold as slaves in the Turkish emirates.

The various enemies of the Empire used this time of civil strife as a favorable opportunity for seizing its territory. Stephen Douchan conquered and annexed most of Macedonia, and, as their part of the spoil, the Genoese acquired Chios and commenced a blockade of Constantinople, the defense of which was intrusted to other Italians under the command of Facciolati. This leader deserted the cause of the regent Anna, and admitted Cantacuzene into the capital. An arrangement was now patched up by which Cantacuzene was to be Emperor until John V reached the age of twenty-five years.

Even now Cantacuzene's troubles as ruler were not over; his plan to form an independent navy recruited from his own subjects and his desire to do away with the commercial monopoly of the Genoese led to a war of five years, 1348-1352. Cantacuzene's Venetian allies were defeated under the walls of Constantinople, with the result that the Greek Emperor was obliged to make peace under most disadvantageous terms. Not long after this disaster civil war broke out again. Souliman, Ourkhan's son, was a subsidized ally of Cantacuzene, and thousands of the inhabitants of the Empire were deported by the Turks to be sold as slaves.

The lessons of these wars were not lost upon the Turkish auxiliaries who were allowed to play such a conspicuous and decisive rôle by both sides; they became acquainted with the country in which they had served, knew its roads, cities, and inhabitants. All this information was put to good use by them when they crossed the Bosphorus to fight for their own interests and to dispossess their former employers at Constantinople.

From the point of view of its economic status the Empire was in no condition to withstand an invasion. As territory was lost the proceeds of direct taxation fell off; increases in the customs duties were opposed and blocked by the Genoese and Venetians; the government lived from hand to mouth. In 1306 when the Catalan mercenaries had to be paid, Andronicus II put an end to the wheat monopoly exercised by the Italians. Another characteristic expedient of this weak government was the debasement of the coinage. But all the ordinary schemes for raising money must have failed by the middle of the century, for we find Anna of Saxony using the treasures of churches to pay for the war against Cantacuzene. Indeed, her court had reached a condition of extreme penury in 1347, when, at a coronation it was found that the imperial jewels had disappeared. The splendid buildings of the city were fast going to pieces. In Santa Sophia there were large cracks, which necessitated the erection of two of the existing great supporting buttresses that have enabled it to survive to our time the frequent earthquakes that disturb the city. In the absence of a centralized government the local administration lost all resemblance to the admirably constructed system of the earlier period of Byzantine rule when, as contrasted with Western Europe, it still preserved the efficiency and smoothness of Roman governmental traditions. The local authorities lived on the country, uncontrolled from Constantinople, except irregularly and ineffectively.

In reality, under the name of empire, all varieties of local organizations existed side by side; some places were ruled by petty tyrants, while others were municipal republics. In the important port of Thessalonika, Italian precedents were closely followed. Here there were four classes of citizens, the notables, the clergy, the bourgeois, and in the lowest class the "populari." Each class enjoyed complete autonomy. They were organized in trade corporations, had their own system of justice, and finally got supreme control of the town, turning it into a democracy under the presidency of their metropolitan. When Cantacuzene undertook to bring the rebels to reason, the archbishop, in pleading the cause of the city-state, declared that his republic was based on equality and justice, and said that its laws were better than those of the Republic of Plato.

There was another factor in this state of anarchy, to wit, the religious dissensions, due to the willingness of some of the clergy to accept union with the Papacy and to introduce Latin customs, an attitude dating from the time of the Latin Empire. Apart from these questions of ecclesiastical policy, there was much discussion of theological subtilties concerning the existence of a supernatural illumination in the soul, a controversy which divided the Church and the imperial court. This trouble was settled by a synod, which decreed that those espousing the new doctrine should be imprisoned.

In a land so situated and so far fallen from its earlier estate, the rapid conquests of the Osmanlis appear as due not so much to the valor and intelligence of the adherents of Islam as to the inability of the Christians to act or work together. The one security of the Empire was the comparative weakness of the Turkish sea power. The Ottoman ships were good enough for piratical expeditions, but there was no Turkish fleet at all able to cope with the navies of Genoa or Venice.

At the very beginning of Murad's accession, a consistent plan of attack was inaugurated, designed to cut off Constantinople from its "hinterland"; the objective being the trade road between the capital and Adrianople. Several of the important points on this line were taken, Murad making his residence temporarily near Demotika. According to Turkish custom, each spring brought a new expedition and a further enlargement of the existing boundaries. The siege of Adrianople itself soon began. (1360.) The Greek chronicles speak of its fall being due to a betrayal of a secret path used by peasants inside the walls to get to their fields. But the Turkish annals tell of an engagement between the garrison and the Osmanli soldiers. In the city Murad took up his residence, being attracted to it by its importance as a trading place frequented by Venetians, Genoese, Florentines, and Catalans, as well as by Turks and Greeks.

Following soon the course of the river Maritza, on which Adrianople stands, the Turkish invaders moved farther into the land until they came to Philippopolis, which had been taken by the Bulgars not long before. But the Slavs showed no greater capacity than the Greeks for united action, and the town was taken from them without difficulty. Other places were added, including Berrhœa on the Hæmus, and this whole section of country for some time made up the northermost borders of Ottoman dominion in Europe.

In the south the same kind of successes took place; again a trade route was selected, this time the road to Thessalonika, and a considerable stretch of the territory through which it passed was annexed. In one place the sea coast was reached at a point opposite the Island of Samothrace. Murad returned now to Broussa, interrupting a farther advance towards Trnova and Sofia, places in the hands of the Servians, whose power in war he respected and feared more than that of their allied race, the Bulgars.

The menace caused by the Ottoman conquests was now being appreciated in Western Europe, where, through the preaching of a crusade by Urban V, a league was formed between Louis of Anjou, King of Hungary, and several of the most powerful princes of the Balkan peninsula, both Roumanian and Slav, for the purpose of driving out the Turks from their newly acquired European possessions. With an army of 60,000 men the Christian leaders reached the river Maritza, two days' journey from Adrianople. Murad was in Asia, besieging a Greek city on the Propontis, but he was not needed, since a small detachment of the army of his general, Lala-Schahin, came in contact with the Christians near Kermianon, and put them to flight in a panic, in which the two Servian leaders lost their lives. (1371.)

This victory is set down in the Servian records as a great national disaster, and deservedly so. It ended their resistance, and it handed over to the Turks the rest of Thrace, Bulgaria, and a part of Servia. Significant of the impression made by the conquest was the action of the people of Ragusa, who signed a treaty of peace, inspired by a desire to gain commercial advantages from the new Turkish conquests. They agreed to pay an annual tribute of 500 golden ducats, and thus they inaugurated a policy imitated by many of their stronger neighbors, who preferred to make a good bargain with the Ottomans rather than try the fortunes of war under the auspices of rival Christian states, whose political aggrandizement, in case a victory were won over the infidel, was dreaded even more than the expansion of an alien race.

Yet the theory of a united Christendom was maintained despite its pitiable outcome in the Balkans. Elsewhere there were brilliant feats of arms, but they were isolated, and being directed by no consistent plan, proved of no lasting advantage. Peter of Cyprus, a representative of the Latin dynasty which had held the island since the days of the earlier Crusades, regarded himself as the guardian of Christian hopes in the Orient because of his titular dignity of King of Jerusalem. He took Alexandria in 1365, and helped by Rhodes, Genoa, and contingents sent by the Pope, he later took Satalieh (Attalia), a place situated in one of the Seldjouk emirates. Some advantages were gained, too, on the coast of Syria.

There was little chance of permanent success so long as the princes and states of the West with their divergent interests, dynastic or commercial, confronted such a solidly compacted power as that raised up by Osman. The Turks had a single aim, simple and direct, and they kept hammering away at their enemies, putting in telling blows at the right moment and the right place. On the other hand, the Christian cause suffered both from the leadership of the Papacy, with its rigid insistence on establishing Western ecclesiastical rule in the East, and from the sordid self-seeking of the Genoese and Venetians. From both points of view the conquest of the Greek Empire was generally regarded as a necessary preliminary for making headway in the restoration of Christian control over the Holy Land.

The hard case of the Eastern Emperor, whose few remaining possessions were in the fast-closing grip of the Ottoman Sultan, is sketched indelibly in the narrative of the Western journey of John V, who, while the Turks were absorbing the Slavic lands about his empire, visited Rome to ask the Pope's aid. In the desperate state of his resources he had borrowed at Venice, at exorbitant rates of interest, money to pay the expenses of his trip. On his return empty-handed he was stayed at Venice by his creditors, and the republic put him in prison. His son, Andronicus, associated with his father in the Empire, had been left behind at Constantinople. When the Emperor appealed to him for aid, the reply came that the treasury was empty. The unfortunate sovereign appealed with more success to a younger son, Manuel, who mortgaged his estates and enabled his father to return home.

In May, 1372, the Pope again took the initiative in organizing an anti-Ottoman league by writing to the Republic of Venice and the King of Hungary a letter which described the achievements of the "Saracens" in Thrace, their defeat of the "Servian lords in Greek lands," and the prospects of a farther advance of the infidel towards the Adriatic. Bad news had come from Greece, too, of the possibility of the Turkish invaders penetrating towards the south. A congress of the Balkan states was called to meet at Thebes, a place under Frankish and Roman Catholic rule; and it was a significant fact that no member of the Eastern Church was asked to be present. A gathering of such a restricted character could do nothing. There were at Thebes only a few representatives of the small Latin principalities in Continental Greece and the islands. Immediately after this gathering the Byzantine clergy put forth in Constantinople a formal protest against the See of Rome and appealed for help to the Knights of Rhodes.

Peter of Cyprus had been murdered by his barons in 1369, and the island had fallen into the hands of the Genoese. In 1374 the small Frankish kingdom of Armenia, an enclave between the Turkish and Mongol lands in Asia, had come to an end with the capture of Sis. In 1378 the great church schism in the West brought about a situation that prevented the Papacy from taking further thought for what was now left of the Christian East. Four years later Louis of Hungary died, leaving his kingdom, a land especially interested in preventing the extension of Turkish power in Europe, a prey to a civil war induced by the division he had made of his dominions between his two daughters. There was no longer even the semblance of a chance that European forces would unite on a large scale to resist the Turks. The contest was left to the weak and divided efforts of the small Frankish states in Greece; to the Bulgars and Servians in the Balkans, who followed only desultory, haphazard methods, and to the Greeks of the Empire, who were living on the traditions of a great past.

Meanwhile, the Osmanlis were not disturbed by questions of religious orthodoxy, and they were also spared the necessity of calling congresses to decide the next step in their stealthy progress. In 1372, under the personal supervision of Murad, expeditions were made by which the whole of Roumelia to the Black Sea was not only made subject to his rule, but Moslem families were settled in the conquered lands and a regularly ordered system of local military government provided. Then came the turn of the few remaining provinces still held by the Greek Emperor. When Vizya (in Turkish, Wissa), an important city, fell into Murad's hands, John, whose bitter necessities had forced him to pay tribute to the Turk and even to furnish a contingent for military service, tried to recover his lost city. A punitive expedition appeared in consequence near Constantinople, and some strong castles were annexed; but nothing near the sea coast was taken, for the Sultan had no desire to bring down upon himself the ill will of the Venetians and other Italians, who would not tolerate any interference in their control of the important waterways near Constantinople. For the same reason, though constant additions were being made to Turkish territory close to Thessalonika, no attempt was made to close in on the city for fear of complications with the Latin powers, complications which might excite such an outbreak of the crusading ardor that the Italian navies might be used.

Considerably more important were the operations of the Sultan's lieutenant, Lala-Schahin. There were internal dissensions between the Bulgars and the Roumanian Layko, a feudatory of the King of Hungary. Allying himself with Layko, Lala-Schahin succeeded in capturing Sofia, and for a while even Nisch was occupied. No attempt was as yet made by the Slavs after their earlier defeat to protect themselves on a large scale. At this point the method and aim of the pacific penetration policy of the Sultan, which alternated with carefully devised methods of military aggression, can be seen in the picturesque story of the plot entered into by Andronicus, the son of John the Emperor, and Sandschi, the son of Murad, to take the lives and the crowns of their respective fathers. The conspiracy was detected and defeated, and the young Turkish prince died from the effect of having hot vinegar poured in his eyes. Andronicus, escaping from his prison, after the common Byzantine penalty of blinding his sight had been, perhaps intentionally, inflicted with such mildness that he regained it, made a treaty with the Genoese and with Murad. He agreed to confer special privileges on the Turks if they would help to secure for him the imperial crown. For three years the usurpation lasted, and John and his faithful son Manuel were only restored to their rights by Murad's friendly connivance, which was secured by the promise of 3000 ducats a year. Of less value must have been the additional agreement that the Byzantine princes would serve in the Sultan's army.

Andronicus had fled to the Turkish lines and, through the intervention of Murad, he received later Thessalonika as an appanage. He was aided by the Genoese, while his father had as allies the Venetians, a division of interests out of which grew the celebrated naval war, called that of Chioggia, between the two rival cities of Italy. Murad preferred to keep quiet while the two Italian naval powers were in force in his neighborhood, and he devoted himself with much sagacity to fishing in the troubled waters of the Asiatic emirates, with results both in war and diplomacy that were eminently satisfactory.

In 1387 after there had been such successes of the Turks to record as the surrender of Monastir, and Prilep, and Schtip, and even the temporary seizure of Thessalonika, the Servians undertook, under the direction of a feudal lord, Lazar, to organize a systematic plan of resistance. Lazar was first aided by a Bosnian king, Tourtko, who had, however, ambitious designs on certain lands under the Hungarian crown, designs that soon robbed his promised co-operation of its influence. Schischman of Bulgaria was drawn into the league, and in Lazar's army there appeared also contingents of Albanians and Roumanians standing side by side with the Slavs. The crisis was fully appreciated by Murad. He summoned new troops from Asia, and all the greatest generals took part in the campaign, in addition to his two sons, Bajesid and Jakab. The decisive battle was fought on ground that was part of Lazar's own domains near Prischtina, on the wide plains called Kossowopolje. Murad was surrounded by his band of Janitschars; to hold back the enemy the camels of the Asiatic troops were drawn up in front. The Christians were confident in their superior number, for they had 200,000 men under arms ready to begin the attack.

From a contemporary account comes the narrative of the death of the Sultan. It is there told how ten young men of distinguished birth, bound by oath to stand by one another, succeeded in forcing their way to the tent of Murad. One of these, Mulasch Obilitsch, managed to inflict two fatal wounds on the neck and body of the aged ruler. But this successful stroke did not end the fight, for Bajesid, who was renowned for the rapidity and daring of his generalship, drove his wing of the Ottoman army into the Christian ranks, broke through them, and put them to flight at the very moment they thought themselves victorious. It is said that in the panic Lazar lost his life; probably he was captured and subsequently sacrificed in revenge for the murder of Murad. (June 15, 1389.)

Both armies withdrew after the battle. Murad's fate made him a martyr to the faith, and he is one of the Sahibs or Elect of Islam. Even the Greeks praise his character as being benevolent towards the conquered, whom he understood how to win over to his side after he had conquered them by the irresistible force of his arms. He laid the foundations of the Moslem state, adapting it shrewdly for rule over conquered populations. They were accepted as tenants of the new owners of the soil, paying tithes. The Sultan himself received the Kharadsch or tribute money. At the same time the subject races retained their faith, their customs, their church, their courts, and their aristocracy. The warrior class was made up of native Turks and some renegades. These became the sole owners of the land and had to take their place in the regular yearly campaigns. There was, besides, a standing army of young foot soldiers composed of captives taken in war, the Janitschar class, who looked up to the Sultan as their father. For administrative progress there was a corps of officials, whose functions descended from father to son, composed of "Begs." At the top of this bureaucracy was a Beglerbeg for each half of the kingdom, one for Asia and one for Europe, and a Wesir or Pascha, the equivalent in Turkish of the former word, which is Arabic. The administrative divisions under the Begs were called Sandjaks (flags) because these were carried by the Begs as emblems of their authority.

The battle of Kossovo, in which both opposing armies lost their leaders, became in Servian folklore and poetry a source of inspiration of the kind that among Romance peoples gathers about the defeat of Charles the Great in the Pyrenees and the death of Roland. The incidents of the heroic theme take up the tragedy of the battle; Slavic improvisers sing of the death of Lazar, of his father-in-law, the aged King, and his nine brothers-in-law. Mulasch, the slayer of Murad, who met his death in the flight, is not passed over, nor the 12,000 infidels who perished. Like Murad, Lazar, the "Servian crown of gold," is celebrated as a martyr of his faith, a hero who went voluntarily to his death. The legend tells how St. Elias, in the form of a falcon, came from the Holy City of Jerusalem, bringing him a letter from the Mother of God, in which he was offered the choice of the heavenly empire or dominion over the earth. Lazar made the choice which gave him the spiritual kingdom.

III

BAJESID

The first act of Bajesid's accession was the murder of his younger brother, whom he summoned to his presence and caused to be strangled. This deed left Bajesid the sole representative of the house of Osman; there was no rival now for him to fear. He wished to stand alone as creator of his own statecraft, for he refused to respect any of the arrangements or conventions made by Murad. His own ideal was foreign to the loose feudalized system previously established; he desired to clear away all the dependent dynasties, and to substitute for them officers of his own, directly controlled by him.

The first important military operation of the new reign was directed against Mircea, a Roumanian lord, who had seized and occupied Nicopolis, lately surrendered to Ali-Pascha, Murad's vizier, by Schischman, before the battle of Kossovo. All the vassals were called under arms to follow the Sultan, who crossed the Danube to where Mircea was awaiting his attack in a position difficult of access on account of roads and swamps. No details of the fight are given, but Bajesid was the victor. (October 10, 1394.) Mircea fled to the Carpathians.

As one result of their victory the Turks left Bucharest in the hands of an Ottoman garrison under the direction of a Roumanian Boyar Vlad, who was appointed to take the place of Mircea, because of the latter's failure to perform the obligations of a faithful vassal, though he had met with generous treatment from Bajesid after the battle of Kossovo. He was not present at the battle itself, but rendered himself liable to punishment by sending armed contingents of his own men to help the Christian cause. He had been captured and exiled to Broussa; but he was released on condition of paying a small tribute, and retained his right of sovereignty over his subjects. More remarkable still, Bajesid had undertaken not to permit any Turks to establish themselves in Wallachia, or to found mosques in Mircea's country. By presuming on this favorable and exceptional treatment, Mircea again had brought himself into the status of an exile.

Sigismund of Hungary saw the necessity of helping his unfortunate neighbor Mircea with the Turks so close at hand. Moreover, the Hungarian ruler's relations with Western Europe, through his connection with the house of Luxembourg, and his inheritance from Prince Louis of Anjou, placed him in a good position to appeal to the warlike lords and knights of France to aid him against infidel aggression. He turned also to the Republic of Venice as a partner in the undertaking, but the prudent merchants of that commonwealth showed no immediate interest in the projected crusade.

The movement initiated from Hungary put heart into the Byzantines, who, because of the change from the mild Murad to the relentless Bajesid, were now hard pressed in the small corner of territory still left them. There was moral depression as well, for Manuel II, when made co-Emperor with his aged father John, had been obliged to accompany the Sultan in all his campaigns with a contingent. This obligation revealed the desperate straits of the Greek Empire, especially as the contingent numbered only a hundred men. One Greek city, Philadelphia, the single imperial possession in Asia Minor, had been attacked by Bajesid because the citizens refused to receive a Turkish garrison, though John had previously agreed to surrender it to Murad. Among the other vassals who were called to take part in this campaign were Stephen, Prince of the Servians, and Manuel, the Byzantine Emperor. As a further sign of dependence on the Sultan's will, who seemed bent on devising schemes to humiliate the miserable Greek prince, Manuel had been forced to help to repair the fortifications of Gallipoli, and also to coöperate with the Turks in their preparations to send expeditions to Attica and some of the islands of the Ægean. When John V began to restore some of the ruined fortifications around the imperial city, Bajesid ordered him to desist, threatening, if the command were not obeyed, to deprive Manuel of his sight, for the heir, and co-Emperor, was, as usual, doing duty as a vassal in one of the Turkish military expeditions.

On the death of John V, in 1391, Manuel was allowed to succeed to the title, and, officially, good relations were observed between the Sultan and the ruler of Constantinople. Bajesid, however, had no intention of permitting Manuel, whom he knew to be a man of ability and decision, to gain any new ground. The few places contiguous to Constantinople, over which the Greeks still ruled, were constantly being harassed by Ottoman aggressions. Manuel was really being besieged in his own capital. His constant appeals for help were made in vain; the Venetians found it commercially more advantageous to draw closer to the Osmanlis, especially since Bajesid, by absorbing various emirates in Asia Minor, was in control of important trading towns on that coast. A treaty was concluded between the two powers, and the Venetians went so far as to deny their help to the Frankish lords of the Ægean, and were preparing to weaken continental Greece by efforts to gain territory in that quarter at the expense of the Greek master of the Morea, a son of the Emperor.

While Sigismund was seeking allies in the West against the Turks, and Bajesid was elaborating plans for an invasion of the whole country south of his European holdings, Thessalonika was retaken from the Greeks. Without much difficulty Turkish troops in a raid westward penetrated into the Morea, or Peloponnesus, itself, though a wall had been built by the Venetians across the Isthmus. No permanent settlement was made, but still the country suffered, for many of the inhabitants were sold, and, during the course of the expedition, many cities of Greece experienced, for the first time, the barbarism of a Turkish invasion. This expedition to the south was like so many others under the command of the local "Begs," because Bajesid himself was bent on completing the conquest of Bulgaria. After a long siege Tirnovo was taken by assault; its churches were sacked, and it was, in general, made an example by the ruthless conqueror. Even the dead were left unburied. Along with a multitude of prisoners, the Bulgarian Patriarch was taken to Asia. As to Sischman, he is reputed to have died, either on the battlefield or in captivity; his capital, which had been the residence of the Bulgar Tsars since 1200, sank to the level of a small market town, though once it had been famous for its beautiful buildings, constructed to rival or imitate those of Constantinople. Bulgaria, already a poor fragment of its original extent after the first stage of the invasion, now ceased altogether to exist as a Slav state.

At this disastrous conjuncture for the Christian cause (1394), Sigismund of Hungary intervened by sending representatives to Bajesid to ask by what right he had destroyed Bulgaria. As an answer to the delegation, Bajesid is said to have shown the bows and arrows which decorated the hall of audience. Long anticipating the warlike aims of the Hungarian King, Bajesid made ready to complete the siege of Constantinople, and so to prevent any coöperation between the Greeks and the Christian power farther north. Sigismund, who, as we have mentioned, had relied on his influence in the West to get aid adequate to the undertaking he had in hand, now knew that his embassy which had visited France had been well received by the King, Charles VI, and his great nobles, many of whom had agreed to take up arms. As head of the expedition, John the Fearless, son of the Duke of Burgundy, had been selected; there were gathered round him many well-known lords as counselors, and a contingent of 10,000 men, foot and horse. Besides these, there were contingents of knights from Germany, Luxembourg, England, Switzerland, and the Low Countries. Even Venice was induced to supply galleys and money for the cause. The Knights of Rhodes sent their fleet and their Grand Master with it. The Slavs of Poland and the Roumanians also joined the crusade. Even Manuel took heart and promised to keep some of the Turkish army occupied by making an offensive movement.

In July, 1396, the various contingents from the Occident met the Hungarian and Roumanian armies at Bada. Mircea, who had had personal experience with the Turkish military power, advised, with the wisdom that comes from defeat, a policy of defensive action, that the allies should wait for Bajesid's advance into Hungary. But this dilatory program was not acceptable to the Western knights, who declared that they were there to fight, not to waste time in the inaction of a camp. Accordingly the army went down the Danube to Ossovo, and the river was crossed near the so-called Iron Gates.

After winning some initial successes in a land where only the garrisons were Turkish, the crusaders, on September 12, reached Nicopolis, a place well fortified and strongly held by a veteran Ottoman general, Dogon-beg, who commanded a garrison of seasoned troops. At first the French knights tried to take the place by storm; but there were not enough ladders. It was, therefore, resolved to starve it out. The siege was in progress when Bajesid arrived from Constantinople. When he heard of the danger of his general he burnt his siege machines and hastened to Nicopolis. The crusaders would not at first believe that the Sultan was marching upon them; those who first reported the news in the camp were treated as spies and had their ears cut off. When it was found to be true, the Christians massacred the prisoners already taken.

In preparing for the battle there was a fatal diversity of views. Sigismund wished to put Mircea's men in the first line, since they were not regarded as good warlike material; next to this division he wished to station the

Hungarians, and then, as the chief support of the whole, the knights from the West. But the French would hear nothing of this plan, which they regarded as equivalent to an insult; the place in front belonged, they thought, to them by right. A few of the most experienced counselors of John of Burgundy agreed with Sigismund, but nothing could be done to persuade the mass of the French warriors to give way. In the Ottoman army there were no differences of opinion; the Sultan's vassals were answerable to his command, and, it is to be noted, that Stephen, the young Servian despot, with a contingent of trained warriors, fought for Bajesid against the crusaders. But with this exception the Sultan's army, in all reckoned at 110,000, was composed of Moslem troops. Out of the 110,000 ranged on the other side, there were about 20,000 crusaders, of whom 16,000 were French. These, with the bravado that came from the traditions of western chivalry, undertook to bear the brunt of the fighting. Sigismund again tried to secure the adoption of his more cautious plan, but without result. The constable of France, Count d'Eu, gave the signal to advance, and the French knights moved to the onslaught with cries of "Vive St. Denis, Vive St. George." Sigismund's army, composed of trusty Transylvanians, Hungarians, and Tschechs, was in the center, and on the right wing behind the crusaders, while Mircea's men made up the left. The Turks were drawn up in three lines; in the first were irregular troops, "akindji" and "azabs," and a body of mercenaries; in the second Asiatic foot soldiers flanked by two squadrons of "spahis"; behind were stationed what might be called the guard regiments, the Janitschars and the spahis of the Porte; a short distance away in individual formation stood the 5000 Servians under Stephen.

In their reckless dash forward the knights carried everything before them, the irregulars first, and Janitschars afterwards, though these were protected by a line of inclined pointed stakes. The horsemen had no difficulty in leaping over these obstacles, and made fearful execution with their swords on the Turks in the level plain. But, while the French were driving through their enemies in front like a flying wedge, the Turks on the two wings were reforming to make an inclosing movement around the knights. As these could not withdraw, they continued the charge right into the second line of Bajesid, where they put "hors de combat" five thousand Turks. But by this time both men and horses were exhausted, and the ranks were broken. The more cautious leaders advised Count d'Eu to fall back on the Hungarians for support, but he gave orders to renew the charge. The third line of the enemy could not, however, be broken; the Western crusaders were being overwhelmed by fresh bodies of Ottomans.

The Frenchmen might have been aided easily by their allies behind them, but at this moment Mircea, with his Wallachians and the Transylvanian contingent, suddenly deserted the field. This cowardly action threw the rest of the army into a panic. Soon Sigismund was left with but a fraction of his army, the men from the Christian lands in the East lent no aid, nor did they stand their ground. The Hungarian King advanced to rescue the Western crusaders, but a charge made by the Servians, who had as yet kept out of the battle, prevented the union of the now separated portions of the Christian army. The French, though left alone, performed great feats of arms, fighting, as the chronicles say, like mad wolves and frothing boars. Gathering together in small groups of eight or ten, the knights, using their long swords, fortified themselves behind the heaps of dead and wounded Turks. It was told how the standard of the Virgin, defended by John de Vienne and his companions, was six times struck to the ground, only to be proudly lifted again until the heroic Frenchman himself fell, still clasping in his arms the tattered standard. Sigismund also fought desperately, but there was no escape except by retreating northward to the Danube, where the galleys of Rhodes and Venice took on board what was left of the great army of the crusaders.

The splendid equipment of the Western knights furnished Bajesid with immense spoil; but it was a dear victory. From thirty to forty thousand of his men lay dead on the field, as a witness to the prowess of French chivalry. Wherever the French fought, the chronicles record that "for one Christian of those who lay dead on the field, there were thirty Turks or more, or other men of that faith." Maddened by his losses, the Sultan ordered his prisoners to be killed. The massacre went on all day; 2000 were executed; only those escaped who were likely to be ransomed for large sums, and a few prisoners whose age was less than twenty years. It was the soldiers' greed rather than the Sultan's clemency which brought the butchery to an end.

When the news of the defeat was received at Paris, there was universal mourning. Then an embassy was sent, with rich presents for the Sultan, to arrange the ransom of the prisoners. The amount settled upon was 200,000 florins. The Western ambassadors were treated with great courtesy and magnificent entertainments were provided for their amusement. In parting from one of the distinguished captives, John the Fearless, son of the Duke of Burgundy, Bajesid said, "I do not wish to require from you the oath not to bear arms against me again; if, when you return home, you still find yourself in the humor for fighting me, you will find me always ready to meet you on the field of battle, for I am born for war and conquest." As presents for Charles VI of France, in exchange for those that had been sent him, he despatched by the French envoys various warlike accouterments, among others a drum and bowstrings, made of human flesh.

The fancifulness of the Turk was also seen by his sending with those who made the formal announcement of his victory to the Moslem princes of Asia and Egypt, the Western prisoners all equipped in their heavy armor to enable the leaders of his own faith to understand the significance of his success. As a result of the battle of Nicopolis, Bosnia, Bulgaria, and Roumania accepted Ottoman rule; at the same time the adjoining lands of the Hungarian King became the field of Turkish raids.

Constantinople was in a perilous situation, but an attempt to take it failed (1398). Less fortunate, as has been seen, were the inhabitants of continental Greece, who saw Argos taken, and the country of the Peloponnesus ravaged by Bajesid. The troubles of the imperial city were not relieved by Bajesid's failure to capture it, for by the instigation of the Turks, John, the nephew of

Manuel, became a claimant for the crown, and at the head of 10,000 Ottoman troops marched on the city. The result was that Manuel agreed to take his nephew as associate in the Empire, a term which now had only a technical significance, for the imperial dignity meant little more than the rule over Constantinople itself. Bajesid refused to allow this arrangement unless further concessions were made, such as the establishment of a fourth mosque in the city, and the same local autonomy for the Turkish colony as that enjoyed by the Venetians and Genoese. Manuel refused and appealed to Western Christendom. France again showed its sympathy by sending a survivor of the Nicopolis campaign, a knight, Boucicout, who, with only 1200 men, forced the entrance of the Dardanelles, and afterwards won a minor success in Asia, though he failed in his attempt to take Nicodemia. Manuel tried, as his father had done, a personal visit to the West, and remained nearly two years in France. Bajesid, in the meantime, was encircling Constantinople with his fleet and armies, when the situation suddenly changed, owing to the expansion of a new power in the Orient.

The emirates of those Seldjouks, who had survived absorption by the Ottomans, had, at the close of the fourteenth century, formed a defensive alliance against Bajesid, but they were not successful. The Sultan seized their best provinces, and, when they resorted to arms, defeated the Seldjoukian emirs on the battlefield. Gradually the Ottoman dominions were approaching the Euphrates, by which they were brought near the frontier of the newly-organized Mongol empire, the creation of the great conqueror Timur. The growth of bad feeling between the two rival powers was accentuated, when each sovereign began to receive with favor the rebellious vassals of the other. Timur sent to the Sultan a threatening letter, which was answered in the temper in which it was couched. Timur's reply was to cross the frontier, and this step was followed up by the capture of the important town of Sivas. All the inhabitants were massacred, the Christians in it being burned alive, and the governor of the place, a son of the Sultan, was strangled. Timur turned from his invasion of the south to attack Angora with the purpose of drawing the Turks into a trap. He succeeded, for he had between two and three hundred thousand men, while Bajesid, to oppose him, had only 120,000. A great battle took place on July 20, 1402, which ended most disastrously for the Turks, because the Seldjoukians went over to the enemy. Bajesid was captured, and two of his sons were killed. Much of the land to the west was overrun by the Mongols, but a permanent organization of the Mongol Empire was made impossible because of the death of Timur on February 19, 1405. Bajesid had also died of a broken heart, after his terrible defeat.

IV

MURAD II

This change of fortune meant much for the Greek Empire. Manuel took courage, deprived the Turks of their privileges at Constantinople, and making use of the divisions among the successors of Bajesid, succeeded in regaining a part of the territories that had been lost. For some years the Ottomans, under Mohammed, were engaged in regaining their position in Asia; in Europe the tables were reversed. The empire of the Ottomans seemed to be on the point of going through a process of disintegration similar to that experienced by their predecessors of the same race, the Seldjouks. When it was defunct its residuary legatee might well be the Greek Empire.

There were now many Ottoman princes, no longer one sultan. Souliman, who reigned at Adrianople, sought the protection of Manuel, gave him as a hostage one of his sisters, married a niece of the Emperor, restored part of Macedonia and Ionia, and yielded up Thessalonika, the greatest prize of all. When he was succeeded by his brother Mousa, there was an outbreak of hostilities; Thessalonika was again lost by the Greeks, but soon retaken, while a Turkish fleet was resisted by a fleet now manned by Greek sailors; for Manuel had taken care to provide for a navy, and was no longer dependent on the commercial cities of Italy. Mohammed was summoned by Manuel from Asia as an ally against Mousa, and the two succeeded in defeating him. On his capture he met death at Mohammed's hands.

For the next eight years (1413-1421) Mohammed was sole ruler of the Osmanlis, but internal difficulties hindered aggressive action on his part, so far as the Christian powers were concerned. His policy was decidedly philhellenic, Manuel receiving from his hands important territories on the Black Sea and the Propontis; but his main attention was directed to the Asiatic provinces, where, in addition to troubles with the emir of Karamania, there were disturbances, due to religious agitations in Islam. One of the chief agitators was a converted Jew, Torlak-Hin-Kemali, a preacher of the revolutionary doctrines of liberty and equality, who demanded a division of property. This communistic teaching stirred up the masses of the people, and excited the active sympathy of the dervish party.

On the death of Mohammed, his son, Murad II, took up the succession. He was a prince of energy and ability, who devoted himself for thirty years to the restoration of the Empire. The Greek Emperor Manuel still carried on his policy of sowing dissension among the Turks, but with less success than in the preceding period. Mustafa, an uncle of the new Sultan, became the ally of the Greeks, and Gallipoli, the first place taken by the Turks in Europe, was besieged. Murad hastened personally to save the town from capture. His uncle was taken, beaten, and hanged. Murad undertook then to lay siege to Constantinople, this making the fourth time that the city had been threatened by Ottoman armies. (June, 1422.)

The besiegers were a motley host; mixed with the soldiers were dervishes, marabouts (religious teachers), artisans, and peasants, all drawn together by the hope of sacking the rich capital.

They showed much improvement in the siege-methods employed, for they used wooden towers, and tried to get into the city through the aqueduct. The Greek armies were beaten in front of the walls, but Manuel and his son, John, soon found a way for causing the withdrawal of Murad's army, by inviting over from Asia another son of Mohammed, to whom his brother had intrusted the government of one of the Asiatic provinces. He was ceremoniously received in the city, and as soon as it was known in the Turkish camp that he was on his way to the west, Murad withdrew to Adrianople.

This siege is signalized in the chronicles by a narrative of the miraculous appearance of the Virgin on the walls of the city, the very day a general assault had been ordered. The Ottomans, panic-stricken, it is said, hastened to retreat. Both Christians and Mohammedans accepted the authenticity of the apparition, which is not surprising, since, in the ranks of the Sultan's army, there were large numbers of men who had been converted to Islam, but who could not throw aside the religious habits of mind of medieval Christians.

Peace was made on conditions extremely favorable to the Greeks. There was still a tribute to be paid, but some territory that had been taken in the campaign was restored. When Manuel died in 1425 he left six sons, all of whom were in positions of command. One of them, John VIII, was his successor as Emperor, the others were ruling parts of the empire at Thessalonika and farther south.

One of the first acts of the new administration was to endeavor to placate the Turks by restoring some of the towns on the Black Sea. But the efforts at pacification were of no avail. The Morea was invaded by one of the Sultan's generals, Tourakhan-beg, whose progress was not effectively contested, except by the Albanian colonies. The inhabitants of these were, however, mercilessly slaughtered, and on the site of the razed towns the Turks erected pyramids of the heads of their victims. In the north, too, there was successful fighting on the part of the Ottomans, both with the Roumanians and the Bulgarians, and even with the Hungarians, whose King, Sigismund, was defeated near the walls of Kolunbitz.

In 1430, Murad took charge of the attack on Thessalonika, now in the possession of the Venetians, who had taken it from the Greek prince Andronicus. The activity of Venice at this time is in decided contrast to the cautious policy displayed by the republic in the previous century. For one thing, the secular contest with Genoa had been decided in favor of the Adriatic port. Then, too, the objections of the Venetians to occupy continental possessions had been overcome by the exigencies of Italian politics, which had forced Venice to play a larger rôle in advancing her especial interests than ever before. It seemed for a time as if the Venetians would become the natural heirs to the territories of the Eastern Empire in the lands of peninsular Greece, while to the north Hungary had risen to be the main power, around which the Roumanian and Slavic races gathered as their natural protector against the Turk. From now on the establishment of the Ottoman power in Europe would depend on the overthrow of both the Venetians and the Hungarians. The former, as has just been intimated, were slowly and diplomatically acquiring Greek principalities in the south of continental Greece, but were striving, at the same time, not to bear the brunt of Turkish hostility. They relied partly on the strong fleet which had been sent to the East, and partly on the care they had taken to secure the aid of the Hungarians. On the other hand, the Turks had been developing their navy, and they ventured, as early as 1428, to attack merchant vessels belonging to the republic.

The fall of Thessalonika precipitated events and caused the Venetians to recognize that quick action was necessary. The republic entered into relations with the King of Cyprus and with the dissatisfied vassal princes of Karamania, who were ever ready to rebel against the Sultan. Proposals were made to King Sigismund to inaugurate a new crusade, in which he would have charge of the land forces, while the Venetians, keeping the mastery of the sea, would prevent new troops from being sent over from Asia. Unhappily, Sigismund proved apathetic; there were disturbances in the Albanian lands owned by Venice, and a war with Genoa kept the Venetians from having a free hand to deal effectively with the Sultan. Accordingly, a peace was patched up, by the terms of which Venice paid a tribute to the Turks for some of her Greek possessions.

Plundering expeditions were now made by the Turks into Hungarian territory, but before Sigismund could undertake military operations on his side his death occurred. (December 9, 1437.) The work of defense was then undertaken by his successor and son-in-law, Albert. For the first time the Sultan in person led an army in the region of the Carpathians and the Danube, and, although a coalition was formed, consisting of Hungarians, Servians, and Wallachians, the Turkish arms proved, as so often, irresistible. Semendria was taken, and many thousands of prisoners were carried away from the ravaged countries. But Belgrade held out, though Albert died there among his troops on October 27, 1438.

Strong hands were found ready to take up the work of defense. In the city, which was amply protected by a threefold wall, and by many pieces of artillery mounted on the ramparts, there was a garrison of German mercenaries, while in other regions exposed to the invaders, there were Hungarian forces under the command of Johann Hunyadi, the son of a Roumanian peasant of Inidora, whose reputation as a national hero was soon to be made in the victorious leadership of his people against the Turk.

Hunyadi's first aggressive act was an invasion into Bosnia, where he drove out some marauding bands of the Turkish general Isa-beg. A much more important military exploit was the battle of Szt-Imre, where, in 1442 (March 18), the Turks were forced back into Wallachia. Attempts made somewhat later to avenge this humiliation had no final success, for Hunyadi attacked the invading army on its march, winning a victory conspicuous because many well-known Ottoman generals lost their lives.

Spurred by the prowess of Hunyadi, the Western powers prepared to support him in driving the Ottomans from Europe. There was additional ground for hope in the arrangements, lately made, for a union between the Eastern and Western churches, a scheme naturally regarded as a good basis for coöperation against the Moslems. A new crusade was proclaimed, but nothing was accomplished by it, since the Venetians feared the loss of their possessions in the East, if the Slavic races were too actively aided, and since the Pope had no inclination to part with the tithes collected for the crusade, while he had use for them in protecting his temporal sovereignty as an Italian prince.

The Hungarians, left for these sinister reasons to deal with the Turks single-handed, displayed no lack of resolution. Hunyadi, with troops of Roumanians and Hungarians, passed the Danube late in October, 1443. He soon occupied Nisch and defeated several Ottoman armies, but the campaign had no decisive result, for Hunyadi feared to penetrate farther into Turkish territory without additional forces, especially as Murad was now in personal command. This caution was justified, for, in withdrawing, the Christian army suffered a reverse. The Hungarians could congratulate themselves that their advance had given great encouragement wherever the pressure of the Turkish occupation was felt. Yet there was no sincere effort on the part of the Christian powers to work together. The Servians made their own terms with the Sultan, and the Venetian fleet, ostensibly despatched to eastern waters to act with the Hungarians, was put under the command of Loredano, who had private instructions to come to terms with the Turks.

The story of a peace concluded on terms most humiliating for Murad, by which, among other things, the whole of Bulgaria and Servia was evacuated, is rightly questioned. All that is known is that Wladislaw, who was now King of Hungary (1440), solemnly protested that he would undertake a crusade against the Turks, all treaties and truces to the contrary notwithstanding. The expedition was begun, Hunyadi coöperating, and Papal legates testifying, by their presence, that a true crusade was in progress. But, although the army stood for the cause of the whole of Christendom, in the ranks there were almost none but Hungarian soldiers. It crossed the Danube, intending to march straight to Varna, and from there proceed by sea to Constantinople. But it was far too small for the work it planned to do; even after it had been joined by Vlad of Wallachia, it only numbered 15,000 men. Before Varna could be taken, Murad (at the head of an army of 40,000 men) hastened from Asia to arrest the progress of the crusaders. In the engagement that followed all efforts to break through the Janitschars, even when attempted under the experienced leadership of Hunyadi, failed completely, and the Christians suffered a decisive overthrow. Only a few of the 15,000 escaped, among them Hunyadi and Vlad. Among the dead were the King of Hungary and a Papal legate. (October, 1444.)

The news of this disaster took some time to reach the West, and by the time it was known there, information was also received that the indefatigable Hunyadi was again girding himself up for a second expedition. This ended with some small advantages in Wallachia. Again, in 1448, he tried another mode of entrance into the Sultan's territory, passing this time among the Albanians, on whose aid he reckoned without avail, since they were fighting on their own account against the Turks. The Servians, too, held aloof. The second battle of Kossovo (October 17, 1448) ended in a defeat for the Hungarians, although the Turkish losses were very severe. Under the hammering of Hunyadi, the Janitschars were obliged to give way, but they withdrew in good order with unbroken ranks.

There was a truce for three years after this battle, much to the relief of both sides, since Murad had encountered an aggressive Albanian leader in Scanderbeg, who seemed likely to rival Hunyadi as an enemy of Ottoman rule. For some time this Albanian champion, whose name in Albanian is equivalent to Alexander, had been kept as a page at the Sultan's court. During the confusion caused by the campaigns of Hunyadi, the young man had managed to escape, but before doing so, he had forced the Sultan's secretary, under menace of death, to sign an order directing the commander of Croia to give up the place to Scanderbeg. On reaching his home in the mountains, the Albanian chieftain put himself at the head of 600 warriors. Entering Croia alone he presented his written order to the governor, who immediately turned over the place to him. In the night he brought his men into the town and the Turkish garrison was massacred.

Everywhere throughout the land the Albanian people rose to cast out the Turk from their borders. Scanderbeg soon had 11,000 men under him, and won back all the possessions belonging to his family. Even the Venetians, who had tried to seize an Albanian town, were glad to come to terms with him, and to become his financial agents. He was accepted as chief of all the forces operating against the Ottomans, and a relief expedition of 40,000 men, under the command of Ali Pascha, the vizier, was caught in the fastnesses of the Albanian mountains and slowly exterminated. (1443.) Another Turkish army fared no better than that under Ali Pascha, and it lost 10,000 men. When Murad himself undertook to repress the rebellion, bringing with him the overwhelming force of 100,000 men, he took two cities, but left 20,000 of his men dead in the narrow defiles of Albania. Two years afterwards Murad began the siege of Croia, trusting to specially powerful artillery to overwhelm the enemy. But Scanderbeg, by skilful manœuvers, not only held the Sultan in check, but actually enveloped his army. Murad, seeing his danger, offered peace, on condition that Scanderbeg would acknowledge his sovereignty, and pay tribute to him. This was refused, and Murad abandoned his efforts to arrest the stubborn guerrilla warfare in which the Albanian chieftain had proved himself a master.

In the Morea, where the Byzantine princes, the sons of Manuel II, were gaining ground at the expense of one of the Latin feudal lords, the Florentine Acciajuoli, who had accepted the Sultan as his overlord, Murad's army of 60,000 men achieved decisive successes. The wall across the Isthmus of Corinth was taken by the Ottoman artillery, and the Peloponnesus was overrun by the invaders. Corinth was seized and burnt; but Patras, by its stout resistance, held the Sultan in check until terms were made, by which the invaders withdrew, on condition of receiving an annual tribute. (1446.)

But the dynastic disputes of Constantinople weakened the Greek power of resistance as much as did their failure in warfare. On the death of John VIII, in 1448, the dispute between his sons as to the succession was settled by Murad, who decided in favor of Constantine, the valiant defender of Patras. There was, however, no ceremony of coronation; therefore, strictly speaking, the last Christian Emperor of the East appears in the long line of the successors of Constantine the Great,—his namesake,—with a tinge of irregularity in his record. Soon after this elevation Murad died, February 8, 1451. His virtues are celebrated by the western chronicler, Brocquière, in the words, "a mild person, kind and generous in according lordship and money."

V

MOHAMMED II

Mohammed II was only twenty years old when he took up the reins of government. He was ambitious, was endowed with great physical endurance, and, from reading the deeds of Julius Cæsar and Alexander, as they appeared in the folklore tales translated into Arabic, had conceived a strong desire to transform the tribal and loosely organized sovereignty of his people into an enduring political power with a systematic organization. His primary object was the capture of Constantinople, and to get a free hand for this undertaking, he adopted a most pacific policy in the first year of his reign. He renewed the treaties with Genoa and Venice, with the princes of Servia and Wallachia, and with Hunyadi, Scanderbeg, and the Knights of Rhodes.

MEDAL OF MOHAMMED II

He opened hostilities with the Greeks by building, in an extraordinarily short space of time, a fortification on the narrow seas, near the imperial city, which enabled him to collect dues from all the vessels entering the harbor, and served as a point from which issued armed expeditions that captured nearly all the Greek territory outside the city walls. Meanwhile, some slight acts of aggression in the Morea failed to reveal to the West the real purposes of the new Sultan. Those who had seen him spoke of him as a mild and learned young man, not at all the kind of ruler who would walk in footsteps different from his father's. The Western Emperor, Frederick III, thought it was sufficient to write the Sultan a letter, warning him not to attack Constantinople. Those who were nearer understood his temper better, knowing that, when Constantine sent a delegation to protest against the erection of the fortification that had lately been built on the European shore of the Bosphorus, the Greek emissaries had been beheaded.

In the doomed city itself dissensions reigned supreme. Ecclesiastics had come from Rome to look over the religious situation in Constantinople with the purpose of reporting the prospects for carrying out the terms of union, drawn up lately at the Council of Florence. Their appearance in the city disgusted the common people, who called their new Emperor a traitor to the Eastern Church, and an irreligious usurper, who was, after all, they said, not a real emperor, because he had not been crowned.

The Venetians were busy looking after their own interests on the Adriatic coast or in continental Greece. They were busy arranging terms with the Sultan, as to the export of grain from Asia, and were so pleased with their commercial success in this bargain that they only resolved to allow artillerymen to be hired among the subjects of Venice by Constantine, not to aid him officially.

Outside the city the prospects for successful resistance were quite as bad. When a delegation came from the East to beg their help, they were referred by the Signoria to the Holy Father, as the head of the crusading program. Yet they began to suspect something was wrong when one of their ships, coming out of the Bosphorus, was fired on by the Turks, and the crew was taken and massacred. There were a few Venetian merchants' galleys in the harbor whose crews, at the Emperor's request, took part in the work of defending the fortifications. The Genoese, fearful of the fate of their colony at Pera, sent an armed force of 1000 men to help defend the city.

While keeping up a constant blockade, Mohammed was preparing his plans. His success, he saw, depended on siege guns, for he fully appreciated the tremendous revolution in warfare due to the use of gunpowder. From the many renegades in his camp he had heard of the remarkable effects produced by bronze cannon in battles and sieges. His adviser in preparing his siege guns was Urban, probably a Roumanian renegade, who showed great skill in perfecting the technique of projectiles at this early stage of their use. To the inventive faculty of this Christian fugitive in the Osmanli camp, the taking of the great Christian capital in the Orient was largely due. The weight of the new guns is shown by the fact that it took sixty oxen to draw the first one, which was manufactured by the end of February. Fifty similar ones were ordered to be constructed.

Troops from Asia and Slavic contingents from Europe kept gathering round the city during the winter and early spring; there was besides an Ottoman flotilla of 300 vessels. By the beginning of April, 1453, the Sultan, with his court, came to the encampment of the besieging army, and took up a position two miles and a half away from the city walls. To each portion of the fortifications a certain contingent was assigned, specific directions to proceed with the attack being given, according to the character of the ground and the defenses.

In the Sultan's army there were probably as many men under arms as were usually taken in the Turkish military expeditions, between forty and sixty thousand, but the number is not given in the sources. The Emperor Constantine had not more than 7000 men; besides, as we have seen, the population were ill disposed to him, because of his concessions to the Latin Church, and more than once the hostile cry was heard within the walls, "better under the Turks than under the Latins." One of Constantine's chief officials, Lukas Notoras, had already exchanged his Christian headgear for a Turkish turban.

The Latin element in the town took the chief part in the defense; not only were one-third of the soldiers from the West, but the galleys in the harbor, the weapons used, the stores for the siege, all were from the Occident. Only one of the towers on the city walls was in charge of a Greek, and the keys of the four chief city gates were kept by the Venetians. Catalans and Genoese were also given responsible positions; even in the personal entourage of the Emperor, only a few Greek names are noted.

When the siege opened, the character of Mohammed's strategy was soon plain. He had no intention of making a general assault of the ordinary type; instead, his cannon were directed against weak spots in the wall, and the work of destruction began. An unsuccessful attempt, however, was made to surprise the garrison on the 17th of April, and the Sultan was greatly disappointed when his fleet came out worsted from a fight with the imperial ships, which issued from the harbor to protect the entrance of three or four Genoese vessels that were bringing in stores.

While the walls on the land side were being bombarded, the part of the city touching the sea was threatened. Urban, imitating the Venetians, who had transported war galleys across the land to Lake Garda, brought some of the Turkish ships from Galata-Pera to the Golden Horn. All attempts to destroy this hostile flotilla failed; by its presence it divided the Christian forces, and kept the small army of Constantine from concentrating in any strength at a threatened point. When May came, the besieged population began to suffer from scarcity of food. The only hope of relief was to be looked for from Venice; for the other powers in the West had received Constantine's appeals with only verbal promises, or with indifference. Yet even the Venetians proceeded with great deliberation. The twelve galleys that had been ordered to be sent to help Constantinople in February were only ready by May 7th, and the Admiral, Loredano, was given instructions to handle the Turks unaggressively. He was told not to engage in a battle with them unless forced to do so.

Slowly the various details of the siege operations were perfected by the Turks; parts of the moats before the walls were filled up; a bridge was built from Pera to Constantinople, that gave an admirable basis for cannonading the city at close quarters. On the 28th the inhabitants noted such great activity in the Ottoman camp that it was evident the final attack was close at hand. Mohammed rode from point to point giving final directions, and word was proclaimed by heralds that every member of the besieging army should be prepared. The movement in the Turkish camp began three hours before daybreak. The Christian allies and the rank and file of the Moslem soldiers were directed to place ladders at a point in the wall near the Romanos gate that had already especially suffered from artillery fire. The loss of life among the assailants, at this point, was very great, but as the élite of the army did not suffer, the Ottoman leaders were indifferent as to the cost of getting the ladders near the walls and defenses.

The next step was to bring up the Janitschars, who, under the personal direction of the Sultan and the two chief generals of his army, commenced operations near the Romanos and two other gates. Compact in their firm discipline, and protected by artillery fire, with the smoke of their guns concealing from the defenders their rapid motion, they pressed ahead. On the Greek side the Emperor kept out of the tumultuous fighting, leaving the work of active defense to the Italian Giustiniano, who made a heroic resistance in the interior defenses of the city, until, struck in the breast by a bullet, he was carried away to a ship mortally wounded. After this fatality general confusion followed; there was no one to take the commander's place. No words of command were now heard; the Turks, who had been held back from the high walls, filled up the space between the outer lines of temporary palisades and the permanent fortifications that were being dismantled by the cannonading.

At the place where Giustiniano had been shot some ladders were set up, and at the same time a small gate, used by the Genoese soldiers to pass out of the city to protect the outer ring of the defensive works, was occupied. By this way a considerable number of the Janitschars penetrated into the interior of the city. But their entrance was not noticed by the defenders on the walls, who, in the conflict, had no time to leave their posts. The sailors of the fleet now landed, ready to take their part of the spoil. The squadrons of Janitschars rode without resistance through the narrow streets flanked with wooden houses, searching for the first of the booty. Every corner was searched for wealthy citizens, who would be likely to pay large ransoms, and for valuable slaves. Adult men, actually with weapons in their hands, were killed, and, of course, no Franks were spared, nor any of the imperial troops. Small children, too, old men, and invalids, who came in the way of the Ottoman soldiers, were mercilessly slaughtered; they had no marketable value. Whole groups of citizens were dragged off, and then a systematic plundering of churches and private houses began; carpets, stuffs, precious stones and metals, books, whose binding attracted notice, all were carried off. (May 29, 1453.)

In the sacking of the city the Emperor Constantine perished. When he saw destruction going on all about him, he is said to have asked, "Is there no Christian here to cut my head off?" His fate must have come later, for his body was found on a heap of corpses near the gate that had first been entered. His head was set the same day on a column of the Augusteion, a sign to the Greeks that they had no other emperor now but the Sultan. Then it was placed in a precious casket and despatched from one Moslem ruler to another as the convincing proof of the prowess of their Moslem overlord.

Three days had been allowed for the sack; after this period the troops returned to their camp. Some of the streets were then cleaned, and the Sultan made his solemn entry into the deserted city to the Church of St. Sophia, which he transformed into a mosque. The Podestà and a few of the Italians from Pera, who had not actually been under arms, were protected by a guarantee from the Sultan's own hand. But the walls of the suburb were destroyed, all weapons had to be given up, and a slave succeeded the Genoese Podestà as the supreme authority in the colony.

Most of the fleet, taking advantage of the confusion during the capture of the city, succeeded in getting away, taking with them some fugitives who escaped by disguising themselves in a Turkish garb. The head of the Venetian colony and the Catalan Consul were beheaded as disturbers of the peace, and even Lukas Notoras, the chief Greek noble, did not escape, although he had led the opposition against Constantine. The Greek clergy, on the other hand, were treated with great clemency; they had been trained by centuries into habits of servile obedience to secular rulers, and, therefore, they could be turned into useful instruments for ruling the subject Christian population.

With shrewd understanding of the religious situation, Mohammed now appointed as Patriarch in place of the Latin ecclesiastic, who had escaped from the city, the leader of the clerical opposition, Gennadios Scholarios. The new Patriarch dined with the new Emperor, and received rich presents and most courteous attention, befitting his exalted dignity as a churchman. In place of Santa Sophia, he was given as his metropolitan church the building known as the Church of the Holy Apostles. As a new Patriarch, created by favor of the Moslem Emperor, he kept his rights of jurisdiction over the Emperor's Christian subjects.

A Moslem governor was placed in the city to order the administration, with instructions to induce those who had fled from the town to return, and to arrange for the colonization of the Moslem newcomers. Only a small garrison was left; and the Sultan took his road to Adrianople on 18th of June. While the Moslem ruler and his successors spared the population, and left to their Greek subjects a kind of spiritual empire, the conquest of Constantinople proved fatal to the many treasures of ancient art that had survived the Latin conquest of the city in 1204. The bronze statues of the Emperors were made into cannon, the bronze inscriptions on arches and obelisks were coined into money, and the marble statues of pagan divinities were turned into lime.

Valuable antique columns were sawn to make baths, or were transformed into cannon balls.

The Basilica, in which the bodies of the Emperors were buried, became a mosque; the bones were scattered and the sarcophagi turned to the basest uses. Forty-two other churches became mosques, or were secularized; one, St. Irenæus, was employed as an arsenal. Some of the splendid mosaics in Santa Sophia were hidden by whitewash, because of their Christian symbolism; near the structure was built a minaret, and Mohammed's successors added three more. As time went on, new mosques were constructed; also hospitals, schools, and palaces, the Sultan being a great builder. The new population was cosmopolitan, for many Greek, Servian, and Roumanian towns were drawn upon for their several contingents, as the Turkish conquests continued.

At the time of his great achievement, Mohammed was only twenty-five years old. He publicly announced that he had reached maturity by decapitating the Grand Vizier Khalil, the tutor set over him by his father, who was suspected of treasonable communications with the Greeks during the siege. He made it plain, also, that there was to be no repose from war after the taking of the capital, the Servians being the first to experience his heavy hand. Brankovitch's fidelity as a vassal proved no protection to him; for Mohammed wrote claiming his kingdom. In terror the Servian prince fled to Hungary to secure the aid of Hunyadi. The war that followed was hotly contested, with the result that in 1454 the Sultan agreed, on the basis of the large tribute of 30,000 ducats, to recognize Brankovitch.

But this peace was not observed, for the conqueror appeared the next year and took Novoberda. Hunyadi, against whom bitter foes were working at the court of the King of Hungary, had only the support of the Wallachian princely house. When Belgrade was attacked by Mohammed, in May, 1456, only 3000 Christian soldiers were ready to oppose him. When the siege really began, however, 200 boats appeared before the city, containing many thousand men of various nationalities, whom the Franciscan monk, John of Capistrano, had drawn to the crusading cause by his protracted and widely extended journeys in Western Europe. Though over seventy years old, he had displayed remarkable energy, and he was honored by the defenders of Belgrade as a holy apostle.

On July 15 the two welcome allies took possession of the castle, as the city had not yet been cut off from the outside. The first stage of the defense was the defeat of the Turkish flotilla on the Danube; some vessels were sunk and others were captured, so that entrance into the town by water was made safe. In the attempt to storm the defenses made by the Janitschars, who advanced in small divisions, hardly 600 survived; three times Hunyadi, sallying from the castles, forced back the assailants. Capistrano's crusaders proved too much for the Sultan's trained troops; marching right up to the guns and careless of the havoc caused by the cannon fire, those who took part in the sortie cut down the Turks and threw the cannon into the water and ditches. If the crusaders had not stopped on the way to plunder, they would have broken through the Sultan's own bodyguard. As it was the Ottomans were able to withdraw safely from their camp; but they lost some of their best captains, among them Aga, who was killed while protecting the Sultan, who escaped with an arrow wound.

No serious attempt was made to follow up this victory, though Hunyadi boasted that it was now possible "to take possession of the whole kingdom of Turkey." Anarchy prevailed in the motley crowd gathered in the crusading camps along the river; worse still, owing to the unhealthful surroundings in the low lands, a plague began, to which the great Hungarian champion soon fell a victim; not long after Capistrano also died.

Soon after the death of Hunyadi the long career of the Servian Prince Brankovitch came to an end, and with it closed the history of Servia as a vassal state, for his death was followed by long and bloody quarrels over the succession. Finally, the claim of Brankovitch's daughter-in-law, Helena, the widow of his son Lazaras, was acknowledged. Her accession gave Mohammed an excuse for appearing as the champion of an Ottoman pretender. The Sultan's influence over the Servian nobility was increased by the fact that Helena was favorable to the Latin Church; she placed Servia under the protection of the Pope, and married her daughter to the heir of the Bosnian kingdom. But this foreign help availed nothing. Many of the strong places in Servia were captured, including the city of Semandria (1459). The Servian "woiwodes," who preferred the domination of the Sultan to the acceptance of the religion of Rome, showed themselves disloyal to Helena the younger, who was obliged to withdraw, to Hungary first, and then to Rome, where she died as a nun in 1474.

After the destruction of Servia, and its absorption by the Ottomans, came the turn of Bosnia, like Servia disturbed by disputes between vassal princes, which were taken advantage of by Mohammed. King Stephen's pro-Roman policy made him unpopular among his nobles; therefore, when the Turk's army appeared, there was no great difficulty in overrunning the country. The King retired in a panic from his strongly fortified capital, and while in flight was captured and afterwards executed (1464). Herzegovina, which still remained in Christian hands, could not resist the successful aggression of the Turks, and its occupation took place three years after the annexation of Bosnia. As Bosnia was a vassal state of Hungary, its King, Matthias, found himself obliged to look to the safety of his territories. Scanderbeg, who was alarmed at the taking of Herzegovina, and Venice, as the mistress of all the cities in the Morea, had just begun to realize the need of common action to protect their interests.

On the part of the Hungarians war was waged on a small scale, but the Venetians employed a celebrated condottiere, Bertoldo d'Este, to head an expedition of thirty-two galleys and other ships armed by many thousand warriors. After some initial successes, the aim of the expedition failed, because of the death of Bertoldo while he was besieging the Turkish garrison at Corinth. Hitherto the steady advance of the Turks towards the south had been furthered by the anarchy and divisions of the rival races, among which the Albanians and the Greeks showed the most vitality. In Athens the ducal Florentine line brought notoriety to its closing days by the romantic record of its last duchess, the wife of Nerio II, who, when left a widow with the guardianship of her young son, fell in love with Contarini, a Venetian officer in Naples. She promised to marry him if he would get rid of his wife. The condition was accepted, and the young officer, by marrying the duchess, became master of Athens. Those who had acknowledged the old duke as their overlord, resented the introduction of Venetian rule, and appealed to Mohammed to interfere. He bestowed the duchy on a member of the reigning Florentine house, Franco, who caused his aunt, the scandal-making duchess, to be imprisoned and afterwards murdered. The commission of this crime produced discontent, and the Sultan gave orders to one of his captains to take possession of Athens.

Mohammed himself took personal charge of the expedition of 1458, which was conducted with great cruelty. The Albanians were especially singled out for savage reprisals. When Tarsos fell, the Albanian soldiers taken captive were horribly tortured, and at the capitulation of Corinth the leader of the Albanian contingent was sawn asunder. A short respite was at first granted to the Greek princes, members of the house of Paleologi, who were closely allied with the last Emperor of Constantinople, but they were finally dispossessed, and by the year 1460 nothing of Greece was left in the hands of the Christian powers except four Venetian strongholds. But these were not to be spared longer.

In 1463 the Morea was ravaged by the Turkish army, and five hundred Venetian soldiers met death by being sawn apart. In 1467 the island of Eubœa was attacked by both Ottoman fleet and land forces simultaneously. Great preparation was made for the defense of the Venetian citadel, but the plans were spoiled by the incapacity of the commander of the Venetian fleet to defend the approach to the island from the sea. The besieged garrison showed great heroism, and even when they discovered that their leaders were preparing to betray them, they stoutly held out and inflicted severe losses on the Ottomans. For reasons which are inexplicable, the Venetian fleet made no attempt to break down the bridge which connected the island with the continent; the occupation of this passageway finally enabled the Janitschars to enter the city. Its heroic defender, Paolo Erizzo, met the fate of being sawn asunder, because, as a chronicle states, the Turks had promised to save his head but not his thighs.

This heavy blow to Venice stirred the republic to a series of energetic reprisals. With her allies, the Neapolitans and the Knights of Rhodes, and aided by the Pope, she carried the war into Asia Minor. The town of Smyrna was occupied by the Venetian fleet, and the Seldjouk emirates, always ready to rebel against the Ottomans, were encouraged to revolt. When Lepanto was successfully protected by the Venetian fleet, it was felt that Mohammed had at last encountered a power that was ready to contest the imperial ambitions of Ottoman rule. But that there was no sufficient ground for over-confidence appeared when a Turkish general, Omar-beg, invaded Friuli, and began to ravage territories in the immediate neighborhood of Venice. A Venetian general fell fighting the Turks on the banks of the Isonzo, and the citizens of the republic could see with their own eyes the work of the Turks, as they burnt the villages that lie between the Isonzo and the Taghliamento. Scutari, however, withstood two Turkish sieges, though Mohammed himself took part in the operations. Finally, in 1479, Venice, deserted by her allies, was willing to arrange terms of peace. These involved the cession of Lemnos and certain possessions in Albania; but more significant of her humiliation was the payment of a war indemnity of 100,000 ducats, and the agreement to give an annual tribute of 110,000, in return for which sacrifices certain commercial advantages were conceded by the Turks.

Interpreting the treaty in its strictest sense, Mohammed, after arranging a peace with Venice, occupied the Ionian Islands, and soon afterwards showed his contempt for the military powers of Western Europe by sending a fleet of 150 ships to Otranto in Apulia, a province of the kingdom of Naples. The town, entirely unprepared for such a raid, was taken in 1480; the garrison and the archbishop were put to death, and the neighboring country was organized as a Turkish province with its capital at Otranto, where a garrison of 5000 Turkish soldiers was left behind.

The alarm created by this feat of arms was instantaneous. The Italian cities united and soon expelled the Turks from the peninsula, rivaling their enemies in Asiatic deeds of cruelty. Mohammed could not prosecute the conquest of Italy, because his attention was necessarily divided by the troubled state of Turkish rule in Asia, where the Seldjouk principalities still claimed an autonomy which, on crucial matters, made them independent of the Sultan.

In the north of Anatolia, which was directly in the hands of the Ottomans, there still remained the Empire of Trebizond, governed by a Greek prince, David Comnenus. Part of his dominions, Sinope and Paphlagonia, were conquered in 1461, and then the last Emperor of Trebizond turned for help to his Turkoman ally, Hassan, ruler of Armenia and part of Persia. Mohammed struck at his foes rapidly. Marching on Erzeroum, he forced Hassan to sue for peace, and so the Greek Emperor was left to meet the Turks unaided. The city of Trebizond was effectively encircled by land and sea, and David was soon brought to surrender, and afterwards, with many members of his household, was put to death. Equally implacable was Mohammed to the Seldjoukian emirates. At the death of Ibrahim, the Prince of Karamania, the Sultan intervened, while seven claimants were disputing over the succession, and after several campaigns annexed the emirate. Hassan's time soon came. Feeling the insecurity of his rule, he asked help of Rhodes and Venice, especially requesting to be furnished with artillery, by the aid of which so many of the Ottoman victories were won. Two hundred Italian gunners were sent in answer to his call. In 1472 he took the Ottoman town of Tokat, and sacked it. This act caused Mohammed to take up the war against him in person. The two armies met on July 26, 1473, at Outlouk-Bali, near Terdjan, where a decisive victory was won by the Sultan. All the prisoners taken were massacred. The Turkomans had no desire to contest further the predominance of Ottoman rule, which was now extended without question over both Karamania and Anatolia.

It must not be supposed, however, that Mohammed was always successful. Albania held out against him under the heroic leader Scanderbeg, whose earlier exploits have been already chronicled. His success against the Ottomans continued without a break. Even when a nephew proved disloyal and brought an army of 40,000 Turks into the land, he rose up and smote the invaders after the manner of his earlier years (1461). For a time afterward peace prevailed; then, during the Venetian war, he stood as an ally of the republic. His old antagonist Mohammed had another opportunity of testing the valor of the Albanian chieftain at a decisive defeat of the Turkish army under the walls of Croia in 1465. Two years later Scanderbeg died at the age of sixty-seven, and his death was followed by civil strife.

The rounding off of the Ottoman Empire, a process by which the vassal states were absorbed, put an end to the internal movements against centralized rule, and enabled the Sultan to work out his policy of systematic aggression in the regions to the north. After the year 1470 Turkish armies ravaged Southern Hungary, Croatia, Carinthia, Styria, and Carniola; Belgrade, on account of its strong defensive position, was respected. In 1479 the Turks made an expedition in force into Transylvania, where, in the neighborhood of Hermannstadt, they burnt 200 villages. When they were on the point of withdrawing with their booty they were attacked on the Cornfields (Kenyermezo, October 13), and suffered severe losses. Not more successful were the acts of aggression on Hungarian territory in the following year; but the Hungarian King, Matthias, was satisfied with repulsing his enemies; he had no desire to prosecute the war against the Turks on a large scale, for he had none of the ambition or enthusiasm of his famous father, Hunyadi.

In the Greek islands the activity of the Turkish fleet produced positive and permanent results; Lesbos was taken in 1462, and to the list of Turkish successes in these years were soon added Lemnos, Imbros, Samothrace. Much more valiant defenders of their island were the Knights of Rhodes, whom the Sultan was especially desirous of punishing for the part they had taken in the already mentioned Venetian expedition against Asia Minor. In 1480 a large Ottoman fleet of about one hundred ships appeared in sight of the island, and a bombardment was begun, but the fortifications proved too strong for the Turkish guns to make any impression, though the siege lasted from early in May till the end of August, in which time, despite the assaults made on the citadel, only one tower was taken. The Grand Master, Pierre d'Aubusson, and his brother, had prepared most intelligently for the crisis by collecting from all provinces of the Order money, which they used in providing weapons, especially cannon. They had been furnished also by the Pope, just before the siege began, with a large store of food and provisions. Finally, after a heroic defense of eighty-nine days, two Neapolitan ships forced their way into the harbor and broke up the blockade.

In the Wallachian lands the Ottomans met a redoubtable warrior, who, in the annals of the Roumanian people, takes such a high place as a champion against the Turks that the record of his deeds gives him a rank alongside Hunyadi and Scanderbeg. Vlad, the Prince of Wallachia, 1456-1462, called by the Hungarians the Devil, and with equal significance spoken of by the Turks as the Impaler, had a reputation for violence even among his own people. He repressed the internal troubles of his vassals with an iron hand; for after Mircea's death the country had gone through the same period of divisions and intrigues that is found with such frequency in all the Balkan lands, making them, as we have seen, an easy prey for the Ottoman.

It is told how Vlad brought Wallachia to a peaceful state by the execution of 20,000 men, and how, afterwards, in the same drastic style, he resolved to put an end to the annual tribute of 500 children demanded by his overlord the Sultan. Looking for allies in carrying on the resistance to Mohammed, he helped Stephen IV to secure the throne of Moldavia, and married a relative of Matthias, King of Hungary. Mohammed resolved to nip in the bud the independent movements of his dangerous vassal, and sent a renegade Greek official, Catabolinus, with a corps of 2000 Turks to depose Vlad and to replace him by his brother, Radu. Vlad, having surprised this small force, impaled all the prisoners he took; to the pasha who led them was accorded the honor of being impaled on the longest stake. After this outrage the Sultan sent three ambassadors to reinforce his demands; but, when the Moslem delegates refused to remove their turbans in his presence, Vlad ordered their headgear to be nailed to their heads.

This picturesque barbarity appealed to the imagination of the Turkish ruler, who, as an artist in cruelty, conceded that Vlad belonged to a class above him. When the Turkish sovereign made a punitive expedition to Bucharest, he found the approach to the town, half a mile long, lined with stakes, on which were rotting the bodies of 2000 dead Turks. "How," Mohammed said, "can we despoil of his estates a man who is not afraid to defend it by such means as these?" Vlad hung on the invading army, always inflicting losses, without showing himself long enough to be attacked in a formal battle. Using his familiarity with the Turkish language, he penetrated with some companions into the midst of the Turkish camp, and would have succeeded in murdering Mohammed himself, had not a mistake been made in selecting the tent. Instead of the Sultan one of the pashas was killed. Though there are conflicting accounts as to the details of Vlad's versatility in defense, we know that Mohammed gave up his plan of aggression against Wallachia and returned to his capital, Adrianople.

Vlad's career was cut short by the enmity of his neighbor the Moldavian King, Stephen, who, afraid of his influence, drove him from his throne, although he had relied on Vlad to promote his own interests when the Moldavian succession was in dispute. This was, of course, a gross error in statesmanship, for the only possibility of resisting Turkish aggression in these extreme Eastern lands of Europe depended on the close coöperation of Moldavia and Wallachia. If Wallachia were once occupied by the Turks, Moldavia's invasion was certain to be the next step. After Vlad's expulsion, he took refuge at the court of Matthias of Hungary.

His successor, Radu, was entirely devoted to Turkish interests; and soon after this change of rule in Wallachia, Stephen of Moldavia was able to seize the seaport town of Kilia, whose inhabitants were not unwilling to accept an overlord of better reputation than Radu, whose close relations with the Sultan had made him an object of contempt (1465). In the hostilities that followed between Matthias of Hungary and Stephen of Moldavia, the Hungarian King, who had taken up Vlad's cause, was beaten at the battle of Baia. Stephen then invaded Transylvania, captured Peter Aron, the pretender to the throne of Moldavia, and put him to death. Peace was restored with the Hungarians on terms that were advantageous to Stephen, who received two fortresses.

Not long after this Hungarian incident, which, like so many others, weakened the power of resistance to Turkish arms, Stephen invaded Wallachia with the intention of dethroning the Sultan's favorite, Radu. The Moldavian prince prepared for war against the Turks by entering into negotiations with the Venetians, who, as we have seen, were indefatigable in organizing a general league against Mohammed. An ambassador, who had been sent by the republic to secure the coöperation of the Persian King, Louzoun Hassan, visited Stephen, and proposed him as leader in organizing a holy league against the Ottomans, "in order," as he said, "that we may not be left alone to keep up the struggle against them." But before the Venetian envoy had passed beyond the Balkan lands, Mohammed's army, in great force, was already swarming over Moldavia. To meet them Stephen had only some 50,000 men, mostly of his own nation. With these and a few Hungarians he won a brilliant victory over 120,000 Turks at Rakova in 1475, where he killed 20,000 men, took 100 standards, and many prisoners, including four pashas. Pursuing the defeated army, he massacred a large part of them. A church was built to celebrate the battle, and a solemn fast was initiated, followed by the impaling of many Turkish prisoners. This success of Stephen was celebrated as a unique feat of arms in Western Europe, and deservedly so, for the trained troops of Mohammed had been hewn down by a peasantry armed only with pikes, scythes, and axes.

Stephen asked help from the Pope and from Venice to carry on the struggle; but he got no aid, for the Venetians were worn out with the long war against their Eastern foes, and the Pope explained that all money for defense had been turned over to Matthias of Hungary, the overlord of the Moldavian King. Matthias, however, proposed to spend the money at home, as he dreaded the inevitable increase of Stephen's power if he were to inflict another decisive defeat on a Turkish army. When the Turks appeared again, the help of the peasant population could not be secured because they were simultaneously alarmed at the news of a Tartar invasion, said to have been timed to coincide with the passage of the Danube by the Turks.

The Moldavian nobles, however, and their men-at-arms, made an heroic stand against Mohammed's army; their cannon did such execution that the Janitschars threw themselves on the ground to escape the rain of projectiles. The Sultan was forced to lead his men in person to save the day. So stout was the stand the Christians made that the combat lasted far into the night. When most of his nobles had been slaughtered Stephen withdrew from this battle, which was fought at Razboieni, July 24, 1476. After he had been pursued to the forest country in the north of Moldavia, he was finally forced to withdraw to the inaccessible mountain regions. Here, with characteristic enterprise, he gathered together a second army, and the Turks, who already were exhausted by the strenuous campaign in a country ill provided with food, and ravaged as they were by disease, were easily driven back across the Danube. After this success Wallachia was invaded the same year by the Moldavian Boyars, who were joined by the Transylvanians under their new leader, Bathory. The pro-Turkish prince of the country was dethroned, and Vlad, the mighty hammerer of the Turks, now again an ally of Stephen, was replaced by the latter on the throne; but the veteran leader did not long survive his restoration. He died in December, 1477, near Bucharest, in a fight with the Turks, who attacked him as soon as Stephen had withdrawn to Moldavia. He was buried in a monastery founded by him at Snagov, but no inscription marked the resting place of the Christian champion.

Mohammed's own reign was closed on the 3d of May, 1481, in Anatolia. For some time, owing to his excessive weight, campaigning had been difficult and painful for him. In the latter years of his life he was often so incapacitated by gout that he was compelled to give up more than one important warlike expedition, and it was to this disease that his death was due. During his reign the Turkish Empire acquired much new territory; Anatolia was occupied as far as the northern reaches of the Euphrates, and in Europe the Balkan peninsula was made subject to his arms as far as the Danube. Many successful expeditions were also made far beyond these limits, both on the east and on the west. But two great obstacles to Turkish advance he failed to overcome: Rhodes and Belgrade, the latter stronghold commanding the Danube, while the former was the key to the Ægean.

VI

SELIM AND SOULIMAN

In the line of succession were two sons, Bajesid and Djem. Bajesid managed, by rapid marching, to reach Scutari before his brother, and was proclaimed Sultan. Djem, who had occupied Broussa, proposed a division of the empire, but Bajesid refused, and defeated Djem in a decisive battle, fought at Yeni-Chchir (1481). The defeated brother took refuge first in Egypt, with the Sultan of the Mamelouks, and afterwards appeared as a suppliant at Rhodes, where the Grand Master, fearing to keep so valuable a hostage, sent him to France, where he remained for several years in captivity. Djem finally ended his life as a victim of the Borgia Pope, Alexander VI, who is charged with having murdered him to secure the favor of Bajesid. So long as Djem lived, Bajesid was wary of stirring up the enmity of Occidental Christendom; he feared the effect on the stability of his throne by the return of a pretender, backed up by Christian armies. He even refused to answer the appeal for aid sent him by the last King of Granada, only venturing to show ineffective sympathy by sending a fleet to cruise off the Spanish coast.

Charles VIII of France, encouraged by his successful expedition into Italy, planned a new general crusade against the Turk, and secured promises of coöperation from various Western powers. He kept in touch with the Christian population of the Ottoman Empire, and even looked forward to taking the imperial throne of Constantinople by purchasing title deeds to it from the Paleologi family.

After Djem's death, which was soon followed by that of Charles, the Sultan had a free hand. From 1492 to 1495 he warred with partial success against the Hungarians; then came the turn of Venice, whose Italian dominions again saw a Turkish army. In the Morea, also, the republic lost some of the few cities it still possessed. There Nauplia held out, but Modon, Navarino, and Coron passed into the possession of the Turks. Under Papal leadership, an anti-Ottoman league was formed, and the Christian fleet proved its prowess by destroying two Turkish flotillas and by ravaging the shores of Asia Minor.

Internal troubles in Asia Minor, defeats in Hungary, and a long, troublesome war with the Sultan of Egypt brought the warlike enterprises of Bajesid to an end. The Sultan's sons through their dissensions darkened the close of his reign; all three rebelled. Of the three, the most successful in opposing his father's power was Selim, who won the Janitschars over to his side, and through their interference was able to enter Constantinople in triumph, and there enforce his own conditions. Bajesid first offered large sums if Selim would withdraw to the Asiatic province, of which he was governor; finally he consented to accept him as heir and co-regent on the throne; but Selim had secured the influence of the troops, and they demanded the Sultan's immediate abdication. Bajesid was obliged to accede to their request, and only asked that he might be allowed to withdraw to die at Demotica, the place where he was born. The third day after his abdication he died. Because of its suddenness, his death, as was so often the case in those days, was said to be due to poison.

Selim's path after his accession was anything but smooth; the troops were not amenable to discipline, and there were a host of brothers and nephews, who were in no mood to accept him as their lord. Besides his own son, Souliman, there were ten princes who stood near the throne. All were taken and murdered. Though Selim affected to explain their executions as due to reasons of state, his acts were severely judged by his contemporaries. The Turks called him "The Inflexible," while in the West he was entitled "The Savage." Foscolo, the Venetian, described him as the cruelest of men, "a man who dreams only of conquests and wars." He was a well-educated man who favored the pursuit of literature, and it was said that the only individual who was ever able to induce him to revoke a death sentence was the grand mufti, Ali Djemali. His viziers felt the implacable nature of their master; seven of them were executed, for whenever the soldiers were restless the vizier was made a victim of the Sultan's discontent. According to an old report one of them only agreed to accept the dangerous office after Selim had beaten him with his own hands. Intractable at home, Selim, so far as Europe was concerned, proved a pacific prince, his name being recorded only in connection with one expedition against the Christians. His Christian vassals, too, were left undisturbed; all that he exacted from them was the payment of a regular tribute. To the Moslem dissenters in Persia of the Shiite sect, he showed himself an implacable persecutor, all the more because his animosity was excited by the encouragement given to his rebellious brother Ahmed and his three sons by Ismail, the master of Persia. Ismail also negotiated an alliance with the Sultan of Egypt against the Osmanlis. Selim began in his own provinces by organizing a systematic massacre of the schismatics. Then followed a holy war against the Shah, in 1513, in which Selim led an army of 140,000 warriors; and after three campaigns, in one of which a great pitched battle was fought at Tchaldiran (August 24, 1514), he extended the domains of the Ottoman far to the east, bringing to submission Georgia and Kurdistan, and overrunning Mesopotamia and the parts of Syria that were controlled by the Moslem lord of Egypt.

By the expansion of his empire in this direction he soon came into conflict with the Sultan of the Mamelouks. Aleppo was taken, and, when Selim entered the city, he was hailed in the great mosque as the guardian of the two holy cities of Mecca and Medina, a title which gave the Ottoman Sultan almost the rank of the Khalif of the faithful. Damascus also fell into his hands, and so rapid were the successes of the Ottomans, that early in the year 1517 Selim found himself within sight of Cairo. The Mamelouks made an heroic resistance; protected by their coats of mail they charged into the center of the Turkish position, killing the vizier and ten generals. But here, as so often, the superiority of the Turks in artillery decided the day, and Cairo was taken after a prolonged and desperate struggle. Selim proclaimed an amnesty in favor of the Mamelouks; 500 of them, trusting in the conqueror's promises, surrendered and were decapitated, and 50,000 of the citizens of Cairo were massacred. Touman, who led the Egyptian forces, was finally taken and hanged.

Egypt was allowed to retain its ancient organization, with its irregular force, the Mamelouks, and its twenty-four Begs as military commanderies; but the direction of the government was placed in the hands of the Ottoman Pasha. With the possession of Egypt Selim became lord of Yemen, its dependency, and so exercised actual control over the holy places of the Moslem faith. At Cairo he had found a sheik, an obscure and neglected personage, called Elmo-stansir-bi-illah, who was reputed to be in the direct line of descent from the second branch of the Abbasides Khalifs. Selim kept him in confinement until, on the promise of securing his liberty, and for a small money payment and a pension, he agreed to transfer to the Turkish ruler all his claims to the Khalifate.

Selim's victories made a great impression. Venice, whose commercial interests were affected, sent ambassadors to Cairo to arrange for paying the tribute that was due to the Sultan of Egypt for the island of Cyprus. Hungary asked to have the truce prolonged between the two powers, and the Shah of

Persia sent gifts and congratulations. Selim died on September 22, 1520, while he was preparing for an expedition against the island of Rhodes. He was succeeded by his only son, Souliman, a ruler whose long reign, from 1520 to 1566, makes him a contemporary of the great European leaders of the sixteenth century, a fact which Paul Veronese recognized when he placed him in his celebrated painting, "The Marriage at Cana," along with the chief sovereigns of the day.

As the lines of expansion in the East and in Africa had been closed by the remarkable achievements of Selim, Souliman's hands were free to take up the traditional line of aggressive progress of Turkish power. Hungary was attacked on the ground that the payment of tribute was refused. In 1521, after two important battles, Belgrade was besieged by the Sultan; the fate of the city was decided by the defection of its Servian and Bulgarian allies. Twenty assaults were made, and there were only 400 able-bodied men in the garrison, when a mutiny among the inhabitants forced the town to capitulate on August 29, 1521.

The conquest of Rhodes, the center of Christian resistance in the East, was now not long delayed. A large navy of 200 vessels appeared off the island with a summons to the grand master, Villiers de l'Isle Adam, to surrender. Souliman had collected an army of 100,000 men to undertake the siege, but the defenders were not terrified. Every assault made on the great bastions of the citadel caused enormous losses among the Turks; but their prolonged artillery fire and the new supplies of men, drawn constantly from Asia, showed the mere handful of defenders that their struggle could have only one outcome. In December, 1522, the island capitulated on terms that were favorable to the heroic defenders; even the Sultan appreciated the tragedy, for he is recorded to have said to his favorite Ibrahim, that he was loath to force this Christian commander, in his old age, to leave his house and his goods.

The next field of Souliman's military enterprise was Persia, where the Shah, by the defection of an Ottoman official, had recovered some of the territory taken by Selim. Souliman, appearing with a large force, received the submission of many of the Shah's vassals, and, after a long march to the East, during which his cannon had to be abandoned, entered the ancient capital of the Khalifate, Bagdad, in 1535. But several other campaigns were required to establish definite possession of the country. Finally, after many victories, peace was signed at Amasia, on the 29th of May, 1555, a step which implied that the Sunnite Turks acknowledged the legitimacy of a Shiite monarchy. In the mountains of Armenia and Kurdistan the extension of Ottoman power encountered serious obstacles. Native chieftains and princes followed their own caprices and their own interests in changing their allegiance to Shah or Sultan. There was constant guerrilla warfare, without any notable advantage to Turkish arms. In the southern regions at the confluence of the Tigris and the Euphrates, the Ottoman power was firmly established; Turkish vessels were to be seen now in the Red Sea and the Persian Gulf. Aden was occupied and the control of Yemen made effective. But the chief effort of Souliman was directed against the King of Hungary and the Emperor Charles V. A curious and novel development of European diplomacy was seen, when Francis I, the French King, appealed to the Sultan in his difficulties, after his defeat at the hands of Charles in Italy. Souliman sent a gracious message assuring the imprisoned monarch of his support, and spoke of his own throne

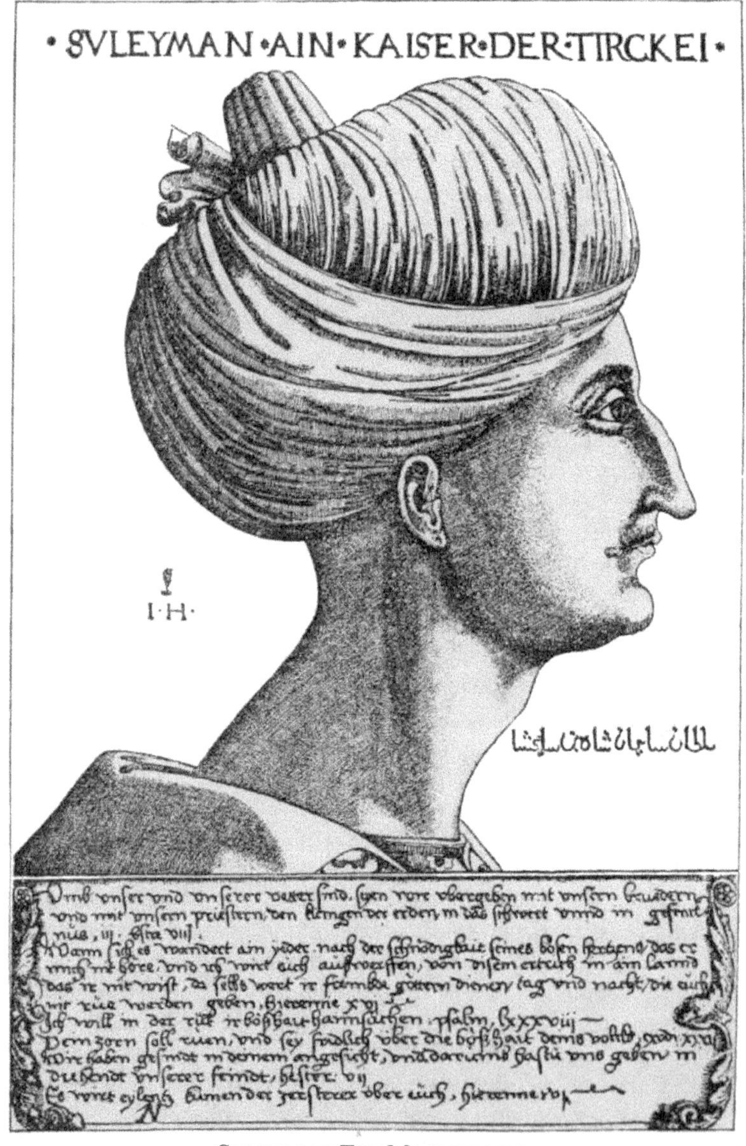

SULEYMAN THE MAGNIFICENT
(In Youth.)

as the refuge of the world; "night and day," he added, "our horse is saddled and our sword girded." In 1526 the Sultan marched from his capital to give battle to Charles, the "hated head of the infidels," with an army of 100,000 men and 300 cannon. There was a great battle with the Hungarian troops at Mohacs (August 28, 1526). After a hot engagement of two hours, the Christians left on the field 20,000 foot and 400 horse, and of the prisoners 400 were put to death.

A few days after the battle Buda surrendered to the Turks, and the Hungarian kingdom was harried by the Turkish irregular forces. Everywhere they went, their path was marked by massacre. Ten thousand captives were taken, and the result of the campaign was almost the disappearance of Hungary as an independent Christian kingdom, because, after the taking of Buda, Souliman called to him the Hungarian nobles and settled who should be their king. The kingdom was now rent by factions, some of the nobles siding with the Sultan's candidate, John Zapolya, while others accepted Ferdinand, the brother of Charles V. When Zapolya appeared at Constantinople, because of the failure of his faction to support his claims, the Sultan, after securing from him a formal engagement as vassal, undertook to place him on the Hungarian throne. The promise was more than made good. In October, 1529, the Turks appeared before the walls of Vienna with 250,000 men and 300 cannon. To defend the city there were only 16,000 men and 70 pieces of artillery. But the defense was conducted with such spirit and intelligence that the Turkish army was compelled to withdraw. When winter approached, the extent of the ravages of the Turkish arms was marked by attacks on Regensburg and Brunn. Later on, another expedition was made into Styria, where the country suffered terrible devastations.

Under the stress of these alarms the powers of Western Europe, irrespective of religious differences, banded together to resist the enemy. Even Francis I was concerned at the rapidity of the success of his ally, the Sultan, and sent an ambassador to Constantinople to entreat Souliman to hold his hand. Finally, owing to the difficulties with Persia, the Sultan agreed to sign a treaty of peace with Hungary in 1533, by which Ferdinand was allowed to hold the land already occupied by him. But the war with Charles V, and with his ally, Venice, still went on, chiefly a contest at sea between the Turkish admiral, Kheir-ed-Din, and his Venetian antagonist, Andrew Doria, without decisive results, except the capture of many of the Venetian islands in the Ægean. In 1541 steps were taken, when dissensions arose again in Hungary between the heirs of Zapolya and Ferdinand, to make the conquest of part of the country effective. A Turkish pasha-lik was formed, with Buda as its capital, and for 147 years Buda remained an Ottoman city. Further conquests were made of Van, or Stuhlweissenburg, the city where the Hungarian kings were consecrated, and Vychegrad, where the royal crown of Hungary was kept. Owing to the valor of the people there were repeated efforts on the part of the Hungarians to renew resistance to the Ottoman domination. A treaty was made in 1567, when the aged Sultan, worn out by constant warfare, was willing to concede to the Emperor Ferdinand an arrangement for the payment of an annual tribute. Although peace was formally declared, disturbances on the frontier still continued, and the seas were not free from acts of piracy.

As Spain had not been included in the treaty of 1562, a Spanish flotilla of twenty-two ships was destroyed near the island of Djerba, which had previously been seized by Spain. Not long afterwards a Turkish armada of 191 vessels sailed against the island of Malta, with the purpose of bringing to the home of the Knights Hospitalers the ruin that had already been inflicted at Rhodes on their brethren. For four months the siege lasted, costing the assailants nearly 20,000 men. Dragut, the Turkish commander, was slain, and finally, on September 11, 1565, the undertaking was abandoned as hopeless, and the Turkish armament withdrew.

Souliman's days were brought to an end in the midst of the siege of a Hungarian town, Sziget, one of the many events of the frontier warfare carried on without intermission, irrespective of the treaty between the heads of the two states. His death was carefully concealed from his men for fear of discouraging them in their assaults on the citadel of the town, which was being heroically defended by Zriny. Three days after the Sultan's death, on the 8th of September, 1566, only the central tower of the fort was left in the hands of the Hungarian champion. He loaded up his cannon to the muzzle, and in the smoke of the cannonade rushed into the thick of the Turkish lines and perished. He had taken care to arrange for the blowing up of the powder magazine at the time he made his sortie. The great tower fell in ruins, burying in the débris 3000 Turks. Souliman, in his life of seventy-one years, had personally led sixteen campaigns against the Christians; despite gout and physical weakness he would not hand over to a lieutenant the work of wiping out on the battlefield the stigma inflicted on Turkish arms by the failure at Malta.

VII
THE DECLINE OF THE OTTOMANS

In the expansion of their empire the main characteristic of the Ottomans had been fidelity to their tribal origin in Asia and to their religion; they showed little elasticity in modifying their system of government to new conditions, but they did recognize the necessity of progress. After their conversion to Mohammedanism their supreme guide was the "cheriat," under which term is signified the religious law of orthodox Moslems in the threefold division of Koran, Sunna, and the Sentences. In addition to this, there were the various official interpretations from the Sultan's hand in the application of the law called the Kanoun. So much importance had this aspect of the Sultan's functions that Souliman is remembered under his title of El Kanouni, that is, as a Turkish Justinian, rather than as a great military leader.

As head of the Empire, the Sultan's various titles are significant of the progressive stages of Ottoman development from a tribe to a great world power. The sovereign was still called Khan, as the head of a Turkish nomadic horde. When the Turks were converted to Islam, there was first added the title emir, an Arabic word, Chief of Believers; then came the name sultan, king; after the conquest of Constantinople, the Persian term padishah, king of kings, came into use. As we have seen, the conquest of Syria, of Egypt, and Arabia, made the Sultan defender of the holy cities and khalif.

After the conquest of the capital of the Cæsars, the influence of Byzantine traditions introduced a rigid system of court ceremonial; the days of patriarchal simplicity were closed; the person of the Sultan was raised in dignity. The change is clearly indicated in an edict by Mohammed: "It is not my will that anyone should eat with my imperial majesty; our ancestors were wont to eat with their ministers, but I have abolished it." The influence of the Byzantine bureaucratic hierarchy can be traced in the method of Ottoman administration; even in small details the permanence of the Roman imperial tradition is noteworthy. The sovereign's documents were, like those of his Greek predecessors, written in gold, purple, and azure. His letters of victory are but a continuation of the "litterae laureatae," while the bakkchich given to the Janitschars is but a reminiscence of the Imperial donation.

But actual assimilation between the Turks and their subject peoples was prevented by difference of religion. Racial differences made no distinction between Greeks, Albanians, Slavs, and Roumanians; they were all orthodox Christians, while the same people, if they became converts to Islam, were turned into Ottomans. The two types of religious allegiance were mutually irreconcilable. The peculiarity of Ottoman absolutism is to be found in the exclusion from governmental offices both of the free Moslem and the free Christian subjects of the Empire. The administration from top to bottom was in the hands of slaves, and these slaves were largely recruited from the children of Christian families of the subject races, who were constantly exposed to a detestable and unnatural form of oppression. The conquered populations were ruled despotically by men of Christian birth, who, during their initiation into slavery, had become Moslems. The famous Admiral Dragut was the son of a Christian of Asia Minor. Many of the famous generals were taken from Christian Albanian, Bosnian, and Dalmatian families. Of forty-eight grand viziers, only twelve were of Moslem birth.

Many Christians also became renegades, since an easy road to fortune was opened to them in this way. The hardy, adventurous, and less scrupulous elements of the conquered races accepted the religion of their conquerors; even a Paleologus, one of the last descendants of the imperial line, became a Moslem. There were conversions on a large scale, accomplished without special pressure among the landed proprietors, who were warriors by tradition, and who refused to endure the restrictions placed upon them by their religious profession.

The absolutism of the Sultan allowed no rival in any of the religious dignitaries of Islam. Even the Cheikh-ul-Islam had no authority over the Sultan; though the supreme ecclesiastical dignitary, he was only an authoritative expert in the law, the head of the body of oulemas, whose opinions could, if necessary, be passed over. At the same time the Cheikh-ul-

Islam's advice carried weight, and we sometimes hear of ambassadors being protected from the rage of the Sultan by his intervention. Legally, the Sultan was altogether above the law, or, rather, outside of it; he had the right to execute his brothers and children "if the peace of the world required it."

While women in the household of the Padishah played no conspicuous rôle, there were exceptions to the rule. Under the institution of the harem the Sultan's wives were slaves, and frequently domestic discords that had an influence on the destiny of the Empire were the result of harem intrigues. Often the sons of the Sultan were children of different parents. It was remarked in the time of Souliman that one of his wives, Roxelane, perhaps a Russian, acquired great ascendency over him. The Venetian ambassador reported that Souliman, contrary to the custom of his ancestors, had taken her for his legitimate wife. She became practically an empress, and was responsible for the Sultan's policy on several occasions. The war with Persia and the undermining of the power of the grand vizier were due to her.

As to the army, it kept the basis marked out for it by Ala-ed-Din. The élite body of the Janitschars still formed the chief protection of the Sultan's power. From the regular tribute of blood only Constantinople, Athens, Rhodes, a few other islands, and the Mainotes, the Laconian mountaineers, were exempted. Every five years the officers of the Sultan passed through the villages where children of the peasants were collected, and each fifth one was taken. Oftentimes Christian families were glad to pay the exaction even before the tax collectors appeared. Many of the members of the corps preserved traces of their early faith, and so drank wine without scruple. The solidarity of the body was maintained by exceptional privileges; their pay was large; they had a special share of the booty, or regular donatives, and the assurance of a pension for old age. The Janitschars were forbidden to marry or to engage in any trade. They could be punished only by their own officers, and even the grand vizier had no jurisdiction over them. In the time of Souliman they numbered 12,000, and as their numbers increased their turbulence grew. Selim attempted to meet this difficulty by incorporating in their body 7000 of the palace servants, and by dividing the command.

In the government of the subject peoples no uniformity was observed. The inhabitants of mountain regions, the Albanians, the Montenegrins, the Mainotes, the dwellers on Mt. Libanus, were protected from tyrannical actions. Where the country was level, there were no bounds to the barbarity of Turkish governmental methods. The vassal states, such as Transylvania, Moldavia, Georgia, were still ruled by native princes. But under Ottoman rule, in spite of the constant wars and the attendant anarchic conditions, there was worked out a crude kind of unity throughout the Empire. At least, with an Ottoman overlord, there prevailed a condition of internal peace between the various portions of the Empire, that gave stability to commercial relations and rendered communication easy between distant parts. Religious persecution in the sense in which it had existed in the Byzantine Empire, and in the Eastern domains of the Italian municipalities, was now unknown. At Rhodes the Greeks preferred the new régime to the rule of the Knights

Hospitalers, who, as Latins, had showed no sympathy with the Orthodox Church. In Crete and Greece the Turks were more popular as masters than the Venetians; and the Servians, Hungarians, and Roumanians preferred Moslem control to that of Catholic Austria.

Economically, the substitution of Turkish for Byzantine rule was a benefit to the Greek industrial population, who were better protected against foreign competition than they had ever been. Customs duties were arranged by an ad valorem scale, under which the Italian merchants were taxed four and a half times as much as the native Christians, although these, in turn, paid more than the Moslem traders who were favored by the Ottoman government. The Greek parts of the Empire entered upon an era of prosperity such as had not been seen since before the Latin conquest of Constantinople. For example, a large colony of Greeks established themselves at Ancona, where, in 1549, they transacted business to the annual value of 500,000 ducats. Moreover, the persecution of the Moors and Jews of Spain brought much capital into Ottoman territory; soon there were numbered 30,000 Spanish Jews at Constantinople, and 15,000 to 20,000 at Salonica. On this commercial basis the national renascence of the Greek peoples was founded. The landed proprietors of their own race mostly became Moslems, while their scholars and literary men found a refuge in the Occident; but the traders made and kept a place for themselves. Hence there was created a new center in which the old ideals of an independent Greek nationality could grow.

The Slav peoples were much worse off than the Greek population, because over their provinces were scattered Turkish garrisons, and through them passed the roads used by the Sultan for the interminable expeditions into Hungary. They retained fewer traces of autonomous existence, and their clergy were more ignorant than the Greek. The higher ecclesiastical positions were never bestowed on Slavs, and their landed gentry mostly became Moslem. The Roumanians, who were more remotely situated, preserved, under the form of vassalage, a complete national organization. They paid a moderate tribute, and were obliged to furnish military contingents, but there were no Turks in their territory, and no mosques were built among them. Wallachia and Moldavia, in the time of Souliman, made more than one attempt to throw off Turkish rule, but both principalities were compelled to submit before the middle of the sixteenth century.

The Turkish conquest of North Africa begins, strictly speaking, with the resistance of the Moslem Berber tribes and princes to the extension of Spanish influence over the African Mediterranean coast towns. This was a primary object of Charles V, who was bent on following up, by his control of sea power, the expulsion of the Moors from Spain. After many vicissitudes, Kheir-ed-Din, who had a powerful rival supported by the Spaniards, became King of Algiers. He turned to ask help from the Sultan of Constantinople, Selim, and he offered, in return, to become his vassal and to incorporate his small kingdom as an integral part of the Ottoman Empire.

Selim sent to Kheir-ed-Din 2000 Janitschars, well realizing the importance of using Algiers to block the progress of Charles V in his North African ambitions. Four thousand men were also recruited in Anatolia to defend the Moslem cause. It was a critical time, when the Viceroy of Sicily (1519), at the head of an armada of forty ships, appeared off Algiers. The Spaniards were beaten off, and many of the ships were lost in a storm. An even greater success for Moslem arms was the conquest, ten years later, of the citadel of Peñon, which commanded the harbor of the city that had for long been in the hands of the Spaniards. The island on which it stood was, by instructions from Kheir-ed-Din, joined to the mainland, and so an impregnably fortified harbor was constructed, which turned Algiers into the lasting home of those Barbary pirates that were for so long the plague of the Mediterranean commerce.

In 1535, Tunis was captured by Charles V in person, that monarch's great expedition of 400 ships and 30,000 men having proved too strong for Kheir-ed-Din, who had hurried to save the place with only 9000 men. At Algiers, the Emperor's next objective, Kheir-ed-Din could not take part personally in the work of defense, since he was not kept in command of the Turkish fleet. The government of Algiers was turned over to Hassan Aka, no idle leader. The Christian Emperor's armada was calculated to inspire terror; when it gathered at Spezzia, in August, 1541, it numbered 65 galleys and 451 transports, ready to embark the 29,000 troops, German, Italian, and Spanish, and the members of the Knights of Malta. In addition to the Emperor, who was in command, there were a large number of high officers of the various arms, and members of the nobility from Charles V's wide domains.

To oppose this brilliant host, Hassan had only 800 Turks, 5000 Moors, some Moriscos from Spain, and a few renegades from the Island of Majorca. There were rumors of treachery on the part of Hassan, but when the actual attack was made, nothing was left undone by him to keep up an effective resistance. He was helped by a severe storm, which caused much damage to the fleet; many ships were driven ashore, where the crews were attacked and the cargoes seized. An attempt to attack one of the forts by which the city was defended failed; the imperial troops got near the walls, but no farther; even the heroism of the Knights of Malta failed to save the day. The Spanish admiral, Doria, insisted that the expedition should reimbark, as his ships could not hold their anchorage. No other attempt on such a scale was made to arrest the progress of the Turkish vassal powers in North Africa. Tripoli was conquered in 1556, and there was incessant warfare with the Sherif of Fez, and also with the Spaniards, who still continued to hold Oran.

After the death of Hassan, the Turkish Beglerbeg at Algiers was Euldj-Ali, the son of a Calabrian fisherman. He had given up his faith and become one of the most dreaded Corsairs in the Mediterranean. He promoted the revolt of the Spanish Moriscos, afterwards winning a great success at Tunis, where, in 1573, Don John of Austria had brought 27,000 men to defend the Spanish citadel in the harbor. Euldj gathered an overwhelming force, took Goletta, and massacred the Spanish garrison. By this decisive victory Tunis became the seat of a Turkish pashalik. His next step was to make the throne of Morocco dependent on the Sultan.

The government of these African provinces was strictly centralized; over the whole was a Beglerbeg, who transmitted to his subordinates the directions which he received from Stamboul. The military strength of the provinces was remarkable, notwithstanding the unimportant part played by the regular Turkish soldiers. In their place there were regiments of renegades, Kabyles, and mercenaries of many nationalities. The navy was made up of corsairs, organized in a kind of guild, whose members made a life business of hazardous expeditions on the sea for the purpose of plundering vessels or harrying coast towns. No effort was made to interfere with the local customs of the tribes in the interior. All that was asked by the Beglerbeg was free passage for military expeditions and the payment of a large tribute.

Turkish rule was maintained with a very small display of military power. The whole country was controlled by little more than 15,000 men, most of them in a small number of garrison towns. Scattered through the country were small divisions of soldiers, whose chief business was the collection of the tribute. For the purposes of local government there were artificial tribes made up of natives, placed under the authority of a sheik or religious personage. The government of Algiers gave these groups certain landed concessions, and they paid some small dues to the sheik. They were expected to support soldiers or travelers when these appeared in their territory. They lived in tents or huts along a highway and the principal group was called a konak. In addition there were the real tribes, of warlike temper, that had once been independent; they paid no tax on their land or herds, but they had the function of collecting the tribute from inferior tribes called raias. This recognized position was enough to secure their loyalty.

The Algerian corsairs became famous for their ravages in the narrow seas, for their ships were models for speed and lightness, and their crews worked under the strictest discipline. Each vessel carried soldiers, cannon, and artillerymen. The merchant vessels they seized were brought back to Algiers, where the passengers, crews, and cargoes were sold at auction. These undertakings proved most profitable to the captains, "Reis," who built themselves a quarter of the town, where they lived in houses resembling fortresses, since their captives were kept in these buildings (bagni) until they could be sold. So was formed a Barbary aristocracy, which ended by winning its independence from Turkish rule. Among the corsairs were many renegades, especially Italians.

Algiers developed from a small town to a city of 100,000 souls. Many of the captives gave up Christianity and won their freedom. With such elements it is not surprising that the hold of the Turks on the inhabitants became weakened, until finally, not long after Greece won its freedom, Algiers was conquered by the French in the reign of Louis Philippe.

After the death of Souliman the Ottoman Sultanate underwent an eclipse. The succession of strong rulers was broken, and the empire was largely under the direction of the women of the harem and slaves. Of the eight successors of Souliman, one only can be called a military leader; many were mere children when they were called to the throne. Even Murad IV (1623-40), the most active of all, took the title of Sultan when he was twelve years old, and his career ended when he was twenty-eight. But even under such unfavorable conditions the progress of Turkish conquests was not arrested.

Of the western powers, the chief rival of the Ottoman Empire, during the sixteenth and seventeenth centuries, was Venice. At the cost of a yearly tribute of 236,000 ducats, she enjoyed great commercial privileges, was mistress of possessions in the Levant and on the Dalmatian coast, and blocked the way to complete Ottoman domination. Though Rhodes had been taken from the Knights, as we have seen, the large islands of Cyprus and Crete were still in the hands of the republic of the Adriatic, and her possessions in the Ægean Sea were a constant source of annoyance to the Turkish lords of the Morea. Piracy flourished in these ports, which became centers of retaliation for the excesses of the Barbary corsairs.

Aggressive measures were taken by Selim, Souliman's successor, who, after long years of peace between the two powers, summoned Venice, in 1570, to surrender the Island of Cyprus. One hundred and seventy-one Ottoman galleys supported the demand. Venice had tried to get the Christian powers to coöperate against the Turks, even calling on the Persians and the Arab tribes of Yemen to aid her in the defense of the island. But the arms of the Turkish generals soon prevailed. The chief fortress of the island, Famagusta, capitulated in 1571; and with its fall the Turks began the occupation of the island, which only ended after the war between Turkey and Russia in 1878.

During the progress of the siege an anti-Turkish league had been completed, composed of Venice and the Papacy, Spain, the Knights of Malta, and many Italian states. The result was the despatch of a large fleet under the command of Don John of Austria, at this time a youth of only twenty-two years. The objective of the armada was Patras, because, in the Gulf of Lepanto, close at hand, all of the squadrons of the Turkish navy were assembled. In all, the allies had 208 ships of war, the Ottomans slightly more, but the weakness of the Turks was due to the lack of soldiers to defend their fleet. There were but 2500 Janitschars on their galleys, the rest were troops raised from continental Greece, 22,000 in all, who were either new recruits or were not trained for naval warfare. Among the Turkish captains were present many older men who desired to avoid conflict with the Christian armada. Of a different temper were Hassan Pasha, the son of the famous Kheir-ed-Din, and Ali-Muezzin-Zade, the new captain pasha of the whole fleet.

The Christian fleet was in an admirable state of preparation for the fight. It was composed entirely of armed vessels directed by skilful rowers; besides the 203 galleys there were six galiasses, great floating citadels carrying heavy artillery and 500 soldiers. Don John had also armed the Venetian vessels with contingents of Spanish infantry. On the side of the Christians there was the additional advantage of superior equipment in armor and weapons for the individual warrior. The soldiers wore helmets and breastplates, and were armed with arquebuses, while the Turks used lances and arrows. There were also superior numbers on the side of the allies, the fighting men numbering between 28,000 and 29,000.

The two fleets took up the same position and adopted the same tactics. In the center on each side were collected the largest ships under the command of the respective chief admirals. Some initial successes were won by the Ottomans over the division made up of the Venetian vessels, but in the center, after desperate fighting, the men under Don John, owing to their superior weapons, got the better of their enemies, and the captain pasha was killed. The Algerian vessels showed much tactical superiority to the Christian right wing, under the command of John Andrew Doria; but, although they inflicted much damage, they could not save the day for the Ottomans. The victory cost the Christians dear, for they lost 12 galleys and 7500 men. But the defeat of the Turks was overwhelming; 15 galleys were sunk, 177 were captured, and many pashas and governors of provinces lost their lives; 12,000 to 15,000 of the galley slaves on the Turkish vessels, Christian captives, were set free.

Such was the remarkable victory of October 7, 1571, remarkable not only for the heroism displayed, and the sensation caused by the success of the Christians, who had for so long been incapable of resisting Ottoman aggression, but also because of the small practical results produced. The Christian armada returned to Corfu, and from there made for the coast of Italy, where it disbanded. On the side of the vanquished, Euldj-Ali, gathering together eighty-seven ships as a nucleus for a new Ottoman fleet, sailed into the harbor of Constantinople, and was welcomed as a conqueror by the Sultan and the grand vizier, Sokoli. New honors were heaped upon him, not altogether undeserved, for during the winter a new fleet, larger and better armed than the one destroyed, was made ready for sea.

The recuperative energy of the Ottoman Empire was not lost on the Venetians, and their agent at Constantinople, Antonio Barbaro, saw that there was more than an empty boast in the words of the Vizier, who said to him, "There is a great difference between your loss and ours. By taking from you the Kingdom of Cyprus we have cut off your arm; by defeating our fleet you have only shaved our beard. A beard grows out thicker for being shaven." This argument appealed to the republic, and in 1573 peace was made. The conditions were the cession of Cyprus, the payment of a heavy war indemnity by Venice, and a regulation of the frontier in Albania and Dalmatia, that secured to the Turks their ancient possessions there. The Venetians also were required to increase the annual tribute exacted for the Island of Zante, which was still in their hands.

Three generations after the taking of Cyprus the long-coveted island of Crete, or Candia, was annexed to the Ottoman Empire. Hostilities began between Venice and Sultan Ibrahim I, because of the seizure by the Knights of Malta of a Turkish vessel carrying high officials of the court to Egypt. The Maltese ships were received in the friendly harbors of Crete, where they took refuge. In April, 1645, a great fleet of 302 ships, and a large army of over 100,000 men, commanded by a Dalmatian, Pasha Joseph Markovitch, set sail for Crete. In June, one of the two chief fortresses of the island, Canea, was invested. After two months' siege it surrendered. In 1648 began the first siege of Candia, but this stronghold proved as hard to capture as Rhodes. During the course of twenty-one years it was the objective of repeated attacks on the part of the Turks, and only fell into their hands in 1669.

As has been seen, the Ottoman Empire began to decay from the top. The Sultan finally became the mere figurehead of palace intrigues, and the effect of the rottenness in the supreme head of a centralized military despotism was widespread. Taxation became extravagantly burdensome; the royal domains were alienated, the coinage was debased, offices were sold to the highest bidder, and this general venality caused the disappearance of the military fiefs from which the armies of the empire had been recruited.

The Janitschars lost their characteristic qualities as warriors when the custom of recruiting them from the Christian population was abandoned. They finally degenerated into a mere rabble of turbulent blackguards, composed of the worst elements of all nationalities, Christian and Moslem, who disappeared from the ranks during a war, or fled from the battlefield and lived normally by blackmail or by illicit trading. The abandonment of this living tithe was due probably to the jealousy of the Moslem families, who objected to the monopolizing by men of Christian birth of the lucrative privileges attached to an élite corps. The last time the tithe was collected was in 1676, when 3000 youths were brought in as recruits. With the abolition of the Janitschars dates the rise of the bands of brigands among both the Slavic and Hellenic populations. The able-bodied members of the conquered races found in this sphere of activity a chance for developing their capacities in guerrilla warfare; with the training and traditions so acquired they were able in later years to act as the leaders in the national movements which, during the course of the nineteenth century, ended in the dismemberment of the Ottoman provinces in Europe.

Spanish Conquerors

I
THE SPANIARD AND THE NEW WORLD

In the century which followed the discovery of America, not only was the lead in initiative taken by Spain never lost, but she practically had no competitors in the conquest and colonization of the New World. If the lines of medieval enterprise had been followed in the opening up of new territories for economic development, it should have fallen either to Venice or to Genoa to undertake the work of exploration and exploitation of these unknown regions. But times had changed, and the Italian republics had changed with them. Under the stress of the Turkish conquests, which had led to the organization of a great military and naval power in the East, Venice could follow nothing but a policy of self-protection that admitted neither of expansion nor of adventure. Internal changes in the Italian peninsula, indicated by the overlordship of Milan, had reduced the power of Genoa, which had already been weakened by her long contest with Venice for the naval mastery of the Mediterranean.

The rise of Spain was phenomenal; nothing exactly resembling it had been seen before, except in the case of those great tribal or national invasions that so often altered the face of Europe. For centuries, like Italy before the advent of Italian unity, Spain was only a geographical expression. Only fourteen years before Columbus' first voyage, the marriage of Ferdinand of Aragon and Isabella of Castile had consolidated the royal power on the Iberian peninsula and made these two Spanish monarchs lords of the whole land south of the Pyrenees, except in the kingdoms of Granada in the south, of Portugal in the west, and of Navarre in the north. A steady policy of aggression and conquest soon brought about the disappearance of the small kingdom of Granada. Between 1486 and 1489 Loja, Malaga, and Baza had been taken; Granada alone held out a few years more. Ferdinand, a most astute monarch of the type of Louis XI of France and Henry VII of England, had already crushed the Portuguese faction in Castile, who had favored the alliance of their queen with the King of Portugal. His ideals were for an absolute monarchy, which, by the elimination of feudal traditions and by the accumulation of wealth, might become the predominant power in western Europe.

There was no reason for Spain to become a colonizing power in the modern sense, since the peninsula was a sparsely populated country, large tracts of land having been opened up for occupation by the Christian conquests of Moorish territory. In preceding centuries, when the Christian princes began to win back, piece by piece, the lands belonging to the Moslems, a conciliatory policy had been adopted towards the conquered race; the Moors had kept their personal liberties and had been encouraged to group themselves in autonomous communities in the suburbs of Christian cities. Even when Granada was taken, favorable terms were given to its inhabitants, although in the end the promises were broken. They were conceded liberty of person, trade, education, and worship, the protection of Mohammedan law, administered by Mohammedan judges, and the benefit of mixed tribunals. But here and elsewhere Ferdinand's methods were a consistent application of the principles of an autocrat, and, when the New World fell as a prize to the Spanish conquerors, the usages of expansion by conquest at home in the Iberian peninsula were mercilessly applied. When Malaga was taken, the captive inhabitants were sold as slaves; one-third of the proceeds of the sale was taken for the redemption of Christian captives in Africa; another was given to those who had served in the army of occupation either as mercenaries or as officials, and the remaining portion was paid into the royal treasury. As to the land, it was laid out for a colony. The large tracts opened to colonization were offered on easy conditions to the Christian inhabitants of Spain.

It was not land hunger, therefore, which prompted the Spanish monarchs to accept Columbus' scheme of a westward route to the rich empires of the Orient. Profit-bringing trade by which stores of specie could be accumulated attracted the founders of Spanish absolutism. The project itself was not viewed with skepticism; its scientific basis was cogent; there were besides widely circulated stories of land existing in the West. But the one practical difficulty in the way of fitting out the proposed expedition was the war with the Moors of Granada, by which the Spanish treasury had been exhausted. After the city fell in January, 1492, several months were spent in haggling over terms. Columbus had made up his mind that if the voyage were sucessful he should be adequately rewarded for his trouble. Apart from conditions as to offices and the administration of the newly acquired possessions, it was agreed that he was to receive one clear tenth of all merchandise, whether gold, silver, pearls, spices, or whatsoever else was gained or gotten for the crown in his new jurisdiction. Moreover, there was a further clause inserted that in case Columbus should choose to contribute to the equipment of vessels employed in the new trade to the extent of one-eighth, he was to be at liberty to do so, thereby entitling himself to one-eighth part of the profits.

The prospects of a great trading adventure seemed altogether alluring. It must be remembered that the discoverer carried with him a letter from the Catholic monarchs to the Grand Khan of Tartary; and that it was this opening up of a direct trade route, with enormous possibilities for commercial profit, that inspired the Spanish conquest of America. Even after the configuration of the new continent had been made out by later voyagers, the fascination of establishing a connection with the Orient remained a strong inducement. Then as it faded away as an immediate possibility, the opportunity of securing large hoards of the precious metals stimulated discovery and exploration. The lust of territorial conquest remained associated with the lust of gold. The Spanish adventurer had no ideal aims; he was not attracted by the American continent because it offered a new home or because it presented a chance for trying political experiments. There was the same single-mindedness in the conquistador ideal as is seen to-day in the trust magnate who is searching for oil wells. The sordid aims called forth by the success of Columbus' expedition were not developed by the contest with the natives occupying the lands whose possession was coveted.

When the Spanish conquerors arrived in those unknown islands of the western sea the American continent was held by a number of the Turanian races which had one time peopled most of the Old World. Only a few relics of their predominance are seen in the Europe of to-day in the Basques, the Finns, and the Esthonians. Long before historical times the process of uniting Asia and Europe with America had begun. Probably thousands of years before the rise of Caucasian civilization along the Nile and the Euphrates, Turanian hordes found their way across the Behring Straits. Little capacity for attaining the arts of civilized life was shown by the American Turanians; there were, it is true, differences in social organization, but the general level of civilization was not far above the savage type, even in the Valley of Mexico or in Quito and Cuzco in South America.

Those who took part in the overthrow of the Aztec and Inca governments magnified their own achievements by describing themselves as the conquerors of great civilized empires. Such fictions were natural in men who desired to exalt the difficulties of a suddenly achieved fame, and the exaggeration was the more easily believed because of their seizure of large stores of those precious metals by which, in the Old World, progress in civilization was measured. From the point of view both of the home government and of those who took part in the first cycle of voyages, there was not much encouragement of profit to be derived in the islands and shores of the mainland touched by Columbus and by those who worked under his leadership and inspiration from 1492-1517—that is, during the first twenty-five years of Spanish conquest.

In the first voyage of Columbus much of the coast of Hayti was explored because of the stories told as to the existence of gold on the island. In the second expedition, made the following year, Dominica, Guadeloupe, Puerto Rico, Jamaica were discovered. The foundation of the first Spanish city on the island of Hayti was laid; then the explorer passed along the north coast of Cuba, which especially interested him because he took it to be the mainland of Cathay and Cipango not far from Malacca. In 1498, after discovering Trinidad, he reached the South American continent at the mouth of the Orinoco River, which was identified by him as one of the streams of the terrestrial paradise. Then followed complaints of administrative abuses which led to Columbus' return to the Spanish peninsula as a prisoner.

There was a fourth voyage in 1502 which extended as far as Honduras. After showing a piece of gold to the natives Columbus inquired of them by signs where the metal could be found. They pointed to the east, and after some further communications Columbus was convinced that the land of Cathay lay in that direction. He spent many weeks afterward in tacking along the shore against adverse winds and currents. Finally he landed at a place called by the natives Veragua, where the signs of civilized life, indicated by the village communities and the numbers of temples and sepulchers constructed of stone and lime, and suitably decorated, and, above all, the abundance of gold demonstrated to him that he had reached the golden Chersonese of the East. This was the land, he was sure, that had furnished King Solomon with his famous treasures. He set out from Veragua certain of discovering after a few leagues' journey the straits of Malacca. After that, to reach the mouth of the Ganges would only be a matter of a few days. When he found the peninsula larger than he expected, he turned back to Veragua, meaning to found a permanent settlement there; but the warlike natives forced him to take refuge on his ships. Disheartened, the explorer withdrew to Hayti, from whence he returned to Spain, where he died on May 20, 1506.

There was a curious vein of mysticism in Columbus' character, which comes out in a quotation made by him in his later years, from the famous medieval Apocalyptic, Joachim of Calabria. "The Rabbi Joachim," he writes, "says that out of Spain shall come he who shall rebuild the House of Mount Zion." His discovery, the explorer explained, would bring about the recovery of the Holy City and of the Sepulcher of Christ by means of the gold which would be found in the Indies. When he returned the first time from Hayti to Spain, he wrote that those whom he left behind would easily collect a ton of gold while he was absent, and that, therefore, in less than three years the capture of the Holy Sepulcher and the conquest of Jerusalem could be undertaken. Later on, he provided that the accumulated income of his property, which was to be invested in shares of the Bank of St. George in Genoa paying six per cent., should to the extent of one-half go to aid the expenses of recovering the holy places in Palestine.

The constant quest for gold that stimulated the voyages of the great explorer had, therefore, its basis in this extraordinary and fanatical revival of the spirit which had once inspired the Crusades. It was almost a mania with Columbus, whose letters contain eulogies on gold: "Who hath this, hath all that can be desired in the world; gold can even bring souls into Paradise." Though the metal could not be found in great quantities, he discovered nevertheless a way by which the New World might be made to yield the gold which was wanted. It was Columbus who started in America the traffic in human beings. The day after he arrived in the West Indies, he talked of the prospect of using the Indians for slave traffic, and he promised to send to Europe a whole shipful of these idolaters. He kept his promise also, for in 1495 he sent five hundred Indian captives to be sold at Seville. The next year three hundred more arrived at Cadiz. It has been not unnaturally supposed that the harsh treatment received later on by the explorer at the hands of the governor of Hayti had a close connection with Columbus' persistent policy of recruiting slave gangs from the natives of the islands he had visited. It is certain that Isabella was so outraged by the constant stream of West Indian slaves which had its source in Columbus' discoveries that she frequently directed their repatriation. It is significant also that Bobadilla, the man who sent Columbus back to Spain in irons, is spoken of by Las Casas as an upright and humane person.

This willingness to allow the inauguration of a trade in slaves in lieu of the export from the New World of the precious metal which was so persistently sought for may be also explained by the strangeness and uncouthness of the inhabitants of the West Indian islands. Apart from the Mexicans and Peruvians, the greatest extent of the New World was inhabited by peoples who had not yet got beyond the hunting stages of culture. They used, of course, articulate speech, they had the knowledge of fire, and employed a few rude instruments of stone and wood, but they were essentially savages, and up to this time man in an actually savage stage was not known to Europeans—even to travelers. Marco Polo, indeed, had told of the existence in the East of races who devoured human flesh, but he was not believed. It was the voyage of Columbus that revealed the practice to be a literal fact and gave it such impressive emphasis that the Indian name Carib or Caribbee, in the modified form of cannibal, came to be used to designate the savage who feeds on human flesh. The smaller islands of the Antilles were all occupied by branches of this parent stock, the Carib, all of whom were distinguished by savage ferocity. The name was given them by a rival race, the Arawaks, who under various designations lived in the four larger islands, Cuba, Jamaica, Hayti, and Puerto Rico. Both peoples had come from the opposite coast of South America, probably drifting to the islands by the help of the equatorial current. On the mainland there was constant warfare between the two, with distinct advantages on the side of the Carib.

When Columbus reached the Antilles, the Arawaks in Cuba and in Hayti were in process of extermination at the hands of the Caribs. The work of subjugation commenced by the savage Carib was taken up by the Spaniard; in a few years the Arawaks of the larger islands were absolutely destroyed. The vigorous race in the smaller islands was never dominated by the Spanish conquerors; even when Spanish domination in the islands gave place to English and French rule, the Carib kept up the contest for more than a century. But the long years of warfare caused their numbers to dwindle away. As late as 1773 a military expedition was ordered to be sent to the island of St. Vincent to exterminate the Carib population, who refused to be reduced. But in place of drastic measures it was resolved to deport them. They were finally removed to the mainland of Honduras, where from this original small group the increase has been so remarkable that to-day their settlements extend from Belize to Cape Gracias a Dios.

Hayti, the island where the first city of European foundation in the New World was established, may be taken as illustrating the point where the island population had reached the most advanced standard of life. It is true that in part of the island the Caribs had effected a landing and were driving the less warlike Arawaks before them. But Hayti, when the Spanish conquest began, was already an agricultural country. It had no dense forests; there was an absence of larger game; the climate was mild and equable, and there were broad open tracts of country well adapted to cultivation. When the island was discovered, the population was estimated to be above a million; a few years later, in 1508, when under the cruel methods of the Spanish conquest the inhabitants must have been very considerably reduced, there were still 60,000 males left. The island was probably therefore more densely populated than any part of the mainland. The natural food resources in the shape of fish and small game could hardly support such a number. The growing of maize was not unknown, but the evidence goes to prove that the natives lived largely on the product of enormous manioc plantations. The root of this plant was reduced to a pulp, the juice was pressed out, and after being exposed to heat, the residue took the form of a meal that could be turned into bread cakes. The preparation of a crop of manioc was not difficult. The great savannah lands of the island, which were covered with prairie grass, were burnt over; the soil was thrown up with a pointed stick, hardened by fire, a few cuttings of the stem were planted in, some slight weeding was done, and after twelve months, without additional labor, there was ready a heavy crop of roots that could be immediately converted into bread. According to Las Casas' estimate the labor of twenty women working six hours a day for a month was sufficient to provide bread enough to last three hundred persons for two years. The ease with which the crop was grown is shown by the naïve offer of a native chieftain to his Spanish masters to substitute for the tribute of gold which his people had no way of providing, an enormous field ready planted, which was to extend across the island from Isabella in the north to Santo Domingo in the south. The bulk of the natives including the males did not work at this primitive method of tillage, nor did they share in the breadmaking, but apparently their freedom from this kind of labor did not encourage other types of industry. The only metal worked was gold, though the island contained both copper and tin. For cutting they used stone implements, and for fishing bone hooks. Owing to the mild climate little clothing was necessary. The cotton plant was not artificially cultivated, both cloths and hammocks being made out of the wild cotton. Little attention was paid to housebuilding, though there were some large joint family houses. There was no stone architecture, and even fortification in its simplest form was not known.

For the purposes of warfare the island was divided into five districts, each of which contributed several thousand warriors under an independent chief, whose office was devolved upon him by hereditary descent. The warlike equipment was inadequate, not equal to that used by the aggressive Caribs, who had the training which comes from the hunting of large game. The Arawaks were therefore completely at the mercy of their savage assailants, unless they fought the Caribs with overwhelming numbers on their side. When the Spaniards began the conquest of the island the mild natives had, therefore, no chance of withstanding even small numbers of Europeans.

As a further test of the stage of culture reached by these, the most advanced of the islanders, we may take their religion, which proves their affinity to the lowest peoples known. They practised a simple form of fetichism combined with ancestor worship. There was a class of wizards, both men and women, who were supposed to control the spirit world. The multitude of spirits were embodied in the form of idols, sometimes in human shape, made of various materials. There were also idols consisting of the wooden figures of dead chiefs set up over their places of burial. The most famous of this type of idol were the images of the two first ancestors of mankind that were kept in the cave from which they had emerged after the deluge. As worship to these divinities, rude hymns were recited and manioc bread was used as a sacrificial offering and afterwards distributed among the worshippers.

The backward condition of the islanders did not discourage the projects of colonization which were inaugurated immediately on Columbus' return from his first voyage. In 1493 the new flotilla showed the expansion of the hopes based on the discoverer's success of the year before; there were now seventeen ships carrying 1200 men: miners, artisans, farmers, noblemen, all bent on the work of colonization. Twelve priests were included in the party. The exploration of the interior of the island was taken in hand by one of Columbus' lieutenants, whose object was to discover gold and to commence the systematic working of the mines.

It was nearly a year before the Admiral returned to Hayti. In the meantime affairs in the nascent colony were in anything but a happy condition. The colonists, dissatisfied probably because fortunes were not coming quickly enough, were sending to the home government petitions and complaints condemning Columbus' administration. A royal commissioner was soon sent out, whose personal inspection of the island resulted in a most unfavorable report being despatched to the Spanish sovereigns. Internal dissensions continued, due to quarrels over questions of jurisdiction, but these difficulties were less serious than the miseries occasioned by the oppression of the natives. Though Las Casas describes them as "the most humble, patient, loving, peaceful, and docile people, without contentions or tumults; neither fractious nor quarrelsome, without hatred or desire for revenge, more than any other people of the world," the advent among them of colonists and adventurers bent on introducing the advanced economic system of Europe changed everything. A tribute was laid upon the whole population of the island which required that each Indian above fourteen years of age was to pay a little bell filled with gold every three months. In all other provinces the natives were to pay an "arroba" of cotton.

It was soon found that these taxes could not be collected. Accordingly, in 1496, a change was made; instead of gold and cotton, labor was substituted. The Indians near the plantations were obliged to prepare and work them. Such was the origin of the "repartimiento" system which, applied to a population unused to regular toil, and administered by harsh and unprincipled masters, transformed the larger Antilles into virtual prison houses. The natives who resisted were treated as guilty of rebellion and were sent to Spain to be sold as slaves. Oftentimes, in order to escape this servitude, whole villages and even tribes would take refuge in the forests. Regular raids were organized against those who tried to evade the tribute; those who were captured were sent to Spain. In 1498 the vessels of Columbus, fleet took home a consignment of six hundred, one-third of whom were given to the masters of the ships to cover the freight charges.

There were scruples on the part of the home government against sanctioning such an arrangement, and on more than one occasion, in applying his policy of "pacific penetration," Columbus acted without waiting for royal sanction. After the two years' insurrection of Roldon, the chief justice, had been brought to an end by mutual agreement, Columbus, in order to institute an era of good feeling, made a generous distribution of slaves and lands among Roldon's supporters. Each man was to receive a certain number of hillocks for the purpose of manioc culture. The operation of tillage was placed in the hands of an Indian chieftain whose people were obliged to dwell on the land they cultivated. Those of the former rebels who chose to return home received from one to three slaves apiece. Fifteen took advantage of this last offer; but they soon found themselves confronted by a royal proclamation which directed that all holders of slaves given them by Columbus should return them to Hayti under pain of death. An unfortunate exception was, however, made in the case of Indians who had been taken as rebels.

Further indications of the attempt of the home government to curb the economic exploitation of the island introduced by Columbus are seen in the instructions given to Nicolas de Ovando, who succeeded Bobadilla as royal governor in April, 1502. He was directed to convert the Indians, not to maltreat them, nor to reduce them to slavery; to require them to work the gold mines, but to pay for their work; to refuse to allow Jews or Moors to have access to the island; to accept blacks as slaves. The idle and the dissolute were to be returned to Spain, and all mining concessions made by the previous governor were to be revoked. Ovando's rule was to extend over all of the West Indies, with his residence on Hispaniola (Hayti).

The expedition conveying the new chief was of imposing size; there were thirty ships and 2500 persons. On board was the famous Las Casas, afterwards the apostle and champion of the Indians, who came now to make his fortune in the New World like so many other adventurers. The attraction of the reported mines of gold was irresistible, and it can be imagined how great was the joy of the Spaniards when the first news they heard in the colony was the report of the finding of a huge nugget of gold thirty-five pounds in weight. This treasure was dug up by an Indian girl not far from the settlement of San Domingo.

Equally reassuring as a foundation for the prosperity of the colony was a second piece of news which recounted how, in a part of the island, there had been an uprising of the natives which had been successfully punished, and in which the victors had reaped the reward of turning the captured rebels into slaves. It was well known that the feeling in the home country was becoming distinctly unfavorable to a colonial polity practised so ruthlessly on the natives. The Spanish sovereigns had declared themselves to be the protectors of the Indians, and had ordered them both to be treated mildly by the civil authorities and to be prepared for Christianity by the representatives of the Church. They were to be civilized, and taught the Spanish language and habits of industry. No arms should be sold to them, nor strong drink; there was to be cultivation of the soil, but it was not to be done under duress. The Indian lands could be bought or sold, and the natives were to be encouraged to adopt autonomous municipal institutions under the direction of the priests. They were also to have the right of appearing in court to act as witnesses or to institute suits. As to the mines, they were permitted to work in them, but were not to be forced. Even tribal customs were allowed to be continued, where they were not contrary to the ethical obligations of a higher type of civilization.

It was an almost idyllic scheme for assuming the white man's burden, but it remained a paper reformation; as the testimony of Las Casas shows. For some time before his ordination this untiring advocate of the rights of the natives lived in Hispaniola the life of the ordinary Spanish colonist. He acquired slaves; worked them in the mines, and devoted himself with such assiduity to the control of the estates previously acquired in the colony by his father that he declares they turned in to him a yearly income of 100,000 castellanes, an enormous sum, considering the purchasing power of money at the beginning of the sixteenth century.

The gold fever caused terrible havoc among the colonists; they were not used to manual labor, they knew nothing of the methods of mining, they were poorly supplied with tools for the work. Often they rushed to the mines without taking with them an adequate supply of food. The tropical climate soon brought on a strange disease, probably pernicious malaria. Under its ravages, in a short period, 2500 of Ovando's men met their deaths not long after they came to the colony. The conditions of life were hard, even food being scarce in the neighborhood of the mines, and, when the royal tax of one-fifth was deducted from the small proceeds after the expenses were paid, the colonist's share was barely sufficient to cover his living expenses. The few who were contented with agricultural pursuits were really better off in every way, but in the mania for gold discovery no thought was given to the magnificent resources of the soil.

Las Casas notes that the worst effects of this colonial policy began in the year 1504, when Queen Isabella's death became known. Ovando's short and easy methods with the natives are described with great vividness by Las Casas, who took part in the warfare against one of the native chieftains. It was, of course, a conflict in which the weaker race could play their part only through ruse and stratagem, for, as Las Casas says, "all their wars are little more than games with little sticks such as children play in our countries." Nor were the natives well qualified even for this sort of hostilities, since they were "most humble, most patient, most peaceful and calm, without strife or tumult; not wrangling nor querulous, as free from hate and desire for revenge as any in the world." Even Columbus, in the hearing of Las Casas, bore witness to their humane qualities. He said that he met with such gentle and agreeable reception and such help and guidance when the ship in which he sailed was lost there, that in his own country and from his own father better treatment would not have been possible.

The escape of the natives to the mountains and their efforts to retaliate started, according to Las Casas, the war of extermination. When the governor Ovando arrived in the part of the island which was ruled over by a woman chieftain, Anacaona, more than 300 chiefs were brought together and assured of the pacific intentions of the Europeans. "He lured the principal ones by fraud into a straw house, and, setting fire to it, he burnt them alive; all the others, together with numberless people, were put to the sword and lance; and to do honor to the lady Anacaona, they hanged her." Death by fire, administered with the most exquisitely devised tortures, was the fate of the Indian chieftains. "I once saw," he continues, "that they had four or five of the chief lords stretched on the gridiron to burn them, and I think also there were two or three pairs of gridirons where they were burning others." The fugitives were hunted down by boar-hounds who were taught and trained to tear an Indian to pieces as soon as they saw him.

Although Cuba had been discovered by Columbus, no attempt was made to occupy the island until 1511, when his son Diego, acting under the powers conferred upon him by the home government, selected Velasquez, one of the oldest and most respected colonists in Hispaniola, to take charge of the enterprise. With only three hundred men he easily occupied the island. Like the Indians of Hispaniola they were not able to organize any effective resistance. There was a repetition of the atrocities by which Hispaniola had been pacified. By 1521 the miserable natives were so brought under control that they were turned into the unwilling and inefficient instruments of the colonial policy of their new masters.

Las Casas was present at the close of this expedition, and he speaks of frequent burnings and hangings of the inhabitants. Many committed suicide to escape the enforced working in the mines. The following item in his indictment deserves to be reproduced: "There was," he says, "an officer of the king in this island to whose share 300 Indians fell, and by the end of three months he had, through labor in the mines, caused the deaths of 270; so that he had only 30 left, which was the tenth part. The authorities afterwards gave him as many again, and again he killed them; and they continued to give and he to kill.... In three or four months, I being present, more than 7000 children died of hunger, their fathers and mothers having been taken to the mines." The concentration of the conquerors on economic success may be gathered from the experience of Las Casas himself, who, though he had done all in his power to restrain the commission of cruel deeds, wherever he was present, did not hesitate to take advantage, priest though he was, of the "repartimiento" system, under which he received a valuable piece of land and a number of Indians to work it, in recognition of the services he had rendered in conciliating the natives.

Columbus, it must be remembered, received an authorization to deport from Spain criminals under sentence of either partial or perpetual banishment. Other delinquents had had their sentences remitted provided they agreed to go to the Indies. The result among such a motley crowd, released from the ordinary pressure of social obligations, was a laxity and dissoluteness such as was seen in the nineteenth century among frontier communities. Even Columbus spoke with no admiration of the colonists. "I know," he said, "that numbers of men have gone to the Indies who did not deserve water from God or man."

Despite the fact that the exploration and subjugation of the larger Antilles went on with feverish energy, Puerto Rico and Jamaica both being taken in 1509, the profits of the colonial system were most disappointing. The expeditions were costly, there was no economy in organization; at home and abroad, there were a host of officials who had to receive salaries. The gold mines were poor in quality. The native population, by war and disease, had been so much diminished that labor became scarce. The smaller islands were then drawn upon to keep up the supply of labor in Hispaniola, and as the death-rate still continued excessively high, the place of the natives was filled by negroes imported from the Portuguese colonies in Africa. Some negroes were taken to Hispaniola as early as 1505. In 1517 the African slave traffic was authorized by Charles V.

A more intelligent side of the colonial system was seen in the aim of the government to acclimatize in America European plants, trees, and domestic animals. From the time of the second voyage of Columbus there had been detailed government orders, according to which each ship that carried colonists should also be provided with specimens of such seeds as might be useful. Though there were very few domesticated animals in America, it was soon found that the European varieties would flourish there. Las Casas often speaks of the astonishment caused among the natives by their first sight of the horse. This animal soon became an economic necessity, and in many places herds of wild horses in unoccupied regions proved how fast the original stock multiplied in the newly discovered countries. Cattle also soon became one of the chief articles of internal trade between the colonies, and hides were one of the staple goods carried on the fleets engaged in West Indian trade. Sheep and European poultry also were introduced with great success. As to plants, the vine was not encouraged because the mother country produced more wine than was needed for home consumption, and it was an article that could be transported easily to the colonists. The introduction of the sugar-cane was a social benefaction, for it set the settlers free from the burden of gold mining under unfavorable conditions. The sugar industry was developed rapidly after the introduction of negro labor.

With the prevailing ideas of state control of industry, colonial autonomy was out of the question. The need of a central body with supreme powers was suggested from the first by the dissensions caused by the conflict of jurisdiction between the various officials, whose spheres of action were not carefully distinguished. In 1509 the king decided to establish at Hispaniola a supreme tribunal which could hear appeals from the decisions of the governor. From this body grew the committee called the Real Audiencia, or royal court of claims, which, after 1521, governed most of the West Indies. The function of this body was to look after the welfare of the natives, to watch over the executive acts of the governor and other functionaries, and to put a stop to abuses. An appeal from the committee lay to the Council of the Indies in Spain. This body was given final jurisdiction in all civil, military, ecclesiastical, and commercial affairs. With the consent of the king it named the viceroys, the presidents of the Audiencia, and the governors, and it had full control of the higher ecclesiastical patronage.

There was also the Indian Chamber of Commerce, the so-called Casa de Contratacion, which was intrusted with the supervision of the West Indian trade. This body saw to the provision of ships, received all goods, and had jurisdiction of all commercial questions between the colonies and the home country. Through the "Casa" passed all the enormous mineral wealth that came from the opening up of the mines on the continent of America. In 1515, owing to the representations made in Spain by Las Casas of the grievances of the native population, Cardinal Ximenes sent three friars of the order of St. Jerome with full authority to act on behalf of the Indians. Las Casas was appointed protector. When the commission was under discussion, he asked specifically for unconditional liberty for the natives and for the suppression of the serf system in all its forms and provisions, in order to enable the European proprietors to work their estates profitably. These humanitarian efforts had little effect in arresting the prevailing methods of exploitation. When the pearl coast near Trinidad in the northeastern region of South America attracted settlers, there was a fresh demand for enforced labor of a new type, and the native tribes were raided in order to secure supplies of pearl divers. Although through the voyages of explorers various widely separated points on the mainland had been touched, no place had been effectively occupied by settlement. Wherever efforts were made, the native population, the Caribs, were found to have such warlike qualities that no successful foothold could be secured. The climate also proved fatal to Europeans. After Balboa made his celebrated passage across the Isthmus, an expedition of 15 ships and 2000 men came to occupy the land, but 600 of these died in a few months.

No point yet visited by European adventurers had offered examples of native civilization higher than the primitive standards attained by the Carib and the Arawak. But in the interior, in the thick forests of Central America, were scattered about the relics of an ancient culture. In a triangular space including some of northern Yucatan, Mitla in Oaxaca, and Copan in Honduras, there are the remains of sixty communities distinguished by temples, tombs, statues, bas reliefs, fragments of buildings, and deserted palaces. These are relics of a race who at the discovery of America had lost their supremacy for many generations. According to some reckonings, at least as early as the twelfth century these celebrated dead cities were founded.

The difficulty of historical research in reconstructing the records of these aboriginal peoples is due partly to poor methods of transmission and also to the fact that so many of the original documents were lost at the time of the Spanish conquest and before. Chronological reckonings were kept for the purpose of marking the days on which tributes and sacrifices were due. To this were added the figures of chieftains, the notices of tribal conquests, and such events as floods, famines, and eclipses. All of this miscellaneous popular lore was embodied in paintings, executed by a large class of artists, some of whom were women, on paper or fiber rolls or on prepared skins. For this picture-writing skins, oblong in shape and of great length, were employed. Along with these "pinturas" there was handed down an oral method of interpretation. Our knowledge of Mexican history has to be derived from the surviving examples of these picture rolls and from the traditional explanations which were taken down in writing at the time of the entrance of the Spaniards into the country.

The tradition existing in Mexico at this period told how the primitive stock inhabiting the land were giants, many of whom had perished by flood, fire, and earthquake. Then came a body of men who wished to reach the sun, and for this purpose they reared a tower. The sun, angered at the presumption of the earth-dwellers in aspiring to share with the gods the dwellings in the heavens, summoned all of the supernatural powers; the building was destroyed; and the guilty mortals were scattered over the earth. A mythical legislator then appears in Central America who teaches the people, the offspring of the giants, the arts of civilized life. The basis of this folklore may not unreasonably be ascribed to the finding of the bones of large extinct animals and, on the site of the Central American ruined cities, of mammoth statues of human beings. The residuum of truth seems to be that the Mexicans of the Conquest were correct in their common tradition that their ancestors had come from the north, and that the country had been gradually occupied by successive swarms of invaders who came south while they were still dependent on hunting game for their food and were finally reduced to settled forms of life by the cultivation of maize. The various tribes who took part in this migration are called by the Mexican word "Nahuatlaca," used to denote those communities who were dependent on agriculture and followed a nahua or rule of life dictated by a custom administered by hereditary chiefs. At the beginning of the sixteenth century the Nahuatlaca had reached the present limits of Costa Rica. That there were aboriginal inhabitants is inferred from the mention of the Otomi, the Huaxtecs, the Totonacs, and the Ulmecs, who at the time of the Conquest occupied districts not overrun by the Nahuatlacan immigration.

In the first stage of the southward movement the Toltecs take the lead; it is stated that, being expelled from their own country, they came from the region of the north by both land and sea. Their chief center in their new land was Tollan, a pueblo which stands on a tributary of the Moctezuma River, a stream which falls into the Gulf of Mexico. This place seems to have been once a center of trade, for the Toltecs had the reputation of being clever craftsmen. In addition to knowledge of preparing skins and of manufacturing clothing and articles of domestic use, they must have become familiar with various metals and with the employment of stone for building. Colored stones and crystals were used in their decorative work; from the coasts were brought the colored shells with which they covered their buildings, and the feathers which were woven into their tapestry. Besides this, they had a reputation for the knowledge of medicinal plants. The ruins of Tollan are extensive; as described by those who saw some of the still extant buildings at the time of the Conquest, they must have been most impressive. Sahogun mentions especially the Chalchiauhapan (On the blue water) because it was built between the two forks of the river. There were richly decorated apartments, four being more magnificent than the rest. One was called the House of Gold, another the House of Green Jade and Turquoise; a third room was covered with colored sea-shells arranged as mosaics, the interstices being filled with silver; the last room was decorated in red stones, combined with colored shells. There were besides four rooms adorned with tapestry made of the plumage of different colored birds. As with Selinus, a famous Greek city in Sicily, the downfall of Tollan must have been sudden, for there was an unfinished building seen in the ruins with remarkable pillars in the form of rattlesnakes, and also a mound in process of construction to be used as a foundation of a building of unusually large size. This fate seems to have overtaken it some centuries before the Spanish conquest, and was probably due to an insurrection among the subordinate pueblos.

The name Toltec came to be used as a synonym for a builder in stone or a worker of metals, and it was due to the influence of this race that the other branches of the Nahuatlaca stock made their progress in the civilizing arts. Not only do they stand out among other peoples of the New World as prominent in the pursuit of useful arts and in artistic achievement, but they deserve a place of honor because the deity they worshipped, Suetzalcohuatl, was not propiatiated by sacrifices of blood, but by offerings of maize, perfumes, and flowers. Probably many of them migrated to the regions of Central America, where they were able to preserve their own traditions. Here can be seen better than in the neighborhood of their ancient capital the specimens of their artistic skill. Some of the Toltecs of the dispersion took refuge at Cholula, which at the time of the Conquest was the chief seat of Toltec arts and religion, and also the center of the slave trade. Not far off is the town of Tlaxcallan.

The dissolution of the Toltec control was followed by a long period marked by successive waves of migration. Some of these nomadic tribes who described themselves as Chichimecs of the sun (Teo Chichimecs) established themselves in the strong places of the mountains, and took possession of Tlaxcallan, making it their center. In time this pueblo and its neighbors became of great importance, emigrants spreading from it over parts of Yucatan and Central America. Even at the time of the Spanish conquest the territory which Tlaxcallan dominated, although it was only forty miles in its greatest length and considerably narrower in breadth, mustered 50,000 warriors.

The spread of the Nahuatlaca race by their various emigrating swarms brought them over all parts of the Mexican plateau, and also to the coast both of the Atlantic and Pacific, but the center of their rule lay in the narrow Valley of Mexico, probably once the crater of an immense volcano surrounded by a girdle of mountains. There were fifty pueblos in the valley placed on or near the four lakes which, by changes in the distribution of land and water, had taken the place of the one large body of water that had once filled the extinct crater. Before the coming of the Nahuatlaca the district was occupied by the Otomis, whose language is still spoken in the neighborhood of Mexico City.

When the migration took place, Tezcuco, situated on the northeastern shore of the lake, became a dominant pueblo, and was at the head of a considerable confederacy. On the western side of the lake was another group of pueblos known as the Tecpanecs, who were rivals of Tezcuco. Here there settled about the year 1200 a vagrant tribe of the Chichimecs; the new arrivals were named by the Tecpanecs crane people or Aztecs, probably from their habit of wading in the marshy shores of the lake while engaged in fishing. The newcomers proved industrious, and in the course of time reclaimed the marshy island, building on the land two towns, the villages of Tenochtitlan (place of a prickly pear) and Tlatelolco (place of a hill). According to Aztec folklore, when they took possession of the island, they found on it a prickly pear tree growing on a rock and on this rock they saw an eagle devouring a snake. This fable is still recalled in the present arms of the republic of Mexico.

The two Aztec pueblos on the lake remained distinct communities until 1473, a fact which suggests their being built on separate islands, according to the traditional account. By help of the Aztecs, who were skilled in the art of war, the Tecpanec confederacy made great advances in dominating the valley. There was a little contest with Tezcuco when the confederates demanded from its people the usual tribute of cotton cloth; Tezcuco was taken and handed over to the Aztecs as a reward for their valuable services. The growing importance of the island pueblos soon, however, aroused the jealousy of the Tecpanecs and they resolved to suppress the two island communities by transferring the inhabitants to the shores of the lake. In the war which followed, though many of the people of the islands were at first reluctant to try conclusions with their powerful neighbors, the counsels of their warlike leader, Ischohuatl, prevailed. Azcapozalco, the center of the Tecpanec confederacy was captured, and with this conquest, which took place in or about the year 1428, Tenochtitlan or Mexico became the dominant power in the valley.

The island pueblos showed a statesmanlike policy in dealing with their neighbors; Tezcuco was restored to something like an autonomous position, and in the group of pueblos in the valley, of which the island communities were now the head, an equitable distribution of the tribute formerly collected by the Tecpanecs was made. Tezcuco also, and Tlacopan, a Tecpanec pueblo, were given a specific district over which to preside, and were allowed to pursue untrammeled their own line of conquest. To secure the dominant power of Mexico, causeways were built in three directions to the shore, and with other works constructed on two of the lakes, by which the straits between the lakes of Tezcuco and Xochimilco were bridged, a strong fortified place came into existence which was practically impregnable. The warlike and aggressive traditions of Ischohuatl were so well maintained throughout the ninety-two years between the formation of the confederacy and the advent of the Spanish invaders that large tracts of country outside of the valley were turned into tributary regions.

A considerable portion of this work of expansion was done by Ischohuatl's successor, his nephew Montezuma the First, who ruled over Tenochtitlan for twenty-eight years (1436-1464). During his reign the limits of Mexican rule were extended nearly to those formed by the Spaniards, the area of conquest being decided largely by commercial reasons. Wherever in the Pacific district there were honey, cacao, tangerines, precious stones, copal gums, cinnabar, and gold, that region was marked out for absorption. These Pacific regions extended 800 miles in length and, because of the value of their products, were the most important of all the Mexican dominion. On the side of the Gulf of Mexico the eastern part of the present state of Vera Cruz was rendered tributary; from this district the most prized object of exportation was the quetzalli feathers used for standards and for warriors' plumes. There was trade from Mexico with the Caribs on the Gulf, for Columbus met, in 1502, a Carib vessel having a cargo of cotton cloaks, tunics, skirts, Mexican swords, stone knives, bronze hatchets and bells, pans for smelting bronze, and cacao. From the time of Montezuma I to the reign of the second of the name, the sovereignty was held by three brothers in succession. During this period there was a revolt of the sister community of Tlatelolco, the suppression of which brought to an end the long existing equality in the confederation headed by this pueblo. Apart from this the boundaries of the tributary area do not seem to have been enlarged.

Altogether there are found in the roll of tributary pueblos 358 names when Montezuma II was dominant chief (1502-1520). These were small industrial settlements in all of which a particular kind of tribute was prepared; some sent cotton cloths, others raw cotton, others timber for fuel or building; from others came weapons, deerskins, tobacco. The tributes were generally paid annually in prescribed quantities. Under this system the great bulk of the population, the Nahuatlacan peasantry, were condemned to a life of severest toil of all kinds done in behalf of the warrior and priestly classes. The warriors, too, every twenty days, had to take the field, partly as a military exercise, partly also to provide the human sacrifices that, according to their old elaborate Mexican ritual, had to be offered to the gods. The priests took charge of the prisoners, prepared them for the sacrifices, divided the flesh of the victims, and arranged their skulls in the precincts of the temple, this being the method of keeping a regular toll of the offerings. There were more commonplace tasks of the priestly order, the Teopixqui, that must have filled up the intervals between the frequent great sacrificial festivals. In each teopan, or temple dedicated to a divinity, the sacred fire was kept ever burning; besides, there was the regular offering of incense, four times a day, at sunrise, noon, sunset, and midnight. To keep up this sequence of devotion and also the prescribed immolations, at stated intervals the heavens were scrutinized with official vigilance day and night. At midnight all those attached to the teopan were aroused for the solemn offering of blood that took place in a penitential chamber, each worshiper supplying his share of blood by tearing his own body with a strap of aloe thorns.

In their religious system the Aztecs, like the other members of the Nahua stock, had reached, in a technical sense, a highly differentiated standard. They had long left behind that stage of the lowest savage life where there is no recognition even of spirits, those substantial and active beings who are made responsible for the changes in the material world that the savage cannot otherwise explain. When the spirit is supposed to be composed, not of flesh and blood, but of some ethereal matter the era of civilization begins. According to savage belief the spirits are made in the image of a man, consisting of flesh and blood like man, and also requiring, like him, nourishment of food and drink. This principle took the widest extension in the Nahuatlacan worship; with the development of tribal life and the organization of confederacies there went hand in hand the regular provision of meat and drink offerings organized on a very large scale to secure the benevolence of the divinities. Various familiar forms of fetich worship were employed. Probably before the fashioning of idols by the hand of man natural objects such as plants, trees, mountains, and animals were worshipped; for example, in Mexico there was a national annual sacrifice to the mountains. In the frequent human sacrifices the victim was slain with a stone knife, on a stone slab, while the neck and limbs were kept in place by a collar and fetters made of stone. From the maize plant developed some of the most important deities in the Mexican religion. There was a long midsummer festival of eight days devoted to this vegetable, one of the prime necessities of life, at which one victim, a slave girl, was offered to the spirit dwelling in the maize. At the end of the eighteenth century the idol before which the sacrificial ceremony was performed was discovered in one of the squares in Mexico, recalling the procession in which it was carried, bound round with skulls, dead snakes, maize leaves, and ears. The toad, as the offspring of water and the symbol of the water spirit, was an object of veneration. The rabbit, as an animal considered totally devoid of sense, was worshipped as a drink god, to whom offerings were made that the worshipper might escape the deleterious effects of an over indulgence in pulque. Like other people in the primitive stage of culture the Mexicans venerated rivers and lakes as manifestations of will.

The common practice of worship of the dead prevailed also in Mexico, where its existence is attested by the preservation of the skull, or by the blocks of stone surmounted by enormous human heads which invariably denote the distinguished dead, because the gods are always represented with all their limbs. There was also a large heavenly hierarchy, gods of the atmosphere and stellar powers, some being associated with particular mountains, but the most important of all was Tezcatlipoca the giver and sustainer of life, the symbol of the wind, the bestower of life and death. Next to him came the sun god, Huitzilopochtli. He being a living person was, as appeared from the natural phenomena seen in the succession of the seasons and the change from day to night, especially in need of food. His vitality frequently shows signs of failing. It is therefore especially incumbent upon man to help him in this struggle for existence. So necessary was the maintenance of this principle of religious faith that the sun always received a share of the human victims offered to the other divinities. But all sorts of vegetable and animal life were offered to this needy divinity, who seemed to the Mexicans to show such constant signs of an impaired vitality. In the pictures of the Aztecs the rays of the sun, significantly represented as long crimson tongues licking up blood, constantly appear. The order of society was so regulated as to keep the sun in full vigorous condition; hence the never ending slaughter of human victims supplied by incessant warfare with neighboring tribes to provide the food supply for the sun. If there had been large animals in Mexico, these ghastly immolations of human victims might not have stained the progress of the Aztec people, for it is an established principle that the search for food is closely related to the development of religion among primitive races.

As the people of Nahuatlaca stock advanced economically and politically, they applied the results of their experience to their primitive tribal religion. Along with the system of tributes which maintained the dominant pueblo, there were expeditions made for securing the tribute to the sun god, called in the language of religious imagery "the plucking of flowers." As the service of the god was connected with military expeditions, Huitzilopochtli was the Aztec god of war, the tutelar divinity of the warrior class. Twice a year in Mexico there were special rites in the building called the Abode of the Eagles, where the warriors assembled to send a messenger to their patron. In the principal court of the building there was a colossal symbol of the sun, in the shape of a solar wheel sending forth rays of gold. Before it was a great stone at the top of forty steps, called the cap of the eagles; the middle of the altar was hollowed out to receive the victim's blood, and here the poor captive was brought dressed in the colors of the sun. He carried a staff, a shield, and a bundle of coloring matter, the purpose of which seems to have been to enable the sun to decorate his face. Just before the immolation the victim was addressed in the following words: "Sir, we pray you go to our god, the sun, and greet him on our behalf; tell him that his sons and warriors and chiefs, those who remain here, pray for him to remember them and to favor them from that place where he is, and to receive this small offering which we send him. Give him this staff to help him on his journey and this shield for his defense, and all the rest you have in this bundle." Those who fell on the field of battle were believed, as a reward, to be transported into the house of the sun, where they became his servants and shared in his constant banquets.

With the eclecticism common to all religions and that specially marks its primitive type, an ancient god of the Toltecs, Quetzalcohuatl, also a solar deity, was adopted as a member of the Aztec divine hierarchy. According to tradition, this divine being left his abode in heaven for the purpose of showing beneficence to mankind. From him man learnt the arts of life, and while he was on earth the age of gold prevailed. Unlike the other deities, his character was mild and kindly, for he was described as being averse to war and sacrifice. Constantly crossed in his purposes by wizards, he floated away on a raft. There was a general belief that he would return and restore the reign of peace, an anticipation which was popular among the tribes who felt the burden of the Aztec domination. Each year, with an inconsistency not foreign to higher forms of religion, human sacrifices were offered under the guise of messengers sent to inform the benign Quetzalcohuatl of the need of a speedy deliverance.

As might have been expected, exaggerated estimates are given by the early authorities of the number of human beings slaughtered in the course of the year; but, in any case, it must have been great, for in the small and poor region of Tlaxcallan from one pueblo 405 captives were sacrificed at the chief feast of the local deity. Naturally, in the dominant pueblo the proportions of the human victims offered to the gods must have far exceeded these limits.

Closely connected with the Aztec religion was the development of an ingenious, if imperfect method of reckoning time. It was apparently evolved independently, for in the Old World there was nothing like it. The basis of time reckoning was the period of twenty days, and each day of this division had a proper sign or name. The periodic expeditions against neighboring hostile tribes were controlled by this division, as were also the holding of markets and the arrangement of tributes. There were eighteen of these divisions, which regulated the various festivals of the religious year. For secular purposes the 360 day year was corrected by adding to it a period of five days, a fractional part of the twenty-day period. On these supplementary five days all public ceremonies ceased. The chronological system consisted of a combination of great cycles, each of fifty-two years' duration. And each great cycle was divided into four smaller cycles of thirteen years.

The economic and political basis of Aztec life was the pueblo, or tribal community, in which frequently each clan of the tribe had a localized quarter, each provided with the temple of the particular deity recognized by the clan as its protector. Through the wars of conquest with weaker pueblos there had grown up a rudimentary feudalism, according to which the distinguished warriors were established in the subject pueblos as proprietors of the best lands in them. The possession of these lands could descend to the sons or might be alienated for the benefit of a distinguished chieftain. The food supply of the country so controlled was regular, hence there was no need of a nomadic life. Wealth was increasing, and the population growing. Habits of industry were encouraged, with the result that the principle of the division of labor to a certain extent existed. Some forms of craftsmanship, too, were cultivated, specialized in particular communities; for example, Cholula was famous for its potters, while the art of the goldsmith was practised at Azcapozalco. Clothing was manufactured, the houses and buildings were decorated internally, and there was an elaborate cuisine. Montezuma's meal is described as consisting of thirty sorts of stews. He used chafing-dishes to keep them warm, and he also drank chocolate and ate fruit as a second course.

There was a system of customary law administered by qualified officials, and, for controlling the conduct of the people, there existed an extremely elaborate rule of life which implied discipline and the recognition of social duties and family obligations. The Aztecs had standards of value, but no coined money and no standards of measurement, nor anything like an alphabet or even a syllabary. In the "pinturas," however, there were a few purely phonetic symbols.

The darker side of Aztec rule is seen in the enforced human labor exacted to supply the tributes in kind, and in the revolting system of organized cannibalism, the outgrowth of their elaborate ritual. Some of the neighboring tribes successfully resisted both these types of oppression, while those who were too weak to do so depended on the mysteriously predicted deliverance from their yoke. In any case, the way for a rapid conquest had been well prepared.

II

THE CAREER OF CORTEZ

In 1517 the governor of Cuba, Diego Velasquez, began to send some of his subordinates to explore the coast of Yucatan. One of them brought back ornaments and vessels of gold and also information as to the extent and importance of the great native power in the interior of the land. An expedition was then put in charge of Hernando Cortez, who for eight years had been an adventurer in the New World. The new leader was a native of Medellin in Estremadura, where he had been born in 1485. He had received a good education, graduating as bachelor of laws, but, after leading an irregular life at home, he had sailed for the West Indies, where he had spent eight years, first in Hispaniola, then in Cuba. Like other adventurers, he had taken part in Indian warfare and had been a planter. Powerful interests worked against his appointment; accordingly, when he left Cuba he was informed that Velasquez intended to supersede him in the command. His fleet carried 110 sailors, 553 Spanish soldiers, 200 Indians, some artillery, and a valuable asset for the conquest, sixteen horses.

On the 12th of March, Cortez' squadron arrived at Potonchan, having previously stopped at Cozumel to pick up Geronimo de Aguilar, who had taken part in an earlier and unsuccessful expedition to the coast of the continent. He had become a member of a native pueblo, had married an Indian, and was especially useful because of his knowledge of the Indian tongue. At Potonchan the inhabitants brought out provisions in boats, but were not disposed to receive the newcomers in their village; indeed, they asked them to accept the food,—bread, fruit, and birds,—and take themselves off. Cortez arranged an ambush near the pueblo and, according to the agreement, two hundred men under Alvarado and Avila rushed upon the settlement when the natives came out a second time to bring provisions. In the meantime the Spaniards on the ships disembarked under the fire of their artillery. There was some sharp fighting, and by the time the pueblo was taken most of the inhabitants had fled to the highlands nearby. The dead were not counted, but there were many wounded and a few captives. Perhaps the actual fighting men on the native side in this first engagement were not more than four or five thousand. Plenty of food was found in the place, but no gold. There was soon another battle, in which eight hundred or a thousand Indians were killed. Apparently they fell into a panic when they confronted cavalry for the first time; "they thought the man and beast were one thing."

From a Drawing Taken from Life

Twenty-two days the expedition now halted, as the pueblo was well supplied with provisions, and the enemy was active outside. Finally the Indians, who were exposed to the prevailing bad weather and were without food, sued for peace, making a rich present to Cortez. But this was nothing, Diaz del Castillo naïvely says, in comparison with the twenty women, who were distributed as booty to the Spanish captains; one in particular was a prize—the celebrated Doña Marina, who spoke the language of the Aztecs, and also, because she had been a slave on the coast, knew the languages of Yucatan and Tabasco. As Aguilar understood Tabasco there was made possible, through Marina, direct communication with the people of the country. "It was a great beginning for our conquest," says the worthy Diaz.

When Cortez received the natives' peace offering, he was careful to inquire where they had acquired the gold and jewels. They replied by directing him to the setting sun, and mentioned the words Culchua and Mexico. This was a sufficient indication, and on the 18th of April, Cortez left Potonchan and in three days arrived at San Juan de Ulua. Here the emissaries of Montezuma, who from the accounts he had received through his messengers, was convinced that the Europeans were none other than the famous divine being Quetzalcohuatl and his companions returning by sea after a visit to the sun, greeted Cortez with extraordinary honors.

There was abundance of food,—chicken, maize, bread, and cherries,—drinks of very good cocoa, and, more welcome still, many pieces of gold, some well worked, and a large quantity of the feathered drapery and jewels. Cortez represented himself as the friendly ambassador of Charles V, sent on a special mission of peaceful curiosity. His chief interest was concentrated on the gold, however, for he particularly inquired of the Aztec Teuhtlilli who spoke for Montezuma whether his master had gold. When he answered in the affirmative, Cortez bluntly said, "Send me some of it." In return for the generous welcome given them the Spaniards amused themselves, in the days following their disembarkation at San Juan, by showing the natives their arms and bloodhounds and explaining how they meant to use them in their passage through the country.

The news of the manners of the mysterious strangers threw Montezuma into a panic; he was more convinced than ever when he heard of the rapacity and cruelty of the Spaniards that Cortez was nothing less than Quetzalcohuatl, the description given being admirably suited to one of the principal divinities of the Aztec theology. To the king's mind the sole remedy lay in incantations; he summoned therefore the most experienced experts to devise powerful enchantments to keep the whites from approaching the Aztec capital. The charms were inefficacious. At his wits' end, the Aztec overlord sent peaceful directions to all his dependents.

After the disembarkation at San Juan de Ulua the adventurers did not pass their time in idle dreams; they found abundance of occupation in collecting gold and precious stones, giving the natives in return objects of small value. Fresh embassies presented themselves to Cortez, not only with the usual presents, but giving useful information. Among them was a representative of

Ixtlilxochitl, the lord of Texcoco, who spoke of the tyranny of Montezuma, who had killed his brother. He welcomed the Spaniards as allies who would help him to avenge the murder. Cortez saw in this an opportunity to encourage dissension among the natives, by taking advantage of which he could make himself master of both factions, and so control the country. He desired to found a settlement at the place at which they had first touched land. There was a division among his followers on this point; some of them regarding his purpose of making himself the captain general of the new colony as an act of disloyalty to Velasquez, the governor of Cuba. He met the situation by putting the most obstinate of his opponents in chains, and finally all the members of the expedition were won over by the generous promises he made, although there was complaint at his proposal to take for himself one-fifth of all the gold that might be gathered from the natives.

The colony Cortez succeeded in establishing received the name of Vera Cruz, because they had reached the spot on Holy Saturday; the words Villa Rica were added to mark the fertility of the surrounding country. Visits were made to neighboring pueblos with profitable results. At Cempoala twenty of the leading men, accompanied by their chief, presented themselves; there were the usual valuable offerings, and Cortez took care to promise his aid in defending and helping his new acquaintances. The chief complained of the oppression of Montezuma, explaining that his people had only lately been conquered and had been deprived of much treasure. They were obliged to carry out his orders, he said, because the Aztec was the lord of great cities, lands, vassals, and armies of warriors. Before leaving the pueblo, Cortez spoke of his philanthropic mission as the representative of the Emperor Charles V, promising that after he had returned to his fleet he would see that their grievances were remedied.

The impression made by the benevolent stranger was so great that at Cempoala 400 natives were offered by the chief of the pueblo as pack-carriers—men of great endurance, the chronicler says, who could carry fifty pounds weight five leagues. This was a great relief to the Spaniards, who had hitherto been obliged to transport the valuables they collected from the villages through which they passed on their own shoulders in small sacks. Other pueblos were treated to the same successful diplomacy.

The more Cortez heard of the country, the more he was convinced that the real objective of the expedition must be Montezuma and his capital. The presents received by the adventurers and the tales they heard showed that their journey must, if their hopes were to be realized, have its termination in Mexico. When the second installment of presents came from the Aztec capital, the astute commander remarked to some of his men nearby, in admiration of the valuable articles so freely placed in his hands, that the Aztec overlord must be great and rich. "If God wills," he said, "some day we shall have to go and see him." This pious aspiration fell on no unwilling ears, and the opportune moment came sooner than even the most sanguine adventurer could have hoped, for Cortez soon succeeded in forming an alliance with thirty pueblos, contiguous to his own settlement, all of them ready to follow him as their leader in an expedition which was to free them from the burdensome yoke of Aztec despotism. The fighting force now available must have been considerable, for we know that one pueblo, Quiahuistlan, half a league distant from Vera Cruz, offered to supply 5000 men.

In the meantime, a ship had arrived from Cuba with seventy Europeans and nine horses. The expedition had now been three months in Mexico, and the demand to push on to Montezuma's city was general. Cortez sent home an account of his experiences, in which he drew up a formal accusation against the Cuban governor, Velasquez, fortifying his own claims by a rich present in excess of the value of the royal fifth, the statutory portion. "It is the first we have sent," the commander said to his comrades in excusing and explaining a generosity that had to be collected from their hoards. This act of loyalty was an additional stimulus to the adventurers, who saw in their march to the interior an easy method of recuperating their losses. When the commissioners were about to leave for Spain, some of Cortez' men proposed to accompany them. Cortez arrested them immediately. Two were put to death; one, a pilot, was deprived of his feet, and the common seamen received each two hundred lashes. Father Diaz would have been punished, too, had not Cortez respected his habit. One of the victims who was executed was Pedro Excudero, who had made charges against Cortez in Cuba before the expedition sailed.

To prevent the recurrence of such attempts at desertion and also to add to his men the crews of the vessels, Cortez resolved to destroy the fleet in the harbor, with the exception of one small boat which was to carry the commissioners back to Spain. The proposal was arranged not to come from the commander himself, because, if he had taken the initiative, he might have been obliged to pay off the seamen out of his own pocket. So, as Herrera, one of the adventurers, says, "if anyone asked him to pay the money, he could retort that the advice was ours, and that we were all involved in settling up the accounts."

Cortez knew that he would meet with no mercy at Velasquez' hands; his only chance, therefore, was to remain in Mexico, and that the destruction of the fleet rendered certain. The daring plan was carried out secretly at night by the master of one of the ships, an intimate friend of the commander. The crews had been removed beforehand, and the explanation made by Cortez' envoy in Spain, Montejo, was that the ships were old and on the point of foundering before they were scuttled. This plausible statement was not more convincing than the rest of the envoy's argument, and the Royal Senate of the Indies condemned Cortez' conduct as "contrary to righteousness and justice." He had acted also contrary to the commands of the governor of Cuba, who, in the meantime, as the case was being discussed by the home authorities, asked that capital sentence be passed. Cortez' view finally prevailed because of the fortunate outcome of his march, and in 1522 Velasquez was directed not to send to New Spain any people or armed forces.

After scuttling the ships Cortez returned to Cempoala to arrange for the expedition. The chieftains of the pueblo advised that the route by the way of Tlaxcala should be taken because the people of that place were their friends and mortal enemies of the Aztecs. A start was made on the 16th of August with 400 Spaniards, 15 horses, and 5 pieces of artillery. In all the chronicles of the expedition there is a discreet reserve as to the number of Indian allies. It seems to have been a fixed policy to obscure this point. But the native contingent must have been very large, for at each pueblo where the expedition sojourned one hears of the acquisition of native warriors; at Ixtacamaxtitlan, a small place, the chief gave 300 soldiers.

On reaching Tecoac in Tlaxcala the invaders found that the attitude of the people was distinctly hostile; in a preliminary skirmish thirty warriors preferred to die rather than yield. The inhabitants of the pueblo were then cut to pieces, as they refused to retire or surrender. This was on the last day of August; the next day there was a hot battle, in which the Spaniards seem to have been saved by their native allies from destruction. Diaz del Castillo says that Cortez thanked them profusely, and adds that the Spaniards were panic-stricken by the wild shouts of their opponents. There was soon after another battle, where the escape of the Spaniards was due to the existence of dissensions in the Indian camp; the people of the pueblo refused to stand by one another. Much damage was done in the second ranks of their warriors by the fire of the artillery, but fifty of the Spaniards were wounded, and one was killed, together with all the horses. Cortez estimated his enemies at 149,000, plainly an impossible figure.

Marauding expeditions were made against the defenseless pueblos, whose fighting men were with the Tlaxcalan army. Women and children were put to the edge of the sword without mercy, and the dwellings were burnt to the ground. Fifty emissaries appeared on the 7th of September to ask for peace, bringing with them presents of food and plumage ornaments. Some were suspected of treachery, and all fifty, by Cortez' orders, had their hands cut off. The same day the Spanish camp was attacked by 10,000 men, warriors of the greatest valor, but even this danger was repelled because the plan was known beforehand. The situation of the Spaniards was almost desperate, for they had lost a hundred and fifty of their number, and the survivors were worn out by anxiety and by the constant physical fatigue. There was depression in the camp, some proposing return to Vera Cruz, where the natives were friendly and where help could be had from Cuba. But the commander's spirit did not falter. He sent three of his leading captives to Tlaxcala to ask for a peaceful passage through their country to Mexico. After deliberation the proposal was granted, although there was opposition, especially on the part of the young chief Xicotencatl, who declared that in another night attack he could take the camp and slay all the Spaniards. The peace party carried the day, and Cortez entered the pueblo on the 23d of September, receiving a royal welcome from the inhabitants, who gave him valuable assistance and an enduring loyalty.

After a month's stay Cortez set out again with 5000 of these new allies, "men much experienced in warfare," as he himself allows. In the neighborhood of Cholula he sent the inhabitants word, on receiving their envoys, that they must become vassals of the Spanish crown, saying if no reply were received within three days, he would attack and destroy them. This menace had its effect, and great hospitality was shown to the Spaniards and their allies. The streets and roofs were crowded with people as the army entered the town, and they were lodged in several large halls. The drain on the stores of the natives was so great that on the third day they brought only water, rushes, and wood. The scantiness of these offerings was to Cortez a demonstration that the townspeople were disaffected and were plotting against their guests. He issued an order therefore that all the chief men of the place should assemble in the court of the temple of Quetzalcohuatl. Suspecting no harm, they obeyed. To strike terror into the natives, Cortez planned to murder the principal men and the priests; but there were a great many other warriors of the pueblo in the inclosure so crowded together they could not move. At the entrance were stationed the Spaniards, who, at a given signal, rushed on the unarmed mass. Some were mowed down; some burnt themselves alive, while others cast themselves down from the temple pyramid, the raised platform on which the altar was placed. In two hours, according to Cortez, 3000 met their death. The massacre was continued in the streets for five hours; none were spared until the pueblo was deserted. The carnage continued the next day, gladly shared in by the Tlaxcalans, who had come in to take their part of the pillage. It was the commander's intention to demolish the place altogether, and the cruel work took two days more.

A fresh start was made on November 1st. The pueblos subsequently visited by the expedition were terrorized by the massacre at Cholula, and there was no stint of offerings. Cortez, too, being now in a better temper because of the jewels, gold, and precious stones so easily collected, did not forget to explain that he had come to save the new vassals of the Spanish Crown from robbery and oppression. In each pueblo he won the inhabitants over by his dexterous diplomacy and pleasing manners, and they readily became his allies. No opposition was encountered during the rest of the journey to Mexico. Meanwhile the news of the massacre at Cholula had completely unnerved Montezuma; "he humbled himself like a reed"; there was no thought of resistance. He sent one of his chief men to impersonate him, as he was afraid to meet Cortez himself. The deceit was soon discovered by the Indian allies, and the substitute for royalty returned in confusion, leaving rich presents behind. Montezuma consulted his magical experts again, but the auspices and enchantments were no more favorable than before. He now saw only death for all his people and for himself; with a fixed fatalism he was convinced there was no escape. Tradition told him that the people from the land of the rising sun were invincible.

It was the eighth day of November when the Spaniards reached the capital of the Aztecs. The army must have been imposing in its size, and perhaps Montezuma's religious scruples may have been reinforced by others of a different character when he saw the number of his enemies and revolted subjects who followed Cortez. Father Sahagun, a most reliable authority, who visited Mexico in 1529, says that "hardly had the rear guard moved from Ixtapalapan when the vanguard was already entering Mexico." The welcome was in harmony with the respect caused by the size of the expedition and by the superstitious fears of the Aztec overlord. A thousand of the principal men came out to greet Cortez a half-league from the town. A quarter of a league from the palace Montezuma presented himself with ceremonious pomp, accompanied by the lords of the greater pueblos. He was supported by Cacomer, king of Texcoco, and Cuitlahuatzin, king of Ixtapalapan, each holding him by an arm on either side. All three were dressed alike, except that Montezuma was shod. When Cortez dismounted to embrace him the two accompanying lords forcibly prevented him from touching their master. Flowers were offered according to the Aztec custom; likewise gold and precious stones.

After reassuring the Aztec ruler of his amicable intentions, Cortez went with his suite to lodgings assigned in the treasury of one of the temples, a residence selected because of their character as divine beings. Montezuma spoke to Cortez of the prophecy of the return of Quetzalcohuatl, expressed his willingness to become the vassal of the great lord of the land of the rising sun; and repelled the charges made against him by the people of Tlaxcala and Cempoala. He made, too, a special point of denying the stories of having houses with golden walls and of being served with gold furnishings and vessels. "The houses," he said, "which you see are stone and chalk and earth; it is true that I have some things of gold left me by my ancestors; all that I have do you take whenever you want it." The offer was made effective immediately. Cortez had received already many different jewels, much gold and silver and feathers, and five or six thousand pieces of cotton goods, very rich and in divers manners woven and worked. After the interview rich presents of gold were made to the commander, as well as to the captains and to each of the soldiers.

The Spaniards kept watchful guard in spite of the sumptuous welcome; the soldiers were restless and desired to sack the town. Their attitude did not escape the attention of the natives, who began to suspect their motives in remaining in the city. Food commenced to give out, and the horses suffered and also the dogs. In a short time the men did not scruple to sack some of the dwellings near Montezuma's palace; they showed also little respect for the native women, many of whom had shut themselves up in terror at threatened maltreatment.

It was a well-known and settled policy on the part of the Spaniards in their conquests in the Antilles to seize the native chiefs in order to reduce the members of the tribe to submission. This is made clear in a letter from several Dominican friars, written home as early as 1516, when the practice is noticed. In mentioning it, they explain that the Indians are a people who love their lords much and are very loyal to them. This strategy was now employed with complete success by Cortez. He determined to force Montezuma to take up his residence in the Spanish quarters by use of fair words, then to threaten him immediately with death if he tried to escape from captivity. As an excuse for putting this daring program into execution, Cortez, who entered the palace accompanied by his captains, after the usual friendly welcome, charged Montezuma with responsibility for the death of two Spaniards at Nautlan.

Cuauhpopoca, the local chief, it seems, had caused them to be executed because of their offenses and excesses. Some time passed in discussing the charge which the Aztec monarch, of course, denied. Cortez' comrades wished to hasten proceedings by killing the Aztec at once. Finally Montezuma, completely terrorized, agreed to accompany Cortez, and also followed his direction that he should tell his people that the step was taken voluntarily at the advice of his priests.

The chief of Nautlan, his son, and fifteen of the principal men of the pueblo were summoned to the capital by Montezuma. Cortez ordered them to be burnt; at the same time directions were given that all the arms in the city should be collected. Fifteen cartloads in all were to be burnt with the prisoners. Before the execution they confessed that they had acted by order of Montezuma. Cortez put his prisoner in chains, and this outrage was allowed to pass unavenged, for the Aztec lords feared that their ruler would be slain. The timorous monarch told his subjects that what he was enduring in the Spanish quarters had divine sanction. Having the king in his possession, Cortez made detailed inquiry as to the location of gold and silver mines. Much gold was collected, and, whenever there was resistance to the orders from the capital, the chiefs who refused to give up their possessions were treated as rebels to their overlord, and either killed on the spot or imprisoned after being summoned to the capital by orders issued through Montezuma.

Cortez was delighted at the willing compliance of the king in playing the rôle of a puppet in his hands, and he wondered because "great lord as he was, that being a prisoner as he was, he was so much obeyed." On his own initiative, Montezuma addressed his chieftains, telling them that the Spaniards were sent by Quetzalcohuatl, and begging them to be obedient to Cortez in every respect, urging them to accept their position of vassalage to Spain. This was the signal for another great collecting expedition among the Aztec feudatories, the chief contributor being Montezuma himself. The chronicler's powers of description are exhausted in enumerating the wealth that poured into the hands of the eager adventurers. There was no scruple in taking what was left after the regular tribute of vassalage had been paid.

The commander, however, was very unwilling to proceed to the distribution, and when he could resist his soldiers' demands no longer, it was found that the greater part of the three and a half million dollars' worth of metal had been retained by the leader and the captains. He met their complaints by telling them that they all would be very prosperous and rich, because they would be the masters of rich cities and mines. As a more practical argument, he went among the soldiers giving them secretly gold ornaments, and making individual promises of reward.

Meanwhile the rapacity of the adventurers and their open display of their wealth did not bring so much odium upon them as their forcible efforts to convert the natives. A Christian chapel was placed in the chief temple, an action which seems to have contributed to destroy the illusion among the people that there existed some relation between the newcomers and their god Quetzalcohuatl. The undisguised enmity soon came to a head in plans for a revolt that included a general massacre of the Europeans. When information of the plot was conveyed to Montezuma, who seemed worried at the fate of his strange guests and advised their leaving the city, Cortez spoke of the destruction of his ships and told the king that, when ships were prepared, the latter must go with them to see their emperor. Workmen were sent to Villa Rica to prepare the vessels, but it was probably with no serious intent beyond the purpose of deceiving the prisoners.

This was the state of affairs after five months' residence in Mexico, when news came that Spanish ships were off the coast, 16 vessels, large and small, 1400 soldiers, 80 horses, and 20 pieces of artillery. When the envoys landed, they summoned the captain of Vera Cruz to accept as superior officer Narvaez, who had been sent by Velasquez to take possession of the country. The four Spanish envoys were hurried off as prisoners under an escort of natives who, by forced marches night and day, reached Mexico in four days. Cortez, with characteristic diplomacy, excused the rude behavior of his lieutenant. Indeed, adequate reparation was made, not only by smooth speeches, of which Cortez was past-master, but by the more telling arguments of gold strips and ornaments. They, in turn, told all they knew of the expedition of Narvaez, and regained the coast, won over by the munificence and the amicable manners of the commander.

No time was lost in heading off Narvaez' expedition from entrance into the interior. Cortez took most of his men and probably a large force of the native allies sufficient to block Narvaez' march to the capital. Only 130 Spaniards were left in Mexico under the command of Alvarado. While Narvaez was sojourning at Cempoala despoiling the neighborhood of the few valuables that remained there after Cortez' march, one of the ecclesiastics from Cortez' army was sent to visit the rival camp. He showed much dexterity in winning over important men-at-arms, especially those of the artillery, by a judicious distribution of gifts, though outwardly he made loud profession of devotion to Narvaez. The work of this skilled emissary was made the easier because Narvaez kept all the spoil he collected for himself; the contrast was not left unnoticed by the men whom the commander had won.

When the work of undermining Narvaez' men had been completed, the Friar Olmedo found it easy to break off negotiations and return to his own camp. There was now little difficulty in settling the affairs between the two captains without bloodshed; Narvaez' men were ready to abandon him. Cortez, as he explains in a letter to Charles V, after drawing near to Cempoala with his army, entered Narvaez' camp with a few followers by night and, before he was observed, took his rival prisoner. There was only a little fighting; two were killed by artillery fire in preventing those who wished to rescue Narvaez from entering a tower where he had his quarters. This strategy seemed to Cortez the best way "to avoid a scandal," but less satisfactory to his men was the division of booty found in the camp. Cortez gave it all to Narvaez' men. "They were many and we were few," Diaz del Castillo regretfully explains; "Cortez feared that they might kill him and his small band of men-at-arms."

With the advent of this new army of marauders in the country there appeared a plague of smallpox, a disease hitherto unknown. It made frightful ravages, and its effects were compared by the Indians to those of leprosy. No mention is made of the epidemic by Cortez; he was too alarmed at the news which came from Mexico to heed the sufferings of the native population, who were dying like cattle. While he had been so successful on the coast, his garrison in the capital had been attacked; their quarters had been partly burned and undermined, and Cortez was afraid that all the treasure would be lost, his men massacred, and the city sacrificed. No word had come from Montezuma; it seemed that the worst must have happened.

The difficult situation in which Alvarado was placed was due to his own brutality. Before Cortez had left the city, he had given permission that the festival of the god Toxcatl should be celebrated with the accustomed ceremonies. Alvarado added as further conditions that they should bear no arms nor offer human sacrifices. This festal occasion lent itself readily to a repetition of the butchery of Cholula, and some authorities go so far as to think that Cortez had given secret commands for the massacre before he set off for the coast. While the chiefs, warriors, and other leading men, more than 1000 in number, were solemnly dancing in honor of their god in the court of the temple, unarmed and covered with gold ornaments and jewels and singing as they moved about, half the men of the Spanish garrison entered and ranged themselves around the wall, after closing the entrances to the courtyard. The Indians, thinking they had come in as curious spectators, made no break in the ordinary ritual; suddenly the dancers and the spectators were set upon, and the patio of the temple was soon filled with dismembered heads, arms, and legs. The court was soon nothing but a human shambles. Some tried to escape by climbing over the side walls or by rushing up the temple steps; others feigned to be dead; only a few saved themselves.

The massacre lasted an hour, and, carefully planned as it must have been, no hitch occurred during its progress. The people outside finally got news of what was happening and, picking up their weapons, they made savage attacks on the Spaniards, forcing them back to their quarters. Alvarado himself was wounded on the head. Finding refuge, the Spaniards barricaded themselves as well as they could, and the Indians turned to bury their dead, an operation which took many days on account of the elaborate ceremonial required by the dignity of those who had perished. After the funeral ceremonies, the Mexicans returned impetuously to the attack on the Spanish quarters.

It would have gone hard with Cortez' men if Montezuma had not interfered in their behalf. Speaking from the roof of the building where he was kept a prisoner, he gave orders to the Aztec warriors to stop the fight. Cortez had heard of the massacre from both sides, as Montezuma had sent to him envoys to complain of Alvarado's wanton slaughter in the temple. He promised to do justice when he arrived, and also spoke, as a proof of his peaceful temper, of the small force he was bringing back with him. As a matter of fact, when he re-entered the city there were over 1000 Europeans and many allies with him; in Tlaxcala alone he enlisted the services of 2000 men. No opposition was made to this formidable force taking up their old quarters.

It was strange that Cortez, who was usually quick to punish any contravention of his orders, took no account of the massacre. He omits mentioning it in his letters to Charles V, and it is not surprising that Friar Sahagun reports that Cortez approved of the crime and told Alvarado he had done well. In the disturbed conditions in the city no market was held, and the Spaniards were no longer provided with food. Montezuma excused the omission because of his imprisonment. Threatening words were spoken by Cortez, and from this time his prisoner ceased to exert any influence to prevent the revolt against the invaders.

A messenger sent out to Vera Cruz returned to his comrades with the news a half hour later that the whole city was up in arms. Even a group of 200 Spaniards could make no headway through the streets. The Indians faced the artillery in close array, and as fast as they were mowed down, the gaps were filled up by others. They fought with a desperation which caused wonderment even from men in Cortez' army who had served against the Turks. Constructions of wood were made to protect the Spaniards from the showers of stones that poured down on them from the housetops, while they tried to clear the streets covered with barricades. But they could make no progress, and finally they withdrew to their quarters, pursued by the Aztecs, who entered the palace in the face of the desperate resistance of the Europeans. They threatened to leave no Spaniard alive, yet they begged as suppliants for their lord Montezuma to be given back to them.

Though there are conflicting details given of the Aztec attack on the Spanish quarters, there is not much doubt but that Montezuma had been killed on the morning of the 27th of August, the day the wooden engines were first used. The monarch was no longer of any use now that he had refused to keep the revolt in check. There are different accounts of the murder, but there seems a fairly general agreement that Montezuma was stabbed to death.

As there was no longer any hope of defending their quarters successfully, Cortez tried to save himself and his men by a ruse. The dead body of the Aztec ruler was taken up on the roof, covered with a large shield so that the fact that it was a corpse could not be seen clearly. Then one of the feudatories, the lord of Tlaclolco, addressed the crowd and bade them, as if speaking in the presence of his master, to give up the attack on the Spaniards, because, if they persisted, he was afraid he would be killed. Little impression was made; injurious words were spoken against the vacillating and effeminate ruler, supposedly still alive before them. There was a volley of arrows, and some say the body was struck by a stone. This is the basis of a story circulated purposely by Cortez and others that the monarch had died from the wounds received on the roof, where he had gone voluntarily to speak to his people. It was a dangerous thing for Cortez to confess to the murder, for Montezuma, be it remembered, had accepted the position of a vassal of the Spanish crown. When the Aztecs showed no sign of taking a peaceful attitude, Cortez himself tried the plan of addressing them from the roof, but his diplomacy was of no avail. The only conditions offered were withdrawal from Aztec territory; as long as he stayed in the city, the Aztecs said, they would keep up the fight.

Further essays at street combats showed this to be no idle threat; forty-six Spaniards were killed and persistent attempts were made to pull down the walls of their quarters, while missiles of all kinds were directed on the defenders day and night. In order to bring some relief to this perilous position, Cortez sent one of the prisoners to announce the death of Montezuma, and offered to give up the body, knowing that the burial ceremonies would keep his enemies occupied for several days. But the animosity of the people was not to be diverted from their prey. Cortez was afraid that the one causeway, that to Tlacopan, would be destroyed and the sole means of escape cut off. His men were discouraged; indeed, those who had belonged to Narvaez' expedition were in a state of mutiny.

One of the Aztec priests and other leading men previously held as prisoners were sent to ask permission for the Spaniards to leave on condition that all the gold should be given up. Timbers were prepared to place across the ditches near the causeway, and a plan of escape was mapped out for the Europeans and their allies. The treasure was carefully guarded by the allies, but before the night appointed for the retreat all the Aztec prisoners were put to death. The soldiers also found a large quantity of gold which they divided among themselves. The exit from the city began just before midnight; there was a severe thunderstorm which kept the Europeans from being observed until they got past the first ditch; here they were seen by a native woman who was drawing water there. She gave the alarm, and before the second ditch was reached the Mexican warriors had gathered to annihilate their enemies. There was immediately a panic, and those who were carrying the gold were forced into the ditch. Diaz remarks laconically, "The gold killed them and they died rich."

The only Europeans saved were those who carried small amounts of gold. On the mass of Indian allies drowning in the ditch the Spaniards threw their loads; using this living embankment a few of them made their way to safety. Everyone looked out for himself, and when Cortez was reproached for deserting his men, he replied that it was a miracle that anyone had crossed the causeway alive. It was some time before Alvarado, with the miserable surviving rear-guard of seven soldiers, all in a sad plight, reached the main body of the army at Tlacopan. (August, 1520.)

As long as they were in Aztec territory, there was little chance of escaping annihilation, for the disconsolate army after their night journey were set upon by the warriors of the neighboring pueblos. Their Tlaxcalan allies guided them along devious trails until they reached Totoltepec, where the fugitives found some temporary security in a temple, which they were glad to use as a fortress. Fortunately they were not actually pursued by the main body of the Aztec fighting men, who remained behind to collect the gold and jewels cast aside by the Spaniards, and to spoil the dead. Besides, a number of Spaniards had either by choice or by necessity remained in the city. According to one authority not all of Cortez' soldiers were acquainted with the plan for the night journey; others preferred not to desert their treasures. It is computed that 270 Europeans kept up the fight in the city and then surrendered. During the rest of the retreat there were some sharp skirmishes, and because of their fatigue and discouragement the army's power of resistance was soon exhausted. Thanks to their native allies, however, they were brought finally to a place of safety in the friendly pueblo of Tlaxcala. The losses had been terrible, nearly 1000 men had perished, besides 4000 of the Tlaxcalans and other natives. At Tlaxcala there was much mourning for the great calamity which had robbed the place of its best warriors, but there was no hesitation in offering Cortez their continued support in resuming the war against the Aztecs.

Cortez was careful to give instructions to his men to treat the inhabitants with consideration and not to rob them of their property. These orders did not cause so much dissatisfaction to the survivors as Cortez' high-handed procedure in appropriating for himself whatever he could find of the gold that had been saved in the panic of the retreat. Many of the Spaniards spoke of returning to the coast to sail back to Cuba. Cortez' iron will now stood him in good stead; he quieted his own men, and arranged to start immediately a campaign against Mexico by the help of the Tlaxcalans, promising as the price of their aid a part of all the conquests he made and various privileges and exemptions from tribute.

This offer proved an attractive one not only to the Tlaxcalans but to other natives who saw a further chance of securing their freedom from their Mexican overlords. Over 100,000 men were collected, either by promises or by methods of terrorism; any pueblo that resisted was sacked and the inhabitants massacred. Tepeacac, the center of resistance, was taken; its men were put to death, and the women and children set apart as slaves. As time went on, various individual adventurers appeared off the coast, and by degrees the losses in Europeans, in artillery, and in horses were made up. This good fortune caused so much satisfaction to the veterans of Cortez' army and their commander that he resolved to undertake the seemingly hopeless task of besieging Mexico itself. Additional re-enforcements and the necessary war supplies were brought from Hispaniola, and in order to attack the Aztec capital in its most vulnerable point brigantines were prepared on the lake, since it was realized that it was impossible to force now an entrance over the causeways.

By the end of December all was ready. The Europeans numbered not quite 700 men, while the native contingent is placed by some at 150,000. From Tlaxcala, 10,000 were asked for, but many more volunteered. As the army proceeded, they found no great difficulty in occupying the places on their route. Some, like Texcoco, had been partially deserted by the inhabitants, who had the forethought to remove their goods. In disgust the Spaniards burnt the town and its palace where all the ancient records in picture scrolls of the Aztec kingdom were preserved. The ravages of the smallpox weakened the Aztec resistance, and among those who died was the implacable enemy of the Spaniards, Cuitlahuac, the brother of Montezuma, who had been chosen as his successor. His death at the end of November was a loss hard to repair.

Even Diaz speaks of him as "a valiant man and very prudent."

As their next chieftain they selected Cuauhtemoc, a cousin of Montezuma, a young man who, during the period of the Spanish occupation of Mexico, had distinguished himself by his active opposition to it. He had taken a leading rôle in the revolt that had brought about the evacuation of the capital, and he now set forward upon the work of defense with great intelligence. Orders were sent to the dependent pueblos to unite in repelling the European invasion, and the tribute was remitted. Care was taken to collect treasures and arms, and Mexico itself was placed in a state of defense by the construction of intrenchments and ditches. Cuauhtemoc's plan of campaign consisted in concentrating all the available forces in the capital, yet offensive tactics were skilfully applied. His hand was seen when the Spaniards occupied Iztapalapa; here the inhabitants deserted the pueblo, and while their enemies were peacefully enjoying the spoil and resting in their quarters, the sluices were opened, and had not the natives of Texcoco warned Cortez in time all would have been drowned.

Desultory warfare continued for a time on the shores of the lake, Cortez' policy being to exact vengeance for the hostility of the lake pueblos during the retreat. Many were razed to the ground and burnt. But strenuous operations did not begin until the brigantines were finished. For their construction Cortez was indebted to the skill and industry of the people of Tlaxcala, who at their own expense cut the wood, and transported it over mountainous defiles by bad roads to their own pueblo, where it was cut into shape for the vessels. Thence the pieces were carried eighteen leagues overland to Texcoco on the lake, where, fastened together, they were transformed into ships ready for navigation.

Futile attempts were made by the Aztecs to set fire to this navy, for they recognized the danger of an attack from the water, but there was no thought of surrender. Untiringly, night and day, they prepared for the siege, making new weapons to meet the attacks of cavalry, and constructing barricades in the streets. The Spaniards also had to do much preliminary work to enable the fleet to get into deep water; 8000 Indians were constantly employed in digging a channel from the shore sufficient to accommodate the draught of the brigantines.

All was ready on the 28th of April, 1521. The brigantines were manned with European troops and artillerymen; but as usual the mass of the army was made of native auxiliaries, probably underestimated by Cortez at 80,000 men. Altogether the Spanish nucleus numbered about 1100, half of them lately come to join the veterans. Efforts were made to arrange terms of peace, but the Aztecs refused to listen to Cortez' complaints of bad treatment and disloyal conduct on the part of his late hosts.

At every point of the advance to the city, Cortez encountered stubborn enmity. There was fighting both on the lake and on the shore, that showed the temper of the people. The brigantines were surrounded by a flotilla of canoes as they proceeded on their way; but it was an unequal combat because the frail canôes of the Aztecs were exposed to the gunfire of the ships. Under the protection of the brigantines a landing was effected on the causeway. Step by step, the defenders were forced back towards the town; as long as they fought on the causeway they were exposed to the raking volleys of the guns on the brigantines.

It was a long, tedious process to take the many barricades of the city, and even when the principal street was reached the determined onslaught of the Aztecs forced the Spaniards back to the causeway bridges. No real ground was gained in these first skirmishes, although there was a concerted plan between Cortez and his lieutenants that they should make for the center of the city at the same time. While the siege was being resisted with such desperation, the straits of the Aztecs induced the neighboring pueblos to send out large contingents of men to break the power that had so long kept them in bondage. Cortez notices especially the support given him from Texcoco both in men and in provisions; they kept on the lake 1000 canoes going and coming with supplies, and 32,000 warriors.

In order to starve the city out, the water supply had been cut off before the siege began, and it was hoped that by guarding the causeways no food could be brought in. Much skill was shown by the Aztecs in overcoming these difficulties; they sent out many canoes by night, a flotilla of specially large canoes filled with warriors who did not hesitate to grapple with the brigantines. One they captured, and they inflicted heavy losses on the equipment of others. The resourcefulness of the defenders was worthy of the skilled campaigners of Europe; but the problem of the food supply could not be solved by deeds of heroism, and famine was more destructive than the weapons of their enemies. They faced not only the actual distress from scarcity of supplies but also the desertion of the city itself by large numbers of warriors who could not be fed within the walls.

The methods of warfare on both sides were worthy of the combatants. Whenever the Spaniards or their allies were taken prisoners, they were treated as victims for sacrifice and offered up in the various temples of the gods with ordinary ceremonial rites. The Spaniards, whenever they entered the streets, burnt and destroyed everything within reach, temples and houses. The rage of the Aztecs at the destruction of all they held dear showed itself in their furious attacks on their enemies as they drew back at nightfall to their camp outside.

There was no thought of coming to terms, although the losses were heavy and the besieging force under Cortez alone was more than 100,000 men, and his flotilla of canoes was 3000. The chief aim of the Spanish ruler was to take the market-place, and plans for a general assault were arranged, now that the blockade of the city was strictly kept. From this center it was hoped all the streets could be cleared. The large number of allies who each time the town was assaulted swarmed over the roofs of the houses and made light of all other obstructions, seemed to promise a speedy termination of the struggle. But before, in the general attack the inclosure of the town was reached, the Aztecs in canoes and on the various land approaches, which had now been partially destroyed, made an unexpected sally. There was a call to arms sounded from the apex of one of the principal temples, the ritual drum being beaten whose tones could be heard at a distance of two or three leagues. Instantly, as the Indians came rushing upon them, the Spaniards were thrown in a panic, and made a precipitate retreat. Cortez was himself in danger and would have been killed, had not his enemies made strenuous efforts to take him alive in order that he might be kept for a sacrificial offering. None of the other captains fared better; Alvarado's men narrowly escaped destruction.

Many European prisoners were made, and from their camp the Spaniards could watch their comrades being offered up to the sanguinary deities of the Aztec religion. They were pierced with stone knives and their palpitating hearts were drawn out as they lay recumbent on the stone altars that capped the temple pyramids. At the same time the men in the camp had to listen to the threats of their foes who, close at hand, promised them the same fate as their comrades. There was no inclination at this point on the part of Cortez and his men to resume the fight; orders were given to restrict operations to the defense of the camp. But the temper of the native allies was not affected by the defeat. The Tlaxcalans especially took the lead in harassing their enemies, while the Spaniards kept to their quarters. They also suggested a plan by which the remaining supplies of food and drink might be cut off.

This gradual process of attrition had its natural effect on the powers of resistance of the Aztecs. Cuauhtemoc was forced to cover up the losses in his army by disguising the women in the city as warriors. Standing on the flat roofs of the houses they were easily taken to be male warriors, and at closer quarters the Spaniards found them to be as brave as the men. Cortez, indeed, tried to induce his opponents to see how desperate their case was. His offers of peace were rejected; when envoys were sent it was always a signal for renewed attacks on the three Spanish camps.

After consultation with his captains Cuauhtemoc resolved to die fighting with his people rather than let them become the slaves of the Spaniards. The chief food of the inhabitants now was the green vegetation growing on the lake shallows, and they drank the saline water from the same source because fresh water was no longer to be had. Numerous must have been the victims of hunger and thirst and pestilence in the Aztec quarters, and great were the losses in the continued combats with an enemy far stronger, whose own losses were being made up by uninterrupted accessions of strength, while there was the whole countryside open from which supplies kept pouring in. It is significant that the success of the Aztecs in blocking the general assault of their capital made no impression outside. So far as we know, no attempts were made to break the Spanish investing lines, nor, on the other hand, did the failure to take the town in any way stop the movement to throw off the Aztec yoke which was plainly the prime motive on the part of the natives in helping the Europeans to take Mexico.

The siege had now lasted forty-five days; it was time, therefore, to make a radical change in the primitive methods of attack hitherto followed by Cortez, methods that recall the Homeric accounts of the siege of Troy. Each day there was hot fighting in the streets or on the lake where the Aztec canoes gathered about the brigantines. At nightfall there was a general return to the camp. The new plan was to destroy all the houses in the portion of the streets where the daily fighting took place. As the horsemen charged, the space was cleared and the work of destruction began. On the exposed part by the lake the brigantines and the canoes of the allies were able to do much effective damage. The scale of the operations is indicated in one of Cortez' letters, where he speaks of using in this kind of fighting 150,000 warriors. Under these conditions, where each day ground for the next stage of occupation of the town was secured, the great market-place was taken.

Finally the Aztecs were confined to an eighth part of their capital; there was no bread to be had; nothing but fetid water to drink; and a diminishing supply of defensive weapons. Cortez himself reports that the Aztecs stood on the housetops, covering themselves with their cloaks but without weapons. The streets and the houses were filled with dead bodies. On the 13th of August the signal for the final attack was given. Crowded together, without arrows or even stones and sticks to defend themselves, the Aztecs were mowed down by the Spanish gunfire. It was a disappointment to Cortez to have to use such extreme measures; largely, it appears from his own words, because there would be no spoil to be taken. Most of the houses had been destroyed, and the people threw their wealth into the lake before they perished.

The sufferings of the besieged made an impression even on the hardened feelings of the Spanish commander. The last fights in the city and on the lake took place amid scenes of horror; everywhere were dead bodies; on the lake they were heaped up around the combatants, and could be seen floating about as the canoes kept up the unequal conflict with the Spanish brigantines. Diaz reports that all the houses were filled with dead Indians; there was nothing green to be found; the inhabitants had even eaten the bark off the trees.

The end came when the cannon, at Cortez' signal, began to fire on the mass of unarmed Mexicans, too weak to move, stretched out one upon the other, dying heroically, still even in their extremity, as Cortez says, "never asking for peace." As the artillery seemed slow in carrying on the work of destruction, the brigantines with the European soldiers and the allies were brought up and ordered to fall upon the remnant of the Aztec warriors, who were either slain on the spot or cast into the water from their last place of refuge.

Cuauhtemoc fled from the city in a large war-canoe, and the Spaniards gave chase. When overtaken he first prepared to sell his life dearly, but seeing his wife and other women in the boat, rather than expose them to risk he gave himself up and was conducted to Cortez, who spoke in a friendly way and praised his valiant defense of his capital, promising at the same time that he should be allowed to rule his people as he had done before. The capture of the Aztec chieftain took place on the 13th of August, 1521, the day that Mexico fell into the hands of the Spaniards.

The losses of the Aztecs in the final battle are set down as 40,000; many chose to die by throwing themselves and their wives and children into the lake rather than surrender. At the close of the siege there followed scenes of pillage of the usual type, with no pretense at discipline. The actual treasure seized was small, and to increase the disappointment, no trace could be found of the lost gold and silver which had been abandoned during "the mournful night" of the previous year. The supposed explanation was that it had been carefully hidden. Accordingly, Cuauhtemoc and others of high rank with him who, like himself, were captives, were tortured by fire. But no revelations were made, and the amount of gold distributed to the soldiers was small, only five pesos to a horseman and less to a foot-soldier. The native allies were paid off even more cheaply; they departed for home taking with them promises of future land grants.

Cortez' plans for reconstructing the city were put into operation immediately after the end of the siege. All the temples and great houses that survived during the street fights were removed. In order to make the conversion of the people to Christianity easier, the records of their past were obliterated. In a few years all traces of the complex Aztec society, with its divisions into nobles and priests and warriors, were lost. But at least the native population in Mexico did not meet the fate of those in the isles of the Antilles: the stock was a hardier one and the systematic working of the mines did not begin until twenty-five years after the conquest, when, owing to the propaganda of Las Casas, protective measures were enforced. Cortez introduced European grains and took care to repair the losses in the food supply produced by the devastation of the conquest.

Incapable of reconciling himself to the humdrum life of peaceful rule after his years of adventure, the commander could not endure to see his lieutenants penetrating into the unknown regions of the south, while he stayed behind receiving their reports of immeasurable treasure. In October, 1524, he set out for Honduras with a few Europeans and a large number of Indian allies. Among his companions were Cuauhtemoc, the dethroned Aztec overlord, and many of his nobles and chieftains. The march was through difficult country filled with dense woods, mountains, and morasses. The expedition suffered from the heat, and had to endure lack of water and food as well as perils from enteric fever. Cuauhtemoc and the Aztec lord of Tlacopan were charged with plotting against their new masters and were, therefore, put to death. Nothing was accomplished in this expedition, and after twenty months Cortez returned to Mexico. Soon after he was recalled to Spain to answer various charges due to his maladministration and to his uncontrolled dictatorship. He was treated with great honor and named captain-general of New Spain, but care was taken that he should no longer be intrusted with the duty of civil administration in the new province. He returned to Mexico in 1530 and again tried his fortune as a discoverer, this time undertaking, either personally or by lieutenants, expeditions to the northwest. Two fleets equipped by him were destroyed; a third was led by him into the unpromising region about the Gulf of California. In 1540, he again left Mexico to secure an indemnity from Charles V for his unsuccessful ventures. He followed the Emperor to the siege of Algiers in 1541, but was not able to secure attention to his demands. The rest of his life was passed in preparing petitions to a monarch whose treasury was being drained by other more immediate claims. He did not return to Mexico, and died on December 2, 1547, at the age of sixty-three years.

III
THE INCAS

It is the custom to associate, when the spheres of Spanish conquest are in question, the Aztecs of Mexico and the Incas of Peru. The parallel is only roughly accurate, for, although the Incas had made a great record in material advancement by the time they came into contact with the Spaniards, the level reached by them was considerably lower than that attained by their neighbors to the north. Their method of reckoning was far more primitive; they used picture painting for ornament; there was no commerce, no division of labor, no standard of value. On the other hand there was no such cannibalism as that found consecrated to the religious usages of the Nahuatlaca.

Among the Incas there was a vast peasant class who had been brought into subjection by the conquering race who entered Peru from the south. Apparently the first home of these invaders was the high land of Bolivia, in a small canton, Cuzco, situated on the natural highway that leads from the Bolivian highlands to the upper tributaries of the Amazon. The origins of Inca history can hardly go back further than three hundred years before the Spanish conquest. When the Spaniards came, consistent traditions were still preserved of the origin of the dominant tribe that told how, when Cuzco was first settled by them, it was already occupied by aboriginal inhabitants whose district was taken possession of by Manco Ccapac, the founder of the Inca rule. From the time of the first occupation eleven sovereign chiefs had borne sway over them for a period which may be justly estimated as three hundred years.

There were no chronological records, but there was curiously unique evidence in the shape of the mummified bodies of the eleven chieftains, who were given the same attention as lords and landowners that they enjoyed when alive. Their estates, herds of llamas, serfs were still treated as belonging to them; food and drink were daily placed before them; new clothing was prepared, and they were carried out for daily exercise in richly ornamented litters.

The rise of Inca domination had not been without serious opposition; there was a powerful coalition formed against them when their aggression became a menace to the neighboring tribes. The Inca chieftains were killed, and the situation was saved only by the appointment of a new leader, Huiracocha, who saw that more was to be won by conciliation than by aggression. This chieftain was one of the four to whom the consolidation of the Inca dominions was due. Under a later Inca chieftain Pachacutic (1435-1471), "the changer of the world," the pueblo of Cuzco dominated the whole of central Peru, and a district 300 miles in length towards the northwest. To the southeast it had a sphere of influence over a district of about equal extent, which was converted into definite subjection by Pachacutic and his allies.

The next stage of conquest was towards the north, where no special obstacles were encountered. The population was sparse, and in a low condition. Here an Inca colony was founded, which, with its capital at Quito, still survives under the form of the republic of Ecuador. From this vantage ground in their northern colony the Incas seem to have been brought into direct connection with the sea coast, for, owing to the long overland journey between Cuzco and their northern possessions, the water route was easier, and owing to the penetration of the land by the gulf of Guayaquil would easily suggest itself to those who as residents of the interior were not familiar before with journeyings by water. The advance into the coast valleys met with stout resistance on the part of a powerful confederacy which had Chimu as its center. The place was of strategical value to the Incas because it commanded important roads leading from the coast plain to the sierras, and was also accessible to the newly acquired northern colony and its hereditary domains.

Because of the successive steps by which the power of the Incas was so rapidly extended, the name of Pachacutic was associated with the whole of the administration of the Inca state as a lawgiver, architect, engineer, economist, and chief priest. His successor Tupac-Yuparqui followed in his father's steps by enlarging the state's borders both on the south and north. Resistance was cruelly repressed, as one sees from the narrative of his war on the coast valley of Huarco, where the Inca's warriors, brought together for three years in a permanent camp, wore out the natives by constant harryings, until they agreed to capitulate on the condition of being incorporated with the Inca nation. Tupac had no scruples in violating the compact by a general massacre of the vanquished. Even at the conquest immense heaps of bones were still pointed out, as relics of the methods by which Inca rule had been built up.

In 1493, Tupac died at Cuzco and was succeeded by his son Huaina Capac under whom the era of expansion came to an end; he occupied himself with temple building, with road construction, and with making punitive expeditions on the savage tribes who dwelt on the outskirts of his empire. Afterwards, in 1525, he fell a victim to an epidemic. There was a civil war due to a rebellion in the northern colony under Tupac-atahuallpa who assumed the government because of the incapacity of Huascar, the new chieftain at Cuzco. The revolt was successful; the warriors from the northern colony steadily advanced until they forced Huascar to leave Cuzco and finally to surrender himself and his family into the hands of the rival chieftain, after which he was taken to Lazamara, the fortified station midway between the northern colony and the original dominion.

The extent of the territory conquered by the Incas, as well as the rapidity with which the conquest was made, gives their annals a unique position in the history of tribal life at a comparatively low state of culture. As soon as they passed beyond the confines of middle Peru, their expansion as a conquering power met with no setback. The peoples who were threatened by their advance did not form a coalition against them, and when new areas were once conquered, new peoples were at once added, who supplied them with additional warriors. The structure of the empire was so simple, so loosely knit that it collapsed as soon as it was confronted by the serious internal difficulties that grew out of the disputed succession. The Spaniards came at an opportune moment and received without trouble the large landed inheritance of the Inca overlord, whose domains covered the territory now occupied by Ecuador, Peru, Bolivia, and Chili.

In estimating the standard of civilization attained by the Incas their theology, which is certainly of an advanced type, is naturally taken into account. The worship of the sun was one of the strongest bonds that kept together their widely separated lands. In each pueblo there was an estate of the sun god that was worked exactly as if it belonged to a chieftain. This economic network of temple estates was primarily intended to provide the sun with such constant supplies of food that the god's beneficent activity on the earth and to man could be sustained. The processes of tillage and the craft of weaving were all brought in this way in close relation to the religion of the dominant people. Portions of the finest woven stuffs, along with the offerings of the ground, were burned in sacrifice at each pueblo; the rest was carried on the backs of llamas belonging to the estates of the sun for the great festivals celebrated annually at Cuzco, where these beasts of burden and all they carried were sacrificed in honor of the god. An essential part of the ritual of sacrifice was the offering of human victims. These were not war captives as in Mexico; they were taken from the women serfs, attached to the estates of the sun, the weavers of the llama wool, who were called "the selected ones." This name was given to them because from each family in the pueblo there was collected a regular tribute of girls, distinguished by their beauty and vigor, who were trained to become members of the communities dedicated to the sun's service. After an education of eight years most of them were distributed among the various temples of the gods, the sun receiving the larger share, while some were given to the Ccapac Inca himself or to his officials.

These offerings of human victims took place at the prescribed sacrifices during the religious year, and also at extraordinary crises—for example, when the Inca chieftain was attacked by disease, when the country was endangered by wars, or when earthquakes and eclipses occurred. To symbolize the sun, images in the figure of a man were carved with an attire resembling that of the Inca chieftain, decorated with a headdress of darts, to resemble the solar rays.

As in Mexico the warrior class in Peru had a special ritual of sun worship not shared by outsiders. In this case the idol represented an infant molded of solid gold, with golden embroidery, shod with golden sandals, and with a headdress copied from that worn by the chiefs. For the purpose of popular worship, as these esoteric rites were not accessible to the common people, great sun dials covered with leaf of gold were set up, where they were exposed to the rays of the sun, and on them simple liquid offerings were made, that were visibly appropriated by the god through the processes of evaporation.

A great center of pilgrimage was the throne of the sun at Titicaca where, in the innermost shrine, there was a sacred rock the summit of which glittered with gold leaf. In the neighborhood of Cuzco and on the road to the rock of pilgrimage there were stations of sacrifice, where burnt-offerings of llamas, cocoa, and maize were made in order to inaugurate the new sun's progress from his ancient birthplace in the south. Sunrise was the time selected for these offerings; a white llama, bearing fuel, maize, and cocoa leaves, was previously led up to the mountain top, fire was kindled, and the victim was slain and consumed in the flames. By the time the sun was about to rise above the horizon, the burning pile was in full blaze. As the sun rose, the Incas chanted the prayer for the protection of their god: "O Creator, Sun, and Thunder, be forever young! Multiply the people, let them ever be in peace."

In the Peruvian religious system much attention was given to the service of dead chieftains by a class of special attendants organized like those who served the gods. There was, therefore, throughout the whole Inca domains, a large class of ecclesiastics well endowed with lands and serfs; at Cuzco at the time of the conquest most of the inhabitants of the pueblo were assigned to the service of some mummy. There was no hope for the living unless they could keep the good will of the dead; in all the affairs of life they had a part, food was set before the dead body at feasts and liquid refreshment was forced between the mummy's lips.

Huascar, the rival of Atahuallpa for the chieftainship of the Incas, lost the support of the warrior class because he was reported to have said that all the dead ought to be buried and their property taken from them. He did not wish to rule over mummies, from less sentimental reasons than those once expressed on a celebrated occasion by the spirit of Achilles. There had undoubtedly originated in Peru a movement against the economic monopoly connected with the temple worship. An effort had been made to meet this difficulty on the part of the Inca chieftains, who apparently, in view of the multiplication of festivals and sacrifices, had adopted the policy of diminishing the worship of the minor divinities and of concentrating the sacrificial offerings as far as they could on the Creator, Sun, Thunder, Earth, and Moon.

Under Inca rule the simple tribal administration was retained throughout the group of districts which were added in rapid succession to the seat of the race at Cuzco. Each Inca pueblo had its local chief or curaca, to whom were assigned a certain number of llamas and those portions of the land that were worked for him by the peasantry, who did all the agricultural labor. Distributions of the same character were made in each pueblo for the use of the head chieftain who dwelt at Cuzco, the so-called Ccapac Inca, and for the service of the tribal chieftains. The products of these reservations were taken to Cuzco and deposited there in store-houses from whence the llama hair was given to the women of the chief pueblo and woven by them into cloth. The food and the cloth so prepared were either kept as stores for military expeditions or used for sacrificial purposes.

As the territory of the empire was enlarged, this original system was applied to it. In each central district there was the same arrangement of buildings secular and religious, the Inca-tampu and the Ccoricancha, to which the produce of the lands belonging to the overlord and the sun was brought at regular intervals. These stations are found generally throughout the Inca domains, except in the coast-valleys. Between them were minor stations where two messengers were kept to carry orders from one stage to the other. Where there were natural difficulties to be overcome, in the long line of communication between the capitals Quito and Cuzco, a distance of 1500 miles in extent, causeways were built, and over streams and torrents enduring bridges were stretched, made of timber laid in strong ropes of twisted grass. There was a second road along the coast of the same length, but here, where the country was sandy, nothing was to be found save direction marks to indicate the correct track to be followed. In Cuzco there are still standing massive, finely-executed foundation walls which attest the skill of Inca builders. The temple of the sun can still be traced in the edifices of the European occupation. On an elevation commanding the road which led to middle Peru, the coast-valleys, and the northern colony there stands an impressive mass of cyclopean masonry, the fortress of Sacsahuaman, which represents the great terraced fortress begun by the founder of the Inca dominion and apparently not yet finished at the time of the conquest.

Though the Incas preserved a systematic administration that worked with mechanical accuracy over the area of their empire, it was at best a despotism, and their chieftains were nothing better than crude and brutal tyrants. The mental capacity of the race seems to have been below that of the people of Mexico, and their culture was certainly lower, as is seen in the absence of artistic advance on their part along with their inability to invent picture-writing, to work out the divisions of time, or to elaborate a system of numbers, although they were acquainted with denary arithmetic, and regularly observed the solstices. As warriors, they seem to have been drilled efficiently but mechanically; they were unable to foresee changes or adapt themselves to them when they came. They were vanquished by the Europeans more easily than the Aztecs had been, and their downfall was brought about by the assistance rendered the Spaniards by hosts of native allies.

IV

PIZARRO

The discovery of the Pacific Ocean and the foundation of the city of Panama on the narrow peninsula, led to the undertaking of voyages of exploration farther south, and this in turn to the entrance into Inca territory. In one of these enterprises progress was made as far as the Gulf of Guayaquil. The unanimous report was that the country for hundreds of miles was in a state of nature, unoccupied, unhealthful, covered with swamps, forests, and lofty mountains; but the voyagers had also heard that farther on to the south there was an empire, Bisu by name, civilized and notorious for its great wealth.

FRANCISCO PIZARRO
(From the original painting in the palace of the Viceroys at Lima.)

Francis Pizarro had been associated with Balboa up to the time of that leader's assassination; afterwards he planned to act on his own account, and his planning ended in the organization of an expedition to acquire this empire of the south. The natural son of a Spanish noble, Pizarro, who was born about 1471 at Truxillo, had had no such advantages of education as those enjoyed by Cortez; he lacked also that conqueror's impetuosity and chivalrous traits. Of the bad sides of the earlier conquistador he had more than a double portion; he was cold, calculating, and inflexible, shrinking from no cruelty and without a trace of the emotionalism which made Cortez so popular among his men.

Before giving a concrete shape to his scheme of conquest, he formed a commercial arrangement with Almagro an adventurer, and Luque a priest and schoolmaster of Panama, for the purpose of getting a financial backing. The first essay made in 1524 ended without tangible results. The coast of Peru was seen, and the adventurers were long enough on shore at Tumbez to see a surprisingly large number of gold and silver ornaments. They were not sufficiently strong to carry them off, but they had seen enough to pay for the hardships of their three years' trip south and back. Pizarro then betook himself to Spain to get further support, and before he returned to Panama he had made personal arrangements with the government with respect to the basis on which he would carry out his plan of conquest. Some jealousy arose because of Pizarro's manifest intention to assume the place of senior partner; the proposed expedition was saved only by the diplomacy of Luque, who again drew together his two comrades.

Finally, in 1532, Pizarro sailed away from Panama with three ships carrying in all 120 men and 36 horses. According to the plan accepted, Almagro was to follow with reinforcements, while Don Luque remained in Panama to prevent outside interference with the combination. News had come, as we have mentioned, to the ears of Huaina Ccapac of the landing of white men at Tumbez in 1525. Between this date and the year of Pizarro's second trip had intervened the period of civil war between the rival claimants, with the captivity of the legitimate son, Huascar, in the spring of 1532. By April, after a two months' trip down the coast, Pizarro arrived off the pueblo of Tumbez. He found it abandoned and dismantled. Spending some time exploring the neighborhood, he founded the town of San Miguel, and was put in possession of the facts that gave him his opportunity for advance into the interior. Huascar, desiring to get the coöperation of the Spaniards in maintaining his hold on the country, sent messengers to Pizarro with such encouraging words that the plan of conquest could already be outlined. Pizarro knew how, by making use of the divisions of the natives, Cortez had taken Mexico; his own opportunity had come sooner than he had expected. "If the land had not been divided," said Pedro Pizarro, "we should have been able neither to enter nor conquer it." On September 24, 1532, only about 200 Europeans, all told, set out; but the number of natives in Pizarro's army was considerable. All the partisans of Huascar in the neighborhood were expected to join the Spaniards, because before setting out Pizarro had announced his intention of supporting Huascar, the "natural lord of the country."

The Spaniards had, however, not made much progress towards the pueblo of Caxamalca when word came from Atahuallpa, the other claimant, that he desired the friendship of Pizarro; to reinforce his friendly sentiments a present accompanied the message. Pizarro spoke, in reply, of his desire for the Inca chieftain to be his friend and brother, and explained that his chief purpose in coming was to teach the principles of the Christian religion. Shortly after this official description of his mission had been given Pizarro moved forward; no opposition was offered, although in one place a large river had to be crossed where resistance would have been easy.

In order to obtain information about Atahuallpa efforts were made, without success, to get some account of his intentions. An Indian chief was tortured; his information was that the Inca was preparing to make war, in three places, on the Christians; later on it was reported that Atahuallpa was near Caxamalca with over 50,000 warriors. Perplexed, Pizarro employed a native notable to go to Atahuallpa as a friendly envoy to make clear to him that the Spaniards were coming as allies. As Pizarro's men began to fear that they would be exposed to attack on the last stage of the journey, they were comforted by their commander's assurance that they were really nothing more than peaceful missionaries of God and representatives of their king to ignorant heathen to whom they wished no harm.

The fears of the adventurers were set at rest by discovering from the natives they passed on their march up the sierras, that Atahuallpa was not preparing to meet them in anything but a peaceful fashion. In the difficult region through which they were being led, their advance could have been checked by a slight display of force. But the friendly attitude of the Inca chieftain was proved on several occasions by the appearance of messengers with food; Pizarro promised, on his side, that he would help to put down any remaining disaffection. On the part of the inhabitants there was no reason to suspect that the orders given by their superiors to serve and obey the newcomers were not reasonable. The general impression among the natives was that the Europeans were children of their god, the sun. Naturally this belief tended to give them a sacred character. Up to the present, indeed, there had been no conflicts with the natives except at Tumbez and at Puna, where the opposition was confined to a few hundred Indians. On the arrival in Caxamalca, Pizarro still kept up the ruse of being an ingenuous tourist; he sent personally to Atahuallpa to beg for an interview, insisting on his willingness to help him, and promising, if enemies were pointed out, he would send his men to reduce them.

Pizarro had now no difficulty in applying the scheme of conquest so successfully illustrated by Cortez in Mexico, but common enough to the conquistadors everywhere. By getting possession of the chief, the Spaniards made sure of the people; like Montezuma in Mexico, Atahuallpa in Peru was adored as a god. To put the capture of the Inca into execution was not difficult. He was invited to be present at a feast given by Pizarro. Under cover of this hospitable act his person could be seized. The risk came from the fact that he had about him 30,000 men. The night before the plot was to be carried out the Spanish camp gave itself up to religious exercises, the captain Pizarro taking the lead in encouraging his men to face the coming danger. Much comfort was derived from the assurances of the ecclesiastics who accompanied the expedition that God was on their side and would aid them to put his enemies to confusion. Careful arrangements had been made that the Spanish men-at-arms should be held in readiness in their quarters, prepared to sally into the square of the town at a moment's notice. The artillerymen were bidden to train their guns on the Inca camp, and fire on it when the command was given. Pizarro took with him twenty men to aid in the seizure of Atahuallpa. In the great square where the Spaniards were lodged no one was to leave quarters until the artillery fire began. Much help was expected from the horsemen in causing a panic among the Indians, and they were told to put little bells on the harness.

The square of the pueblo that Pizarro selected to carry out his plan seemed expressly constructed for the deed. Triangular in shape, there were but two means of egress from it—two doors which gave access to the streets of the town. When the time appointed came, as the Inca chief delayed, Pizarro sent word to him to be expeditious, as the meal was being delayed until he arrived. Atahuallpa, taking an escort of 6000, who were unarmed except for small cudgels and slings, came into the square. Here there was every appearance of festivity; some of the men were dancing and singing; some carried plates and crowns of gold and silver. In a litter, made of gold and silver, Atahuallpa was borne along through the files of his escort, who parted ranks when he appeared, all keeping absolute silence. He then listened to a harangue from a Spanish friar inviting him to obey the Pope and receive the faith of Christ, and also to become the friend and tributary of the King of Spain. Otherwise he was threatened with the fate of an enemy; the Spaniards told him they would abolish all idols, "so that you may leave the lying religion of your many and false gods."

Atahuallpa, in his answer, objected to taking the proffered position of tributary, but wished to be a friend of the King of Spain; he also declined to receive his kingdom at the hands of the Pope, as the friar had told him the King of Spain had done. On theological points he showed himself a skilled disputant, contrasting the Christian God, who had died, with the sun and moon, who had never died. He also inquired of the friar how he knew that the God of the Christians had created the world. The pious friar gave him his Breviary, explaining that he had learnt of the Creator from that book. Atahuallpa looked at it, opened its pages, first thanked him, then threw it on the ground, saying it told him nothing of the kind. Indignantly the friar picked up the Breviary and rushed to Pizarro, crying out, "The Gospels are on the ground. Vengeance! Christians, at them! they do not wish our friendship nor our law! Kill these dogs who despise God's law. Go on, and I absolve you."

At this instant the guns were fired, the trumpets sounded, and the infantry and cavalry came forth from their shelters. The sight of the armed warriors on their horses and the noise of the guns threw the Indians into a panic. In the rush to get out of the square, part of the wall surrounding it, was broken down. The Indians fell on top of one another, closely pursued by the horsemen, who trampled them down without mercy. Those who held their ground inside the inclosure were dealt with by the foot soldiers, and most of them were killed. There was no resistance, for the natives were practically unarmed. Atahuallpa was, as had been agreed, taken alive, many of his nobles giving up their lives to protect his person from attack. As the members of his bodyguard fell, their places were taken with desperate heroism by others of the group.

The massacre was likened by one of the chroniclers to the killing of sheep. The victims numbered more than 10,000, and only 200 escaped. Not a

Spaniard perished nor even was wounded except Pizarro, who had a flesh wound in the hand, inflicted accidentally by one of his own men. Pizarro's act in hewing down this crowd of Peruvians, unarmed and panic-stricken, recalls the worst features of the Mexican conquest, the massacre of Cholula and the attack made by Alvarado on the Mexican chiefs while they were celebrating a religious festival.

The next day was spent in sacking the palace of Atahuallpa, whose rich stores of gold and silver were discovered. Next came the question of the disposition of the captives, 8000 or more. It was actually proposed that the warriors should be killed or have their hands cut off, but Pizarro, who had not been trained in vain to the economic principles of conquest, decided that all should be reduced to slavery. The reduction of Atahuallpa to the status of a prisoner had the desired effect. The subordinate chiefs made their peace. This was a welcome escape from further hostilities, but Pizarro was more interested in arranging terms for the ransom which Atahuallpa was willing to give to receive his liberty. The gold and silver kept coming in; sometimes in one day 70,000 pesos were received.

Pizarro not being satisfied with the industry of the natives in getting treasure, Spanish emissaries were sent to Cuzco. Under their experienced hands the supplies increased; in one day 200 loads of gold and 25 of silver were brought into Caxamalca. Much of the precious metal was made up of strips taken from the walls of the temples, which were tapestried in this way. Some ornaments are mentioned; such as a fountain made entirely of gold and a golden footstool weighing 18,000 pesos. All was melted down except a few objects of small weight, kept and sent to the King of Spain as curiosities.

Despite the paying of this enormous ransom, there was no question of keeping faith with their captive. He was only in the way now that Pizarro had the enormous ransom. His death would remove a dangerous rallying point, and by it his people would be thrown into such confusion that they would submit the more easily to the yoke that was being prepared for them. Like the chief of the Aztecs, Cuauhtemoc, Atahuallpa was charged with disloyalty to the Spanish crown, of which he was assumed to be a dependent. As the zealous representative of his King, Pizarro passed sentence of death on his prisoner, commanding that it be executed by burning. All protests from the victim were unheeded, even when he assured his conquerors that through him they could keep the Indians on terms of good will. "If," he said, "they wished gold and silver, he was ready to hand over twice the amount they had already received." As they did not believe he could keep any such engagement, they refused to defer the day of execution. When the pile was ready, Atahuallpa, on finding that if he became a Christian, he would not be burnt, went through the form of conversion. Pizarro ordered that he should be bound to a stake on the square of the pueblo and strangled. (August 29, 1533.)

One of Atahuallpa's brothers was then proclaimed chief by the Spaniards, and with this "roi fainéant" in tow Pizarro set out on the two months' march to the capital, Cuzco. Before he came to the neighborhood of the leading pueblo, Inca warriors disputed with some obstinacy his further progress; but the presence of their chieftain with Pizarro prevented anything like a serious rising of the people. Disgusted with this most untoward event, Pizarro blamed an Inca general, who had been made a prisoner at Xauxa, for the resistance made on the march. This was enough to prove his guilt; the prisoner was condemned to death and burnt alive a short distance from Cuzco. Even this flagrant outrage failed to move the Incas to any organized effort to stay the European advance; instead of moving aggressively, Manco, the brother of Huascar, came voluntarily to Pizarro asking his protection, hoping by his aid to become the chieftain of the Incas. This alliance made it easy for the Spaniards, posing as the supporters of the regular line, to get within the walls of Cuzco without opposition, on November 15, 1533. The great massive pueblo with the fortress and temple of the sun, and with its extensive population, was a rich prize. Everything in the way of gold was quickly removed, and the humble followers of the modest commercial undertaking so recently organized at Panama found themselves in the possession of wealth. But the great drawback was the high price of provisions by which the adventurers lost some of the treasure that had fallen to their share. Under such conditions of forced hospitality Pizarro arranged for the elevation of Manco as Ccapac-Inca or overlord. At the same time Cuzco received the gift of municipal government, March 24, 1534. Pizarro, not forgetful of his own services, took the title of governor, and everything was speedily changed. Cuzco now had a bishop, a cathedral was built, monasteries and convents arose as if by magic, and all the famous temples were transformed into churches.

Things were moving expeditiously and smoothly in Pizarro's favor, until he learnt of the arrival at a place not far from Quito of an officer of Cortez, Pedro de Alvarado, the governor of Guatemala, with an expedition of 500 Europeans and more than 2000 Indian allies. This interference seemed likely to cause trouble, until Alvarado was persuaded to sell his army and everything in it to Pizarro. The sum handed over to avoid a competitive conquest, which would have meant loss of life and, more important still, from the point of view of these experts in exploitation of subject races, loss of time, was considerable. Alvarado withdrew with something like $2,000,000; gauged by the standards of butchery, rapacity, and knavery in the West Indies and in Mexico, this was a splendid bargain. But, as Alvarado had only set his foot on Peruvian soil, he had not yet begun to reckon imperially; he was certainly far removed still from Pizarro's poetic fancy in finance. Now that there was no longer a chance for such awkward interruptions, Pizarro set about the foundation of a new capital for Peru. Cuzco, being far distant from the seacoast, was manifestly unsuitable, and accordingly Lima was founded on the 6th of January, 1535, to be the center of this new colonial possession. Preparations were already under way for a regular administration with Pizarro at the head, after the model of the rule established by Cortez in Mexico.

The royal fifth of the treasure taken was so large that it removed all obstacles at Madrid. Detailed confirmation was given to the general concessions made to Pizarro, and their territorial extent was amplified by adding seventy leagues of land to the south. Almagro received a concession extending from the southern limit of Pizarro's province 200 leagues. To the northern territory was given the name New Castile, to the southern, New Toledo; but the Indian names, Peru and Chili, were too strongly imbedded in native usage to be forced out of existence.

When Almagro was sent by Pizarro to Cuzco with orders to use it as a starting-point for the southern territory that had been assigned to him, the lieutenant took the opportunity of claiming that the Inca capital was situated south of Pizarro's concession, and, therefore, was a part of his own land. This difficulty being patched up on June 12, 1535, Almagro set out for the conquest of Chili, while Pizarro began the establishment of a new seacoast town, Trujillo, and pushed forward the building of Lima.

The native population was dealt with after the "repartimiento" plan. Under the burden of their new oppressors, the Indians, who had for so long submitted to the cruder tyranny of the Inca chiefs, rose in revolt. Manco, a scion of the old house, placed himself at the head of the anti-Spanish movement, and the first success of the natives was the capture of the citadel of Cuzco, February, 1536. In the meantime the Spaniards who lived in isolated plantations had been massacred. Both the new towns, Lima and Trujillo, were invested. After a time the citadel of Cuzco was retaken from the natives, but Juan, one of Pizarro's brothers, met his death in the fighting. As a relief expedition Pizarro sent to Cuzco more than 400 men, of whom 200 were cavalry, but they never succeeded in crossing the Sierra. Aid was then asked from the neighboring colonies of Panama, Guatemala, and Mexico. With the help of abundant reinforcements, Cuzco was retaken, and the obstinacy of the Spaniards in holding their ground for six months discouraged the Indians from further efforts to cut off the old capital.

When Almagro discovered the unattractive character of his newly assigned province, where the population was hostile and the land largely a desert, he returned along the western declivities of the Andes to reassert his claims on Cuzco. Arriving there in April, 1537, he made a successful night attack on the place, and took Pizarro's brother, Fernando, prisoner. Near Cuzco Alvarado was stationed with 500 men at Xanca, and here a battle took place on July 12, 1537, in which Alvarado was beaten and taken prisoner. Almagro then set out for Lima. He and Pizarro, after a meeting at Mala on November 13, 1537, agreed to submit the question of the limits of their provinces to arbitration, arranging in the meantime that Almagro should hold Cuzco and Ferdinand Pizarro should have Caxamalca. But this arrangement was not carried out. Ferdinand soon after organized an expedition to recapture Cuzco, and another battle was fought with Almagro in April, which resulted in the latter being taken prisoner. After being given the semblance of a trial, he was put to death on July 8, 1538, by Fernando. Francis Pizarro, who denied complicity in Almagro's death, treated the latter's son kindly, but he did not forget to reward his own brothers, after he had made his triumphal entrance into Cuzco, with large landed estates. To Gonzalo he gave the district of Lake Titicaca, which included the mines of Potosi.

The assassination of Almagro stirred up indignation among his friends, who determined, that when the official explanations were presented in Spain by Pizarro's emissaries, their side should be given a hearing. In the mother country, the authorities refused to distinguish between the claims of the two factions. What was plain was that dissensions in the colony could only damage Spanish control, and might lead to a restoration of Indian rule there. Accordingly a royal commissioner was sent out with ample powers.

Before the new official arrived, Pizarro showed his characteristic industry in expanding the sphere of Spanish influence. Groups of adventurers were sent out in different directions, and plans were made which ended in the foundation of Santiago in Chili. One of Pizarro's brothers was sent off with an army of 340 Europeans and 4000 Indians to conquer the country east of the Andes. Led by the usual stories of the existence of gold and precious stones in far-distant regions, the Spaniards in this expedition, overcoming the most extraordinary natural difficulties in their march, succeeded in reaching one of the tributaries of the Amazon. A boat was then built by means of which one of the members of the party, Orellana, with a few companions, made the long trip to the ocean, and finally succeeded in reaching a Spanish colony on one of the islands of the Antilles. This was a unique achievement, for the vessel in which he sailed was constructed of green timber, there was no compass, no pilot was to be had, and provisions had to be collected from the natives along the bank of the river, who sometimes received the strangers with no friendly welcome. Orellana, in relating his achievements, demonstrated the creative power of his imagination as well as his heroism. He told of seeing nations so rich that the roofs of their temples were covered with plates of gold, and also related how he had passed through a republic controlled by women, who by the force of their arms had acquired the rule over a considerable tract of country. From these fictions of Orellana originated the belief in the existence of a region called El Dorado, and the conviction that somewhere in the center of South America there existed a community of Amazons.

In 1545 the silver mines of Potosi were discovered, an event which played an enormous rôle in the colonization of the country, because its wealth realized the most sanguine hopes of the adventurers. Upper Peru—or as it is now called, Bolivia—became the greatest silver mining country in the known world. Meanwhile the success of Pizarro's administration stirred up among Almagro's friends increasing bitterness, for they saw no chance of receiving a share of the good fortune which was being showered upon the governor, his brothers, and his favorites. Almagro's son, who was in Lima, made that town the central point of the faction that was bent on Pizarro's ruin. The governor, though aware of the existence of these intrigues, affected to treat them with disdain. He relied on the possession of absolute power as the complete protection against any plot. This foolhardy attitude was taken advantage of by the conspirators, who, without much difficulty, penetrated into his house and put him to death June 26, 1541. Even Pizarro's own followers, the men who had shared with him the dangers of the conquest and the spoils of victory, raised no hand to avenge his murder. His Borgia-like character had alienated all, except his immediate relatives whom, as has been said, he had elevated to high positions.

When the governor from Spain, Vaca de Castro, reached the country, he proceeded to inflict strict justice on the conspirators. After an armed conflict near Cuzco, between the partisans of Almagro and the upholders of the authority of the home government, most of those who were guilty of the murder of Pizarro fell into the governor's hands, who promptly executed them as rebels (1542). But the country was not destined to enjoy tranquillity long. Gonzalo Pizarro, the brother of the "conquistador," acquired by force the possession of the colony, and succeeded in extending his rule over Peru and its various dependencies. He even sent north a fleet which captured Panama and so got command of the western ocean. But the usurper's rule did not last long, for, when he was disowned by the home government, he found himself unable to maintain his authority over the colonists. Like his more famous brother, Gonzalo died the death of a malefactor, and the vast possessions acquired on the west coast of South America by the adventurers of the earlier period of Spanish conquest came under the systematic and regular control of the Spanish bureaucratic machinery.

By the middle of the sixteenth century the spectacular features of the conquest of Spanish America vanished away. Large and unexplored territories were indeed added to the monarchy of Spain, but as the lands so annexed were populated by Indian tribes in no higher state of culture than those found in the lesser Antilles, the methods of conquest were but a repetition of those employed by the adventurers of an earlier period. On the whole it may be said that the treatment of the natives improved, especially in those districts where there was no mining or where gold could be discovered near the surface. Long after the complete administrative organization of the conquered lands in Mexico, of Central America, of the northern portions of South America, and of the Pacific slope of that continent, the colonies on the Atlantic side, even if they were founded earlier, were less attractive to the colonist. The Jesuits first appeared in Paraguay in 1586, though Uruguay was opened up for settlement some time before. The town of Buenos Ayres was established in 1538 amid surroundings which gave little hope to colonial settlement. The original group of 3000 Europeans who entered the new Province of La Plata were almost exterminated by disease and by the fatiguing and incessant warfare with the savage races about them.

From the point of view of the old mercantile system of political economy, Spain's colonial policy was advantageous to the home government. It is usual to expose the failure of the government of Madrid to manage its vast empire under any other ideals than those of absolutism, but when one considers the size and novelty of the experiment that Spain was making in these Western lands, and when one estimates broadly the stage of civilization so soon reached in a large number of new communities, it must be allowed that to the government of the peninsula is to be ascribed the credit of accomplishing a task practically unparalleled in modern history. The work was not thoroughly done; there were grave and deplorable defects. Yet without accepting at all the truth of the dictum that whatever is, is right, it can be said that no colonial possessions of other powers during the same century offered the same problems as those confronted by Spain, and nowhere in North America was the progress of extensive occupation and intensive civilization so definitely marked.

The Spanish colonial empire has had the misfortune of being exposed to much the same sort of depreciation as the Byzantine Empire; in both cases investigation has diminished the weight of conventional hostile criticism. Doctrinaire theories of government, and unfounded social contrasts, are apt to produce false standards. It is easy to detect faults in Spain's management of her colonies, but it is not easy to reconstruct for her a policy that might have produced on Spanish soil the sturdy independence of the New England town meeting, or the collective wisdom of the founders of the American Constitution.

NAPOLEON

I

EARLY YEARS

Corsica, during a large part of the eighteenth century, had drawn upon itself the attention of Europe, on account of its heroic struggle for independence. Its champion was Pasquale Paoli, whose character and patriotism provoked the same sort of enthusiastic attention from his contemporaries that centered upon Garibaldi 100 years later. The cause of the islanders against the city of Genoa, which exercised the right of overlordship over them, was so successfully defended that had not the kingdom of France interfered as the ally of Genoa, the establishment of an independent Corsican republic would have been assured. But unfortunately the Genoese surrendered the sovereignty of the island to France. The French occupied the harbors, the Corsicans were defeated in a pitched battle, and Paoli retired as a fugitive to England. All further resistance was abandoned, and the island was annexed to France.

In the Corsican deputation sent to Paris to arrange terms with the conquerors was Carlo Bonaparte, a member of a noble Tuscan family, whose ancestors had established themselves in Ajaccio 200 years before. Some time before this visit to Paris his wife, Maria Letitia, had given birth to a son, Napoleon. There has recently been a question raised whether the traditionally accepted date, August 15, 1769, is correct, and some French investigators are in favor of antedating it by one year. There were eight surviving children, five of them boys, out of a family of thirteen. Napoleon describes himself as an unruly child despite the iron discipline exercised in the home by his mother. "I was," he says, "self-willed and obstinate, nothing awed me; nothing disconcerted me. I was quarrelsome, exasperating; I feared no one, I gave a blow here and a scratch there. Everyone was afraid of me. My brother Joseph was the one with whom I had most to do. He was beaten about and scolded; I complained that he did not get over it soon enough."

The father, a lawyer by profession, was engaged in unending litigation in his own behalf, which required frequent trips to Paris, where he was well known on account of his efforts to recover an estate, deeded by some relative to the Jesuit order, and also as a representative deputy of the Corsican nobility. On one of these trips the head of the house died in 1785; seven years before that date he had been successful in getting a scholarship for Napoleon at the military school of Brienne, where the young soldier had just completed his course and received his commission as lieutenant at the time of his father's death. At school Napoleon had made little reputation as a scholar; he stated himself later on that it was the general opinion that he "was fit for nothing except geometry." He was unsociable, with an imperious temperament that parted everyone from him. One of his schoolfellows writes of his characteristics as follows: "Gloomy and even savage, almost always self-absorbed, one would have supposed that he had just come from some forest, and unmindful, until then, of the notice of his fellows, experienced for the first time the sensations of surprise and distrust; he detested games and all manner of boyish amusements. One part of the garden was allotted to him and there he studied and brooded, and woe to him who ventured to disturb him. One evening the boys were setting off fireworks and a small powder-chest exploded. In their fright the troop scattered in all directions, and some of them took refuge in Napoleon's domain, whereat he rushed upon the fugitives in a passion and attacked them with a spade."

NAPOLEON I
(From the portrait by P. Delaroche.)

He had wished to enter the navy after his studies were finished, but there was some delay until, as his family were in straitened circumstances, he decided to enter the artillery, where the applications for admission were fewer. So he passed from Brienne to Paris, where he again seems to have made no very favorable impression, except on the mathematical instructor at the military school, Monge, whose report on Bonaparte at the time he was leaving school reads as follows: "Reserved and studious, he prefers study to amusement of any kind, and takes pleasure in reading the works of good authors; while diligent in his study of abstract science, he cares little for any other; he has a thorough knowledge of mathematics and geography. He is taciturn, preferring solitude, capricious, haughty, and inordinately self-centered. While a man of few words, he is vigorous in his replies, ready and incisive in retort; he has great self-esteem, is ambitious with aspirations that stop at nothing. He is a young man worthy of patronage."

The new officer, who was assigned to duty at Valence, found garrison life very tedious; promotion was slow, there were no drills, camp life, nor manœuvers; he spent, he says, a good deal of his time reading novels, planned even to write one, and took some part in the local life of the town, making friends among the society of petty officials, lawyers, and other persons of middle-class station. He did some solid reading also, making himself acquainted with Rousseau, Adam Smith, and Raynal, the last having so much influence over him, that he acknowledged himself as Raynal's disciple in his views as to the need of social reform in France, which, among other things, implied the abolition of class privileges and the purification of administration. His literary attempts were various; he was prompted to make them because his pay of 100 livres a month, though adequate for himself, was not sufficient to help out his relatives in Corsica, where his mother and the rest of the family were in a position of financial difficulty.

During the early years of the revolutionary movement in France, Napoleon spent a large part of the time in Corsica, where the nationalist party hoped to take advantage of the civil disturbances of their new rulers, and reclaim their independence. For a time he made their cause his own, and developed a scheme for driving the French from the island. But conditions soon changed after Paoli returned to Corsica. Napoleon, who hoped for high military command among his own people, failed to secure the support of the old leader, who suspected the young officer, on account of the radical sympathies he manifested for the revolutionary party in France. Paoli believed in a constitutional monarchy, and refused to side with the Convention which had put Louis XVI to death. Most of the Corsicans followed their conservative statesman, and in May, 1793, Napoleon and the whole Bonaparte family were declared outlaws.

After an unsuccessful attempt to take Ajaccio from the Paolists Napoleon, with the rest of his family, abandoned the island and withdrew to Toulon. His scheme of self-advancement at home had failed; he had now only France to look to as the field of his ambition. It was fortunate for him that during this period his irregular connection with the French army, in which he still held the rank of officer, was tolerated. He had made himself marked by his openly declared sympathies with the anti-monarchical party, and for this reason, his independent action in visiting Corsica and remaining there as long as he liked was passed over without criticism from his superiors in Paris; indeed, his captain's commission was dated February 6, 1792, a time when he was devoting his attention altogether to Corsican affairs, in his own interest.

His arrival in France coincided with the establishment of the Reign of Terror, and the government at Paris had on their hands an insurrection in the southern part of the country which sided with the Girondins, many of whose leaders had been put to death by the Jacobins. Napoleon resumed his military service at Nice, and immediately took part in repressing the Girondin insurrection. He also expressed his full agreement with the Jacobins in a dialogue entitled the *Souper de Beaucaire*, a pamphlet intended to win adherents to the cause of the Terrorists at Paris. His apology called public attention to him,—the dialogue was printed at the expense of the state, and its author was soon on friendly terms with the younger Robespierre, one of the commissioners of the Convention in southern France.

In various towns, Marseilles included, the insurrectionists were losing their foothold. The last important place left to them was Toulon, where they were being actively supported by English and Spanish allies. It was necessary to win the place, for preparations were being made on a large scale by both England and Austria to use Toulon as a starting-point to invade southern France. Napoleon was given the command of a battalion of artillery, and it was his scheme for arranging the batteries around the town that led to the taking of the city by the French. His services were recognized by promotion to a brigadier generalship, a fitting reward, for it was his strategy which had compelled the allied troops of Spain and England to evacuate the one place on French territory which they occupied.

The younger Robespierre spoke of him in a report to the Committee of Public Safety as a man of transcendent merit. Bonaparte was intimate with the commissioner, and that he impressed those who knew him as an ardent sympathizer with the Terrorists is borne out by a statement contained in Mlle. Robespierre's memoranda: "Bonaparte was a republican, I should say that he was a republican of the Mountain, at least he made that impression upon me from his manner of regarding things at the time I was in Nice [1794]. Later his victories turned his head and made him aspire to rule over his fellow-citizens, but, while he was but a general of artillery in the army of Italy, he was a believer in thorough-going liberty and equality." Yet the fanatical side of the Robespierre government, with its policy of ruthless massacre, evidently did not win his sympathy, for there is good ground for believing that, after the capture of Toulon, he was one of those who counseled moderation towards the vanquished and opposed the wholesale execution of the rebels. What attracted him to the Robespierre régime was its directness and its energy, and there is no doubt that he had a much higher opinion of the personal capacity of Robespierre than is held by a later school of historians of the French Revolution, who see in him a somewhat commonplace and decorative tool of the obscurer members of the Committee of Public Safety. In a conversation with Marmont, after Robespierre's downfall, he said, "If

Robespierre had remained in power, he would have been able to strike out another way for himself, he would have systematized the laws and made them permanent; we should have attained this result without shocks and convulsions because it would have proceeded from the exercise of power. We are now trying to reach this goal through a revolution, and this revolution will give birth to a monarchy."

As a friend and counselor of Robespierre's younger brother, who had already become interested in Napoleon's scheme for an invasion of Italy, the prospects of his securing an independent military command were most encouraging, especially as he had just been so flatteringly recommended by the younger Robespierre to the Committee of Public Safety. But all chances of such advancement were lost with the downfall and execution of the revolutionary dictator in July, 1794.

Napoleon was involved in the general ruin of the Robespierre party; he lost his commission as general and spent a month as a prisoner in a military fortress. He fortunately had friends who interceded for him, among them Salicetti, the Corsican, a member of the Convention, by whose efforts the charge of disloyalty to the Republic was shown to be baseless and the prisoner was released, reinstated, and given the important mission of restoring French sovereignty in Corsica, which had lately declared itself a constitutional monarchy under the protection of England. The expedition failed on account of the weakness of the French fleet. For some time after this misadventure Napoleon remained without a command; the government at Paris was not inclined to forward the interests of a former partisan of Robespierre.

There were besides a number of young officers quite capable of filling important army commands, and all that Napoleon could secure was an assignment in the west under Hoche, who was engaged in repressing the insurrection in La Vendée. He had no taste for such work, nor did he desire to serve in a subordinate capacity. Taking advantage of the weakness of the administration, he delayed his departure from Paris, although he had received peremptory orders to leave for his command. He hoped by the influence of friends such as Barras, whom he had known at Toulon, and who was now a man of weight in the counsels of the party predominant in the Convention, to secure the acceptance from the ministry of war of his plan for the invasion of Italy. He was not only disappointed in this hope, but he found himself again stricken from the list of French generals because of his refusal to proceed to the post already assigned him.

There was no encouragement to be got out of the prevailing political tendencies, which were showing a marked antagonism to the radical revolutionary party, with whose program Napoleon had been allied from the first. A restoration of the monarchy seemed not improbable, for the common people of Paris were showing signs of restlessness under the régime of the Terrorist factions. The members of the Convention, after providing for a stable government with an executive power vested in a Directory of five members, were fearful of the consequences of the proposed changes they had themselves provided, and they proceeded to pass a measure by which the newly elected legislative body, the Council of Five Hundred, should be composed, to the extent of two-thirds of its membership, of those who had served in the Convention. This action caused an open revolt. Forty-four out of the forty-eight sections, into which Paris was divided, were in arms against the continuance of the tyranny of the Convention. On one side stood the National Guard of the city; on the other there were only 8000 regular troops willing to obey the mandate of the government. Barras happened to be one of the commissioners of the Convention appointed to preserve order. He was then chosen commander-in-chief of the army, and, acting with the reluctant consent of the other members of the Committee, he selected his friend Napoleon as second in command, with full power to act in defense of the Convention.

No time could be lost, and everything depended on getting artillery into the city to the Tuileries. Here the guns were stationed, before the National Guard commenced to advance on the 5th of October. No one knows who fired the first shot, but the engagement that followed soon ended in a complete disaster for the insurgents, who were driven from position to position by the volleys of grapeshot which swept the streets in the vicinity of the Seine. In recognition of his services rendered at such a crisis, Napoleon was almost immediately advanced to the post of commander-in-chief of the Army of the Interior, the way being made easy for him by Barras' appointment as one of the Directors in the new government. Napoleon's analysis of the situation, made the day after this fight in the streets of Paris, was characteristically clear-headed. "Fortune is on my side," he writes to his brother Joseph, and from this sudden change in his prospects may be dated that belief in his star signalized by his favorite motto, "Au destin," which became the axiom of his career, as well as its explanation and justification.

Barras' services did not end here; he realized the young general's capacity, seeing in him a man whom it would be useful to have bound to him by personal obligations, and he suggested, and it is said, even arranged Napoleon's marriage with Mme. de Beauharnais, a well known member of Parisian society, the widow of a nobleman who had fallen a victim of the Terror, and herself a native of Martinique. She had fascinated the soldier by her charm of manner and was now prepared, despite the objections of her friends, to give him the social position that Barras insisted was necessary for his further promotion. This advice of Barras was not necessarily disinterested, for there were, it seems, reasons of a different nature, which may have prompted him to relieve himself, by making use of Napoleon, of further personal responsibilities he had incurred towards the lady in question. The marriage had an immediate influence in advancing the fortunes of the bridegroom, for two days before it was solemnized (March 4, 1796), Napoleon attained the long-coveted position of commander-in-chief of the Army of Italy; and on the 11th of the same month, he set out for his new post.

II
ITALY AND EGYPT

Of the great Continental Powers which had formed a coalition against the revolutionary government of France, Austria and Russia were actively inimical, and there was no prospect of coming to terms with them, unless all the conquered territories recently acquired by France were sacrificed. The idea of natural boundaries had become by this time a dogma of political faith, and even the Directory, confronted as it was by a demoralized administration, by bad business conditions, and by an inflated currency, had no thought of making peace. Armies were operating along the eastern frontiers; and as soon as Napoleon reached Nice, he prepared, along the lines he had so frequently urged, to take the offensive against the vulnerable Austrian provinces of northern Italy.

The force he took over now numbered 38,000 men, out of a nominal six divisions of 60,282. They were poorly equipped, insufficiently nourished, and had not received their pay. The manifesto issued to them, according to Napoleon's report of it at St. Helena, held out an immediate change of fortune. It is a document characteristic in contents and form of the new era of glory and conquest on which France was now to embark under Napoleon's leadership. "Soldiers," he said, "you are ill-fed and almost naked; the government owes you much; it can give you nothing. Your patience, the courage which you exhibit in the midst of these mountains, are worthy of admiration; but they bring you no atom of glory; not a ray is reflected upon you. I will conduct you into the most fertile places of the world. Rich provinces, great cities, will be in your power; there you will find honor, glory, and wealth. Soldiers of Italy, will you be lacking in courage or perseverance?"

These promises were made good in the remarkable campaign that followed, in which Napoleon's soldiers found their material wants amply satisfied and their ambitious wishes for a career of glory more than answered in the brilliant victories of their general. Napoleon's plan of operations was guided by the principles he had outlined two years before to the Robespierre régime. "In the management of war, as in the siege of a city," he said, "the method should be to direct the fire upon a single point. The breach once made, equilibrium is destroyed, all further effort is useless, and the place is taken. Attacks should not be scattered, but united. An army should be divided for the sake of subsistence and concentrated for combat. Unity of command is indispensable to success. Time is everything."

The last mentioned condition was fully vindicated, for before the end of April the French had beaten in a succession of quickly delivered attacks and effective battles, the Austrian army occupying Piedmont and also their Piedmontese allies. With the retreat of the Austrians from his kingdom, King Victor Amadeus made peace, and Napoleon hurried on to deal finally with the Austrians on their own territory in Lombardy. With the winning of the battle of Lodi on the 10th of May, Lombardy was soon evacuated by the enemy, and Napoleon entered the capital of the province, Milan, on the 16th of May. The commander of the victorious army paid little attention to the policy outlined at Paris for his conduct in Italy; he negotiated independently of the Directory and oftentimes contrary to their expressed wishes. When they proposed to divide his command by sharing it with General Kellermann, he wrote, "Each person has his own way of making war. General Kellermann has had more experience and will do it better than I; but both together will do it badly." By this plain statement, the Directors were brought to terms; they were unwilling to let Napoleon resign his command, for the campaign was giving the government the prestige it badly needed, and what was equally valuable in their eyes was Napoleon's novel method of conducting warfare without making any demands on the central treasury.

In the meantime there were further successes to be recorded against the Austrians. Wherever they made a stand they were defeated; a large number of their men were blocked up in the great citadel at Mantua, and, for months, armies in succession were sent down from the Tyrol to relieve that city. The ability of Napoleon was tested in many hard-won fights against superior numbers; he was often in critical situations, especially at the battle of Arcola where, for three days (November 17-20, 1796), the stubbornness of the Austrians held the French in check. During one of the critical incidents of the fight, Napoleon had personally to rally his men, and, when they were thrown into confusion by the Austrian fire, he was in danger of capture and was saved only by the presence of mind of his aide, Marmont, and of his own brother Louis.

Further attempts on the part of Austria to preserve its Italian possessions proved unavailing. After a decisive engagement fought at Rivoli early in the year 1797, the Austrian garrison at Mantua capitulated, and with the fall of this fortress, Austrian rule in Italy was brought to an end. Later on Napoleon followed up these successes by moving towards Vienna with a force of 34,000 men. He was ably seconded by his subordinate generals, among whom was Moreau, with the result that the remaining Austrian forces, gathered to defend their capital, were defeated, and by the preliminaries of peace signed at Leoben, Austria lost her Italian possessions, was deprived of her predominant influence in the peninsula, and agreed to the cession of Belgium. As a compensation she was to receive the possessions of Venice on the mainland, on both sides of the Adriatic.

These manipulations of territory, so far as Italy was concerned, were directed entirely in accordance with the personal will of Napoleon, who had already acted on his own initiative in his dealings with the petty Italian states. During the course of the campaign he had forced Tuscany and Naples to accept French sovereignty in the peninsula practically on his own terms, he had deprived the Pope of a large part of his territory and, after the terms of the treaty were signed, but before they were publicly announced, he had sought a quarrel with Venice, in order to put an end to the republic and so to find an excuse for annexing part of her territory to France. In this way he could hand over to Austria the fragments that had been secretly assigned to that power at Leoben. The brilliancy of these military operations, by which the whole face of the traditional situation in Italy was altered in the short space of one year, set Napoleon in such a secure position that his critics and detractors hesitated to call in question his autocratic acts, though Mallet du Pan tells us that the praise showered by the Directory on the young conqueror was recognized as insincere, adding, "There were voices in favor of sending the young hero to the Place de la Révolution to have a score of bullets lodged in his pate."

Napoleon himself, contrasting his success with the inefficiency of the Austrians, describes his victories in the following passage: "My military successes have been great; but then consider the servants of the Emperor! His soldiers are good and brave, though heavy and inactive compared with mine; but what generals! a Beaulieu, who had not the slightest knowledge of localities in Italy; Wormser, deaf and eternally slow; or Alvinzy, who was altogether incompetent. They have been accused of being bribed by me; these are nothing but falsehoods, for I never had such a thing in view. But I can prove that no one of these three generals had a single staff on which several of the superior officers were not devoted to me and in my pay. Hence I was apprised not only of their plans but of their designs, and I interfered with them, while they were still under deliberation."

With the states wrested from the Pope, there were taken from the Duke of Modena and from Austria territories sufficient to found a republic entitled the Cisalpine, and with this, there was a new rearrangement of the territories on the west coast by which the ancient republic of Genoa ceased to exist and reappeared with the Napoleonic brand as the Ligurian Republic. Both of these creations were after the French model, but the general of the army drew up the constitutions, chose the officials, and exercised the irresponsible powers of a dictator. The final terms of the treaty with Austria were not settled till October, 1797, but nothing was gained by the shrewd diplomatic fencings of the Viennese representatives. Napoleon, in a theatrical scene, at which he passionately broke in pieces a valuable porcelain vase in the presence of Coblentzl, the Austrian envoy, threatened to smash the Austrian monarchy if the parleyings were too long continued. The liberation of Italy appealed to the patriotic sentiment of the Italians, until the political realism of their conqueror manifested itself by enforcing on them contributions of money, art treasures, valuable manuscripts, all of which were sifted and collected by the experts Napoleon carried with his army. Even mathematical instruments and natural history collections did not escape his vigilance.

In the imposition of these exactions, the Papacy fared no better than the secular princes. While the dukes of Parma and Modena paid 12,000,000 francs and 20 pictures, the Pope was mulcted to the extent of 21,000,000 francs, 15,000,000 in cash, the rest to be made up by the surrender of 100 pictures, 500 manuscripts, and the bust of the patriot Brutus. This original method of making war pay for itself pleased the Directory. Great fêtes were prepared for the conqueror, when he appeared in Paris, to celebrate his victories. The official orator of the occasion was Talleyrand, who selected as the chief points of his eulogy Napoleon's modesty, his taste for the poems of

Ossian, and his fondness for mathematics.

But to the clear intelligence of Napoleon, forms of adulation, real or insincere, meant little. He was making rapid progress towards the goal of personal rule. The government already suspected his loyalty to them, but they were weak and without moral influence. Besides, they were under obligations, even more binding than those based or the money contributions which flowed in from Italy, for when the reactionary party was about to get the upper hand, both among the Legislative Body and among the Directors themselves, it was Napoleon's agent, Augereau, who had coöperated actively with the radical element and made its continued predominance in the control of national affairs possible.

There was no intention to diminish the weight of the military element as the predominant partner. By the premature death of Hoche, Napoleon was left without a rival, and he did not hesitate to speak of the Directory as a makeshift government. The immediate question was to prevent an outbreak between the victorious general and his superiors, by which a return to the monarchy might be made easy. France was still at war with Great Britain; therefore, when Napoleon proposed to attack the vulnerable point of British influence in Egypt, with the ultimate purpose of advancing from there on the British domains in India, the plan was eagerly accepted by the Directors, despite the obviously utopian character of the proposal. Napoleon spoke in his best sententious style of the East as the only place where real glory could be acquired. The Directors were willing that he should absent himself from France, glad to purchase freedom from his control by assigning him a new important command over the best troops in France.

It is not probable that Napoleon was at all in earnest in planning an expedition to India; he appreciated the weakness of the home government, and from Egypt it would not be difficult to return, whenever he was needed, in the rôle of the sole savior of the country. The scale of preparation for this unique military adventure was most imposing; there was an air of mystery about it; people talked of its destination being Constantinople or India. Ships, to the number of 500, were gathered at Toulon, manned by 10,000 sailors and fitted to transport 35,000 veteran troops, taken mostly from the army of Italy. All of Napoleon's best generals were to be with him, Berthier, Murat, Lannes, Davout, Marmont, Duroc, and the two popular commanders from the army of the Rhine, Kléber and Desaix. Great care was given to the material and scientific side of the expedition. Scholars and scientific experts were to accompany it, either for the purpose of antiquarian research in Egypt, or to develop the unused powers of the soil of the fertile Nile valley. There was plenty of money, for Berthier was sent to Rome to exact additional contributions from churches and convents. He called himself the treasurer of the Egyptian expedition and promised to fill his treasure chests.

The great fleet set sail on the 19th of May, 1798; only when the ships were at sea did the troops know what was to be their destination. The first point reached was Malta, where the famous Knights, so long the residuary legatees of the great crusading tradition, surrendered without resistance and received a French garrison. By good fortune the French armada escaped the vigilance of the English fleet which was cruising in the Mediterranean; and the army was landed at Alexandria on June 30th.

At this time Turkey had only the nominal sovereignty in Egypt, the real power being in the hands of a military caste, the Mamelouks, who exercised an oppressive rule over the cultivators of the soil, and the Arab chieftains, who represented the ancient conquerors of the country. Napoleon proclaimed himself as a liberator, promising to respect the customs and religion of the land, and offering his help in the development of its natural resources. After the easy capture of Alexandria there was a long, weary march across the desert to Cairo, during which the troops so suffered from intense heat, fatigue, and lack of food that there was discontent among both officers and men.

The final stand of the Mamelouks was made near Cairo within sight of the Pyramids, where they tried to rush the French squares with their cavalry. But the French artillery with its murderous fire decimated the advancing squadrons before they could come in contact with the French troops, with the result that on the French side the loss was only about thirty men, while the Mamelouks reckoned theirs by the thousand. Many of them, too, were drowned in the Nile. The French soldiers bent their bayonets and fished the bodies out in order to get the gold pieces in the belts of the dead warriors. Napoleon grimly reported that "the army was becoming reconciled to Egypt." In the midst of these brilliant achievements, the victory of Nelson at Aboukir on the 1st of August came like a bolt from the blue, for the French admiral's fleet was virtually annihilated, and by this disaster the French army was cut off from its base and, as it were, imprisoned in the land it had conquered. Yet Nelson could not follow up his victory; he had no frigates and, therefore, could not enter the harbor of Alexandria to destroy the provisions and the transport ships which were collected there.

One of the results of the naval battle was an uprising at Cairo, which was ruthlessly repressed, 5000 of the insurgents losing their lives. After an expedition had been sent into upper Egypt as far as the cataracts of Syene, the country was reduced to some kind of order, but there were further difficulties to deal with from another quarter, for, under the instigation of England, the Turks were preparing to retake Egypt, and two armies were now on the way with this object. One of them was to proceed through Asia Minor and Syria; to meet the enemy Napoleon, with the bulk of his army, advanced through Syria, conquering towns as he proceeded with his usual unbroken fortune. The march was signalized by spectacular deeds of personal prowess on the part of his subordinate generals. But he also shocked his admirers by the horrible massacre of 3000 prisoners at Jaffa. The excuse for this deed of bloodshed was that the victims had been previously released on parole and had broken it by taking part in the defense of Jaffa. The first failure in this unexampled course of success came at St. John d'Acre, an important seaport which was obstinately defended by its Turkish garrison, aided by an English commodore, Sidney Smith. After two unsuccessful assaults had been made by the French, with heavy losses, Napoleon withdrew in unconcealed disgust at his failure. He never forgot Sidney Smith, and spoke of him always as the man who had spoiled his luck; "that idiot [bicoque] was the only thing," he said, "that prevented me from entering India and striking a deathblow at England."

After the raising of the siege hope of further progress through Syria was abandoned, and the army, suffering from illness and discontent, had a miserable march back to Egypt, their route being marked by dead and dying. Napoleon showed great constancy in this disastrous experience, exposing himself to the ravages of the plague and restoring the confidence of his men by his coolness. On reaching Egypt the French found that a Turkish army of 18,000 men had disembarked at Alexandria; these, however, were soon disposed of at the second battle of Aboukir, fought almost a year after the first (July 25, 1799). The Turkish soldiers who refused, or were not able, to reembark on their transports were thrown into the sea.

While the expedition was marked by such deeds of barbarism, it had a more justifiable side because of the civilized and progressive administration given to Egypt by its French conquerors. Intelligent efforts were made to conciliate the Mussulman population; justice, finance, and administration were reformed; even a beginning was made in establishing something resembling representative government. Works of public utility were encouraged, some planned on a large scale, such as the building of a canal at Suez, a project only realized many decades afterwards. Remarkable also were the scientific results attained through the foundation of an Egyptian Institute consisting of French specialists in archeology, architecture, and art. Among its members were men who devoted themselves to promoting an industrial reformation, while others accomplished hygienic improvements for the cities. Indeed, the most durable result of this extraordinary scheme of Oriental conquest was the primacy of culture it gave to France in Egypt, a primacy she has continued to maintain even in the face of the military occupation of the country by England.

III
THE FALL OF THE DIRECTORY

During the long absence of Napoleon from France, the incapacity of the government of the Directory at home and abroad had been continually manifested; there were internal disorders due to royalist insurrections, which seemed for a time most threatening in the southwest, in the Garonne valley, while at Paris the radicals, who represented what was left of the Terrorist element, were restless under a system which they charged with disloyalty to the revolutionary tradition. There was, besides, no harmony between the legislative and executive organs of government; the Directors were not respected, some being manifestly incompetent, others, like Barras, mere intriguers.

With this weakness at home there had been displayed towards other European powers a consistent policy of provocation and aggression. To all of its weaker neighbors, France, in the hands of the Directory, played the rôle of an absolute dictator; all of them were to be forced, willing or unwilling, to organize themselves on the model of the French Republic. Napoleon had set the fashion in Italy; this example was followed through French influence and by French aggression. When the Swiss cantons rose to defend their ancient rights, they met with no more consideration than the absolute monarch, King Charles Emmanuel IV of Piedmont, whose Italian dominions were annexed to France, or the clerical oligarchy of Rome, who had to see themselves despoiled of their temporal power, when the Roman Republic was proclaimed from the Forum by General Berthier.

A new European coalition was brought into existence to resist the general movement of French expansion and to restore the Bourbon monarchy by invading French territory. Much was hoped from the accession of Russia, which along with Austria, engaged to put in the field the largest masses of men. At the opening of the campaign the French met discouraging defeats; Italy was soon lost through the inability of the French generals to withstand the united Russians and Austrians. In Switzerland, Masséna, by brilliant strategy kept the coalition armies in check; while by the superior initiative of a much smaller French force, a British army, operating in Holland, was obliged to sign an ignominious treaty and to evacuate Dutch territory.

With some of these vicissitudes of the Directorial government, Napoleon became acquainted at a dinner, at which he and Sidney Smith met to discuss matters relative to the exchange of prisoners and where the commander of the French army in Egypt received the public papers and letters intended for him which had been seized by English warships. Napoleon saw the necessity of leaving Egypt, where he was cooped up by an English fleet, and also he must have realized that the chance of a permanent French occupation was infinitesimal. With a few of his generals he left the country suddenly on the 22d of August, 1799, and, avoiding by skilful navigation the danger of being captured by the British warships, disembarked on French soil at Fréjus on October 16th. All parties greeted his return; his trip to Paris was a triumph; the *Moniteur* reported that the crowd on the roads was so great that vehicular traffic was completely blocked. All the places through which he passed from Fréjus as far as Paris were illuminated. Even the Directory disguised their real feelings and gave the hero of the Egyptian campaign a cordial welcome back. Bonaparte won much favor by a discreet modesty of demeanor, ingratiating himself with the generals who were defending France against the coalition, while he represented the Egyptian campaign as an affair undertaken simply for scientific purposes. His popularity was as unrestrained as it was real. The press was filled with stories about him; he dressed as an ordinary citizen rather than as a soldier, wearing a semi-civilian costume at social functions.

But under this ingenuous pose much political intriguing was being set in motion. Napoleon, who was described by one of his brothers as "just as much a manipulator as a general," was planning with Director Siéyès, now recognized as the chief political expert, to be called in to prepare a new constitution. Napoleon cared nothing for constitutions, but he was glad to have Siéyès's influence in overturning the Directory. Siéyès, on his side, recognized the civic virtues of his friend, General Bonaparte, but at the same time anticipated that the result of all this scheming would be to establish him in a position where he would exercise sole autocratic rule.

As to whether the opportunity was favorable, there was a difficulty. France was no longer directly menaced by the coalition since the splendid campaign of Masséna in Switzerland; besides, the royalist insurrections had been suppressed, and the extremists muzzled. The middle classes, to whom the wealth of the nation now belonged, felt secure. At this time the Prussian Minister at Paris wrote that confidence was being restored throughout the country, and that even religious dissensions had become less acute. Some of the most questionable and unpopular legislation, passed against the fortunes and persons of citizens who were suspected by the Directory, was on the point of being withdrawn by the legislative body. The debate on these measures was to conclude on the 17th Brumaire.

There was a difference between the two bodies of the legislature on the question of the change of the constitution. The more popular chamber distrusted Siéyès and passed upon him an indirect vote of censure of a severe character, by threatening with death anyone who proposed to alter the existing form of government. Apparently Napoleon's share in Siéyès's scheme was not suspected, for the Five Hundred named as their speaker Lucien Bonaparte, who had taken an oath to stab to death anyone aiming to make himself dictator. The complicity of various generals being assured by Bonaparte, Siéyès, who could count on the inactivity or sympathy of his fellow-Directors, proceeded to set the machinery in motion by which the government was to be overthrown. When the Ancients met, they listened to a vague harangue by one of Siéyès's adherents, who spoke of a conspiracy, by which the country was threatened, the intimation being conveyed that it was instigated by some foreign power. To escape from impending danger a resolution was offered that both houses should meet outside Paris on the 19th of Brumaire at St. Cloud, and that the command of the troops in Paris should be turned over to Bonaparte.

As soon as this was done, there was a great display of military activity. The city was placed in a state of siege, and care was taken that the minority of the Directors should be kept as virtual prisoners in the Luxembourg. The opponents of the change in the Five Hundred had time enough to prepare for resistance, and they did not propose to annul the existing constitution on the basis of a rumor. Napoleon appeared first before the Ancients, where he made an incoherent speech, and showed himself unable to name the conspirators he charged with disloyalty against the country. When he was ushered into the Hall where the Five Hundred were in session, the whole body had just sworn allegiance to the Directorial Constitution. Walking between four grenadiers, his diminutive figure added no gravity to the scene; he was pale, disturbed, and undecided. The members refused to listen to him, and cried "outlaw" or "down with the traitor." It is alleged that in the tumult daggers were drawn, and that Napoleon was in personal danger, as his adversaries closed round him. But all that happened, according to the most reliable witnesses, was that Napoleon and his escort were jostled and finally ejected from the hall. One grenadier, it is known, had the sleeve of his coat torn. Lucien, who rose to defend his brother, was hissed, and finally gave up his place as presiding officer. Another conspirator, when he refused to pass a motion depriving Napoleon of his command, was replaced by Lucien Bonaparte, who, on his part, collapsed from the nervous strain when he was bidden to put the motion declaring Napoleon an outlaw. He was allowed to go out and find his brother, so that the whole matter might be peaceably settled without extreme measures being taken.

In the meantime the leading conspirator, Napoleon, was suffering from a nervous crisis. When he was outside the hall, he appeared to observers as if he were walking in his sleep; upon trying to address his troops from horseback, he fell to the ground. Lucien just then came on the scene and conveyed him to a room in the palace, where Siéyès said to him: "They wish to put you outside the law; we'll put them outside the hall." The story of the display of daggers was now concocted, and Napoleon's troops were told of the danger their commander had been in. Lucien directed the soldiers to go into the hall and clear out the legislature. This order was executed by two companies of armed grenadiers, who, despite the protests of the deputies, pushed them good-humoredly out of the building, taking some of the members who resisted, in their arms.

The Ancients set forward their part of the revolution by voting the suppression of the Directory, by appointing an executive commission of three members, and by demanding the adjournment of the whole legislative body. But to give the transaction a specious form of legality, Lucien called some of the members of the Five Hundred together, and they, under his direction, proceeded to behave as if they were a majority. An executive consular commission was appointed, composed of Siéyès, Ducas, and Bonaparte, to be called the Consuls of the French Republic. During the adjournment of the legislature, the powers of that body were to be exercised by a commission composed of twenty-five members of each branch. These two commissions were to decide on the measures initiated by the Consuls in matters of administration and finance and also on the changes in the constitution required to free it from its imperfections. This proposal was accepted by the Ancients, and the three Consuls swore to be faithful to the republic, one and undivided, to liberty, to equality, and to the representative system.

The news of the suppression of the Directorial régime caused suspense, but little excitement. People were puzzled rather than alarmed; there had been so many transformations since 1789 that one more seemed hardly irregular. Besides, the Directory had often violated their own constitution; hence the illegality in their suppression was regarded as nothing strange. The Paris workmen stayed quietly in their quarters; there was no Jacobin Club to champion the cause of the radicals or to act as a center of protest. Financial circles were reassured, when government securities rose; there was a difference of seven francs between the quotations on the 17th Brumaire and 24th of the same month.

The royalists were happy, for they were naïve enough to believe that Napoleon would play the rôle of General Monk in a Bourbon restoration. On the whole, at Paris and in the country, the masses of the people were apathetic; some clubs here and there protested and called upon the citizens to arm themselves in defense of the dead government, while some departmental officials were dismissed, because they questioned the legality of the changes at Paris. But nowhere was there anything like an uprising in behalf of the Directory, which too forcibly recalled the terrible years of revolutionary experience.

IV

THE FIRST CONSUL

The provisional consuls remained in control from November 11 to December 24, 1799. Napoleon presided at the first meeting because his name began with "B," it having been arranged that the consular power should be exercised in alphabetical order. The Consuls seemed to have no more authority than the Directors they had superseded. Governmental policy was still anonymous. Napoleon never appeared in public life except with his two colleagues, and his influence was exerted altogether in military affairs, in which he exercised the functions that Carnot had held under the Committee of Public Safety. He dressed as a civilian, not as a general. Moreover, the Consuls showed themselves most conciliatory; they published no magniloquent program and behaved as if the lawlessness which had ushered in their rule was something foreign to their own desires. No one talked of a military dictatorship; there was, indeed, a studied moderation in the new government. It is true a few Jacobins were placed under police supervision, but some of the members of the revolutionary convention were used as agents to reassure the good republicans throughout the country. Among the deputies who had been expelled on the famous 19th Brumaire, several made their peace with the government, while the irreconcilables carefully avoided any overt acts in opposing it. The republican tradition was maintained by manifestoes against superstition and the émigrés. An era of good feeling was now ushered in most auspiciously.

Napoleon seemed to be content with the rôle of a Washington, but the moment he saw there was no fear of resistance he took steps to secure the adoption of a constitution fitted to make him the master of France. The machinery for this purpose was near at hand in the two legislative commissions mentioned above. Siéyès was working hard on a model constitution which was to be a marvelous harmony of various democratic principles. According to this scheme the people were to draw up a list of candidates, while an elector chose from the list those who should carry on the administration. The government was placed in the hands of a Council of State, there were additional bodies to act as representatives or as checks to keep the proper balance and to repress personal ambition and demagoguery. There was, besides this, a scheme to revive the Directory with the names of its constituent parts changed.

Bonaparte, who saw no chance for personal rule in either of these proposals, organized a small sub-committee to which he presented a scheme of his own, that never really went before either of the committees in a regular session, but was signed individually by the members under pressure from him. It was carefully planned, but the project that had such an irregular origin was nothing more than a sham constitution. It contained no declaration of rights and had no reference to liberty of the press. But the most shrewdly planned scheme for centralizing the power in the hands of one man was revealed in the so-called electoral provisions, by which the citizens of each district prepared, by voting for one-tenth of their number, a communal list from which all officials were to be selected. This system was carried through several gradations, until a national list was reached, from which all the higher popular representatives were to be chosen. The right of nomination from these various lists was conferred, in vague and ambiguous language, upon the First Consul. After the lists were once drawn up no further change could be made in these provisions.

Bonaparte transferred to himself the right of appointing all the local officials, the members of municipal and departmental councils, and so by a stroke of his pen deprived France of all trace of local government. His plan brought into existence an intensified centralization such as the country had not known, even under the ancient monarchy. All laws had to be proposed by the executive government; among the various representative bodies, the Senate, Council of State, Tribunate, and Legislative bodies, power was so divided that no single one had an effective initiative.

All the real power was placed by the constitution under the control of the First Consul. According to Article 41, the First Consul promulgated the laws; he nominated and recalled at will the members of the Council of State, ministers, ambassadors and chief foreign agents, the officers of the army and navy, the members of the local administration, and the legal solicitors of the government. He named all the civil and communal judges of the Court of Appeal. As to the second and third Consuls, they had only a consultative share in the executive power; to the Senate was given the function of selecting the three Consuls, but the constitution itself designated those who were to be invested with the authority for the first period of ten years. They were Bonaparte, Cambacérès, and Le Brun.

The constitution was presented to the people for a "plébiscite;" that is each citizen was to inscribe opposite his name on a register "yes" or "no." But this was not done everywhere on the same day; in fact, it lasted several weeks, and so there was time to put pressure on different localities, and also an arrangement was made by which the new government was installed before the plébiscite was completed. Most Frenchmen wanted peace at home and abroad, and as the government was adopting a general policy of reconciliation, they were glad to give it their support, all the more because they had no real constitutional traditions and were sick of emotionalism and rhetoric. The result of the voting was 3,011,007 ayes and only 1562 noes. Among those on the affirmative side were a number of sturdy Jacobins.

In his administration, Bonaparte relied chiefly on the Council of State; he was in close relations with them, because all laws had to be drawn up in this body. He often presided at their meetings and in his remarks to them explained his ideas and his program. He did not hesitate to treat their projects as actual laws, although the constitution provided for a submission to other representative bodies.

One of the first acts of the new régime was the passing of severe press laws. Thirteen papers were allowed in Paris, but they were threatened with suppression if they published articles contrary to the respect due to the social compact, the sovereignty of the people, and the glory of the armies; or if they published attacks on the government or on nations friendly or allied with the Republic, even if the articles in question were taken from the foreign press. This enactment of 27 Nivose, year VIII, may be justly said to have inaugurated the Napoleonic despotism.

Another law presented and accepted was a measure which destroyed all communal and local rights, and turned over the whole administration in town and country to prefects and sub-prefects, appointed by, and responsible to, the central government. Mayors, acting mayors, and town and county councilmen were all appointed by either the First Consul or his appointees, the prefects.

The body known as the Tribunate, which discussed the laws and gave its opinion upon them, and the Legislative Chamber, which voted upon them without discussion, adopted this measure, the first with a strong minority against it, who voiced, by vigorous speeches, their protests against the suppression of all liberty. But the press was muzzled, and there was general satisfaction because of the admirable selection made by Napoleon for the subordinate officials. The new administration was simple and effective, and had not yet shown the possibilities of tyranny it contained.

As to the First Consul, though he took up his residence in the Tuileries, there was no consular court; republican etiquette was observed, and the title of citizen was still retained. When the news of Washington's death reached Paris, mourning was ordered in the name of the principles of liberty and equality. But the new tendencies were shown in the favor extended by the First Consul to men of strong monarchical sympathies. Napoleon, however, was soon occupied with more momentous questions than the discovery of fresh means to paralyze republican institutions in France.

After the withdrawal of Russia from the anti-French coalition,—a step which was due to the victories of Masséna,—Austria, England, and some of the lesser states of Italy and Germany, kept up the conflict. Bonaparte had no desire to see the war terminated, but he so far bowed to public sentiment as to write letters to the King of England and to Francis II, the Emperor, suggesting a cessation of hostilities. England refused to make peace except on the condition that the Bourbons should be restored, and Austria declined to take any action without the consent of her ally. The publication of the correspondence appealed to French patriotism, and the answer of the nation was a vote of 200,000 conscripts to carry on the war.

For the purpose of invading France, Austria had two armies in the field, each of 120,000 men. The French forces under Moreau and Masséna were told off to keep the Austrians in check in Germany and along the Italian Riviera; Bonaparte himself planned with a third army to drive them out of Italy, in a second campaign which was to be the replica of his first in Italy. Both Moreau and Masséna showed great capacity in carrying out the strategical plans assigned to them. Bonaparte gathered together an army of 60,000 and suddenly crossed the St. Bernard pass by a march in which the French engineers showed remarkable skill in overcoming the natural difficulties of the way. The commander-in-chief made the passage on the back of a mule, as many tourists still do, led by a peasant-guide of the neighborhood. On the top, the soldiers were hospitably received at the famous monastery. The chief problem was to get the artillery over, and this was done by dismounting the guns and fastening them within hollowed-out trunks of trees. They were then dragged along the precipitous path by relays of 100 men.

While the Austrian general, Melas, was looking for the French along the Riviera road, Bonaparte was making his entrance into Milan, where the stupid excesses of recent Austrian rule had made the population forget the more intelligent or subtle tyranny of the French conqueror. Instead of rescuing Masséna, who was suffering the extremities of a siege at Genoa, he preferred to leave him to his fate and to risk deciding the campaign by a pitched battle with an enemy much stronger in numbers than himself. These hazards were plainly seen in the engagement that followed at Marengo on June 14, 1800. Three times the French were forced to withdraw, and Melas was sending off couriers to announce his victory, when Desaix, who had been sent, the day before, to Novi to prevent a turning movement on the part of the Austrians, heard the cannonading and came to the aid of his leader. A fresh charge was made, and the ground that had been lost was regained. The first to fall was Desaix, the man who had saved the day. The effect of the victory was instantaneous, for the day afterward, Melas signed an armistice, by which warfare was to be stopped for five months, in which time the Austrians were to evacuate the whole of Italy as far as the Mincio.

When the war was resumed later, French successes continued, until finally the whole of the Italian peninsula was brought once more under French control. After Marengo, the decisive battle of the campaign, which brought Austria to sue for peace, was Moreau's victory at Hohenlinden, the 2d of December, 1800, on which occasion the Austrians lost in killed and wounded 20,000 men. The victory brought forth from Bonaparte the public acknowledgment, made before the legislative body, that Hohenlinden was one of the finest achievements in history, and he also wrote to Moreau saying that he, Bonaparte himself, had been outdone. He afterwards criticised Moreau, and ascribed his victory to mere chance, saying that his opponent, the archduke, had shown greater strategical ability than the commander of the French army.

As the result of these various operations, came the peace of Lunéville, February, 1801, which marked the complete humiliation of Austria. In its main lines it followed the stipulations of Campo Formio, but it added the demand that the Dutch and Swiss republics should be recognized as states under French protection. Moreover, the Pope was allowed to retain some of his territory, and the King of Naples also benefited by Napoleon's moderation towards monarchical governments.

England, now left alone as the sole enemy of France, had been enabled, by her control of the sea, to make a clean sweep of the French colonies. She acquired Malta, and forced the French to abandon Egypt. But English supremacy at sea was resented on the Continent, a league of neutrals was formed, and the Russian government showed distinct signs of drawing towards France, after the refusal of England to restore Malta to its ancient owners, the Knights of St. John. Portugal was detached from England, and Spain was brought into such friendly relations that she ceded to France the territory of Louisiana, which had been in her possession since 1763.

England's isolation was unpopular at home because the enormous accumulation of war debts was dreaded, and the threats of Napoleon to invade the country were taken seriously, after he had established an armed camp at Boulogne. William Pitt, the soul of resistance to France, had left the government on account of differences over the Irish question. His successor, Addington, was not averse to coming to an agreement. After the signing of certain preliminaries in London the terms of peace, as the result of a five months' discussion between Lord Cornwallis and Joseph Bonaparte at Amiens, took the form of a treaty named from that place on March 25, 1802, between France, Spain, and the Dutch republic on one side, and England on the other. Most of the colonial conquests made by England were restored to their owners. Egypt was returned to Turkey, and England agreed to return Malta to the Knights of St. John and at the same time undertook not to interfere in the internal affairs of Holland, Germany, Switzerland, and the Italian republics.

Bonaparte became the hero of peace as he had been already of war. His popularity, due to his splendid achievements on the battlefield, was now enhanced by the victories of French diplomacy. His rule was firmly established; a new era of harmony and happiness seemed to be opening up under his auspices. His unconstitutional methods of government were forgotten in the brilliancy of his successes. But there were many things that showed his anti-republican animus, and his mania for autocratic rule. Before he set out for the Austrian campaign three Paris papers were suppressed, and censorship for the theaters was reintroduced. His taking command of the army was a step not contemplated by the constitution of which he was the author. While he was absent, it is true that the executive power was placed in the hands of Cambacérès, who proved so efficient that Bonaparte hurried back to Paris, immediately after Marengo, in order to resume the reins of government.

The members of the Tribunate showed their feelings by eulogizing the heroism of Desaix and relegating the First Consul to a second place. But Bonaparte's return from Italy called forth a great wave of enthusiasm throughout the masses of the nation, that showed him he could go far in repressing the opposition of the republican party, which was strongly intrenched in the Tribunate. On December 24, 1800, the life of the chief executive had been endangered by a plot, and while Bonaparte was driving to the opera there was an explosion by which four people were killed and sixty wounded near his carriage.

Though it was clear that the authors of the outrage were royalist sympathizers, Bonaparte insisted that the Jacobins were its instigators, and took this opportunity of diminishing the ranks of the opposition by an edict of the Council of State, executed without the sanction of the Tribunate and Legislative Body, that deported 130 republicans to distant colonial possessions. Towards other less known opponents harsh measures were used, some of them being executed on charges of conspiracy, trumped up by the police. Even the wives and widows of former revolutionary leaders were imprisoned without trial, and fifty-two citizens notorious for their democratic sentiments were forbidden to reside in Paris or its neighborhood.

In certain parts of the country royalist brigands were at work, wreaking vengeance on individuals who had taken an active part in the revolution or pillaging the houses of those who had bought confiscated property. Taking advantage of the demand for increased security against such outrages, Bonaparte created special tribunals, in which the judges were partly army officers, authorized to deal with all crimes of a nature calculated to disturb the government. With such elastic provisions, it was easy to turn the machinery of these courts against obnoxious republicans. There was no appeal against the decision made by this body except on the ground of jurisdiction. In this way a sort of revolutionary tribunal was erected, which Bonaparte could use for the purpose of wreaking his own personal vengeance.

Opposition in the so-called representative bodies was crippled by various clever devices. For example, after the return from Italy, when the period had come for the retirement by lot of a fixed number of representatives in the Tribunate and the Legislative Body, the Senate, which was loyal because filled by nomination of the second and third Consuls, intervened and designated those of the representative chambers who should continue to hold office. In this way 320 men, who had made themselves obnoxious by their criticism or by their opposition, were got rid of. Yet even after this purification all independence was not destroyed. It was necessary to employ devious methods to secure for Bonaparte, after the peace of Amiens, his appointment as Consul for life. When the matter was proposed by Cambacérès, so often used as the First Consul's agent rather than as his colleague, the Tribunate intimated that the recompenses for the First Consul's services should be purely honorary. Even the Senate contented itself with re-electing Bonaparte for another term as First Consul in advance of the expiration of his first term of office.

Upon this Bonaparte wrote to the Senate that he preferred to appeal to the people to know if he should impose upon himself the sacrifice of prolonging his magistracy. Using the more pliable Council of State, Cambacérès extracted from them an edict for a plébiscite to be submitted to the people, who were asked whether the First Consul should be named for life and whether he should be allowed to designate his successor. After these illegal preliminaries, for there was no formal authority for the plébiscite from the representative bodies, the single question of the consulate for life was voted upon on August 2, 1802, with the result that there were 3,568,885 affirmative votes and 8374 negative. The increase in affirmative votes of 500,000 over the plébiscite of two years before, shows how many royalists had rallied to the consular system, in response to the favor shown them by the amnesty lately given to émigrés and to manifest their appreciation of the Concordat by which the First Consul had made his peace with the Church.

It is significant that on the registers almost none of the names of members of the Constituent Assembly or of the Convention appear. The men of 1789 had accepted the Consulate two years before, but they now abstained from voting. Of the negative votes most came from the army. At Ajaccio, Bonaparte's native city, out of 300 men of the garrison there were 66 noes. Among others, Lafayette voted against the project, stating in a letter to Bonaparte that the 19th Brumaire had saved France, that the dictatorship had healed its ills, but that he did not wish to accept, as the final result of the revolution, an "arbitrary government."

The next step was to secure the right of appointing a successor. Bonaparte had shown at first an apparent reluctance to accept the suggestion, when it was made as a proposition to be submitted to the people. Now, when it was made a part of a measure entitled "Organic changes in the Constitution of the year VIII" (i.e., 1800), it was passed without any real debate by the Council of State and accepted by the Senate without discussion. At the same time it was arranged that nominations to the Senate were to be made from a list prepared by the First Consul; this practically meant, as the Senate's membership was still far short of its full quota, that the right assigned to it of accepting or rejecting the successor of the First Consul was only nominal. This situation of dependence made the Senate a useful body to Bonaparte; accordingly its constitutional powers were increased, it being given among other new prerogatives the right of dissolving the Tribunate and the Legislative Body. The Senate's omnipotence simply concealed the figure of the First Consul, who set his puppets there in motion.

So reconstructed, the whole machine worked marvelously. The Council of State, after showing signs of independence, was made a purely decorative body, its real power being handed over to a private council named by the First Consul. The Tribunate was to be reduced to fifty members after a short interval. All relics of direct popular election disappeared, and to the functions of the First Consul were added the rights of ratifying treaties and remitting judicial sentences.

As a sop to public opinion, the number of electors, who chose the lists of candidates from which were selected the officials in the local and central government, was increased, largely by doing away with the property qualification, a curious feature of the early more radical republican constitutions. There were, it is true, elections, electors, and elected candidates, but all were under the direct or indirect control of the arch manipulator, the First Consul, who crowned the whole system.

From this period begins the departure from the external signs of republican simplicity. The First Consul was no longer Citizen Bonaparte, but Napoleon Bonaparte; the anniversary of his birth was celebrated by a ministerial decree. Like a sovereign the new ruler had his civil list, and in his residence, the Tuileries, he began to display the ostentatious character of court life. Military dress was abandoned, and it began to be the fashion again to wear one's hair in a cue and to use powder, although the First Consul still appeared with his own hair dressed in the revolutionary manner. Josephine took much interest in reorganizing her household after the model of the old régime; in the exercise of her taste she was allowed to go far, but it was remarked that women had no political influence in the new court.

Judged by contemporary opinion, one of the plainest steps taken by Bonaparte towards a monarchy was the inauguration of the Legion of Honor, having at its head the First Consul, assisted by a great council, subordinate to which there were 1500 posts, each with 27 officers of various degrees, and 350 legionaries. This institution, which was endowed by national funds, was composed of members distinguished by their services to the Republic either as soldiers or as civilians. They pledged themselves among other things to oppose any enterprise tending to re-establish the feudal system, or proposing to reproduce the titles and the characteristics by which feudalism was marked, and to do everything in their power to maintain liberty and equality.

But these republican sentiments did not protect the measure from criticism. It was opposed both in the Council of State and in the Tribunate, where there was only a majority of sixteen in its favor when it was finally passed. Even the Legislative Body made difficulties, as is seen in their recorded vote of 170 for and 110 against. But it was not only from such shadows of representative government as were still permitted to linger on, that opposition came to Bonaparte's personal rule. Moreau, the hero of the Hohenlinden campaign, was known to have sturdy republican sentiments. Moreover, there was Bernadotte, the commander of the eastern army, who was openly discontented and was supposed by many to have instigated a plot against the First Consul at Rennes. There were, indeed, a series of military plots at this time, but the knowledge of their existence was suppressed by the government, whose object it was to impress on public opinion at home and abroad the popularity of the consular system.

The Legislative Body and the Tribunate busied themselves with subordinate affairs such as laws governing the practice of medicine and the organization of a notary public system. In the Senate the hand of the First Consul was seen in the liberal financial provisions for certain senators, who were allowed a suitable house and 25,000 francs annual income. Of course the selection of the beneficiaries of these favors was left to the First Consul. There was no reluctance in voting money and troops for the defense of the state, for by this time Bonaparte's personal policy and the national interests were closely identified.

This feeling of loyalty was all the more intensified when, after war broke out again with England, the British government took a hand in encouraging the schemes of various royalist groups. Among these were some irreconcilable survivors of the Vendéan insurrection, led by Cadoudal, who planned to remove Bonaparte by assassination, after which it was assumed that a Bourbon restoration would follow as a matter of course. Pichegru, an old revolutionary general, was an accomplice, and the conspirators made an effort to secure the coöperation of Moreau, but failed. Learning through his spies of this invitation, and glad of a plea to rid himself of a rival, Bonaparte had Moreau arrested, though he knew his innocence, and instigated a bitter press campaign against him. Police agents encouraged the plot, hoping that some of the Bourbon princes, certain of its success, might cross from England to France, in expectation of Bonaparte's death.

In this atmosphere of plots, Bonaparte seems to have lost his head, and to have descended to the weapons of revenge handed down among the clansmen of his native island when they settled their domestic feuds. One member of the Bourbon house was from this point of view as good as any other, when it was a question of proving the capacity of the government to deal with its monarchical enemies. The nearest victim was selected for a stroke worthy of Cæsar Borgia—the Duke d'Enghien, a distant relative of the direct heirs of the old monarchy, who had been living quietly for two years at Ettenheim in Baden. A detachment of dragoons was sent across the frontier, into the territory of a small state, at peace with France, and arrested the young prince, March 15, 1804. The papers that were found showed clearly that the Duke was not involved in the plot in any way, but in spite of this evidence of non-culpability, he was tried by a commission made up of colonels of the regiments of the Paris garrison.

The prisoner was shot six days after his arrest, the sentence being executed at the château of Vincennes. Though freed from any complicity in the Pichegru plot, the Duke d'Enghien had tried to enter the service of England against France; he had also fought against the French Republic as an émigré, so whatever may be said in criticism of the abject subservience of the officers who acted as judges in the court-martial, it must be remembered that the law of the revolutionary period, by which the death penalty was inflicted upon any Frenchman engaged in open warfare against his country, had never been abrogated. Probably it was to this justification of his act that Napoleon referred when he refused to listen to Josephine's entreaties in behalf of the Bourbon prince. "I am," he said, "a man of the State. I am the French Revolution, and I shall uphold it." These words were spoken in a moment of typical exaltation. After many years had passed he commented in the following way on his action: "The deserved death of the Duc d'Enghien hurt

Napoleon in public opinion, and was of no use to him politically." There soon followed a report of Pichegru's suicide in his prison, a way of accounting for his death which, after the execution of the Bourbon Duke, it was hard to accept as satisfactory. Many believed that he was assassinated at Bonaparte's command because the publicity of an open trial was dreaded.

V

THE INAUGURATION OF THE EMPIRE

From the excitement caused by these conspiracies came the movement which led to the inauguration of the empire. Petitions were drawn up asking that the consulate should be made hereditary in the Bonaparte family; there was considerable reluctance in using explicitly the word "empire," and there was much wavering and intrigue before a member of the Tribunate, Curie, offered a resolution on the 23rd of April, 1804, according to the terms of which Napoleon Bonaparte, the then First Consul, should be declared Emperor of the French, and the imperial dignity should remain hereditary in his family. Carnot was the only member who argued against the change, but his plea in behalf of a régime of liberty found no supporters, though he pointed out in frank language that the movement in favor of hereditary monarchy was fictitious, because freedom of the press no longer existed. The Senate acted quickly on the motion from the one popular body that now was in session, for the Legislative Body was adjourned. A decree establishing the imperial constitution was passed on May 18, 1804. The measure was to be submitted to popular approval, but from the date of its passage Bonaparte received the title of Emperor of the French, and the empire actually came into existence. The international situation played a considerable part in forcing the abandonment of the few remaining vestiges of a republican system. Bonaparte had no desire to maintain for any length of time the pose of an apostle of peace, which for the sake of popularity he had assumed, while the negotiations at Amiens were in progress. England, too, had no wish to fulfil the engagements of that treaty, by which her power would be diminished. She was interested in keeping both Malta and Alexandria, and her promise of non-intervention on the Continent was very liberally interpreted by her government.

In the light of Bonaparte's own policy a strict interpretation of engagements would have been indeed a counsel of perfection, for his plans for the expansion of France were not modeled on the traditions of the eighteenth-century system of balance of power. He had schemes for controlling the Mississippi valley, and he also elaborated a revival of French colonial policy in which the possession of San Domingo was the chief factor. When the revolted slaves of that island made it impossible for the French troops to keep French administration intact, Bonaparte gave up the enterprise, and sold Louisiana to the United States for 80,000,000 francs. French agents and officers were sent to the east of the Mediterranean and to India, with instructions obviously intended to work for the downfall of British power and influence. Only a month after the treaty of Amiens was signed, General Decaen, notorious for his Anglophobia, was despatched to India, with secret instructions to get into touch with the Indian princes who were hostile to England's rule, with the object of forming an alliance among them. Moreover, the official government paper, the *Moniteur*, took no pains to disguise the intention of the First Consul to organize, on the first opportunity, a second expedition for the conquest of Egypt.

On the continent of Europe, too, French aggression proceeded without any disguise. Holland had virtually become a French dependency; and it was now endowed with a consular régime. In Italy, Victor Emmanuel, the King of Sardinia, was deposed, and his territories were annexed to France. Not contented with being president of the Cisalpine Republic, Bonaparte treated the rest of the peninsula as a subject territory and sent garrisons to the south to important points in the Kingdom of Naples. Just as plain was his attitude towards Switzerland, where he made use of the internal dissensions in the cantons to increase French influence. He told the Swiss delegates, when he had selected himself to act as mediator in their disputes, that Europe recognized Italy, Holland, and Switzerland as being under French control. "I will never tolerate," he added, "any other influence in Switzerland but mine, if it is to cost me 100,000 men."

As to Germany, the rôle of protector and disposer of the smaller German states was ostentatiously assumed. Russia, which had been given by the treaty of Lunéville conjoint power with France in the rearrangement of the petty German principalities, was treated with small consideration. The work was done by Bonaparte, and its drastic character can be measured by the statistics of the changes carried out under French direction. In the eighteenth century there were from eighteen to nineteen hundred autonomous sovereignties in Germany; only thirty-nine survived in Bonaparte's "New Model," among them being six free cities and one ecclesiastical domain. By these changes Prussia profited considerably, but even more so Bavaria, because of its well-known friendship for France.

Under the cover of the Peace of Amiens, Bonaparte had become dictator of a large part of Europe. Accordingly, when Lord Whitworth, the English ambassador, protested in the name of the existing treaties, Bonaparte replied, "I suppose you refer to Piedmont and Switzerland; they are trifles; this could have been foreseen during the negotiations." The German publicist, Gentz, summarized the situation, without exaggerating it. "France," he said, "has no longer any frontiers, since all that surrounds it is in fact, if not yet in name, its property and domain, or will become so at the first opportunity."

On its side, England was far from scrupulous in observing the terms of the Amiens convention, and showed notorious unfriendliness to France in encouraging the various royalist plots against Bonaparte's life. Besides, the terms of the treaty were not carried out as regards the evacuation of Malta or as to the conditions made for restoring to the French certain towns in India. What was especially irritating to the British government and people was Bonaparte's plan to develop French industry by adopting a protective system.

He not only refused to sign any treaty of commerce with England, but took active measures to close the ports of France and of the states dependent on her to the products of English industry. A violent press campaign was inaugurated in London against the policy of the Consulate, couched in unsparing language against Bonaparte's character and ambitions. He, on his side, took up a truculent attitude, saying in so many words that England's effort to secure new allies would force him to conquer Europe and to revive the Empire of the West.

In the spring of 1803, the final rupture came with a message from George III that the security of England was menaced by France. The outbreak of hostilities was marked by the seizure on England's side, without any declaration of war, of 1200 French and Dutch merchant ships. Bonaparte replied to this act of piracy by another in kind, though a more original violation of international justice; he arrested all the subjects of England who were to be found on French territory, and prohibited the purchase of any article of British manufacture. The next step was to prepare for an invasion of England from the Channel ports and for the military occupation of Hanover, an appanage of the British crown. On the Continent, Pitt formed an alliance against the aggressions of France, known as the Third Coalition. Austria, Prussia, Sweden, and Naples prepared to act together, the chief military contingents being supplied by Austria with three armies amounting in all to 130,000 men, and by Russia, which promised four armies.

As England controlled the sea power, Bonaparte's preparations to invade it were futile, though 2343 transports were collected, and for many months an army of 120,000 were kept in training for the passage over the Channel. But there was no adequate protecting fleet, and the French officers showed no ability in using the vessels under their command. The entrance to the Channel was guarded by English ships; all the French ports were blockaded, and Villeneuve, the French admiral, in an engagement off Trafalgar, was decisively beaten by Nelson, with a loss of twenty men-of-war, out of a combined French and Spanish fleet of thirty-five. Villeneuve was made the scapegoat for the failure of the plan to invade England, but the scheme was a chimerical one from the start, viewed in the light of the experiences of French armies in San Domingo and in Egypt, where they were cut off from their base. Many critics are, therefore, willing to believe that Napoleon was not sorry to have been relieved by the loss of his fleet from undertaking a spectacular but most hazardous adventure.

Before the battle of Trafalgar, October 20, 1805, while Napoleon was at Boulogne, he dictated a plan evidently the result of long consideration, containing the most exact details for the march of his army to the Danube. In the meantime, the Austrians had invaded Bavaria, had taken possession of Ulm, and were awaiting the French in the defiles of the Black Forest. With wonderful speed, precision, and secrecy enveloping operations were carried out, by which Mack, the Austrian general, who supposed the French army was near Strassburg, when it had already cut his communications far to the east of his forces, was surrounded and forced to capitulate. In this short campaign of three weeks, 100,000 Austrians had been dispersed by remarkable strategical movements, extending over a stretch of country several hundred miles wide. Not an error had been committed, not a combination had failed. The soldiers truly said, "The Emperor has beaten the enemy by our legs."

Now that the Austrians were destroyed as a military entity, the Russian armies in Austria remained to be attacked. By a series of forced marches Vienna was reached by the middle of November without any general engagement. The plan of the Austrian and Russian generals was to cut off Napoleon, when he advanced farther into the heart of the empire, in much the same way as he had treated Mack. They had the advantage in numbers, for the French army now was only 68,000, while the allies had 90,000. The co-operation of Prussia was expected by the allies, if the Russians could win a victory, and with this additional strength it was hoped that the whole French army would ultimately be forced to capitulate.

But Napoleon moved from Vienna with great rapidity and brought on a decisive engagement at Austerlitz. Everything was done to increase the confidence of the allies. They knew that the French were reduced, by the detaching of thousands of men, needed to occupy Vienna and to keep in check various divisions of the Austrian forces. In some skirmishes the Austro-Russians were allowed to win small advantages, to put them off their guard, and to induce them to offer battle on unfavorable terms. Their two wings were adroitly separated from the center by the French troops giving way at an opportune moment. Napoleon took advantage of this weakness of the enemy's center, while his commanders were preventing the detached portion of the enemy's forces from returning to the main body, to drive the Russians, opposite him, on the frozen surfaces of various ponds in the battlefield. He then used his artillery to break the surface of the ice and so drowned several thousand of the enemy.

This brilliant engagement, fought on December 2, 1805, cost the allies 15,000 men in killed and wounded, 20,000 prisoners, 45 standards, and 140 cannon. Napoleon, delighted that the allies had walked into the trap prepared for them, commended in the order of the day following the battle, the conduct of his men. "I am contented with you," he said. "You have, on the great day of Austerlitz, justified what I expected from your valor. When I lead you back to France, my people will see you again with joy. It will only be necessary for you to say 'I was at the battle of Austerlitz' for the reply to be made, 'There is a brave man.'" The Emperor might well be satisfied, for the renewal of warfare had not been popular in France, where the defeat at Trafalgar had caused depression and anxiety. Now all was forgotten in the glorious victory which again placed the Austrian Empire at the mercy of the conqueror.

As the Austrians had been equally unlucky in defending their Italian territories, the Treaty of Pressburg, December 20, 1805, showed how greatly the traditional balance of power was altered, giving place to Napoleon's scheme for dominating the whole of Europe. Austria lost the territories of Venice, Istria except Trieste, Dalmatia; she recognized Napoleon as King of

Italy and was forced to surrender valuable possessions to the German princes who were allies of the French. There was also a titular diminution of power, because Francis II now surrendered the title of Emperor of the Holy Roman Empire, which gave him a theoretical sovereignty over the German states, and accepted the territorial title of hereditary Emperor of Austria. To these extreme measures of humiliation Napoleon obstinately adhered, though his foreign minister, Talleyrand, wisely preached moderation to him, urging with unique diplomatic vision that if Austria were to be deprived of so much territory in the west, there should be compensation made for her losses by handing over to her Turkish provinces in the lower valley of the Danube. France, he pointed out, would profit by this act of generosity, for Austria would give up looking to England for support, and, as a power in the East, would be certain to excite the jealousy of Russia, because Russia had always looked to inherit the Ottoman domains. But Napoleon's plans would tolerate no scheme by which any European state would be helped to preserve more than a fictitious independent existence.

After Austerlitz the Confederation of the Rhine was created, a league of sixteen dependent German princes, of which the French Emperor was the head. Bavaria and Wurtemburg were especially favored, receiving the title of kingdoms, while their royal houses were drawn close into the orbit of French influence by marriages with members of the Bonaparte and Beauharnais families. Italy being now absorbed, Napoleon's sisters were rewarded with Italian principalities, while his brother Joseph took the place of one of the Bourbons on the throne of Naples. Only the Pope was left as an independent sovereign in the much reduced temporal dominions of the Church. Holland, in accordance with the fully developed imperial system, became a kingdom, in place of a republic, with Louis, the Emperor's brother, as its sovereign. Only one member of the family proved recalcitrant to Napoleon's plans, and, therefore, was not rewarded in this division of the spoils of conquest. This was Lucien, who had saved the day on the 19th Brumaire and had made it possible for his brother to climb into absolute power. He refused to divorce his wife and marry a princess, and, therefore, he shared none of the favors that were being distributed. Napoleon's mother, Letitia Bonaparte, who took Lucien's side in this quarrel, was never declared a princess, and had to be satisfied with the honorary title of Madame Mère. Napoleon had conferred upon himself officially the title of Great (1806). His birthday was kept as a national and imperial holiday on which was celebrated a quasi-religious feast of apotheosis, modeled after the precedents of the Roman Empire.

Although Austerlitz called forth a new distribution of the map of Europe, and elevated, as if by a miracle, the members of the house of Bonaparte, it did not give peace to France. Russia had not shared in the Treaty of Pressburg, and even the English government, which, after the death of Pitt, was headed by the liberal pro-French statesman Fox, could make no satisfactory peace terms with the Emperor of the French. Prussia, whose neutrality was suspected, was treated with little consideration and no frankness by Napoleon's government. It is true that he handed Hanover to it, but he made no secret of the fact that he would withdraw his gift provided that, if he restored Hanover to England, that power would consent to make peace. There was an active war party in Prussia who were anxious to try conclusions with the French army, because they relied on the traditions of the perfect military machine established by Frederick the Great. They boasted of their ability to destroy Napoleon's army which had only conquered Austrians and Russians. Alexander of Russia was also anxious to renew the conflict, and England poured out its treasures to the extent of 6,000,000 pounds.

The result was the Fourth Coalition against France, made up of England, Prussia, Russia, and Sweden. Hostilities began with an inflated ultimatum from the King of Prussia, ordering Napoleon to evacuate Germany and to give up the Confederation of the Rhine. The declaration of war on the part of Prussia was most ill-timed, for the Austrians had not yet recovered from the defeat of Austerlitz, and the Russians were not prepared to act the part of effective allies at the beginning of the campaign. To this carelessness in selecting the time for commencing hostilities was added over-confidence in the military superiority of the Prussian army. As a machine, it presented the outward semblance of the creation of Frederick the Great; but there was an absence of intelligent direction. The soldiers were badly treated under a régime of poor diet and strict discipline, while the officers were a privileged class, who remained in active service long after they had passed the prime of life. This artificial system collapsed like a pack of cards; as Heine said, "Napoleon breathed on Prussia and Prussia ceased to exist."

In preparing for this new campaign, Napoleon repeated the strategy of the Austerlitz campaign. He disguised, by feigned hostile movements and by ostentatiously remaining in Paris, his intention of striking one of his rapid, certain strokes at the enemy's weakest spot. Led into a false self-confidence, the Prussians took the offensive with 150,000 men. By means of quick concentration, Napoleon's army was brought up to a strength of 175,000. With this force, instead of coming into contact with the Prussians on the northwest, as had been expected, he turned their army on the southeast and threatened their communications with Berlin. The victory was won by two skilfully conducted pitched battles, at Jena and also at Auerstadt (the 14th of October, 1806), where Davout, with an army much inferior to that opposed to him, specially distinguished himself. The Prussian armies were reduced to a mass of fugitives; there were 20,000 killed and wounded and 18,000 prisoners, but the victory cost the French 12,000 men, for the Prussians had fought bravely, though their generalship was poor.

There was later a spectacular entrance into Berlin by the victorious army, arranged after the manner of a Roman triumph, with the Prussian regiment of the guards disarmed and following their conquerors. Napoleon interpreted his victory as giving him a chance to show his power of wreaking a personal vengeance on those who had so rashly questioned his power. "I will render this court nobility so small," he said, "that they will be obliged to beg their bread." He acted in the spirit of these words, and outraged public sentiment by carrying off, as part of the booty of Berlin, the sword of Frederick the

Great. Over the conquered country was extended a network of officials, intrusted with the duty of collecting large money contributions. No community was allowed to escape the imposition, and all were made to feel their responsibility for the war. There was also a rearrangement of German territories, under which Jerome, the Emperor's youngest and least competent brother, was provided with a throne under the title of King of Westphalia.

After the defeat of Prussia, the Russians, who had been slowly drawing together great masses of men, kept up an obstinate struggle against Napoleon's generals, and little progress was made by the French. Marbot describes the campaign in all its hardships; the weather, he says, was terribly cold, but the troops seem to have suffered even more in their marches from the thaws which rendered the bad roads impassable. While the French army was encamped for the winter, Benningsen, the Russian general, tried, early in February, to force his way between the two divisions of the French army under Ney and Bernadotte. The plan failed because Bernadotte was not taken by surprise; his defense was a brilliant one, and gave Napoleon an opportunity for attempting a turning movement on Benningsen's army. This purpose could not be carried out because the despatch announcing it to the French subordinate commanders fell into the hands of the Russians, who got away in time. In the pursuit, the Russians turned on the French, and the result was a "soldiers' battle," fought at Eylau, February 8, 1807, in which for a time the Emperor's position was most critical, for his army was half encircled and suffered terribly from the enemy's artillery fire. The day was finally saved by a remarkable cavalry charge, led by Murat, who passed through three Russian lines and broke up their attack. But despite this terrible massacre of men at Eylau,—10,000 French and 30,000 Russians,—no final result was attained by it. Neither side could claim to be victorious; it was something, however, to prove that Napoleon was not invincible, and, as Eylau was not a Russian defeat, the Russians interpreted it as a victory. The two powers, Prussia and Russia, agreed not to make a permanent treaty with France until the banks of the Rhine were accepted as her frontiers.

During the spring each side remained inactive, for both were in need of reinforcements. Benningsen with 100,000 men took the offensive, but after some preliminary hard fighting, placed himself, still on the offensive, in an unfavorable position near Friedland. He had brought his army into a narrow ravine with the river Alle behind him, so that in case of a check he had only the bridges to depend upon for withdrawing his men. These bridges were cut in a turning movement, made by Ney, while Lannes, with 26,000 French against 82,000 Russians, kept Benningsen from leaving his position, during a space of thirteen hours. By the evening the Russian army had but 25,000 men under arms and was hopelessly demoralized.

After this defeat the Fourth Coalition was at an end. The Peace of Tilsit was drawn up as the result of a personal interview between Alexander of Russia and Napoleon on a raft anchored in the river Niemen. After several private meetings Napoleon succeeded in attracting to himself the enthusiastic sympathy of his obstinate opponent. There was outlined a common plan of action by which both sides were to benefit, Russia was to gain territory in Finland, at the expense of Sweden, and in the East, at the expense of Turkey. Even more important was the winning over of Alexander to agree to Napoleon's continental blockade against England, by which all English goods were to be kept out of continental ports.

But even by making this volteface in Russian policy, Alexander could secure no favorable terms for his late ally, Prussia. That power was denuded of territory to the east which it had originally acquired in the partition of Poland; for of this was constructed one of Napoleon's new creations, the grand duchy of Warsaw, of which the elector of Saxony, approved by Napoleon for his pro-French policy, became sovereign with the title of King. On the west, all lands beyond the Elbe were taken, to be added to the new kingdom of Westphalia. Frederick of Prussia had besides to accede to the anti-British economic measures of Napoleon, to pay a war indemnity of $20,000,000, and to be humbly grateful for the return of four provinces in the northeast that had been detached from Prussia after the battle of Jena.

VI
AT THE ZENITH OF POWER

After Tilsit it was plain that Napoleon was no longer a French monarch; his schemes of conquest were now not made in the interest of France, for France, like the other powers of central Europe, was to be only a province of a vast territorial empire, managed for the personal profit of a single individual, who bestowed and took away power and territory, according to his caprice. England still stood in his way after his diplomatic success at Tilsit, but no armies were left to oppose him. It seemed, therefore, a comparatively easy matter to master England by cutting her off from the sources of her wealth. No power or state was allowed to be neutral, for those who declared themselves so were proscribed along with England (decree of Milan, 1807). A hard fate awaited any refractory nation, for nationalism now lived only on sufferance. To suspend the economic life of millions of people, to transform habits of industry peculiar to sea-going populations was to Napoleon's mind no greater task than to annihilate armies and partition kingdoms. From Tilsit dates the effort to attain the impossible, and with it begins, in a succession of rapid changes, the decline of the imperial system, the strain being greater than any such artificial construction could bear. Externally the establishment of peace consolidated Napoleon's power and influence at home; the last campaigns had been a severe drain, but the diplomatic success of Tilsit compensated for the losses in the battlefield.

Napoleon's familiar method of using a period of peace for extending his power at every weak point of contact was now resumed. Portugal, as a state closely connected with England, was to be detached from British influence by force of arms. Nor was any consideration to be paid to Spain, loyal though she had been to France, her ally. A loyalty which had cost her dear already became more fatal still when Napoleon began to plan for a cession of Spanish territory and the substitution of a member of his own house for the Bourbons. In the north, Denmark was to be required to renounce her position of neutrality and to hand over her valuable fleet of twenty ships to coöperate with the French. It was in anticipation of this step, that an English fleet, outdoing the lawless code of their adversaries, bombarded, in July, 1807, Copenhagen, the capital of a state with which it was at peace, and seized the Danish ships in the harbor.

This was the act which drove Alexander into closer relations with Napoleon, who adroitly used the opportunity for arranging a formal alliance, by which common action against the English in the East, as well as the West, might be secured. His plans in their full scope are given in the following letter addressed to the Czar of Russia in February, 1808: "An army of 80,000 men, Russian and French, perhaps a few Austrians, which will advance on Asia by the road of Constantinople, will not have to reach the Euphrates, to make England tremble and bring her to our feet on the continent. I am ready on the spot in Dalmatia, your Majesty is on the Danube. A month after we have agreed to act, the army can be on the Bosphorus. The news of it will be heard in India, and England will give in. I do not refuse to accept any of the preliminary stipulations necessary to attain an end so great. But the mutual interest of our two states should be well combined and balanced. All can be signed and decided before the 15th of March. On May 1, our troops can be in Asia, and at the same time your Majesty's troops in Stockholm. Then the English, threatened in India, chased out of the Levant, will be broken under the weight of the events by which the atmosphere will be charged. Your Majesty and myself would prefer the enjoyment of peace and to pass our life in the midst of our vast empires, busied in vitalizing them and making them happy by the methods and benefits of our government. The enemies of the world will not have it so. We must be greater in spite of ourselves. It is the part of wisdom and policy to do what fate ordains and to go where the irresistible march of events is leading us.... In these few lines I am expressing to your Majesty my whole mind. The work of Tilsit will regulate the destinies of the world. Perhaps so far as your Majesty and I are concerned, a little pusillanimity would have us prefer a certain actual good to a better and more perfect condition. But since, after all, England does not wish it, let us recognize that the time for great events and for great changes has come."

This vision Alexander desired to transform into hard realities without delay; the first step was to divide the dominions of Turkey. The question arose as to what disposition should be made of Constantinople and the Dardanelles. But while the Russians were arguing as to the proposed increase of territory in the Orient, Napoleon, without consulting his correspondent at St. Petersburg, was manipulating the situation in the West by the virtual annexation of Spain to France. The haggling with Russia was dropped, and Napoleon hastened to embark in the adventure which was ultimately to lead to his downfall.

Disgust with Godoy, the court favorite, had brought about a revolutionary movement in Spain, which aimed to substitute for the reigning monarch,

Charles IV, his son Ferdinand. These family difficulties were laid before Napoleon, who traveled to Bayonne, post haste from Paris, to act as arbitrator. With a duplicity worthy of a profound student of Machiavelli, he caused to be placed in his hands an abdication, signed by both the royal father and his son; the impartial arbiter handed over the crown to a third party, his brother Joseph, King of Naples. So, by a juggle that a sporting gamester might have envied, a Bonaparte came to reside in the royal palace of Madrid, and if kingships went by personal capacity, and not by descent, it must be said that, mediocre as was Napoleon's elder brother, he was far better fitted for governing Spain than either the feeble Charles IV or his scoundrelly son and heir, Ferdinand.

Alexander heard of these transactions from the pen of his assiduous correspondent, but he cared for none of these things; his mind was filled with the spoliation of Sweden and Finland as a preliminary step to realize his dream of Oriental conquest. It was arranged that the two emperors should meet at Erfurt to settle the terms of their proposed dual domination of the world; only by a personal interview could the question as to the possession of Constantinople be decided. In the meantime there were elaborate plans for the sailing of fleets to Egypt, and around the Cape of Good Hope, to overawe the English.

Events in Spain put an awkward stop to this program. The population of the country had never been awakened by the French Revolution; they hated foreign interference, and, when their Bourbon king was dethroned, they rose *en masse* in revolt, with the spirit of the Vendée. News soon came to Paris of the defeat of a French army in which 18,000 men surrendered. This defeat, the capitulation of Baylem, was soon followed by a disaster to the army corps which was operating in Portugal against a combined Portuguese and English force. The effect of the Spanish resistance was enormous; in all parts of central Europe it revived the hope of successful revolt against the domination of the French system. It stirred Prussia and Austria to renewed efforts; there was great activity of secret societies in Prussia, directed against the French occupation, and Austria was busy in reorganizing its military forces for a fresh struggle.

Napoleon realized the critical situation; antedating his letter to Alexander, to give the impression that it was written before the bad news from Spain had reached him, he announced his purpose to withdraw the French troops from Prussia, and promised to give up the Danubian principalities, without compensation, provided Russia would be willing to see that the Germans were kept quiet, and would influence Austria to abandon her warlike preparations. Alexander showed much complacency, even going so far as to express his sympathy for the eclipse of the French arms in Spain.

Nothing was spared at Erfurt, where the two emperors met, to impress upon the world the security and the extent of Napoleon's rule. It was the fête of a cosmopolitan society, where men of distinction in all spheres of life were brought together at the bidding of the Emperor of the French. Goethe was present, also Talleyrand, who left on record his impression of the atmosphere of adulation that prevailed. The two central figures, Alexander and Napoleon, showed marked cordiality to each other. Alexander spoke of his friend as not only the greatest but the best of men. Yet there were visible rifts in the friendship; Alexander refused to show hostility to Austria, an attitude which was secretly encouraged by Talleyrand, who had begun to fear the result of Napoleon's grandiose schemes, and wished to make friends before fortune turned. Napoleon proved obdurate, when Alexander urged upon him a more generous treatment of Prussia.

In the formal treaty, the result of the meeting, there was incorporated a proposition of peace with England on the basis of the *status quo*—i.e., Finland and the Danubian principalities for Russia and the deposition of the Bourbons in Spain. Alexander would go no further as regards Austria than the prospect of armed coöperation, if Austria went to war against France. Among the subjects proposed was the marriage of Napoleon with a Russian princess. He had been considering for some time a divorce from Josephine, a plan now resolved upon after the birth of an illegitimate son had convinced him that there was the possibility of a direct heir. Alexander, encouraged by Talleyrand's advice, refused to make a frank engagement to forward this scheme, saying that to his mother alone belonged the disposition of his sisters' marriage arrangements.

After the meeting at Erfurt, Napoleon hastened to Spain, where, fighting several successful battles, he restored his brother to his capital at Madrid, and forced an English army under Moore to retreat towards the sea coast. This was in January, 1809. Then Napoleon was obliged to withdraw from Spain because of the threatening attitude of Austria, now firmly resolved on opening hostilities with France. There were also evidences brought him of a plot in Paris, the responsibility for which rested on Talleyrand and Fouché, both long in service under him. It was arranged between them that in case of a reverse or a successful attempt on Napoleon's life, they were to take charge of the government, giving it a figurehead in the person of Murat, Napoleon's brother-in-law. Long before he was expected, Napoleon appeared suddenly in Paris, having ridden from the north of Spain in six days. For a while Talleyrand was in disgrace, but acts of personal revenge were forgotten in the preparation for crushing Austria. It was a most distasteful task, for he feared to break up his friendship with Alexander, the necessary result of dismembering the Austrian Empire. He therefore tried to secure the intervention of Russia, but Alexander refused to act at all vigorously.

Hostilities broke out in April, 1809. There was no longer a question of purely dynastic interests in this armed protest of Austria against the Napoleonic system; the army of 310,000 men represented a general patriotic movement of self-defense that had penetrated all classes of society in the Hapsburg dominions. It stood ready to resist the power that was crushing out racial and territorial distinctions; it spoke for a nation in arms conscious of its national right to exist. At home the French Emperor had to deal now with a population that was weary of warfare and satiated with military glory. To meet, on Austrian territory, this massive attack of the Fifth Coalition, which was made up of England, Spain, and Austria, there was no longer the material at hand that had secured for the conqueror the brilliant achievements at Austerlitz and Marengo. His latest army consisted of new recruits and old soldiers from France and of levies from dependent states.

Napoleon thoroughly appreciated the dangers of his position, as his correspondence with his agent at the Russian court shows. He was most urgent in inviting Alexander to play the part of an effective ally by sending troops to Hungary and Galicia, a movement which would have taken Austria between two fires. There were no longer vague promises of reward held out, but specific engagements were offered as an inducement for the Czar to act. "The three crowns of Austria could be separated. When these last-mentioned states have been thus divided, we can diminish the number of our troops, substitute for these general enlistments of troops, which are tending to call even the women under arms, a small number of regular troops and so change to the system of small armies, as introduced by the late King of Prussia (Frederick II). Our barracks can become poor-houses and the conscripts can stick to their tillage. Even if it is wished after the conquest to guarantee the integrity of the monarchy, I will agree to it provided there is a complete disarmament."

Alexander showed a lack of interest in these proposals; on the other hand, he let the Austrian government know that he hoped they would be successful, promising at the same time that his alliance with the French would be interpreted so formally, that the Austrians would have nothing to fear from Russian armies. Yet in spite of these diplomatic discouragements Napoleon lost none of his technical skill in the campaign that followed. In five days (April 19-23, 1809) with an army of 120,000 men, though the main Austrian army consisted of 175,000, he took 40,000 prisoners and 100 pieces of artillery. He divided the enemy's forces into separate divisions, both of which were defeated, and so he opened up the road to Vienna. But the close of the campaign was obstinately contested by the Austrian commander, the Archduke Charles. In the neighborhood of the Austrian capital there were desperate engagements at Aspern and Essling (May 21-22). For a time Napoleon's lieutenants, Masséna and Lannes, were hard pressed near the island of Lobau in the Danube. The French advance was checked thirteen times; Essling was taken and retaken, and, according to general opinion, the primary result of this serious contest was only a repetition of Eylau.

Reinforcements were summoned from all sides; Lobau was transformed into a strong citadel with impregnable redoubts to insure the passage of the river. In July, Napoleon had under him 150,000 men and 450 cannon. On the 5th and 6th of the month a decisive battle was fought at Wagram, according to a carefully planned program. The Austrians were first of all outnumbered; the whole French army was so dispersed and concentrated over a distance of not more than four miles that it could be directly under the Emperor's eyes. On the other hand, the Austrians were scattered, had no reserves at hand, and orders had to be given in writing. Successful as was Napoleon's strategy, which contained his favorite expedient of breaking the enemy's center by an overwhelmingly strong concentrated attack on the weakest point, it was plain to him that there was no longer in his army the cohesive action that had made the earlier victories so complete. The battle cost from 20,000 to 25,000 men on each side. "These are no longer the soldiers of Austerlitz," he explained; and he showed his lack of confidence by giving up bayonet charges and trusting to artillery fire to break up his opponents' lines.

The Austrian archduke withdrew from the field in good order, but Napoleon had no desire to pursue and force another engagement in the interior of the country. He trusted to the general influence abroad of the success at Wagram, and was glad to sign a treaty of peace at Vienna on the 14th of October, 1809, by which Austria was denuded of large sections of territory, that were taken to reward the fidelity of the Bavarians and Poles to their French allies. Under this reorganization Austria occupied a territory smaller than that of pre-revolutionary France. She was required to reduce her army to 150,000 men and to pay an indemnity of $17,000,000. Russia's share of the spoil was measured by her apathetic position as an ally. There was an addition of territory containing a population of 400,000, but this was a small gain that by no means outweighed the favor shown to the Poles by the annexation of western Galicia to the grand duchy of Warsaw. Annexed to the French Empire were Fiume, Trieste, Croatia, Carniola, and a part of Carinthia, so that Napoleon's eastern dominions extended practically without a break in their eastern border from the mouth of the Cattaro to Dantzic. Austria seemed to have become as much a satellite of Napoleon's empire as Holland or Italy.

VII

THE BEGINNING OF THE END

During the course of the contest with Austria, the war in the Iberian peninsula went on in a prolonged series of obstinate campaigns between Napoleon's marshals and an allied force composed of English, Portuguese, and Spanish contingents. Even after the victory of Wagram the Spaniards held on in the face of several disasters; and helped by the English fleet they managed to retain a foothold in Cadiz. The temper of the population was judged to be so hostile that the French army of occupation was raised to the enormous number of 270,000 and the whole country was placed under martial law. The King, Napoleon's brother Joseph, was only the nominal executive; he aptly called himself the porter of the Madrid hospitals. As the country was harassed with guerrilla warfare, and as the Cortes refused to recognize Joseph as their sovereign, Napoleon threatened to annex the whole kingdom to France.

In Portugal, a French army under Masséna failed to win a decisive victory. It was met by an Anglo-Portuguese force under Wellington, who so strongly intrenched himself at Torres Vedras that Masséna finally withdrew, followed by the English. In his retreat the French general was unable to change his fortune, and the effort to occupy Portugal failed. Masséna was then superseded in his command. Later on the French cause was much injured by the mutual jealousies of the commanders of the various army corps, who, if they had zealously coöperated, might, with the superior forces at their command, have driven Wellington back to the sea coast. By the year 1812, the French armies were stale, and although there were 230,000 French soldiers in the peninsula, Wellington was allowed to invade Spain with an army of only 60,000 men.

Napoleon was indignant at the mismanagement of his subordinates, and sent Jourdon to take charge of the military operations. The new commander not only found the various generals under him unwilling to act together, but also had to deal with a situation in which the troops were demoralized by habits of pillage. Their pay was in arrears, field artillery was scarce, the large siege guns had fallen into the hands of the English, there were no wagon trains and no supply service. Napoleon himself could not from a distance undertake any intelligent supervision of the Spanish situation, since he was obliged to depend on indirect information, and when he interfered his commands were rarely carried out with common sense or good will. His own hands were not free when the Spanish affairs became most critical, for the alliance with Russia, on which so much hope was placed, proved only temporary. On both sides there were grievances; Napoleon was indignant at the apathetic attitude of his ally during the Wagram campaign, and he felt irritated also at the hesitation and delay of the Czar in arranging a marriage for him with a Russian archduchess, after the divorce from Josephine. A distinct Austrian trend was given to French policy when Napoleon found the Austrian Emperor willing to sacrifice his daughter, for the purpose of perpetuating the Napoleonic dynasty. Intimation was given in plain terms that in the questions relating to the Balkan peninsula, Russia's scheme of aggression would be no more encouraged nor supported.

In Alexander's domains the continental blockade against England was unpopular and disastrous. With English vessels barred from Russian ports there was no more an outlet for the raw materials of the country. Many of the landlords were in a bankrupt condition; reprisals were made by increasing the tariff on French goods. In a military sense the only benefit accruing to Russia from the French alliance was the conquest of Finland. No good came from French help either in the war with Persia or in that with Turkey. On the other side, the constant extension of French territory and influence placed a sinister but natural interpretation on Napoleon's promises to share with the Russians the dominion of all European and Asiatic lands as far East as India.

The last step in annexation illustrated the character of Napoleon's present temper. Hamburg and Lübeck were incorporated with the French Empire and along with them the duchy of Oldenburg, whose duke was closely allied to the Russian royal house. The Czar protested formally, but without moving the Emperor of the French either to recede or to give adequate compensation for annexing these German territories.

But the severest blow to Russia came from the favors shown the Poles, to reward their valorous coöperation in the Wagram campaign. The Czar, who feared the restoration of the kingdom of Poland, attempted to secure from Napoleon the promise that that kingdom should never be reëstablished. Napoleon's reply was that he would only pledge himself not to give any assistance to any revolt tending to restore the kingdom of Poland. The Czar's anxiety was misplaced, for the provinces of his empire that he feared might be taken, were in no sense Polish socially, though they had formed a part of the ancient kingdom of Poland. There was no likelihood of a popular movement in favor of the Poles, nor would the population have endured a pro-Polish rearrangement of their territory against the Russians, with whom they, as members of the Orthodox Church, were closely in sympathy. There was also a pro-Russian party among the Poles which Alexander encouraged, by proposing a scheme to establish an enlarged autonomous Poland with a constitution under Russian protection. In 1811, Russian troops were massed together, to invade the grand duchy of Warsaw, and so to encourage the Russian partisans to carry through Alexander's scheme.

In the spring of 1811, Napoleon, who had at first made light of the intimations of the hostile purposes of the Czar, that kept coming to him from Polish sources, realized that there was a substance behind these reports and began to collect forces from all parts of his empire to protect the grand duchy. Napoleon told the Russian representatives of his gigantic preparations, and at the same time declared that he wished for peace; he asked also whether Alexander thought he was ready to sacrifice 200,000 Frenchmen to re-establish Poland.

But the final rupture arose over Napoleon's economic policy. Alexander refused to give up the right of trading with neutrals. "I am ready," he said, "to withdraw to Siberia rather than accept for Russia the situation now occupied by Austria and Prussia." When the Russian ultimatum was handed in, its conditions were the settlement of Alexander's grievances with Sweden, the evacuation of Prussia, and the right of commerce with neutrals as preliminary to the question of tariffs and indemnity for the seizure of Oldenburg. Napoleon's unwilling allies, Prussia and Austria, smarting as they were from past defeats at his hands, were not to be depended upon. On the other hand, Russia's hands were made free by subsidies from England, by a treaty of peace with Turkey, and by the valuable aid of Sweden, whose crown prince was now Bernadotte, a kinsman of Napoleon and one of his ablest marshals.

In May, 1812, the French Emperor appeared in Dresden, ready to undertake the invasion of Russia; he was the personal ruler of 130 French departments, and under him, in the relation of vassals, were seven kingdoms and thirty princes. In Poland, he was greeted with great enthusiasm, but the actual contingents supplied to his army from Polish sources did not amount to more than 70,000 men. Much of the Grand Army with which Russia was now invaded, 678,000 in all (among the items being 480,000 foot, 100,000 horse, and 80,000 artillerymen), were composed, to the proportion of nearly half, of foreign contingents. Besides the force taken with him to Russia, he had at his command, under arms, 150,000 soldiers in France, 50,000 in Italy, 300,000 in Spain. The plan of campaign was to penetrate into the interior of the

Russian Empire, leaving ample forces to guard communications and protect the flanks, as the French advanced. On the Russian side the forces were much less numerous, and there actually faced the 400,000 French who crossed the Niemen the last of June, only 147,000 Russians.

Napoleon's plan depended for success on quick action. He hoped to attack and overcome the two chief Russian armies, before they had effected a junction. But the country was not like the plains of central Europe; it was marshy and broken by forests. His commanders, especially his brother Jerome, whose position at the head of an army corps was an absurd concession to the clan spirit of the Bonaparte family, showed dilatoriness in executing important strategical movements. The troops also suffered in their discipline from the constant marauding expeditions. Desertions were numerous, many lagged behind, and there were epidemics in the invading army owing to the extreme heat. From these various causes the divisions lost a large percentage of their effective strength, so that by the middle of July the invaders were faced by a reduction in the original number of their army of 150,000 men. Napoleon won no decisive victory, for after every engagement the enemy contrived to get away, drawing the invading forces farther into the interior of the country.

At Smolensk and Borodino there were battles that recalled the Eylau campaign, the losses were heavy on both sides without producing any change in the position of the opposing armies. On September 7, a murderous battle took place at Borodino near Moscow; the victory for the French might have been complete, if Napoleon had not at a critical time refused to let his guard charge, saying that he did not want to destroy it, 800 leagues away from France. The loss on both sides was frightful; of the French 30,000 were "hors de combat," while the Russians counted their losses at 60,000. Among the killed on the French side were three generals of division, nine brigadier generals, and ten colonels. The Russians lost their heroic commander Bagration.

The road was now opened to Moscow, but there was no rejoicing among the victors, for on the field of battle lay 30,000 dead and 60,000 wounded. On the 14th, Napoleon entered the city, the ancient capital of Russia. Most of the inhabitants had fled, leaving only the lower classes and the occupants of the prisons, whom the governor of the city had released, when he heard of the victory of the French. While the army was halted in expectation that Alexander would sue for peace, a fire, started by Russian incendiaries, soon consumed most of the city, the houses of which were constructed entirely of wood. Fifteen thousand of the Russian wounded, who had been brought on in ambulances, were burnt to death. After the fire had spent its course Napoleon took up his abode in the Kremlin, which was only saved by the efforts of the Imperial Guard. He still hoped that terms of peace might be arranged, but Alexander continued inflexible.

Napoleon for a time contemplated spending the winter in Russia, since he recognized the practical difficulties of the retreat and the loss of prestige due to his withdrawal. Finally he decided to return by the southern provinces. The start west began on the 19th of November, 1812, with a force of 100,000 men; the way south was made impracticable by the obstinate resistance of the Russian general Kutusoff, with his army of only 50,000 men. Therefore the route over which they had come had to be taken for the return. The rearguard was constantly harassed by the enemy, and early in November there was a battle at Viazma, in which the French lost from 15,000 to 18,000 men. Snow began to fall, food was scarce, the troops were badly prepared to endure the wintry weather; out of 100,000 men there were soon only 40,000 left able to bear arms, and at Smolensk on the 12th of November only 34,000 were left.

No French army corps actually surrendered, but they suffered terrible losses, some of them losing half their effective strength. The Russians who followed the retreat were also reduced from 60,000 to 30,000. At the Berezina, where three Russian armies were joined to dispute the passage, the French with unheard-of bravery rescued themselves from capture by forces three times as numerous, and inflicted on the Russians a loss of 14,000 men. When the remnants of the army reached Lithuania, Napoleon left them there in order to make a rapid return to Paris and to counteract by his presence in his capital the bad effect of the news of the defeat in Russia. New armies had to be raised, for it was practically certain that a large part of Germany would soon be in revolt. Though temporarily strengthened by the various contingents left to protect the communications eastward, the final stage of the retreat from Russia, which was conducted by Murat, bore witness to the frightful straits and demoralization of the French. The sick and wounded were abandoned; there were no provisions for carrying the artillery or the pontoons; even the army treasure and the secret archives had to be left behind. Before the end of the journey west Ney, who commanded the rearguard, had with him no more than 500 or 600 men, and when the Old Guard entered Königsberg, it was reduced to 1500 men, of whom only 500 were fit to bear arms.

The extent of the Russian disaster may be measured by a few statistics; 533,000 soldiers crossed the actual frontier into Russia in the summer of 1812; 18,000 of the main army returned in the December following; about 130,000 men had been made prisoners in Russia, 55,000 had deserted at the opening of the campaign, and there were 55,000 survivors of the various corps that had been stationed as reserves along the line outside of the Russian territory. Altogether 250,000 must be reckoned as having perished during the course of the march to Moscow and the retreat from that city. The disaster meant that Napoleon's schemes of European domination were checked and his military resources much diminished. It was no longer a question of new conquests, but of turning to face the nations who had suffered so long from French despotic rule.

VIII
DEFEAT AND EXILE

From every quarter came the word that, with the Grand Army destroyed, the French Cæsar must now yield; his system, it was said, had expired on the plains of Russia. The hostile spirit of a subject population was seen as the straggling French passed through Prussia; soldiers who dropped out of the ranks were disarmed by the peasants, insulted and badly handled. The Prussians and Austrians made separate arrangements with the Russians, by which hostilities, so far as each were concerned, were to be suspended. Most of Prussia was abandoned; there were only 40,000 French left to oppose a revolted Germany. Even Murat, Napoleon's brother-in-law, abandoned the failing cause and retired suddenly to Naples, to make from there arrangements on his own account with the Austrian Prime Minister Metternich.

The activity of Napoleon in such a desperate situation was marvelous. As to money, he collected nearly $100,000,000 by using his own private treasury and selling large amounts of communal estates. Every available man was placed under arms, including the National Guard and even by anticipation the conscripts of 1814—there were already 140,000 of the conscripts of 1813 under training—the sailors in the seaports were enrolled as soldiers; and many regiments were taken from Spain. Altogether there was collected and sent in detachments to Germany an army of 500,000 men, mostly made up of youths less than twenty years of age. In order to give them discipline and stability, veterans were incorporated in the new regiments.

Napoleon was not so alert as he had been; he was suffering from an internal disease, and sometimes for weeks he was incapable of effort. There were frequent attacks also of drowsiness, all indicative of exhaustion of his powers. He was more intolerant than ever of criticism, refused to take advice, was suspicious of his counselors, and contemptuous of the ability of his commanders, an attitude somewhat justified by the fact that many of his best marshals were now replaced by men of second-rate ability, while others, who were fitted to command, were unwilling from jealousy to work together. Marbot declared that, "if the Emperor had wished to punish all those who were lacking in zeal, he would have been obliged to dispense with the services of nearly all his marshals."

The service of supplies for the army was most defective. In the beginning of the year 1813, by the carelessness of the administrative work in this department, the Prussians got possession of over $6,000,000 worth of supplies, intended for the French armies. The consequence was that the soldiers depended on pillage; even the officers lived on what they could get from the country. Worse than all was the inability of the Emperor himself to gauge the changed conditions produced by his defeat. He still behaved as if he were invincible, and refused to make terms with Prussia or to conciliate Austria by well-timed territorial concessions. To the end he would not believe that his father-in-law, the Emperor of Austria, would take up arms against him. If, at this time, he had accepted a smaller, compact France, confined to its natural limits, he might have avoided the disasters of 1813 and 1814, and yet ruled over a territory larger than that ever held by Louis XIV.

In the new coalition Prussia was most anxious to restore her prestige; the uprising against the French was a national movement common to all classes of the population. Finally, even the timorous King was induced to side with the Russians and to issue an appeal to his people. There were 150,000 Prussians under arms, and in order to receive the help of other German states, proclamations were issued under Russian auspices, making generous promises of national independence and personal liberty. So were transplanted to German soil the watchwords of the French Revolution. Austria made many open professions of fidelity to the alliance with France, but Metternich was actively intriguing with the smaller German courts. He even tried to detach Jerome of Westphalia and Murat of Naples from the French, and he did all in his power to urge Frederick William, the Prussian king, to take up arms in behalf of the independence of Europe.

In the military operations of 1813, while the French were opposed only by the allied forces of Prussia and Russia, the advantage continued on the side of the French Emperor; by the autumn, however, Austria and many of the German vassal states had joined the coalition and the defeat of Napoleon was the certain outcome. As a result of a series of battles around Dresden, the cause of the allies was in a critical position; both sides had lost heavily but Napoleon was much chagrined that there had been no signal positive advantage from the constant butchery of his men. He was weak in cavalry, and so could not follow up his successes; the terrible loss of horses in Russia had not been made up. But at any rate he was steadily getting back the territory in Germany he had previously held. On the other side, the Russian and Prussian generals were blaming one another for their failures, and so making the continuance of the coalition problematical.

At this point Metternich intervened after an armistice had been signed at Pressnitz early in July, 1813. He agreed to support the coalition, unless the French consented to give up Holland, Switzerland, Spain, the Confederation of the Rhine, Poland, and the larger part of Italy. Napoleon was indignant when Metternich laid down these terms during a personal interview at Dresden. "You want war," he said; "well, you will get it. I will meet you at Vienna. How many allies have you got, four, five, six, twenty? The more you have the less disturbed I am. What do you want me to do? Disgrace myself? Never. I can die, but I shall never give up an inch of territory. Your sovereigns who are born on a throne can let themselves be beaten twenty times, and always return to their capital. I cannot do it, because I am an upstart soldier. You are not a soldier, and you do not know what takes place in a soldier's soul. I grew up on battlefields, and a man such as I am cares little for the lives of a million men."

When a congress met at Prague to arrange the terms of peace, they proved far more favorable to France than those first proposed, for she was granted her natural frontiers and Italy in addition. It was nothing short of madness on Napoleon's part to refuse such concessions; only a portion of them had even been dreamed of as possibilities under the Bourbon monarchs at the height of their ambition. Even from his own point of view, he might have trusted to the certainty of future jealousies between the central European powers and

Russia, by which his place as the arbiter of Europe could be regained. Metternich, indeed, was as insincere in his profession on behalf of peace as Napoleon himself, because the congress closed before a special messenger with the French counter proposals reached Vienna. War was resumed on August 11th.

The situation was now as follows: the French were about to be surrounded by three great armies; 130,000 Austrians, 240,000 Russians, and a mixed host, composed of various contingents from all the allies great and small, under the former French marshal, Bernadotte, numbering 180,000 men. Moreover, there were 200,000 combined English and Spanish soldiers ready to cross the Pyrenees. Altogether 1,000,000 men were ranged in arms against the French Emperor. The plan as developed by Bernadotte, now King of Sweden, was to wear Napoleon out. A decisive battle would be avoided, but his lieutenants would be destroyed in detail. Moreau, the victor of Hohenlinden, was brought from the United States, where he had been living in exile, to assume the command of the allies.

To oppose the vast allied forces, Napoleon had altogether no more than 550,000 men, of whom 330,000 were in Germany. At Dresden, at the end of August, an attack on the place was successfully resisted, and Moreau, the generalissimo of the allies, lost his life. But Napoleon's scattered marshals fared badly, and the French army suffered heavy losses just at a time when no man could be spared. The enveloping plan was successfully carried out. Napoleon, at Leipzig, realized his hopeless position, for he tried there to arrange an armistice. With his 155,000 men he had against him 330,000 of the coalition. The situation was rendered worse because the German troops serving with the French deserted and joined the enemy; some, like the Saxons, during the very course of the terrible battle which raged for three days around Leipzig (October, 1813). At the end, 15 French generals and 25,000 men were made prisoners, and 350 cannon were taken; 13,000 of the French were massacred in the houses of Leipzig. The losses on both sides were frightful, for 130,000 was the sum total of the killed and wounded, 50,000 of whom were French.

In the retreat which followed, the demoralization was so great that only 40,000 men reached the Rhine, yet nearly 200,000 men were left, by Napoleon's orders, in various German fortresses, most of them, too, experienced troops who were unable to take further part in the war when their country was invaded in the next year's campaign. Some attempt was made to arrange terms of peace now that everywhere the Napoleonic system had fallen to pieces. The French armies were driven out of Holland. In Italy alone Eugène Beauharnais was manfully and loyally supporting the Emperor's cause, but he had only 30,000 men.

The people of France had no heart for more warfare, and the allies let it be known that they were fighting Napoleon and not France. But still the great mass of the people had no wish for a change of dynasty; the war was unpopular, but not its author. As soon as it became known that the cause of the allies meant a restoration of the Bourbons, and that France would be invaded, in order to displace Napoleon, the answer of the country, exhausted though it was and drained of its male population, was spontaneous and unmistakable. From the autumn of 1813, to March, 1814, France placed in the field under Napoleon's orders, 350,000 men. This is a marvelous record, not to mention the tremendous financial drain caused by the equipment of a fresh army.

The new recruits were not trained, well armed, or sufficiently clothed; there was not time to prepare them for warfare, for the allies crossed the frontiers of France in midwinter (1813). There was no resistance to their progress until Napoleon with an army of 122,000 began to conduct his last extended campaign in the neighborhood of Châlons. By reason of a success gained near Rotheise the allies hoped soon to be in Paris. This over-confidence exposed them to a series of defeats, inflicted upon several of their generals in succession, by Napoleon, in a remarkable exposition of his strategy that recalled the early days of his career in Italy. By the end of February the principal army of the allies retired near Troyes, afraid, though numbering 150,000 men, to face a stand-up fight with Napoleon, who had only 70,000 men. Public confidence was restored in France, especially among the country people, indignant at the brutal treatment they received at the hands of the foreign soldiers. There was now stirred up a spirit of national resistance, which recalled the early days of the French Revolution. The peasantry arose, and inflicted severe losses on the marauding troops. Attempts were made in the spring to arrange terms of peace, but on neither side was there a sincere belief that the war could be brought to an end by mutual concessions. The Congress of Châtillon lasted from the 4th of February to the 19th of March; it was only a concession to public opinion, for the allies really wished for a Bourbon restoration, while Napoleon, depending on his marriage with the daughter of Francis I of Austria, felt certain that he could ultimately detach the Austrians from the coalition. At one time the allied armies were so discouraged, after fighting ten battles on French soil, that they contemplated a retreat eastward.

Confidence was restored to them, not by their military successes, but by the capture of some private despatches from various officials to the French Emperor, which spoke in no uncertain terms of the discontent of the people of Paris and of the general depression throughout a country that was no longer able to bear the material exhaustion caused by the war. So encouraged, the allies marched to Paris; Napoleon anticipated this step, and had ordered the government to withdraw towards the Loire, feeling sure that in time he could drive his foes from French territory. Yet he realized to the full the bad effect of the seizure of his capital.

In approaching the city the allies had only to deal with the marshals, not with the master hand of the Emperor, who first heard of their march westward three days after it had begun. The end soon came; there was a murderous engagement near the city, after which the arrangements for an armistice were made with Joseph Bonaparte, acting for the regent, the Empress Marie Louise. When Napoleon heard the news of the capitulation, he indignantly prepared to annul the action of his brother, and to call the people to arms for a hand-to-hand struggle in the streets of Paris with the foreign soldiery. In a few days, owing to the shrewd persuasions of Talleyrand, who induced Alexander of Russia to accept no alternative government for the country but a Bourbon restoration, Napoleon found himself forced to abdicate.

This step was not taken until after long hesitations, for even to the last he believed in the possibility of continuing hostilities. The troops were still enthusiastically loyal, and eagerly listened to his appeal to them to march upon Paris. But his marshals insisted that he must abdicate. This he finally did in a conditional form, reserving the rights of Napoleon II, and the regency of Marie Louise. This form, owing to the refusal of the Czar to accept it, was finally altered until it read as follows: "The allied powers having proclaimed that the Emperor Napoleon was the sole obstacle to the restoration of peace in Europe, the Emperor Napoleon, loyal to his oaths, declares that he renounces in behalf of himself and his heirs the thrones of France and Italy, because there is no personal sacrifice, even to the extent of his life, that he is not ready to make in the interest of France."...

For several days after abdicating, Napoleon remained in Fontainebleau practically deserted by his old comrades in arms, who were anxious to make peace with the new government, now that Louis XVIII had been proclaimed king. On the night of the 12th of April he tried to poison himself, but the attempt failed, for the toxic drug, which he had always carried on his person since the retreat from Moscow, had lost its power. He soon recovered, however, from his depression, and on the 20th of April, 1814, signed the treaty of Fontainebleau, by which he was given the sovereignty of the island of Elba, and retained the title of Emperor.

The story of the Spanish campaign, which had a potent influence in causing Napoleon's ruin, is marked by many brilliant feats of arms on the part of the French, but the country could no longer be held. Finally, by the successful advance of Wellington, the Spanish war became merged in the general defense of French territory, when France was invaded by the coalition in 1814. On Spanish soil the final disaster came at the battle of Vitoria, June 21, 1813, where the French lost 7000 men, 180 pieces of artillery, and nearly all their baggage trains. One of the great mistakes of the Peninsular War was Soult's refusal to give battle to Wellington in 1812, when all the advantages in numbers were on his side. Later on, though he was in a far inferior position, he proved a most obstinate opponent, contesting Wellington's march north at every step with an army inferior to that under his opponent. He gave way slowly, and while Napoleon was fighting the allies in his last campaign before his abdication, Soult had been forced to withdraw from Bayonne, and then from Toulouse, which Wellington entered on the 12th of April, 1814.

It is generally held by critics that the war in Spain was a most serious mistake from start to finish, and was the chief cause of Napoleon's ruin. Whatever share in the failure of the imperial policy in the Peninsula may be assigned to the mediocre capacity of Joseph and to the confused strategy of the French armies due to the jealousies of the marshals, a large part of the responsibility falls to the account of Napoleon himself. He left his work half done in the Peninsula, where he underrated the difficulties of conquest. He reckoned that it would cost him but 12,000 men! As a matter of fact, it kept a large number of his best troops occupied at a time when they were most needed. It was sheer folly to undertake the Russian campaign while Spain was still far from being pacified. It was also culpably bad tactics to allow Wellington to destroy the prestige of French soldiers and generals, and it was close to madness, in 1813, not to withdraw altogether from Spain, when every man was needed in France to defend its frontiers from the coalition. On the other hand, while Spain's resistance to French arms was a glorious record of patriotism, modern Spain has paid very dear for its glory. All the elements of reaction were interested in the downfall of the Napoleonic régime, and in no other country, not even Italy, did the restoration of the Bourbon dynasty produce such deplorable maladministration and civil disorder.

The dramatic farewell of the Emperor to his troops at Fontainebleau makes a picturesque "mise-en-scène" for the close of a tragedy; it is unfortunate that the spectacular instincts of his genius induced him to accept the ridiculous rôle of sovereign of the island of Elba. It would have been more dignified for him to have refused the offer of the allies, and to have exchanged the rôle of a "roi fainéant" for that of a private individual. Nothing illustrates the parvenu traits of his character more than his desire to preserve the shadow of the royal dignity, even if he had to accept bounty from the hands of a Bourbon king to maintain it.

The allies fully realized the danger of his proximity in Elba, and unofficially there were various plans discussed with a view to rid themselves of their dangerous neighbor. Talleyrand was plotting to have him imprisoned, while the English urged deportation to an inaccessible island. Napoleon, who was an admirable actor, accommodated himself to his Lilliputian kingdom and to his mimic court, and adopted the pose of a modern Timoleon. "I wish to live henceforth," he said, "like a justice of the peace. The Emperor is dead, I am no longer anything. I think of nothing outside of my small island. I exist no longer for the world. Nothing now interests me but my family, my cottage, my cows, and my mules." His demands were not so modest as his words appear, for he spent nearly 2,000,000 francs at Elba in eight months.

He complained bitterly at being separated from his son and his wife, both of whom Francis kept in Vienna. There was no intention that they should be allowed to rejoin the Emperor; indeed, Marie Louise, who was of a very passive disposition, was content not to see her husband again, especially after Metternich had supplied her with an admirer, General Neippberg. It might have been wiser, certainly it would have been more humane, if the allies had adopted a less stringent policy of isolation. Whatever one may think of the sincerity of Napoleon's sentiments, he struck a true note, when he wrote the words "my son has been taken from me, as were formerly the children of the vanquished, to adorn the triumph of their conqueror. One cannot find in modern times an example of such barbarity." He was not entirely dejected, for he was visited by his mother and his youngest sister, and though the king of Rome was withheld from him, an irregular heir was brought to Elba by the Countess Walinska, whom Napoleon had met some years before in Poland.

There were financial embarrassments, which made impossible the idyllic life the exiled monarch had mapped out for himself; the income stipulated by the treaty of Fontainebleau was not paid. But there were more weighty reasons for the flight from Elba, which occurred early in 1815 (February 26). For some time Napoleon had been in secret communication with Murat, probably with a view to restoring the kingdom of Italy, through coöperation from Naples. This scheme promised more difficulties than a return to France, where the Bourbon restoration was not popular, and where the army and its generals were far from being satisfied with their new situation, under a king who favored the lifelong supporters of his cause. Plans had been concocted during the winter to dethrone Louis XVIII, in which both the Bonapartist sympathizers and some of the old revolutionary leaders had acted together. On hearing of this, Napoleon considered that the moment was opportune for his reappearance on French soil. With 1100 of his veterans who had acted as his guard at Elba, he reached southern France in safety. As the prevailing sentiment in this region was royalist, he made his way with his small band through the Alps to Grenoble, marching sometimes as much as thirty miles a day. By the peasants of the country he was welcomed everywhere with enthusiasm. From Paris orders were sent to treat him as an outlaw.

The critical time came at Grenoble, when Napoleon's dramatic qualities helped him to secure the allegiance of his old troops. He marched impressively at the head of his veterans to within gunshot distance of a regiment drawn up in his way. "Soldiers," he said, "look well at me. If there is among you one soldier who wishes to kill his Emperor he can do it. I come to offer myself for you to shoot." The effect was instantaneous, and the answer to his appeal was the old familiar cry, "Long live the Emperor."

The enthusiasm increased as he proceeded farther north. Nothing could arrest it or prevent the defection of the troops, not even the appeals for loyalty to the Bourbon king, addressed to their men by the marshals, who strove to outdo one another in their official abuse of the enterprise. Soult spoke of Napoleon as an adventurer; others called him a public enemy or a mad brigand, while Ney undertook to bring him to Paris in an iron cage. The army cared nothing for these criticisms or warnings; even Ney himself joined the movement and turned over his troops to the "man from Elba." By the 20th of March Napoleon was in Paris at the Tuileries; his marvelous progress was a restoration, not based on diplomacy, but made possible by the enthusiastic loyalty of the population, and the rank and file of the army. Not a gun had been fired. At Grenoble it had been the soldiers who had refused to obey their officers' command, when told to shoot. Afterwards there was no officer found willing to repeat the command.

The question of establishing a new government was solved by inaugurating a liberal constitutional rule. Napoleon seemed once again to remember that he was the creation of the Revolution. As an evidence of his sincerity to the tradition of the Republic, he selected as his chief adviser, Benjamin Constant, the old Jacobin leader, whose independence a few years before Napoleon had so much resented when Constant had led the opposition in the Tribunate. All these things were now forgotten. "Public discussions, free elections, responsible ministers, liberty of the press; I want all this. I am a man of the people! If the people want liberty, I am bound to give it." Under the new government, which was accepted by a small vote, owing to the number of those who stayed away from the polls, the elections returned a majority of liberals and republicans, who were not in sympathy with the restored empire. Many preferred to have a regency with Napoleon's son or the Duke of Orléans. But the real hopelessness of the situation came from the implacable attitude of the allies. At the Congress of Vienna, where the great powers were rearranging the map of Europe amidst much jealousy and intrigue, they at least agreed on one subject: the refusal to allow Napoleon to rule France. That devoted country was put under an interdict. The four powers agreed to fight the French Emperor with a coalition army of more than 1,000,000 men. To oppose this immense force Davout, acting under Napoleon's directions, had in a few weeks got together for the purpose of national defense 500,000 men to be ready by the end of June. Elaborate plans were made to protect the frontiers, and Napoleon proposed to take the offensive without waiting for the allies to invade the country.

The nearest allied army was in Belgium, composed of 100,000 English and Dutch under Wellington, and 150,000 Prussians under Blücher. Napoleon set out to oppose these forces with 180,000 men, intending to get between the English and the Prussians and beat them separately, trusting to the well-known rapidity of his movements to keep them from joining. Strategically the plan was a brilliant one, but it was not capably executed. Ney, at Quatre Bras, did not win a complete victory over the English because the engagement was begun too late. At Ligny, Napoleon attacked Blücher, who fought obstinately, though he lost 20,000 men, and was not completely crushed as had been planned. Instead of withdrawing in confusion, as had been expected, Blücher set out to join Wellington's troops. Grouchy, who was sent in pursuit of the Prussians, did not know of this operation and was under the impression that he was carrying out properly his instructions to pursue the Prussians alone, whereas the greater part of the Prussian army had already come in touch with Wellington, and Grouchy failed, therefore, to bring his men back in time to Waterloo where they were needed. Wellington was strongly intrenched and all attempts to take his position failed. The battle, begun at 11 A.M. on June 18, 1815, was not decided until five o'clock, when Blücher effected his junction with the English forces. It was a most desperate engagement, for Napoleon realized what depended on it. The losses were 32,000 French and 22,000 of the allies.

A second act of abdication was now imposed upon Napoleon, who accepted it, resigning in favor of his son. He even offered to serve as a simple general to prevent the allies from capturing Paris. This was not an absolutely chimerical proposal, for there was an enormous mass of men gathered by Davout, ready to fight even after the defeat of Waterloo. But the elected representatives would not hear of continuing the struggle. Napoleon lingered for several days near Paris, at Malmaison, and it was only when he was advised by the temporary government that they could not be responsible for his personal safety, that he traveled towards the west, where his friends were arranging that he should be taken on an American vessel to the United States. The sea coast was watched by British cruisers, so the defeated conqueror decided to surrender himself to the British, intending to claim their hospitality and protection as a guest, not as a prisoner. Apparently, Napoleon rejected the plan to cross the Atlantic "incognito," for the more spectacular one of throwing himself on the mercy of his most bitter antagonists, because he counted on finding a protection under the constitutional régime of Great Britain, and especially on the ability of the liberal opposition to prevent him from being treated with exceptional harshness. He realized, too, that it would be most dangerous for him to fall into the hands of any of the allied Continental Powers, who might have had him condemned to death by a court-martial or immured in close confinement. It is known that the British premier, Castlereagh, hoped that Napoleon would fall into the hands of Louis XVIII and be treated as a rebel. Therefore, when the vessel which carried him reached the English coast, there was some hesitation as to the treatment he would receive.

Finally, at the end of July, the problem was solved by arranging to send the prisoner to the Island of St. Helena, because, on account of its isolation, there would be little chance of escape. The climate was healthy, close confinement would not be necessary, and Napoleon was permitted to take a suite of servants and friends with him. During his residence at Elba, the plan of a removal of the Emperor to St. Helena had been discussed by the Powers at the Congress of Vienna; perhaps the knowledge of this fact may have contributed largely to induce the flight from Elba and the short-lived attempt to restore the empire.

Acting under international agreement, England became responsible for the guardianship of Napoleon, who was called the prisoner of the Powers. In October, 1815, began the captivity at St. Helena. It was naturally a trying experience to a man who had lately played so great a rôle in the world, and Napoleon did not have the temperament to endure so conspicuous a change in fortune. He instantly began a campaign to secure his release from captivity. Reckoning on the action of public opinion in England working in his behalf, he left nothing undone to exaggerate the onerous conditions under which he lived as an exile. On its side, the British government, which was being administered by men who represented a selfish oligarchy, and who had to their credit a long record of inefficiency, corruption, and attacks on popular rights, was not likely to show especial consideration to a fallen antagonist at St. Helena. A regular system of persecution, inane and petty, was invented, and in applying it the governor of the island, Sir Hudson Lowe, a man of morose temper, whose character is admirably indicated by his name, showed himself a master.

There were various plans for aiding an escape, many of them originating in the United States. Even an attack on St. Helena was discussed by Napoleon's followers, some of whom were on the American continent as participants in the Brazilian war of independence against Portugal. But Napoleon refused to consider any such methods of relief. "I could not be in America six months," he said, "without being attacked by the murderers, whom the royalist committees, that returned to France in the train of the Count d'Artois, have hired against me. In America I see nothing but murder and oblivion, so I prefer to stay on at St. Helena." He saw truly that, in a life of freedom on the other side of the Atlantic, there would be little chance of posing as the victim of misfortune and maltreatment, and it was on the maintenance of this pose that he built his hope of relief from captivity, perhaps even of a return to his old place as ruler of France, for he counted on the expulsion of the Bourbons and a reaction of popular feeling in his behalf. A change of ministry in England also he looked forward to as the opening of an avenue of escape to Europe. He refused to take exercise because, in his walks, according to regulations, he had to be accompanied by an English officer; therefore, he blamed his bad health on the British government. Care was taken by publications in London to detail at length the sufferings of the captive. Incessant complaints were made of the trying climate of the island, the aim being to represent the banishment to St. Helena as nothing but a plan to get rid of Napoleon by the toxic effects of a tropical atmosphere. Indeed, the bad climate of St. Helena has become an inseparable part of the Napoleonic legend, yet we know that Napoleon said to members of his own suite, that if he had to live an exile, St. Helena was, after all, the best spot.

As the years passed, nothing was changed, for the Whigs in England were not strong enough to get any measures though Parliament favorable to Napoleon, and in 1818 the five Great Powers issued a signed statement that they approved of the strict treatment of the prisoner by the British government, and resolved that all correspondence with Napoleon, such as sending money or other communications, which was not submitted to the inspection of the governor, must be regarded as an attack on the public safety and punished accordingly.

Under the régime of no exercise imposed upon himself by Napoleon, his health became impaired; his manner of life accentuated the symptoms of a disease, cancer of the stomach, which had appeared long before the period of his exile. It was an inherited malady, for his father had died of it, also his eldest sister. Some relief was secured by his adopting a more active life in 1819; but with the beginning of the year 1821, the progress of the disease was rapid; exercise was no longer possible, and even occasional dictation was found to be an exhausting task. In April the condition of the prisoner was evidently hopeless, and after he was assured on this point by a surgeon of the British army, Napoleon dictated his testament to Montholon, one of his faithful companions. After his death, which took place on May 5, 1821, the body of the great captain was buried not far from Longwood, his residence. Nearly a generation elapsed before it was carried to its present resting place beneath the dome of the Invalides at Paris.

IX
THE NAPOLEONIC REGIME

During the captivity at St. Helena much attention was given by Napoleon to the dictation of his memoirs. These, however, cover only a short portion of his career and are confessedly apologetic in character. They are shrewdly constructed, often with a gross disregard of accuracy, in order to influence public opinion in his favor. In his conversations also he made good use of his interlocutors, to build up that legend of Napoleonic infallibility and good faith that soon found a receptive atmosphere in the prevalent romanticism of European society. He was convinced to the end of his life that Bourbon rule in France could not last, and he looked forward to a time when his son would be restored. In summing up his own career, he claimed that his dictatorship was a necessity. "Should I be accused of having loved war too much, the historian will demonstrate that I was never the aggressor. Should I be censured for desiring universal empire for myself, he will show that that was the product of circumstances, and how my enemies drove me to it, step by step."

In many passages in the same strain Napoleon curiously manifests his adhesion to the principles and phrases of the idealogues, on whom as a ruler he heaped so much scorn. It may be doubted whether the base metal of his rhetoric would have become current, if the Powers who participated in the Congress of Vienna had not introduced as their maxims of political morality the inflated and transparently insincere professions of the Holy Alliance. Indeed, from the beginning to the end of the Napoleonic period, the point of view that the coalitions against him were fighting in behalf of nationalism and liberty is little short of absurd. At almost any time France under Napoleon might have arranged an alliance with England by offering her the bait of commercial concessions; and even more unsubstantial than the Napoleonic legend is its antithesis, that the Tory oligarchy of England were spending hundreds of millions of pounds of their good money for the benefit of the peoples and states on the Continent.

Napoleon's inferiority cannot be discovered in his lack of morality as a ruler, if morality be determined according to the standards of the allied Powers; his chief opponents were trained and acted according to the principles adopted in the partition of Poland. His lack of scruples carried him farther, simply because of the immeasurable distance between his own genius and the commonplace characteristics of any of his antagonists. He built up his personal rule on his military skill by consistent and well-directed effort. France was made the instrument of his ambition; it was in his interest, not in the interest of the country he ruled, that Germany, Italy, and Spain were made dependent states. France would have been more solidly established, if, in spite of all military success abroad, her ruler had been satisfied with her natural frontiers.

Under Napoleon the divorce of national from personal aims is seen in the changed character of the French army; there was no longer a general levy as in the time of the Revolution, for in 1800-1804, service was regulated by lot and by permission to provide substitutes. Middle-class families as a rule took advantage of this permission, and there were plenty of opportunities, because old soldiers were anxious to re-engage for the service. War had become a profession. The mass of the troops were made up of children of the people, while the officers were mostly scions of well-to-do families. As time went on, owing to the exhausting character of the wars, one year's conscription was not enough. Sometimes there was an anticipated enrollment of the conscripts of the two following years. Then came the turn of the National Guard, made up of men from forty to sixty years, and of those from twenty to twenty-six who had been relieved from regular army service, because of their poor physique or because their families were dependent on their work; these, too, were placed on the active list.

Altogether 3,153,000 French soldiers were called upon for military duty from 1800 to 1815. The losses from wounds and disease, apart from the fatalities on the battlefield, were enormous. In all, the victims of these wars are reckoned at 1,750,000 men. Oftentimes, those who desired to escape military duty had to buy themselves off as many as three times, and yet, even after spending $4000, they were obliged to take part in the campaigns of 1813 and 1814. Finally, owing to the scarcity of officers, requisition by force was resorted to. Lists were made of special families in Paris and the departments, whose children between the ages of sixteen and eighteen were constrained to prepare themselves for service at the military school at St. Cyr.

In the complicated system of the Napoleonic army, a place had to be made for the various national elements and groups, who served in it. But the characteristic feature was the Imperial Guard. In itself it was a replica on a small scale of the whole force, because the various arms of the service all found a place within it. It grew out of the consular guard, first numbering 7000 men, then increased to 50,000, until it was finally brought to 92,000 in 1813. The Guard was always with the Emperor in a campaign, it fought under his eye, and was ordinarily kept in reserve for a critical point of the battle. The section of the Guard which was closest to the Emperor, was the mounted scouts or "guides," who wore a green uniform, the imperial color, and were first commanded by his son-in-law, Eugène, and then by another member of the Beauharnais house, Lefebre-Desnouettes. Napoleon described them as a body of brave men who had always seen the enemies' cavalry flee before them. A part of this division was a corp of Mamelouks, recruited in the Eastern campaign, from the Coptic and Syrian volunteers, a picturesque body of men that still continued to wear Oriental dress, though later on many Frenchmen were added to their number.

In the infantry divisions of the army little change was made; there were grenadier regiments composed of the tallest and best proportioned soldiers, and companies of slight, undersized men intended for the kind of work done in the present Italian army by the bersaglieri. Experiments with dismounted dragoons proved a failure. Napoleon's special work was the reorganization of the cavalry, an arm of the service which had almost altogether disappeared at the time of the Revolution, because large numbers of the cavalry officers went into exile on account of their monarchical sympathies. The most conspicuous branch of the cavalry was the hussars, who gained a reputation for dare-devil bravery, and whose charges with drawn sabers were the dramatic feature of an engagement. They were led by generals of the type of Murat, Marbot, and Ségur.

As to the French artillery and engineers, their already high reputation among European armies was fully maintained. In many of Napoleon's hardest contested battles, such as Eylau, Friedland, and Wagram, the cannonading of the French played a decisive part. In the later campaigns troops of the allied states came to be a more important element, and they gave the army a cosmopolitan character. There were German, Swiss, Italian, Spanish, Polish auxiliaries; even Albanians, Greeks, and Tartars were represented in the enormous masses of men drawn about the Emperor, in his final efforts to subjugate the European continent.

The weapons used by the army showed no technical advance on those employed in the last half of the eighteenth century. The guns were flint-locks of the model of 1777, and the cannon were of the type employed in 1765, most of them pieces of 12 and 6 with mortars that had a carrying power of between 800 and 1900 feet.

Owing to the years of incessant warfare, the administration of the army was the chief care of the government. It was under the supervision of the Emperor himself, who was untiring in attending even to the most minute details. He made frequent inspections, kept in personal touch with his soldiers, and looked out for their comfort. In preparing for a campaign he knew with accuracy all matters relating to the equipment of his troops, the actual resources of the arsenals, and the amount of military stores. But the army in the field was expected to provide its own rations. "I made eight campaigns under the empire," De Brack said, "and always at the front; I never saw during this whole time a single army commissary. I never touched a single ration from the army stores. The soldiers depended on requisitions from the inhabitants or on pillage."

It was the Emperor's maxim that war must support war. When in Spain he wrote to Dijeon, the administrative director of war in Paris: "Send back the reserves of cattle; I don't want any foodstuffs, I have an abundance of everything. What I need are caissons, military transports, hats, and shoes; I have never seen a cavalry in which the troops had as much to eat." The requisitions that had been found so profitable in the Italian campaign were continued without any regard for their effect on the conquered country. Enormous stores of money were accumulated in this way. After the treaty of Tilsit the treasury of the army was credited with about $70,000,000, and Napoleon reckoned that he could continue to make war for five years without increasing French taxation or asking for a fresh loan.

As companions in arms Napoleon had under him a large number of able generals, formed just as he had been, in the wars of the Revolution. When the empire was constituted many became marshals. These were selected from all classes of society: Davout, MacDonald, Marmont, Grouchy, Clarke, from the old nobility; Monery, Bernadotte, Soult, Mortier, Gouvion, Suchet, Brun-Junot, from the middle classes; Jourdan, Masséna, Augereau, Murat, Bessières, Ney, Lannes, Victor, Oudinot, Lecourbe, Sebastian, Driant were all children of the people. It was the policy of the Emperor to have young men in command of his troops; by 1813 there were forty-one cavalry generals alone, who, though less than fifty years old, were on the retired list. The life of an officer was so strenuous that there was little chance of resisting for long the tremendous demands made on the constitution by the long marches and frequent battles. Advancement was speedy and the rewards were munificent; many of the marshals received princely titles with pay suitable to their rank. For example, Berthier's annual income was over $250,000. Masséna, Davout, and Ney were almost as well provided for. After the battle of Eylau each guest at the Emperor's table found under his plate a 1000-franc bill. But these personal rewards were not at all confined to those in high command. The Emperor was careful to retain the devoted loyalty of his men by words and acts of personal note, which by their spontaneity kept the army from being turned into a mere mechanical organism. He went among the men, rewarding those who had distinguished themselves on the field of battle, and showing consideration to the wounded and the weary. The weak spot in the army was the practice of pillage. The soldiers were forced to it and regarded it as their right. Their exactions, too, were imitated on a large scale by the commanders and marshals. Masséna made millions by selling trade permits during the blockade against England. Soult despoiled Spain of works of art and exacted large contributions from rich monasteries.

In his economic policy, Napoleon followed the principles of the Bourbon princes; he was a thorough-going disciple of the mercantilist school. It was his purpose to ruin England; hence the severest enactments were promulgated against colonial products and cotton, both prime articles of English trade. Vessels touching English ports were excluded; not only were high duties imposed on coffee, sugar, and cocoa, but cotton fabrics were entirely prohibited. In 1806, when the English government declared all the French ports from Brest to the mouth of the Elbe closed, and subjected neutral vessels to search, Napoleon issued the decree of Berlin by which the British Isles were declared to be blockaded. All commerce with England was prohibited and no ship which touched the English shores was admitted to a French port. Then came from London the so-called Orders in Council by which neutral ships were required to go to London, Malta, and other places subject to England, to have their cargoes examined and to get permits to trade which had to be paid for at high rates. The next stage in this economic war was Napoleon's decree of Milan, 1807 (December 7), which declared that every ship which had been visited by English officials or had touched at an English port should lose its nationality and be regarded as a lawful prize.

These drastic measures were never rigidly applied, for there grew up a system of exemption by special permits excepting certain articles.

Smuggling, practised on a large scale, acted also as an ameliorating factor; indeed, after 1810 colonial products were admitted into France, though at a high rate of duty, but the war against cotton continued. Everywhere it was found, it was seized, and confiscated or burnt. The result of this system for France was worse than for England, for by her mastery of the sea the latter power was able to maintain both her industries and her credit, while France had to pay more for raw products and, the export of her goods being hampered, the price in the home market was artificially lowered. In 1802, foreign commerce reached a sum total of 790,000,000 francs, of which exports accounted for 325,000,000; ten years later the figures were 640,000,000 and 383,000,000, respectively.

In finance the Napoleonic régime showed no disposition to make innovations; only in details was the fiscal system altered. There was no regular budget in the modern sense of the term; the accounts for each year were kept open, and in order to make the yearly balance, the resources of other years were drawn upon. Apart from these financial irregularities, which, in the absence of any real legislative representative system, were not criticised or counted, the administration of the finances of the empire was carefully directed. The officials were required to do their work well; there was no red tape, and full value was received for every franc expended. Napoleon was vigilant in defending the interests of the treasury, and he treated it as his own patrimony.

In no phase do his gifts as a ruler shine more conspicuously than in his refusal to increase the public debt to any considerable extent. At the fall of the Directory there were 46,000,000 francs of Rentes in French government bonds; his government added only 17,000,000 to this amount. He did not trust to credit to carry on his wars, the bankruptcy of the Revolution being too fresh in the minds of French bondholders. We have noticed before how he expected the extraordinary expenses of warfare to be supplied. His forethought in raising contributions, hard as it was for the conquered countries, was a blessing to French investors.

This care for a sound financial position sustained confidence in the Napoleonic régime, even when its master was engaged in the most hazardous military adventures. In the autumn of 1799 government five per cents. were quoted at seven francs. In 1800 the lowest quotation was 17.37, the highest 44. Each year the rise continued until it attained its extreme limit in May, 1808, when it marked 88.15 francs. Then there was a gradual fall. In March, 1814, the quotation was 45 francs, a year later it had risen to 81.65. Napoleon gave as much and as watchful attention to the maintenance of public credit as he did to the details of army administration. At the beginning of the Consulate he proceeded to restore public confidence by abolishing forced loans and by introducing specie payments. His only questionable financial operation was the employment of the money allotted to the sinking fund, to sustain artificially, at critical periods, the price of government securities, in order to deceive public opinion as to the importance of French defeats.

One of the first steps taken by Napoleon on his attainment of the supreme executive power was to make peace with the Church. Under the anti-religious legislation of the Revolution, in which most of the clergy and bishops had been declared outlaws, the social order had added to its other ills religious chaos. After the battle of Marengo in 1800, Napoleon, in an address to the clergy of Milan, laid down the following principles for his church policy: "No society can exist without morality, and there can be no good morality without religion. Religion alone gives the state a firm and stable support. A society without religion is like a vessel without a compass; France, taught by her misfortunes, has finally opened her eyes; she has recognized that the Catholic religion is, as it were, an anchor, that alone can keep her steady, in her time of stress."

He had no purpose, however, to allow the Church to secure for itself an organization, that might appeal to the people, apart from or contrary to the government. His ideal was an ecclesiastical machine which could be controlled exactly as if it were a government department. Under such assumptions a concordat was arranged with the Papacy, whose power Napoleon respected. He ordered his agent at Rome, who conducted the negotiations, to treat the Pope as if he had 200,000 men. For some time the discussion dragged, because Pius VII refused to accept certain reforms which seemed to threaten the independence of the hierarchy. Finally, the terms were arranged under which the First Consul gained his two chief points: the introduction of an entirely new episcopate with a reduction of dioceses and the recognition of the alienation of church property during the Revolution.

Among the most important features of this instrument was the declaration that the Catholic religion should be freely exercised in France, but that it was to conform itself to such police regulations as the government should judge necessary for public tranquillity. The new bishops were to be presented by the state and instituted by the Pope. Parish priests were to be appointed by the bishops, but the appointment could be vetoed by the state, and the payment of the bishops and priests was undertaken by the government. A number of the former constitutional bishops, who had been in schism with Rome, were appointed in the new hierarchy which now numbered sixty members. The introduction of the clause mentioned above relating to the police powers of the state was used as a ground for a whole series of "organic articles" by which the French Church was bound hand and foot to the Napoleonic system; they were but a revival of the Gallican principles adopted by Louis XIV to help him to become the supreme administrator of the Church in France. Rome naturally protested, for these articles interfered with the autocratic system of the Curia. Acts of the Holy See and decrees of councils were not legalized in France unless they were verified by the government. Bishops could not consult together without a license from the government, or retire from their dioceses temporarily, without a permit. In many other details episcopal jurisdiction and church autonomy were interfered with. But all protests were in vain, and Pius VII conformed reluctantly to the will of the master of Western Europe, hoping that the slow-going diplomacy of his Secretary of State, Consalvi, would secure future concessions.

The first friction between the Emperor and the Pope occurred over the introduction of religious orders. None were authorized except certain orders for women, engaged in charitable or relief work. On December 2, 1804, after much hesitation, the Pope agreed to come to Paris to participate in the imperial coronation. He was treated with respect, but during the ceremony, when he was about to place the crown on Napoleon's head, the Emperor with a show of displeasure took it out of his hands and crowned himself. On one ground or another Pius was kept in France for several months, as Napoleon was glad to have the head of the Church placed in a subordinate position before the world as a kind of Grand Almoner to the Emperor of the French.

New difficulties arose over the Pope's refusal to annul the marriage of Jerome Bonaparte with Miss Patterson, an American, who had been married to Napoleon's youngest brother in Baltimore in 1803 by the Roman Catholic bishop of that city. There were fresh grounds of alienation when, in 1806, Napoleon wrote to the Pope, who wished to be neutral, to close his ports to English vessels and to expel from his court English, Russians, and Swedes. "You are," he said, "the sovereign of Rome, but I am the Emperor; my enemies should be yours." As the Pope still proclaimed his neutrality, Napoleon seized the Papal States, and finally occupied Rome in February, 1808. For fourteen months the Pope was kept a virtual prisoner in the Quirinal under a guard of honor; he was not allowed to communicate with the cardinals, twenty-four of whom had been, by Napoleon's orders, deported. Finally, in May, 1809, a decree was issued by which the States of the Church were annexed to the French Empire. Rome was proclaimed a free imperial city, the Pope being allowed to keep only his palace and his estates with an income of 2,000,000 francs.

Napoleon spoke of himself as revoking the Donation of Constantine; his intention was to make of Paris the religious head of the world with himself the director of its religion as well as of its secular affairs. Pius VII's reply was a bull of excommunication against the Emperor, who, however, was not mentioned by name in the document. It only spoke in general terms of those who were guilty of deeds of violence in the States of the Church. Napoleon affected to pay little attention to the Papal protest, but he acted promptly, first by appealing to the old principle of the Gallican Church, that denied the right of the Pope to excommunicate a sovereign of a state. Then he had the person of the Pope seized by the commander of the Roman gendarmerie. No resistance was offered, and Pius was conducted as a prisoner, in a closed carriage with drawn shades, to Savona on the western Riviera near Genoa. Here he was kept carefully guarded, but he refused all terms of settlement that insisted on his surrender of the temporal power. No one was allowed to see him except in the presence of his guards. When Napoleon desired canonical institution for some newly appointed bishops, the Pope refused, on the ground that he was deprived of the advice of his cardinals. The situation was embarrassing, for there were, in August, 1809, twenty-seven vacant sees in France. Efforts were made to find a solution by calling a council at Paris; but the ecclesiastics, on assembling there, declared that the Pope's consent was necessary. Napoleon then ordered the bishops to take charge of their dioceses without institution from the Pope. But a brief came from Savona to Cardinal Maury, the archbishop designate of Paris, enjoining him from administering his diocese without the Pope's consent. The Emperor now treated the prisoner of Savona with even more rigor, put in prison the clergy whom he suspected of bringing the Papal brief, and deprived Pius of all means of corresponding with the outside world.

At this time the divorce of Napoleon from Josephine took place. The difficulties of the civil law were got over easily, although the Emperor had to violate the provisions of his own code, and the ecclesiastical committee of the diocese of Paris showed itself equally obliging, by recognizing the two imperial claims, that there had been an absence of consent to his religious marriage of 1804, and that there were defects of form in the ceremony itself. When the marriage with the Austrian archduchess was celebrated on April 2, 1810, thirteen of the twenty-six cardinals present in Paris refused to be present at the religious ceremony. This behavior excited Napoleon to an act of personal revenge, by which the recalcitrant princes of the Church were deprived of the insignia of their office, were placed under police supervision, and had to forego their allowance.

In 1811, a council was held in Paris to decide on the question as to the rights of the Pope in the matter of institution. Some of the bishops showed independence, urging the Emperor to restore Pius to liberty. There was a general agreement that Papal consent was necessary. In the meantime the Pope had been cajoled or bullied into accepting a clause, to be added to the Concordat, that canonical institution should be given within a fixed period, and if it were not given, it might be granted by the metropolitan or oldest bishop of the province. Just before the invasion of Russia the aged Pope was brought incognito from Savona to Fontainebleau. During the trip, though he was seriously ill, no consideration was shown him, and for many months after his arrival he was confined to his bed. Only cardinals and prelates who were partisans of Napoleon were allowed to see him. The defeat in Russia brought about a radical change; Napoleon now saw the advantage of arranging some terms of peace, because the harsh treatment of the venerable head of the greatest Christian communion was being used against his persecutor, both at home and abroad. Negotiations were resumed, and under personal pressure from Napoleon, Pius, on condition that the domains of the Holy See were restored to him, made large concessions. He gave Napoleon the right to fill all the bishoprics of France and Italy, except those in the vicinity of Rome, and he allowed metropolitan institution. Afterwards, on consulting with his advisers, the Pope published a retraction of his consent, by which the provisions he had made were annulled. No attention was paid by the Emperor to this change of attitude except that he ordered the imprisonment of the Cardinal de Pietro, who he thought had persuaded Pius to change his mind.

In 1814, before the last campaign on French territory, Napoleon gave the Pope permission to leave Fontainebleau, and shortly before the final defeat he restored the Papal States. There were no further relations between the two, the restored Pope and dethroned Emperor, except that Pius VII, after the Hundred Days and Waterloo, magnanimously offered the Bonaparte family an asylum in Rome, and later on made representations to the English government with a view to reduce the severity of Napoleon's captivity at St. Helena.

It is customary to ascribe to Napoleon creative originality as a lawgiver. This is a part of the Napoleonic legend that has been upset by the industrious investigations of the partisans of the French Revolution, working under a famous professor at the Sorbonne. In many ways these scholars have rescued from obscurity the positive achievements of the Revolutionary statesmen, and it is now certain that the various codes of Napoleon carry out the principles of procedure and justice foreshadowed in the preliminary work done by the Constituent Assembly and the Convention. Napoleon's own temperament is seen in the influence he brought to bear upon his lawyers to provide for rapidity in procedure and in execution of judgment, and in the increase of tribunals in which business men played an important rôle.

In education the Emperor's influence was not so beneficial. He had little sympathy with any type of training that was not practical, and he had no sympathy at all with professorial free speech. Indeed, he expected the teaching profession to take its model from the Grand Army. There was to be little chance for personal development, each man marched in an appropriate rank under orders from a superior. The result of the iron-clad educational régime is acknowledged to have been most unsatisfactory, and it has been one of the most brilliant and most arduous achievements of the Third Republic to abolish the Napoleonic ideals of university teaching, and to substitute for them a system which encourages local and personal freedom. The change has already justified itself, for France is now close to Germany as the home of erudition in many fields of research in which Germany for years justly claimed an uncontested primacy.

The supreme position of Napoleon as a military commander has often led his admirers to affirm that he was infallible in his strategy. He encouraged this tendency at St. Helena, for, when he was composing his Memoirs, he invariably shifted the responsibility for errors in his battles to the shoulders of his lieutenants. He was an expert in manipulating figures, and he had such a good memory that he could always compose a most plausible lie. For years people supposed that the Russian expedition failed because of the extreme cold, and that the defeat at Waterloo might have been turned into a victory if the Emperor's orders had been strictly carried out by Grouchy and if Ney had advanced more rapidly, as he was bidden to do by his commander-in-chief. These are misrepresentations—are the efforts of a man who wished to manipulate history for his own benefit. When, however, he was not dictating as an exile, Napoleon often enough expressed the truth about himself spontaneously. He allowed, for example, that he had been repeatedly defeated, and on more than one occasion he conceded to his marshals the possession of military talent superior to his own. One year after the Russian disaster he owned that the invasion had been ruined by blunders of his own.

He was just as sweeping, too, in condemning various critical phases of his policy. He condemned the attack upon Spain not only as a wholesale blunder, but as a series of blunders in detail, and he characterized the invasion of Russia, while the Spanish War was unfinished, as a hopeless undertaking. Once, speaking to Talleyrand, he said, "I have made so many mistakes in my life that I am not ashamed of them." It was a characteristic trait of his outlook on his own career that he imagined himself carried on as the instrument of deeds and acts which he could not justify. "I am not," he once exclaimed, "a man, but a thing."

Napoleon's lack of appreciation of moral standards both in public and in private life is notorious, but he was no hypocrite. The one pleasing side of his character was his devotion to his family. Here the clear light of his intellect could not reach. It is true he made grotesque mistakes in putting his brothers into positions for which they were manifestly unfitted, but this sign of weakness shows that, after all, Napoleon was not entirely selfish. He seems to have had little actual patriotism. He was not a Frenchman either by descent or by sympathy, and what he accomplished was done at the expense of the French people. He understood some of their characteristics, but his own point of view was so practical that there were whole fields of achievement signalized in the records of French genius that he never appreciated. On lower planes of action, however, his driving power was immense, and the very terror he created by the success of his concentrated individualism prepared the way for that progressive acknowledgment of public justice and social righteousness which characterized the civilization of the nineteenth century. In spite of all his limitations, it seems impossible to point to a more marvelous career in the annals of humanity.